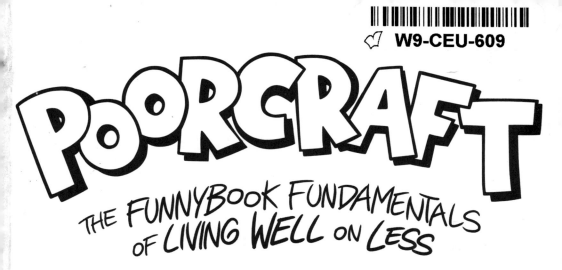

POORCRAFT

THE FUNNYBOOK FUNDAMENTALS OF LIVING WELL ON LESS

Writer, Additional Art ·········· C. Spike Trotman

Artist ·· Diana Nock

Book Design ······························· Matt Sheridan

TM

Published by Iron Circus Comics
ironcircus@gmail.com
www.ironcircus.com

First Edition: May 2012
Second Edition: April 2017
ISBN: 978-1-945820-01-4
Printed in Canada

TABLE OF CONTENTS

Prologue
What Is Poorcraft?

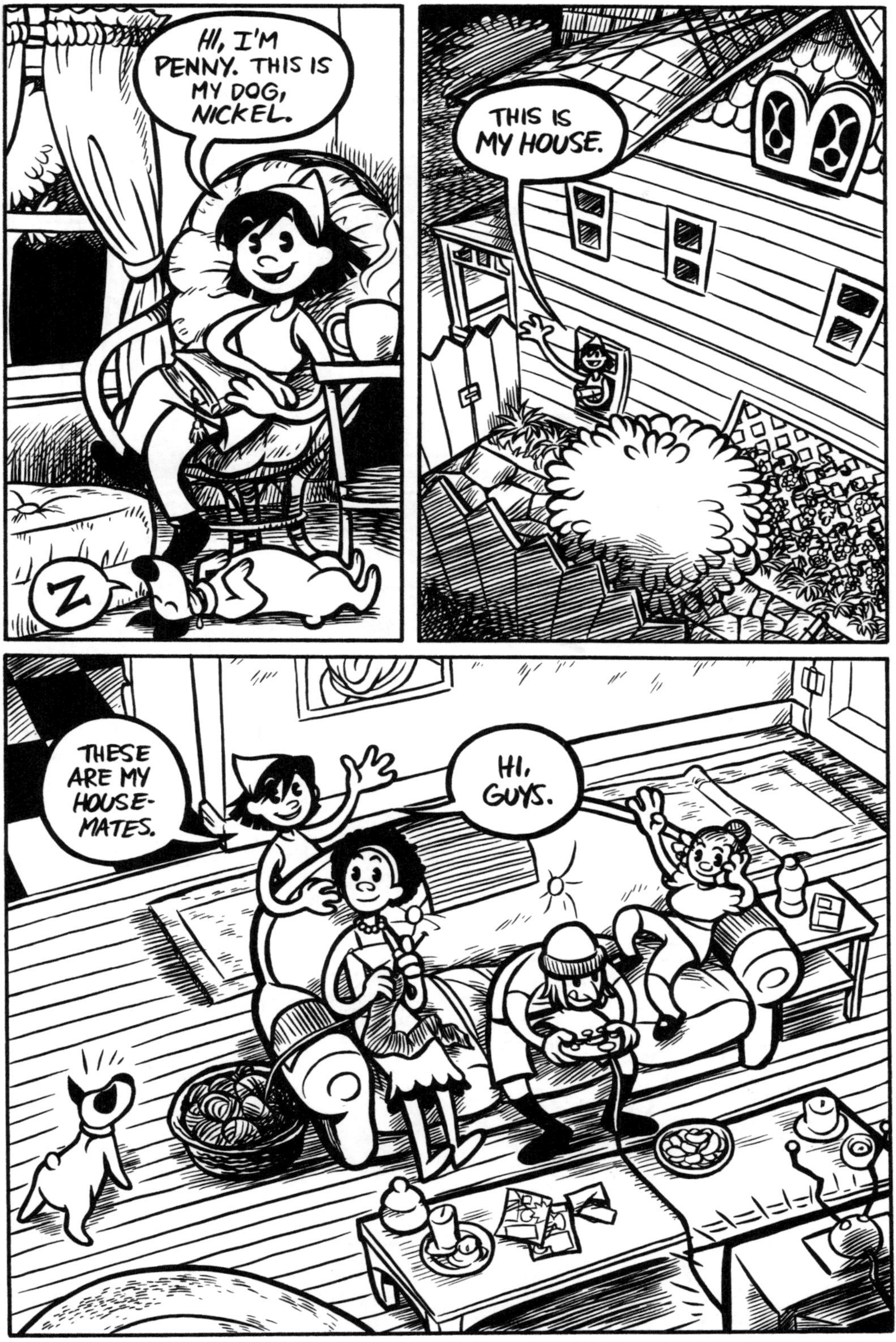
HI, I'M PENNY. THIS IS MY DOG, NICKEL.
Z
THIS IS MY HOUSE.
THESE ARE MY HOUSE-MATES.
HI, GUYS.

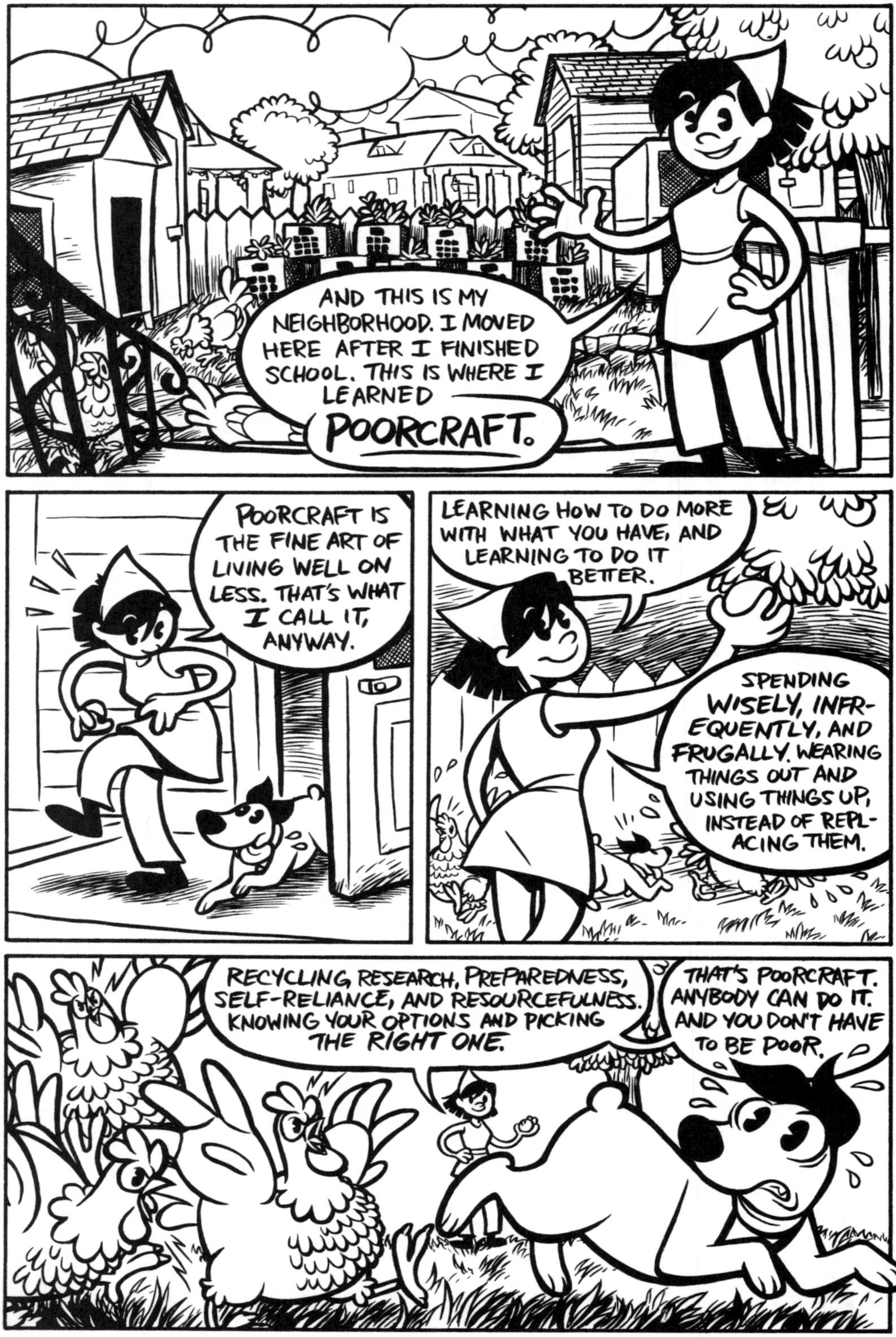
AND THIS IS MY NEIGHBORHOOD. I MOVED HERE AFTER I FINISHED SCHOOL. THIS IS WHERE I LEARNED POORCRAFT.
POORCRAFT IS THE FINE ART OF LIVING WELL ON LESS. THAT'S WHAT I CALL IT, ANYWAY.
LEARNING HOW TO DO MORE WITH WHAT YOU HAVE, AND LEARNING TO DO IT BETTER.
SPENDING WISELY, INFREQUENTLY, AND FRUGALLY. WEARING THINGS OUT AND USING THINGS UP, INSTEAD OF REPLACING THEM.
RECYCLING, RESEARCH, PREPAREDNESS, SELF-RELIANCE, AND RESOURCEFULNESS. KNOWING YOUR OPTIONS AND PICKING THE RIGHT ONE.
THAT'S POORCRAFT. ANYBODY CAN DO IT. AND YOU DON'T HAVE TO BE POOR.

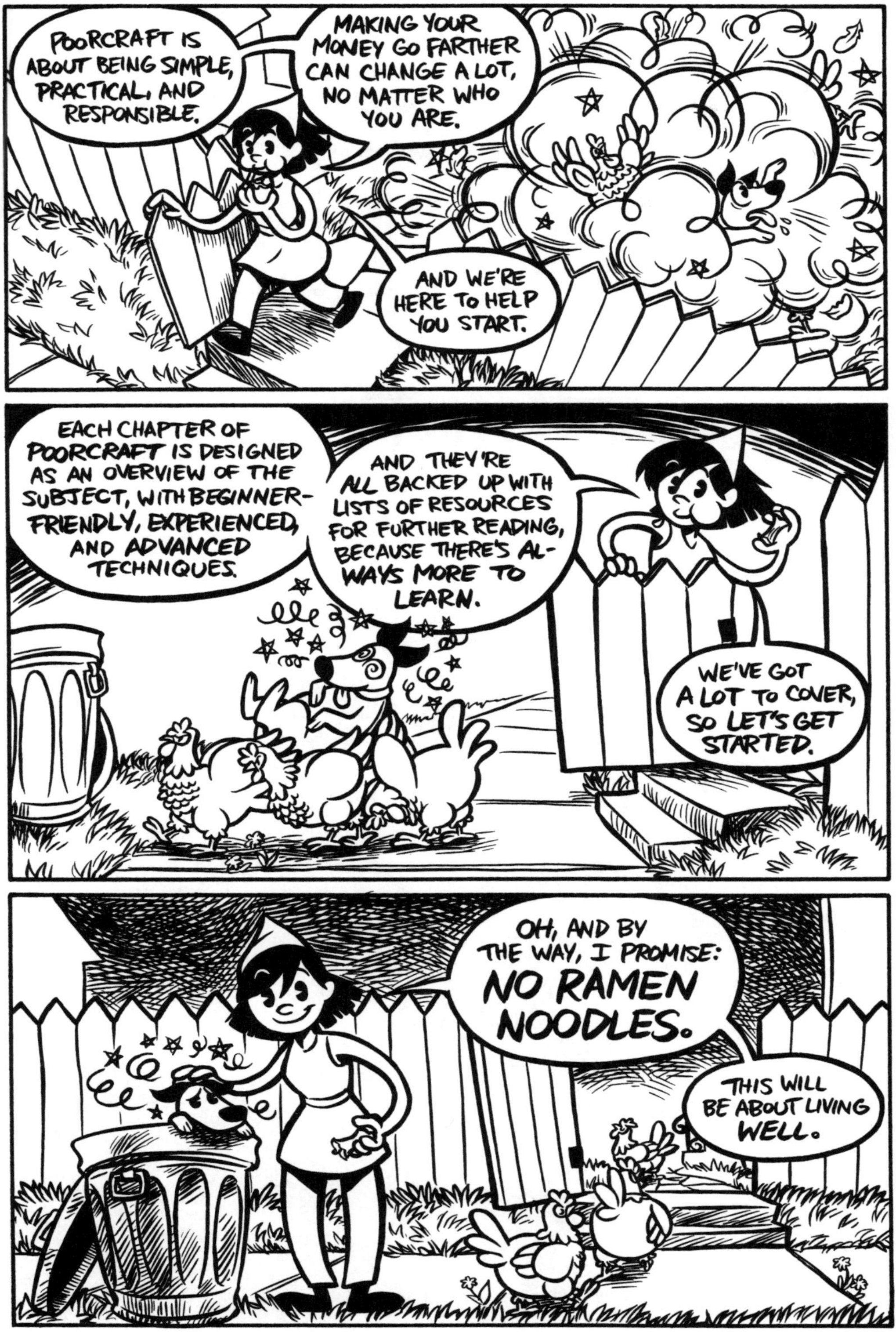
POORCRAFT IS ABOUT BEING SIMPLE, PRACTICAL, AND RESPONSIBLE.
MAKING YOUR MONEY GO FARTHER CAN CHANGE A LOT, NO MATTER WHO YOU ARE.
AND WE'RE HERE TO HELP YOU START.
EACH CHAPTER OF POORCRAFT IS DESIGNED AS AN OVERVIEW OF THE SUBJECT, WITH BEGINNER-FRIENDLY, EXPERIENCED, AND ADVANCED TECHNIQUES.
AND THEY'RE ALL BACKED UP WITH LISTS OF RESOURCES FOR FURTHER READING, BECAUSE THERE'S ALWAYS MORE TO LEARN.
WE'VE GOT A LOT TO COVER, SO LET'S GET STARTED.
OH, AND BY THE WAY, I PROMISE: NO RAMEN NOODLES.
THIS WILL BE ABOUT LIVING WELL.

Chapter One
First Things First

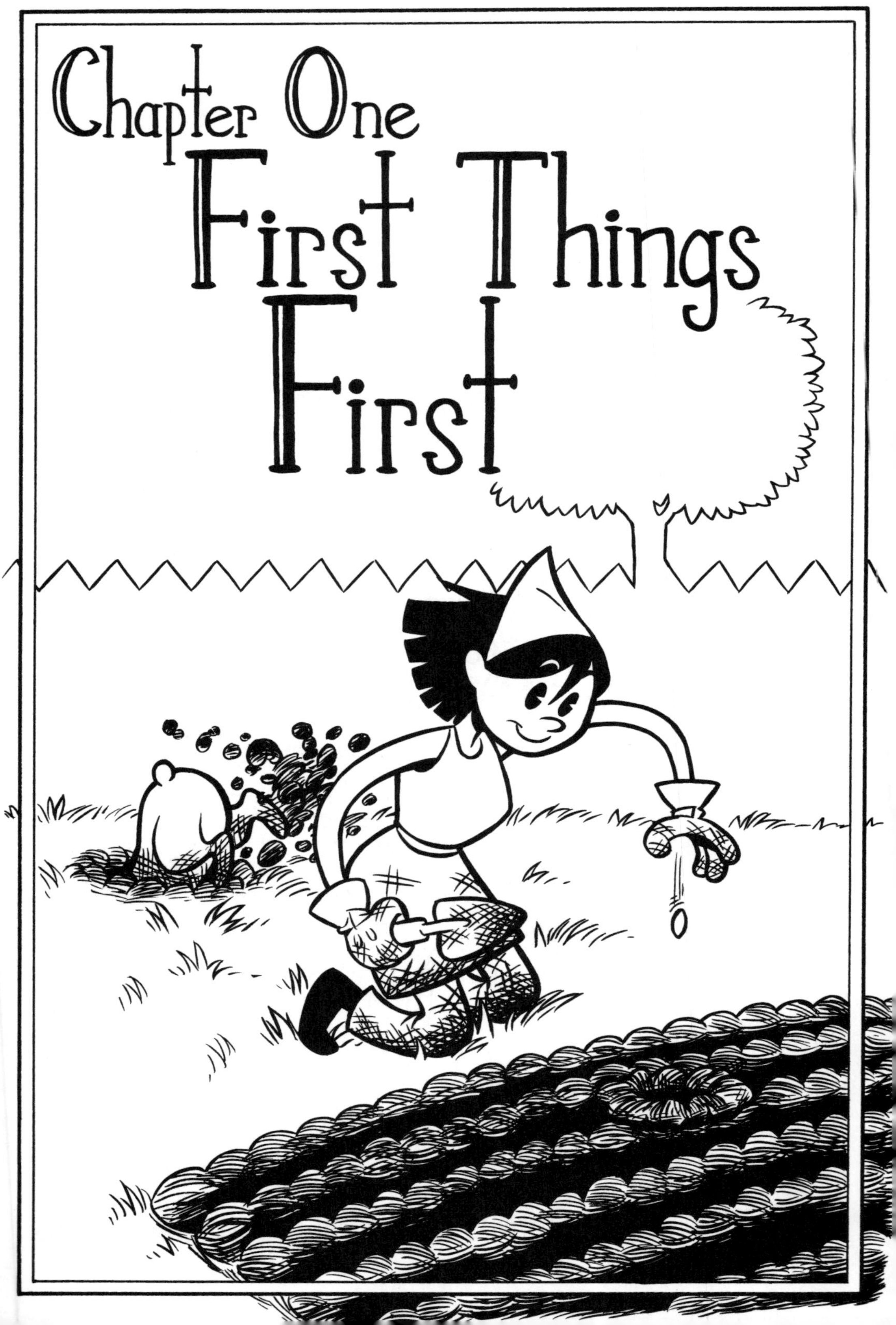

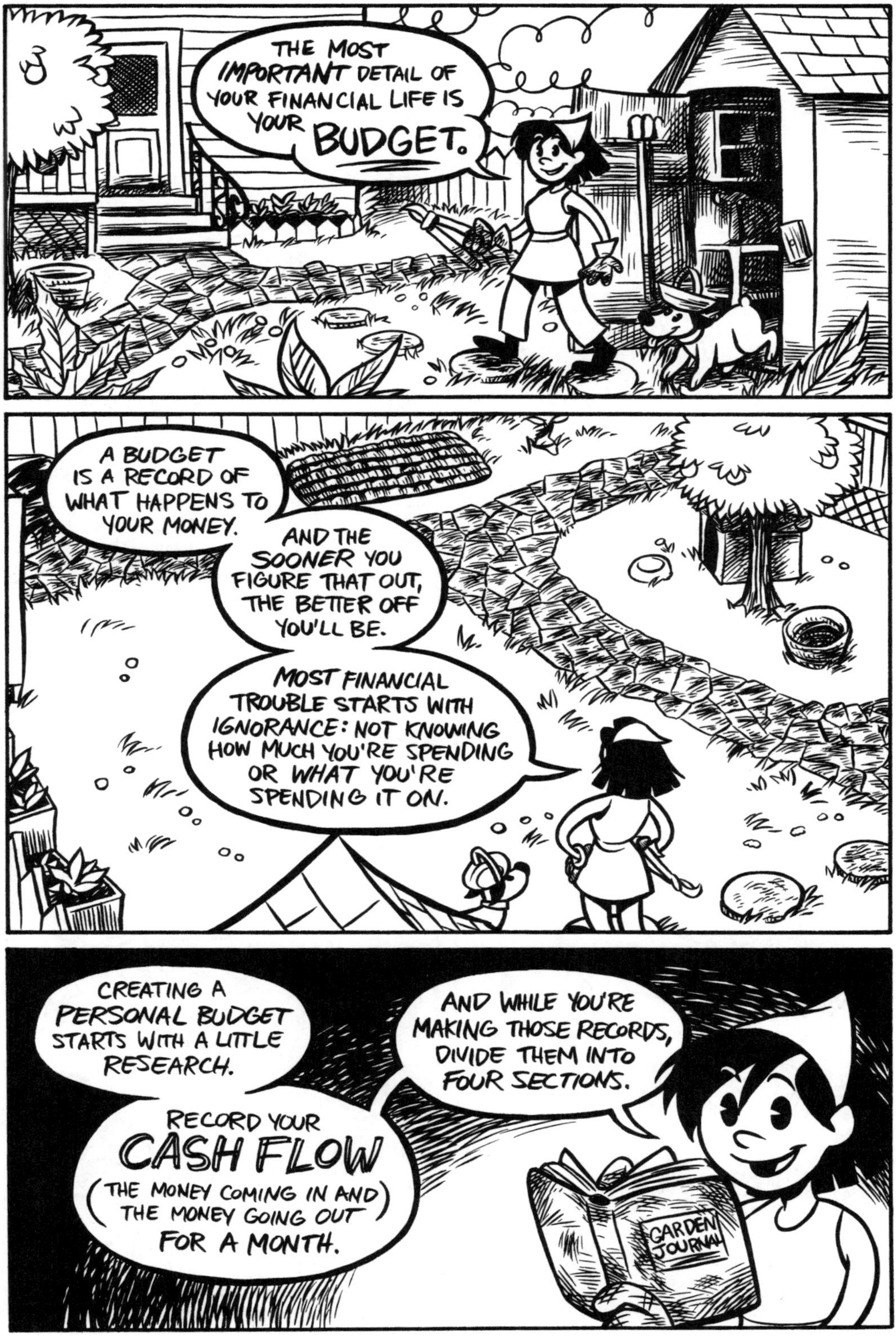
THE MOST IMPORTANT DETAIL OF YOUR FINANCIAL LIFE IS YOUR BUDGET.
A BUDGET IS A RECORD OF WHAT HAPPENS TO YOUR MONEY.
AND THE SOONER YOU FIGURE THAT OUT, THE BETTER OFF YOU'LL BE.
MOST FINANCIAL TROUBLE STARTS WITH IGNORANCE: NOT KNOWING HOW MUCH YOU'RE SPENDING OR WHAT YOU'RE SPENDING IT ON.
CREATING A PERSONAL BUDGET STARTS WITH A LITTLE RESEARCH.
RECORD YOUR CASH FLOW (THE MONEY COMING IN AND THE MONEY GOING OUT) FOR A MONTH.
AND WHILE YOU'RE MAKING THOSE RECORDS, DIVIDE THEM INTO FOUR SECTIONS.
GARDEN JOURNAL

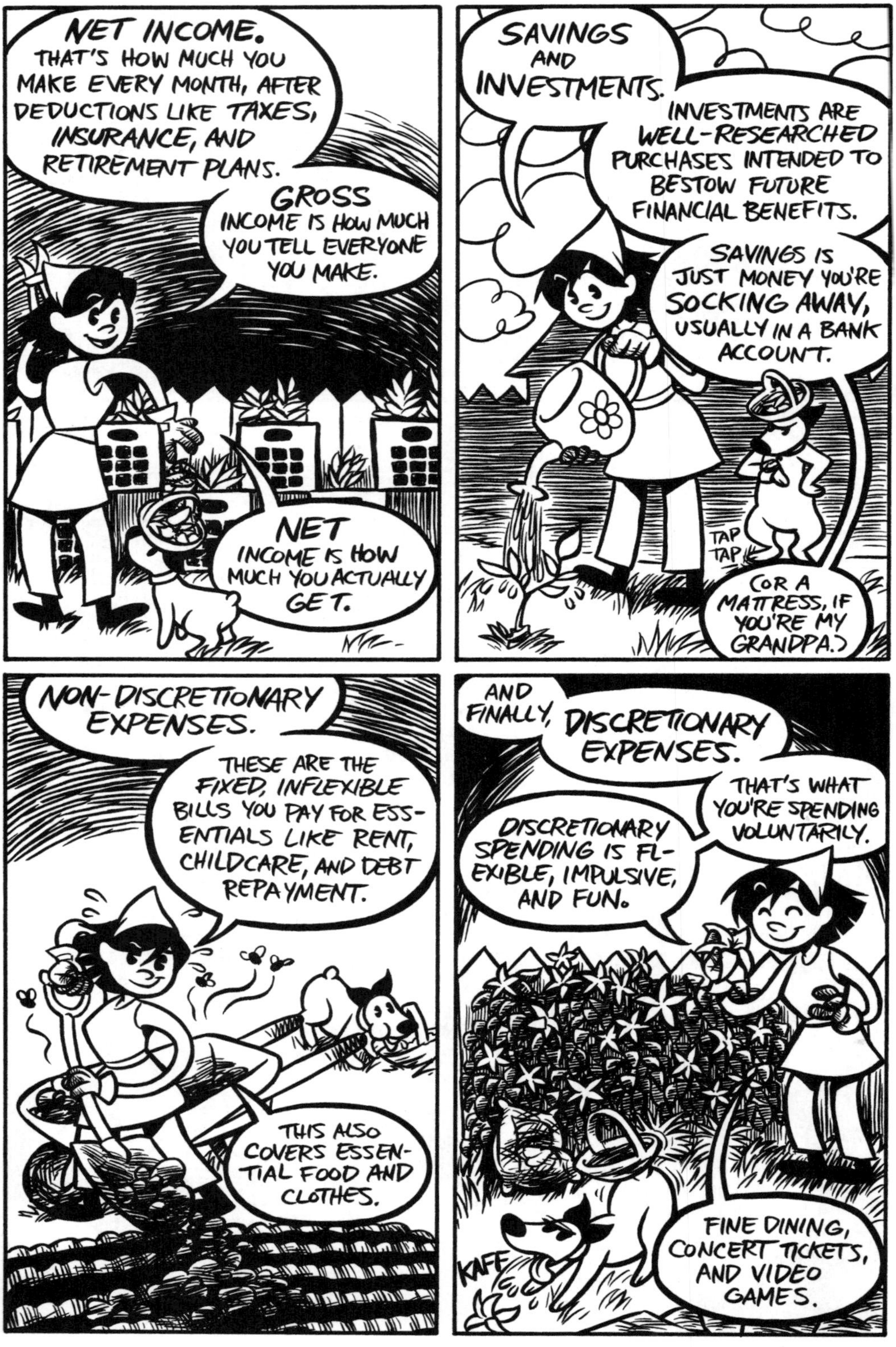
NET INCOME. THAT'S HOW MUCH YOU MAKE EVERY MONTH, AFTER DEDUCTIONS LIKE TAXES, INSURANCE, AND RETIREMENT PLANS.
GROSS INCOME IS HOW MUCH YOU TELL EVERYONE YOU MAKE.
NET INCOME IS HOW MUCH YOU ACTUALLY GET.
SAVINGS AND INVESTMENTS.
INVESTMENTS ARE WELL-RESEARCHED PURCHASES INTENDED TO BESTOW FUTURE FINANCIAL BENEFITS.
SAVINGS IS JUST MONEY YOU'RE SOCKING AWAY, USUALLY IN A BANK ACCOUNT.
TAP TAP
(OR A MATTRESS, IF YOU'RE MY GRANDPA.)
NON-DISCRETIONARY EXPENSES.
THESE ARE THE FIXED, INFLEXIBLE BILLS YOU PAY FOR ESS-ENTIALS LIKE RENT, CHILDCARE, AND DEBT REPAYMENT.
THIS ALSO COVERS ESSEN-TIAL FOOD AND CLOTHES.
AND FINALLY, DISCRETIONARY EXPENSES.
THAT'S WHAT YOU'RE SPENDING VOLUNTARILY.
DISCRETIONARY SPENDING IS FL-EXIBLE, IMPULSIVE, AND FUN.
KAFF
FINE DINING, CONCERT TICKETS, AND VIDEO GAMES.

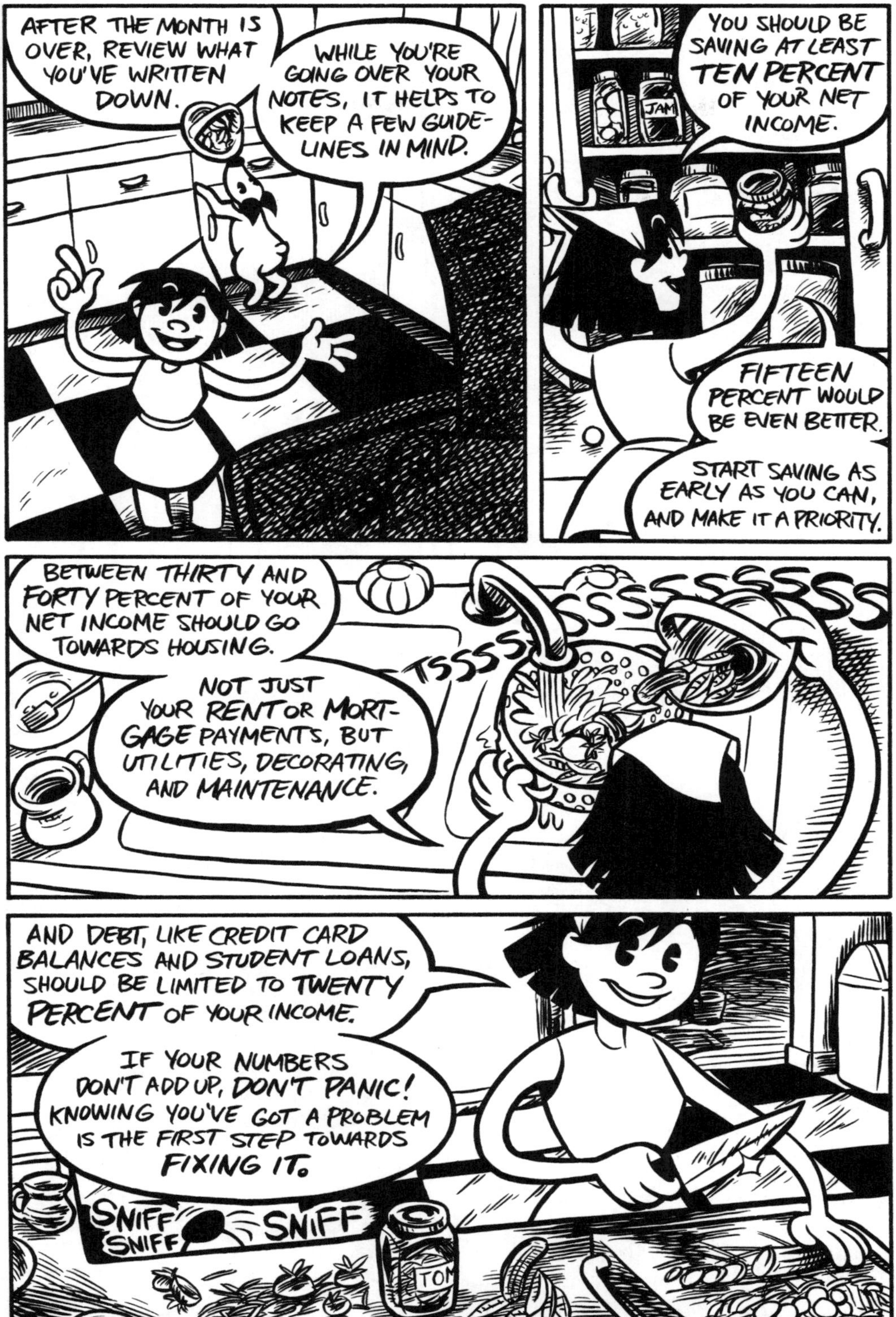
AFTER THE MONTH IS OVER, REVIEW WHAT YOU'VE WRITTEN DOWN.
WHILE YOU'RE GOING OVER YOUR NOTES, IT HELPS TO KEEP A FEW GUIDELINES IN MIND.
YOU SHOULD BE SAVING AT LEAST TEN PERCENT OF YOUR NET INCOME.
JAM
FIFTEEN PERCENT WOULD BE EVEN BETTER.
START SAVING AS EARLY AS YOU CAN, AND MAKE IT A PRIORITY.
BETWEEN THIRTY AND FORTY PERCENT OF YOUR NET INCOME SHOULD GO TOWARDS HOUSING.
NOT JUST YOUR RENT OR MORTGAGE PAYMENTS, BUT UTILITIES, DECORATING, AND MAINTENANCE.
TSSSSS
SSSSSSSSSS
AND DEBT, LIKE CREDIT CARD BALANCES AND STUDENT LOANS, SHOULD BE LIMITED TO TWENTY PERCENT OF YOUR INCOME.
IF YOUR NUMBERS DON'T ADD UP, DON'T PANIC! KNOWING YOU'VE GOT A PROBLEM IS THE FIRST STEP TOWARDS FIXING IT.
SNIFF SNIFF
SNIFF
TOM

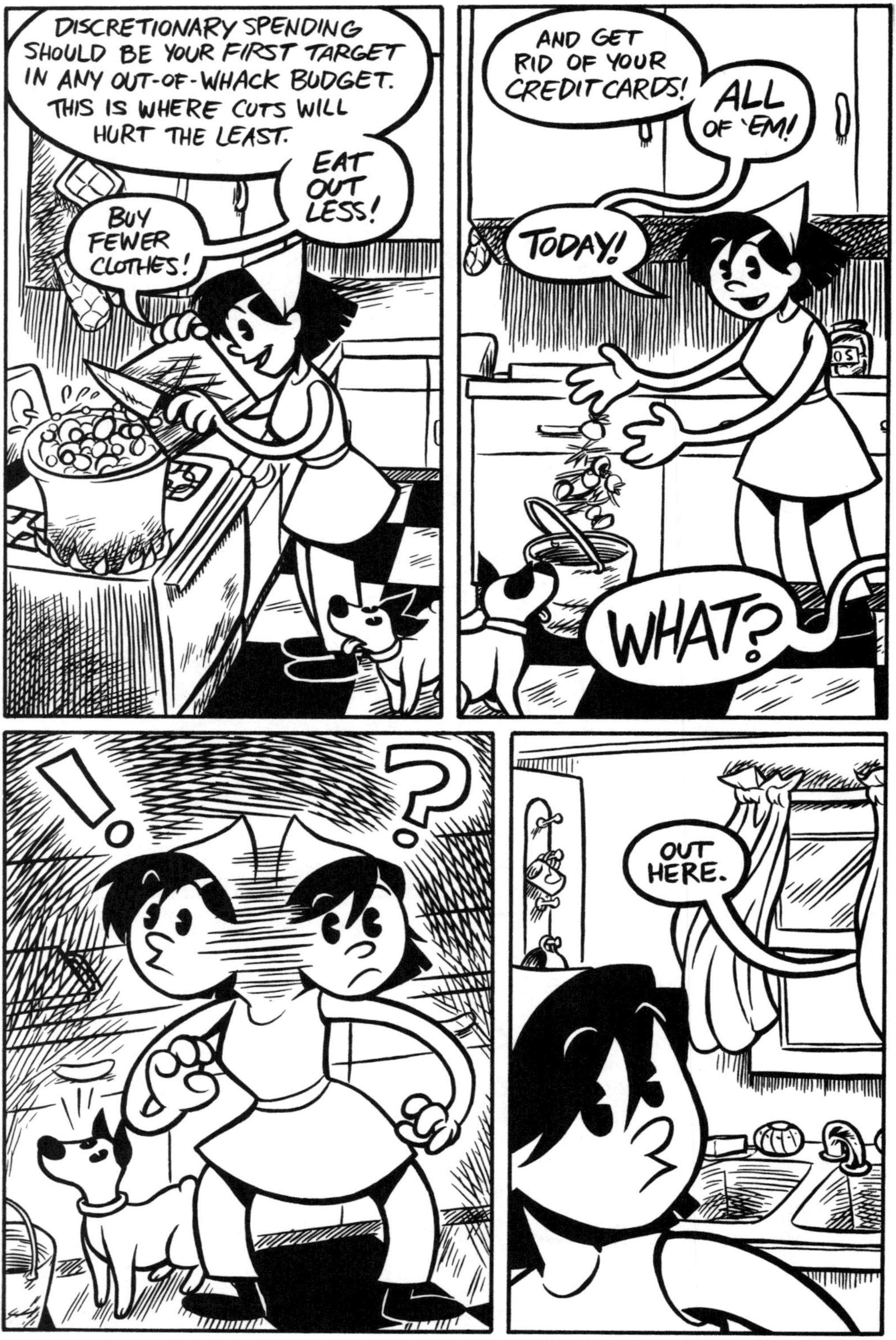
DISCRETIONARY SPENDING SHOULD BE YOUR FIRST TARGET IN ANY OUT-OF-WHACK BUDGET. THIS IS WHERE CUTS WILL HURT THE LEAST.
EAT OUT LESS!
BUY FEWER CLOTHES!
AND GET RID OF YOUR CREDIT CARDS!
ALL OF 'EM!
TODAY!
WHAT?
!
?
OUT HERE.

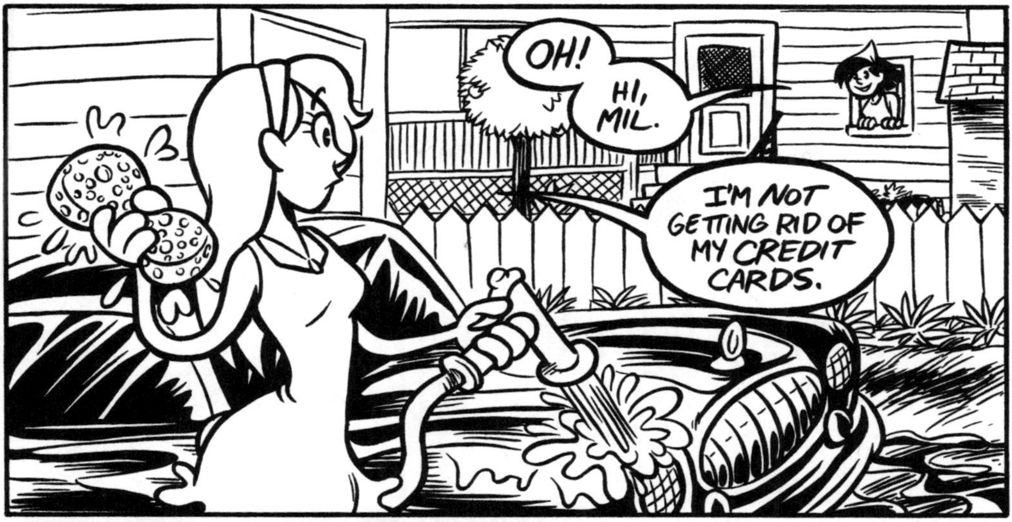
OH!
HI, MIL.
I'M NOT GETTING RID OF MY CREDIT CARDS.

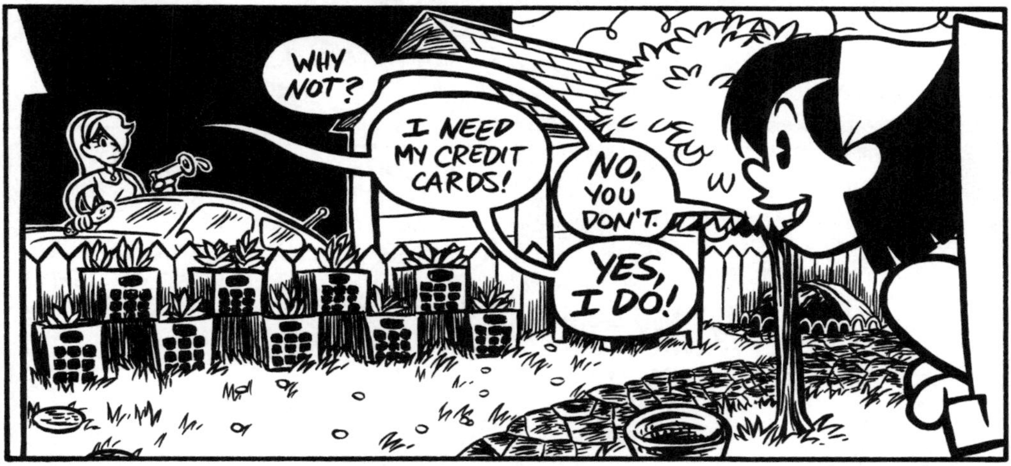
WHY NOT?
I NEED MY CREDIT CARDS!
NO, YOU DON'T.
YES, I DO!

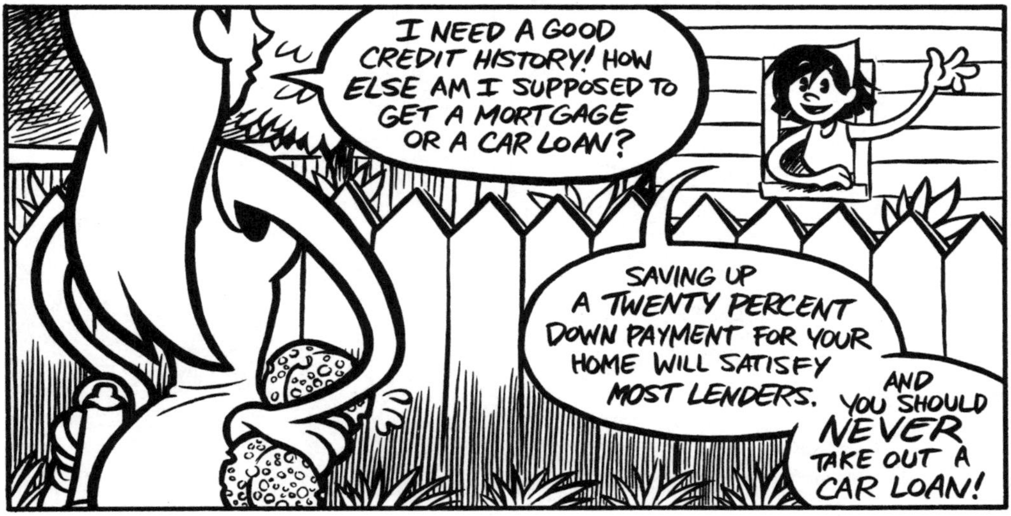
I NEED A GOOD CREDIT HISTORY! HOW ELSE AM I SUPPOSED TO GET A MORTGAGE OR A CAR LOAN?
SAVING UP A TWENTY PERCENT DOWN PAYMENT FOR YOUR HOME WILL SATISFY MOST LENDERS.
AND YOU SHOULD NEVER TAKE OUT A CAR LOAN!

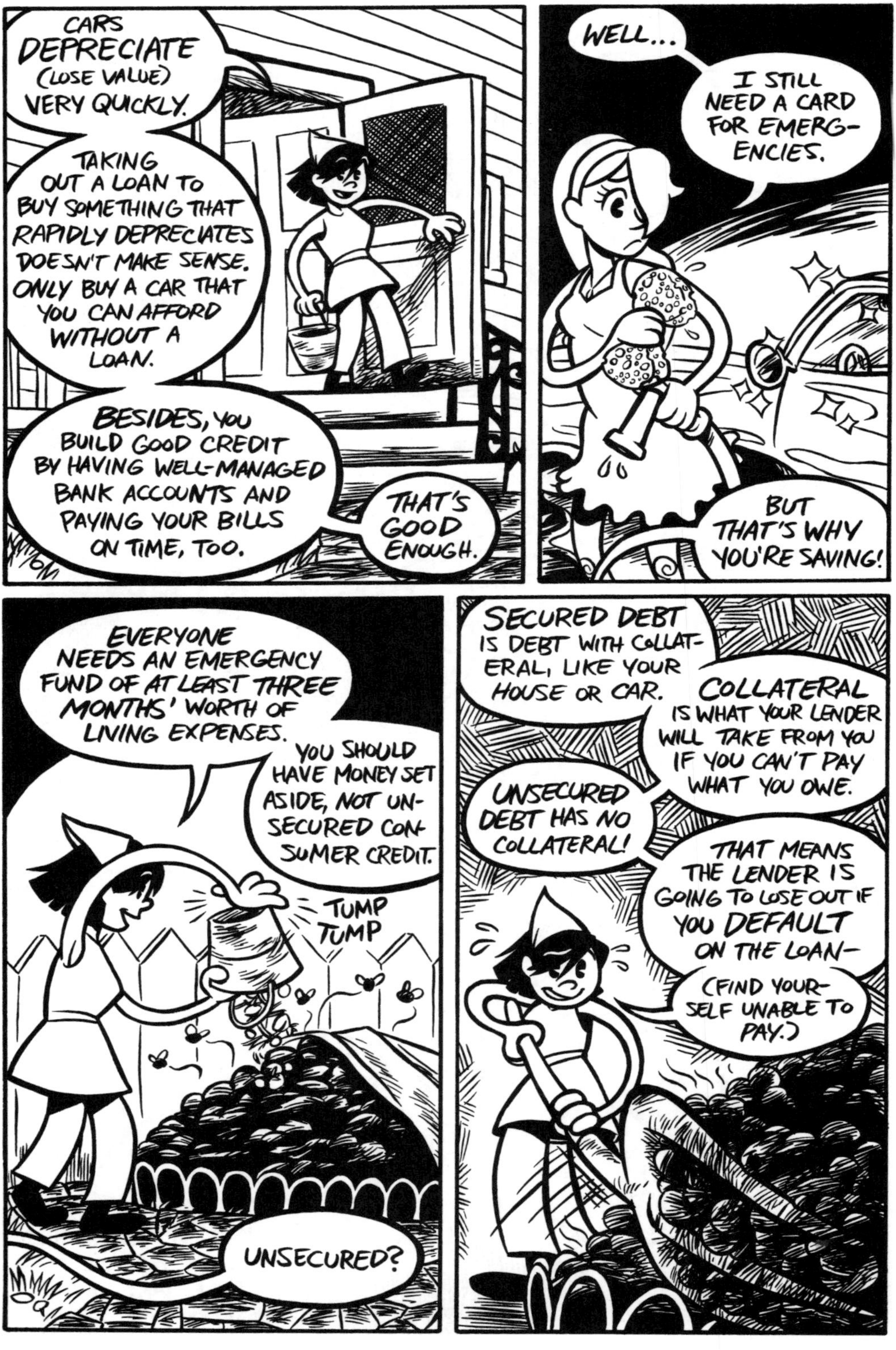
CARS DEPRECIATE (LOSE VALUE) VERY QUICKLY.
TAKING OUT A LOAN TO BUY SOMETHING THAT RAPIDLY DEPRECIATES DOESN'T MAKE SENSE. ONLY BUY A CAR THAT YOU CAN AFFORD WITHOUT A LOAN.
BESIDES, YOU BUILD GOOD CREDIT BY HAVING WELL-MANAGED BANK ACCOUNTS AND PAYING YOUR BILLS ON TIME, TOO.
THAT'S GOOD ENOUGH.
WELL...
I STILL NEED A CARD FOR EMERGENCIES.
BUT THAT'S WHY YOU'RE SAVING!
EVERYONE NEEDS AN EMERGENCY FUND OF AT LEAST THREE MONTHS' WORTH OF LIVING EXPENSES.
YOU SHOULD HAVE MONEY SET ASIDE, NOT UNSECURED CONSUMER CREDIT.
TUMP TUMP
UNSECURED?
SECURED DEBT IS DEBT WITH COLLATERAL, LIKE YOUR HOUSE OR CAR.
COLLATERAL IS WHAT YOUR LENDER WILL TAKE FROM YOU IF YOU CAN'T PAY WHAT YOU OWE.
UNSECURED DEBT HAS NO COLLATERAL!
THAT MEANS THE LENDER IS GOING TO LOSE OUT IF YOU DEFAULT ON THE LOAN—
(FIND YOURSELF UNABLE TO PAY.)

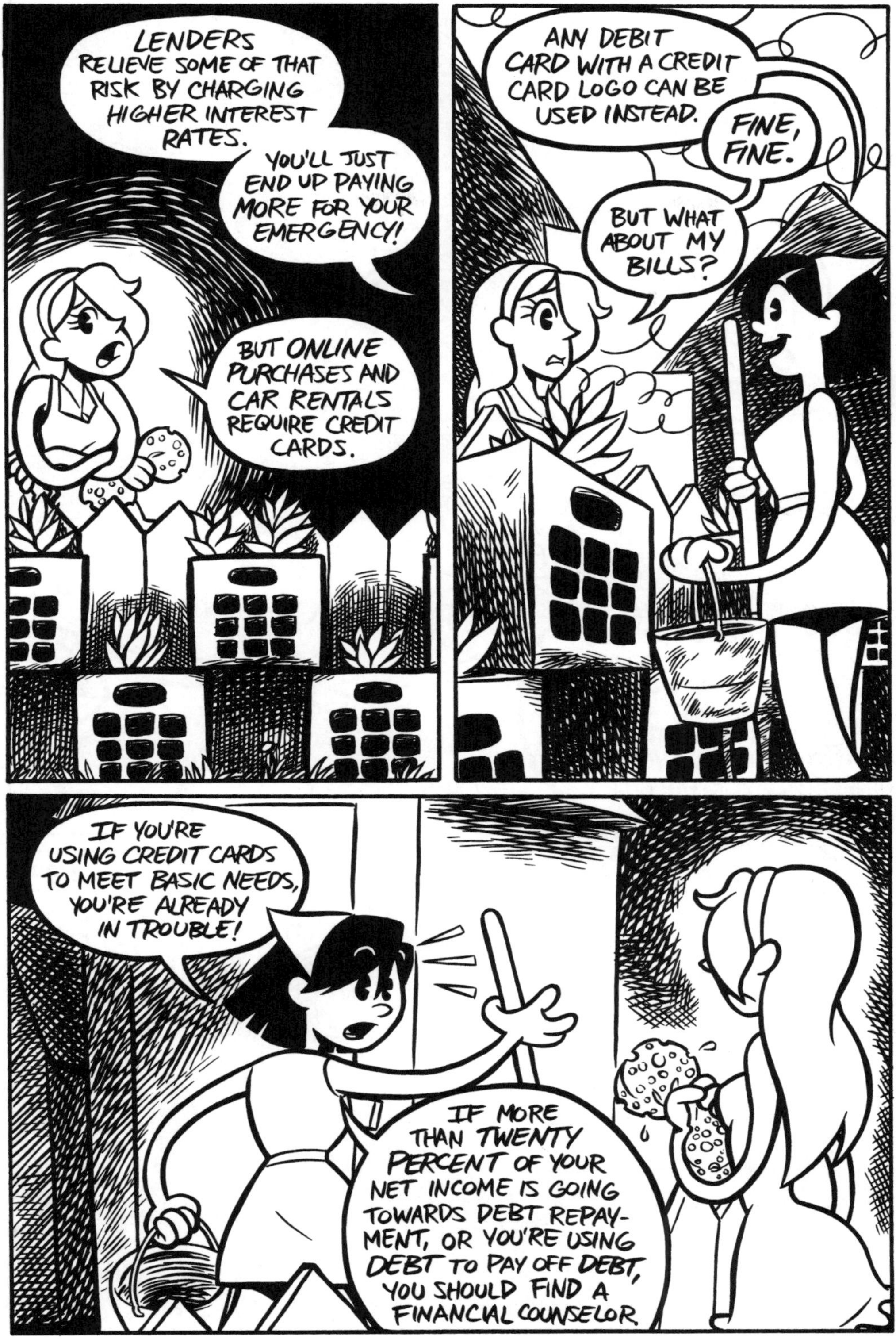
LENDERS RELIEVE SOME OF THAT RISK BY CHARGING HIGHER INTEREST RATES.
YOU'LL JUST END UP PAYING MORE FOR YOUR EMERGENCY!
BUT ONLINE PURCHASES AND CAR RENTALS REQUIRE CREDIT CARDS.
ANY DEBIT CARD WITH A CREDIT CARD LOGO CAN BE USED INSTEAD.
FINE, FINE.
BUT WHAT ABOUT MY BILLS?
IF YOU'RE USING CREDIT CARDS TO MEET BASIC NEEDS, YOU'RE ALREADY IN TROUBLE!
IF MORE THAN TWENTY PERCENT OF YOUR NET INCOME IS GOING TOWARDS DEBT REPAYMENT, OR YOU'RE USING DEBT TO PAY OFF DEBT, YOU SHOULD FIND A FINANCIAL COUNSELOR.

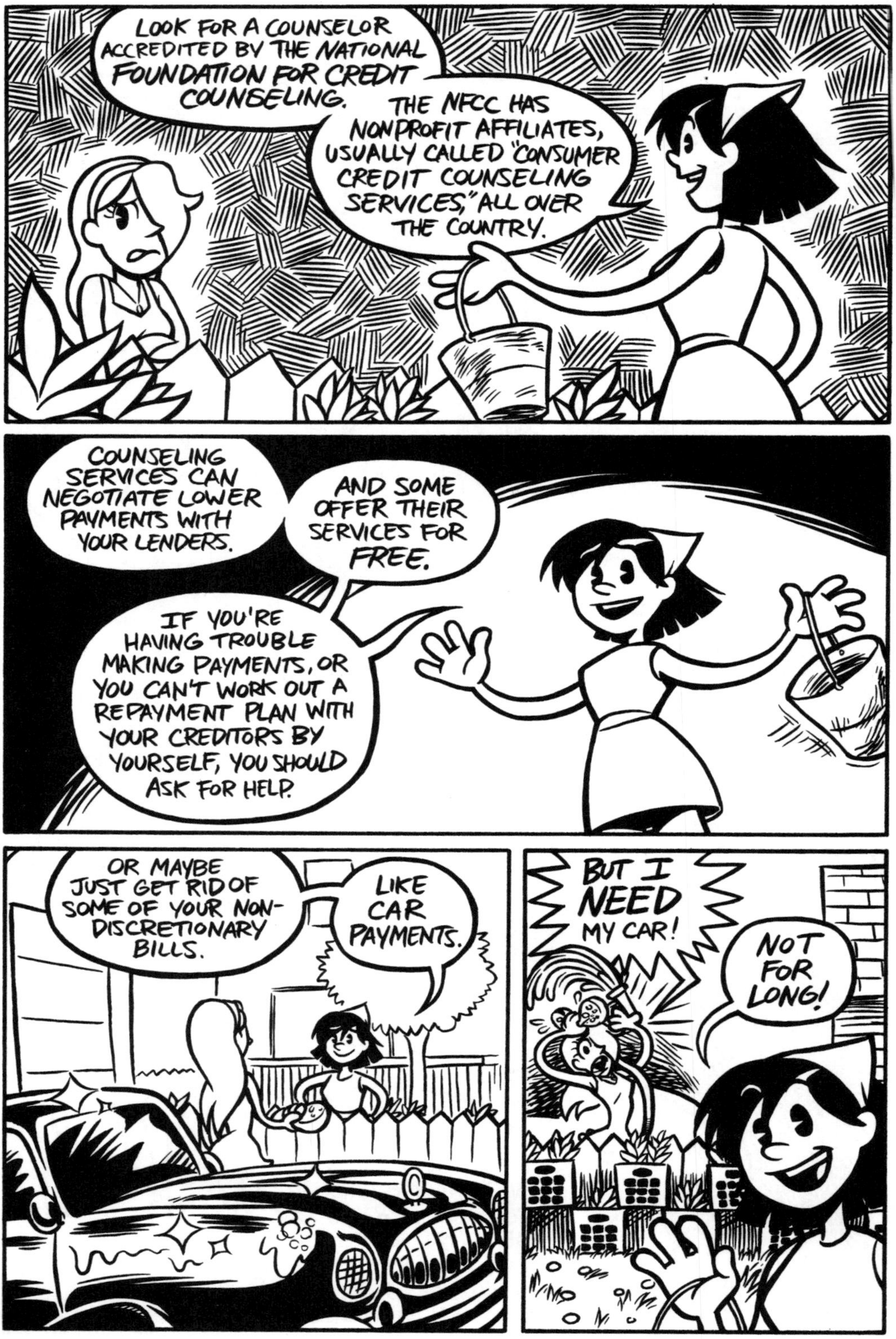
LOOK FOR A COUNSELOR ACCREDITED BY THE NATIONAL FOUNDATION FOR CREDIT COUNSELING.
THE NFCC HAS NONPROFIT AFFILIATES, USUALLY CALLED "CONSUMER CREDIT COUNSELING SERVICES," ALL OVER THE COUNTRY.
COUNSELING SERVICES CAN NEGOTIATE LOWER PAYMENTS WITH YOUR LENDERS.
AND SOME OFFER THEIR SERVICES FOR FREE.
IF YOU'RE HAVING TROUBLE MAKING PAYMENTS, OR YOU CAN'T WORK OUT A REPAYMENT PLAN WITH YOUR CREDITORS BY YOURSELF, YOU SHOULD ASK FOR HELP.
OR MAYBE JUST GET RID OF SOME OF YOUR NON-DISCRETIONARY BILLS.
LIKE CAR PAYMENTS.
BUT I NEED MY CAR!
NOT FOR LONG!

Chapter Two
Housing

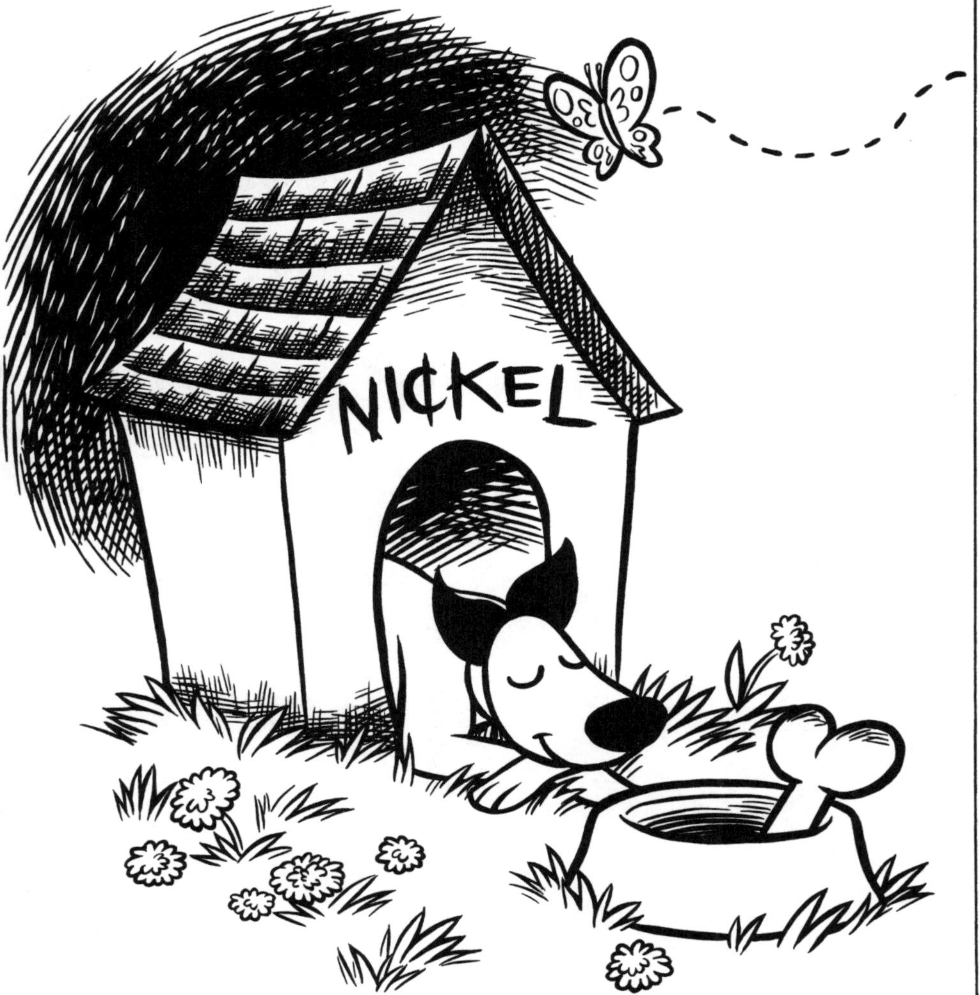
NICKEL

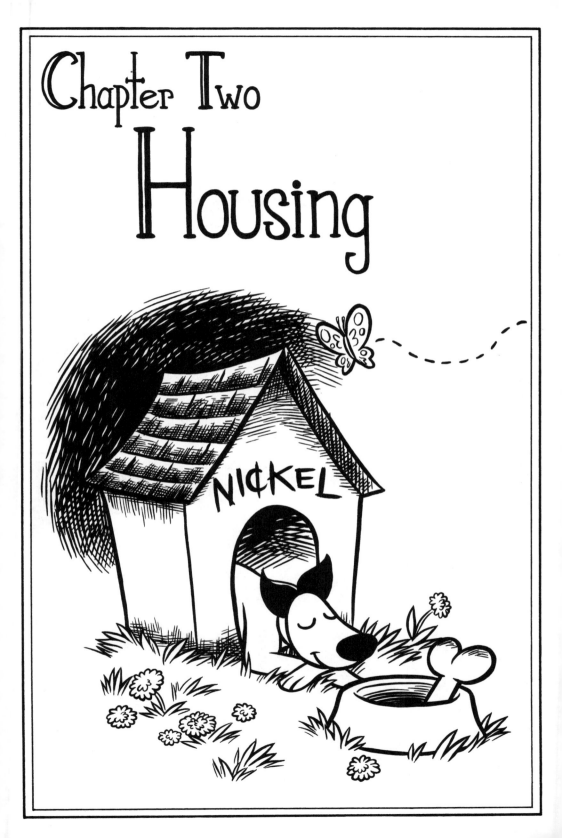

1: GETTING THERE

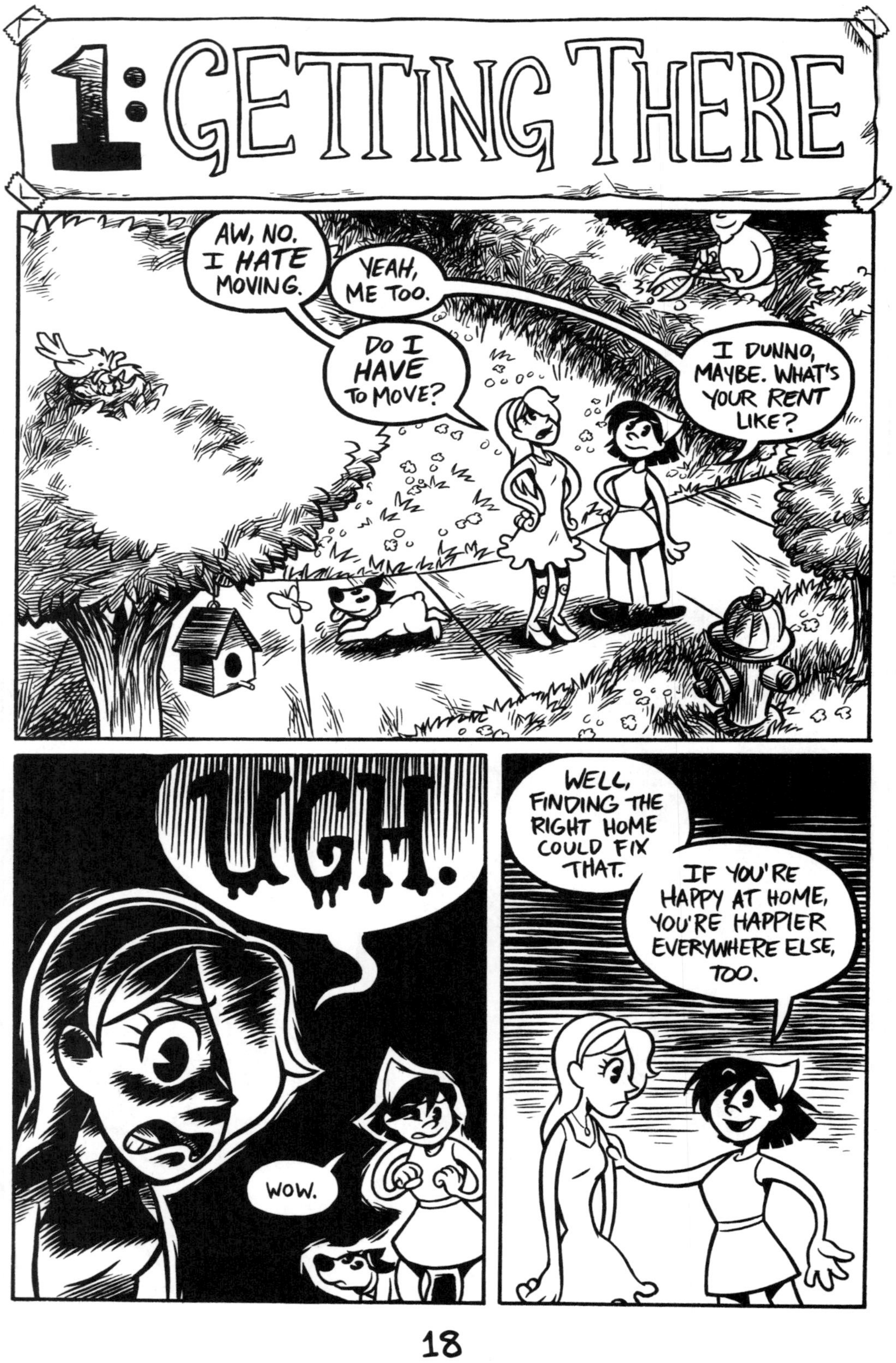
AW, NO. I HATE MOVING.
YEAH, ME TOO.
DO I HAVE TO MOVE?
I DUNNO, MAYBE. WHAT'S YOUR RENT LIKE?
UGH.
WOW.
WELL, FINDING THE RIGHT HOME COULD FIX THAT.
IF YOU'RE HAPPY AT HOME, YOU'RE HAPPIER EVERYWHERE ELSE, TOO.

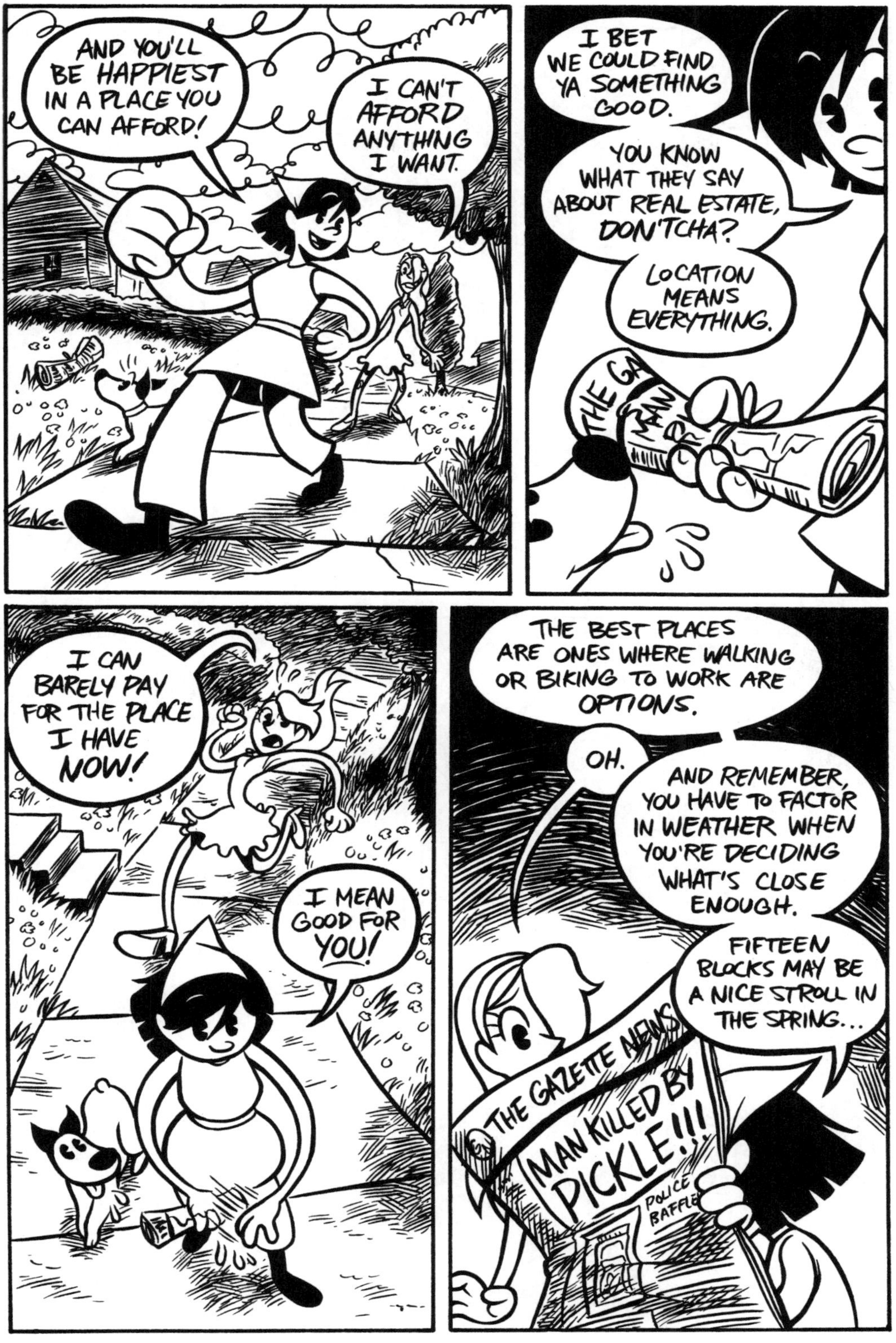
AND YOU'LL BE HAPPIEST IN A PLACE YOU CAN AFFORD!
I CAN'T AFFORD ANYTHING I WANT.
I BET WE COULD FIND YA SOMETHING GOOD.
YOU KNOW WHAT THEY SAY ABOUT REAL ESTATE, DON'TCHA?
LOCATION MEANS EVERYTHING.
I CAN BARELY PAY FOR THE PLACE I HAVE NOW!
I MEAN GOOD FOR YOU!
THE BEST PLACES ARE ONES WHERE WALKING OR BIKING TO WORK ARE OPTIONS.
OH.
AND REMEMBER, YOU HAVE TO FACTOR IN WEATHER WHEN YOU'RE DECIDING WHAT'S CLOSE ENOUGH.
FIFTEEN BLOCKS MAY BE A NICE STROLL IN THE SPRING...
THE GAZETTE NEWS
MAN KILLED BY PICKLE!!!
POLICE BAFFLE

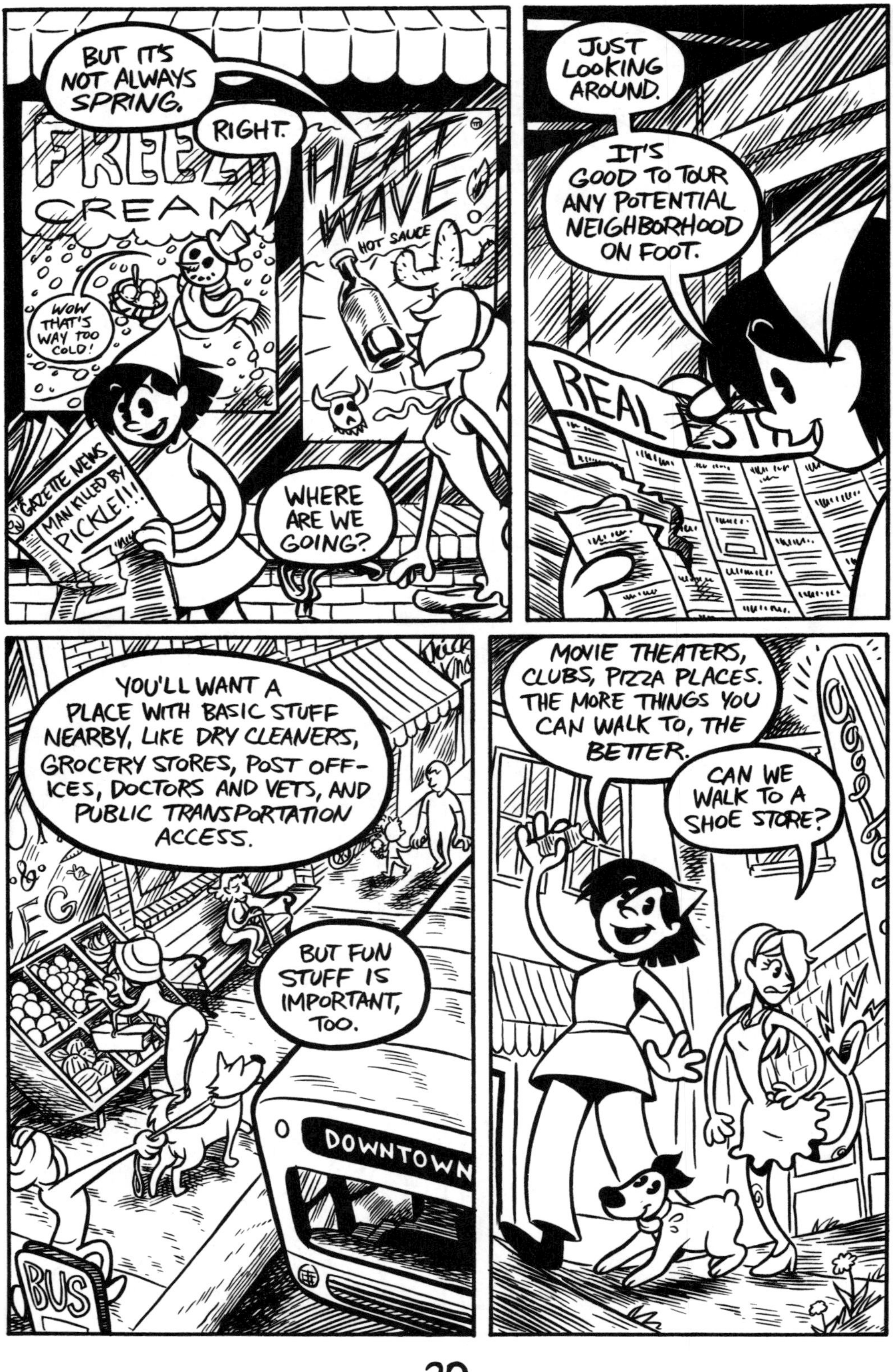
BUT IT'S NOT ALWAYS SPRING.
RIGHT.
FREEZE CREAM
WOW THAT'S WAY TOO COLD!
HEAT WAVE
HOT SAUCE
GAZETTE NEWS
MAN KILLED BY PICKLE!!!
WHERE ARE WE GOING?
JUST LOOKING AROUND.
IT'S GOOD TO TOUR ANY POTENTIAL NEIGHBORHOOD ON FOOT.
REAL EST
YOU'LL WANT A PLACE WITH BASIC STUFF NEARBY, LIKE DRY CLEANERS, GROCERY STORES, POST OFF-ICES, DOCTORS AND VETS, AND PUBLIC TRANSPORTATION ACCESS.
BUT FUN STUFF IS IMPORTANT, TOO.
DOWNTOWN
BUS
MOVIE THEATERS, CLUBS, PIZZA PLACES. THE MORE THINGS YOU CAN WALK TO, THE BETTER.
CAN WE WALK TO A SHOE STORE?

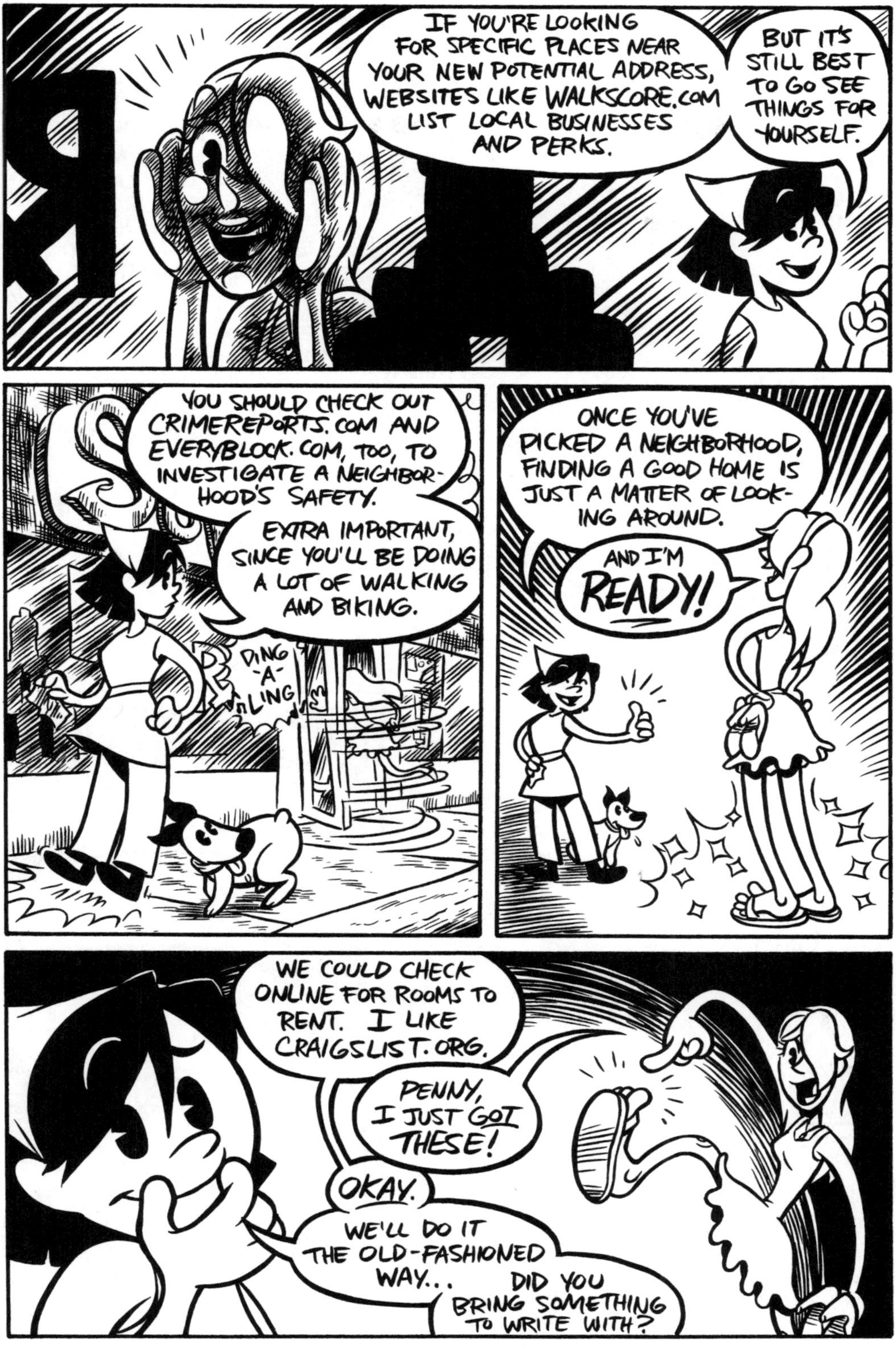
IF YOU'RE LOOKING FOR SPECIFIC PLACES NEAR YOUR NEW POTENTIAL ADDRESS, WEBSITES LIKE WALKSCORE.COM LIST LOCAL BUSINESSES AND PERKS.
BUT IT'S STILL BEST TO GO SEE THINGS FOR YOURSELF.
YOU SHOULD CHECK OUT CRIMEREPORTS.COM AND EVERYBLOCK.COM, TOO, TO INVESTIGATE A NEIGHBOR-HOOD'S SAFETY.
EXTRA IMPORTANT, SINCE YOU'LL BE DOING A LOT OF WALKING AND BIKING.
DING -A- LING
ONCE YOU'VE PICKED A NEIGHBORHOOD, FINDING A GOOD HOME IS JUST A MATTER OF LOOK-ING AROUND.
AND I'M READY!
WE COULD CHECK ONLINE FOR ROOMS TO RENT. I LIKE CRAIGSLIST.ORG.
PENNY, I JUST GOT THESE!
OKAY.
WE'LL DO IT THE OLD-FASHIONED WAY... DID YOU BRING SOMETHING TO WRITE WITH?

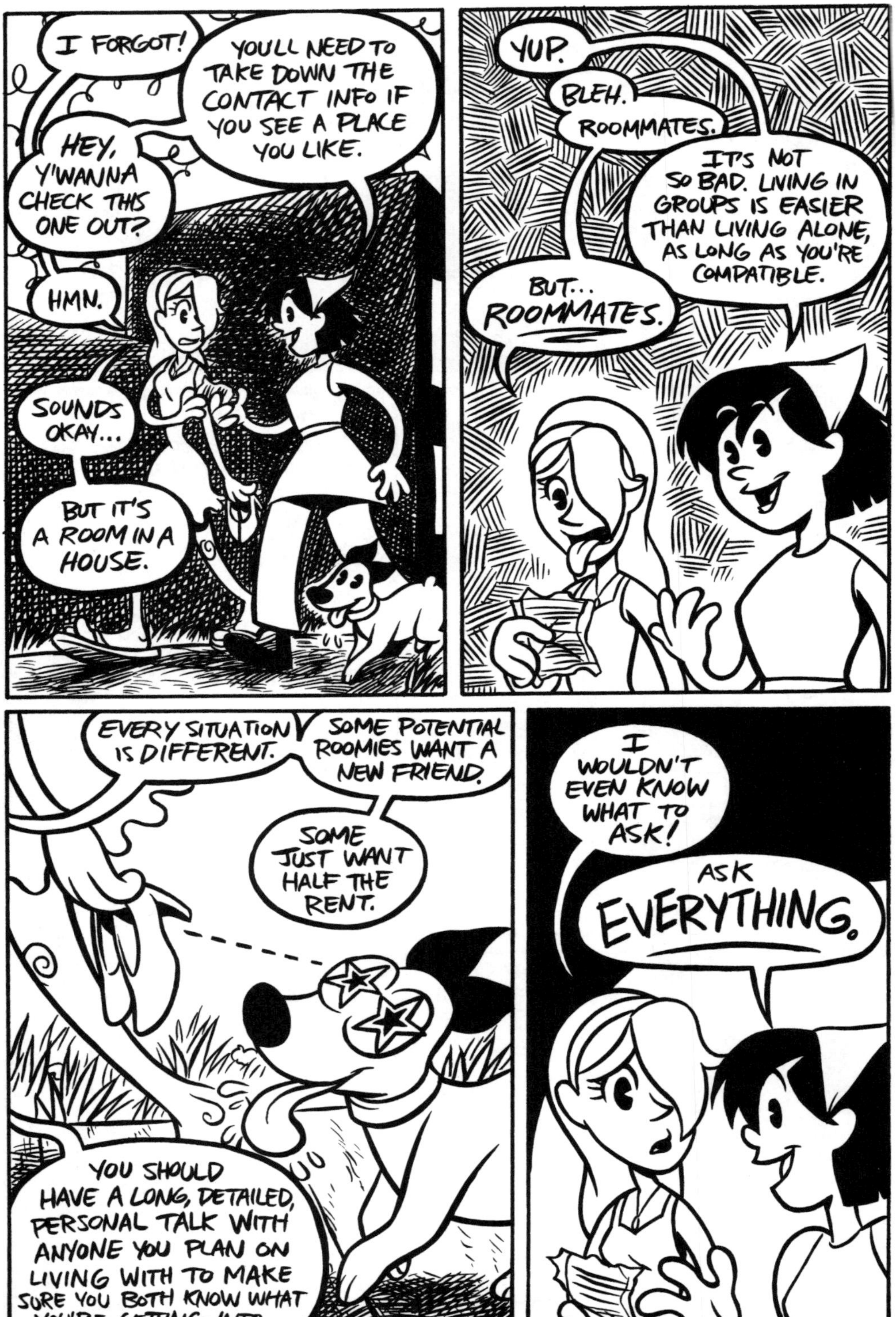
I FORGOT!
YOU'LL NEED TO TAKE DOWN THE CONTACT INFO IF YOU SEE A PLACE YOU LIKE.
HEY, Y'WANNA CHECK THIS ONE OUT?
HMN.
SOUNDS OKAY...
BUT IT'S A ROOM IN A HOUSE.
YUP.
BLEH.
ROOMMATES.
IT'S NOT SO BAD. LIVING IN GROUPS IS EASIER THAN LIVING ALONE, AS LONG AS YOU'RE COMPATIBLE.
BUT... ROOMMATES.
EVERY SITUATION IS DIFFERENT.
SOME POTENTIAL ROOMIES WANT A NEW FRIEND.
SOME JUST WANT HALF THE RENT.
YOU SHOULD HAVE A LONG, DETAILED, PERSONAL TALK WITH ANYONE YOU PLAN ON LIVING WITH TO MAKE SURE YOU BOTH KNOW WHAT YOU'RE GETTING INTO.
I WOULDN'T EVEN KNOW WHAT TO ASK!
ASK EVERYTHING.

2: Sharing Space

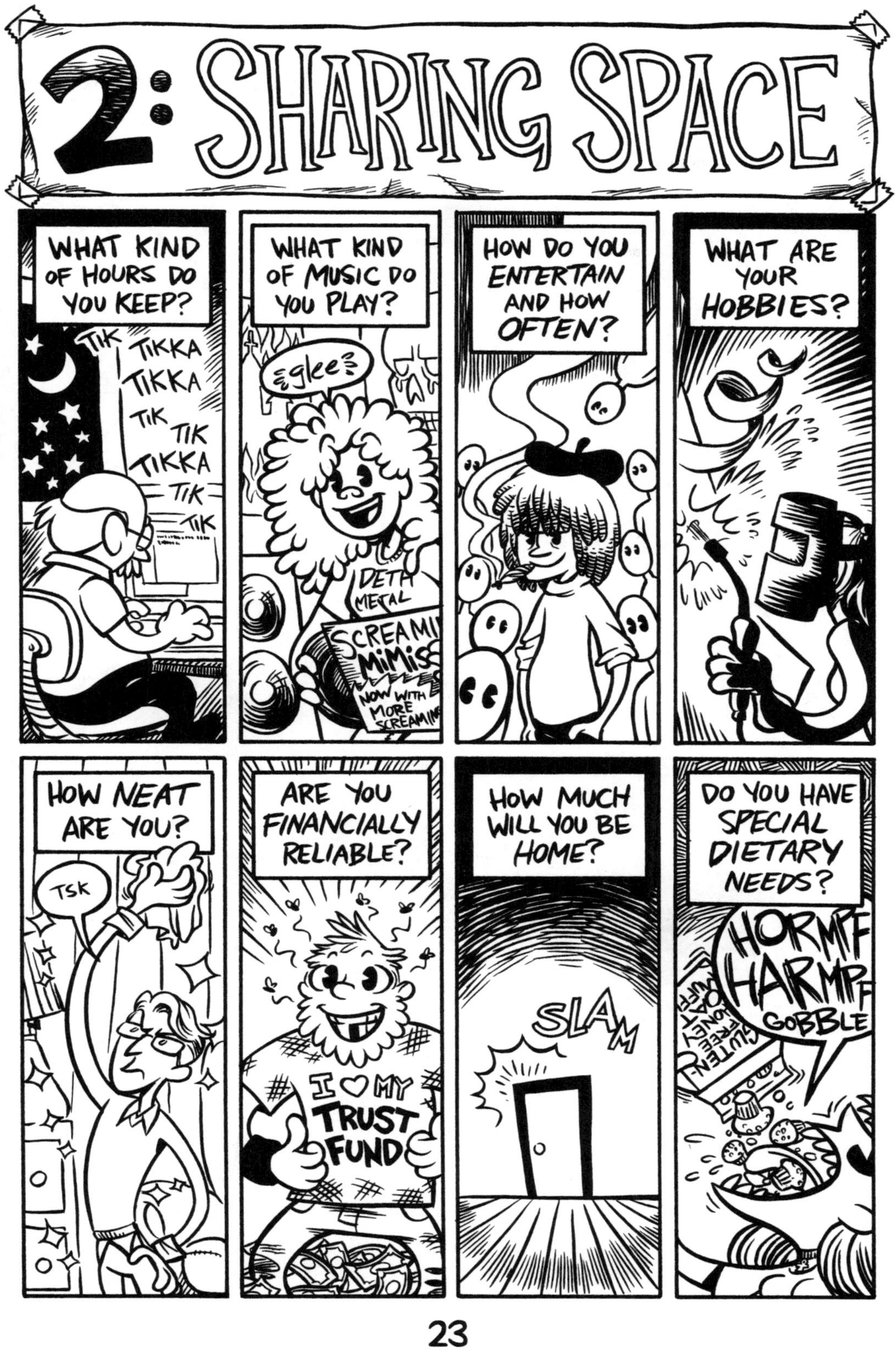

WHAT KIND OF HOURS DO YOU KEEP?
TIK TIKKA TIKKA TIK TIK TIKKA TIK TIK
WHAT KIND OF MUSIC DO YOU PLAY?
glee
DETH METAL
SCREAMI MIMIS NOW WITH MORE SCREAMIN
HOW DO YOU ENTERTAIN AND HOW OFTEN?
WHAT ARE YOUR HOBBIES?
HOW NEAT ARE YOU?
TSK
ARE YOU FINANCIALLY RELIABLE?
I ♥ MY TRUST FUND
HOW MUCH WILL YOU BE HOME?
SLAM
DO YOU HAVE SPECIAL DIETARY NEEDS?
HORMPF HARMPF GOBBLE

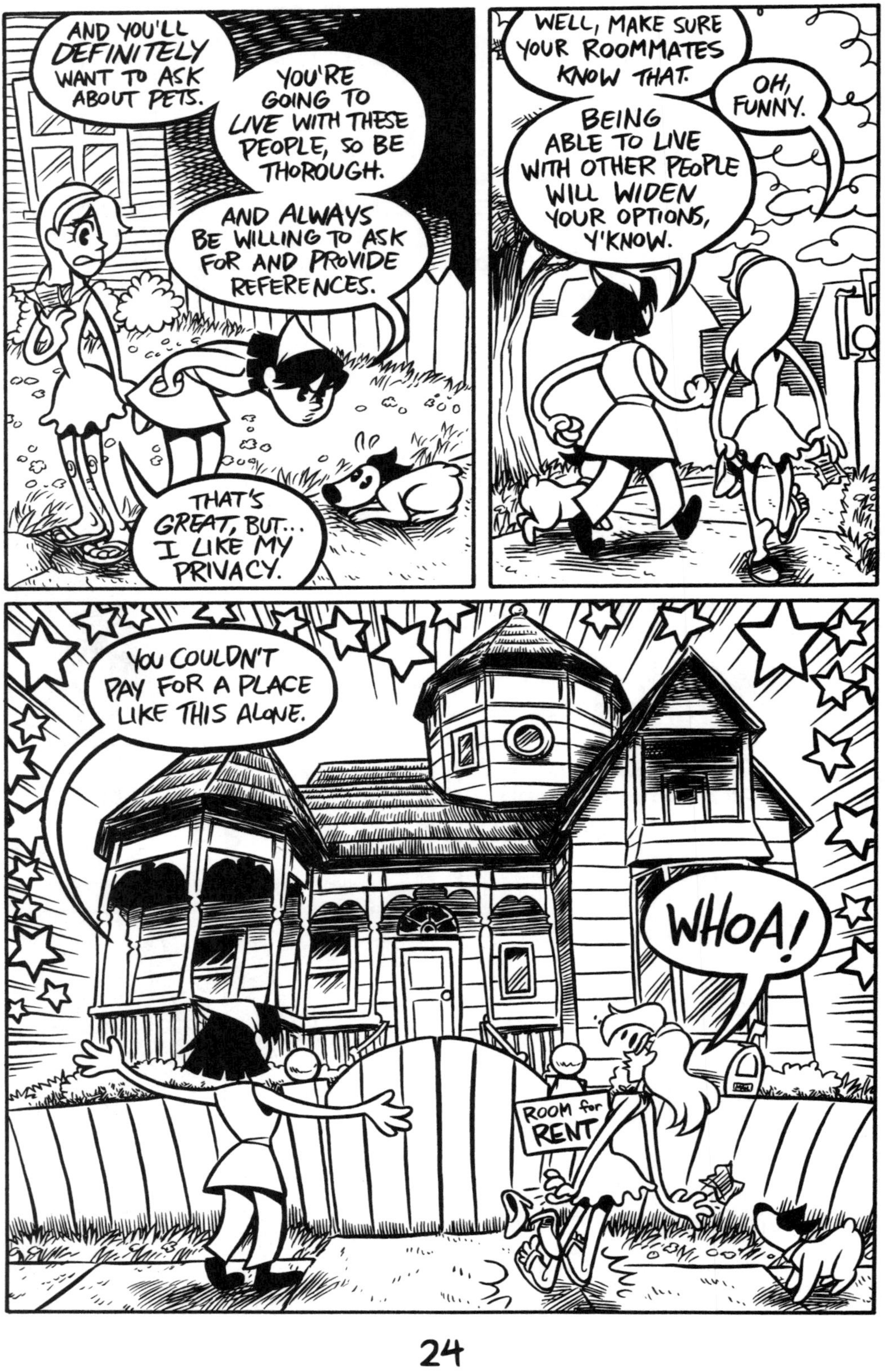
AND YOU'LL DEFINITELY WANT TO ASK ABOUT PETS.
YOU'RE GOING TO LIVE WITH THESE PEOPLE, SO BE THOROUGH.
AND ALWAYS BE WILLING TO ASK FOR AND PROVIDE REFERENCES.
THAT'S GREAT, BUT... I LIKE MY PRIVACY.
WELL, MAKE SURE YOUR ROOMMATES KNOW THAT.
OH, FUNNY.
BEING ABLE TO LIVE WITH OTHER PEOPLE WILL WIDEN YOUR OPTIONS, Y'KNOW.
YOU COULDN'T PAY FOR A PLACE LIKE THIS ALONE.
WHOA!
ROOM for RENT

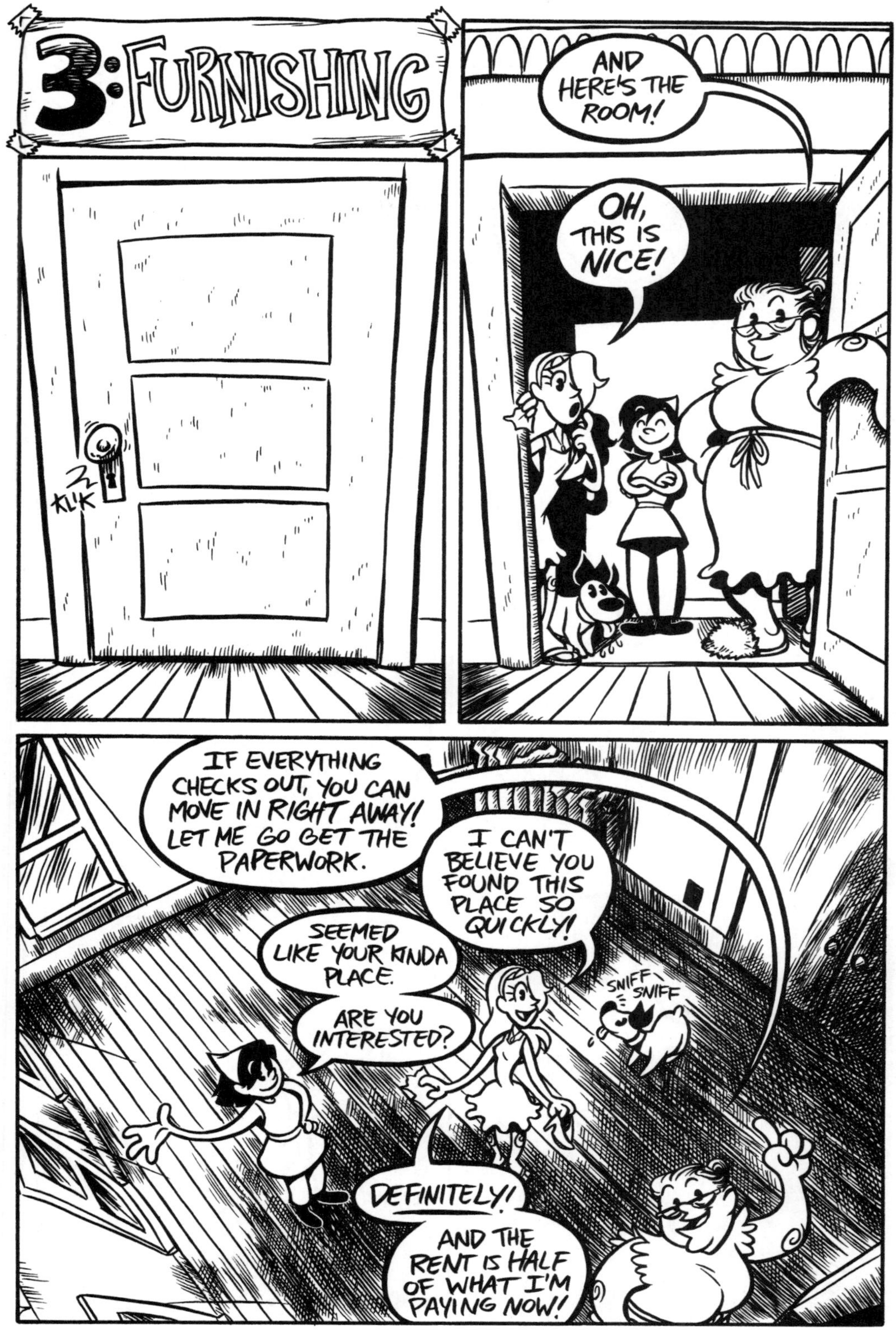

3: FURNISHING
KL'K
AND HERE'S THE ROOM!
OH, THIS IS NICE!
IF EVERYTHING CHECKS OUT, YOU CAN MOVE IN RIGHT AWAY! LET ME GO GET THE PAPERWORK.
I CAN'T BELIEVE YOU FOUND THIS PLACE SO QUICKLY!
SEEMED LIKE YOUR KINDA PLACE.
ARE YOU INTERESTED?
SNIFF SNIFF
DEFINITELY!
AND THE RENT IS HALF OF WHAT I'M PAYING NOW!

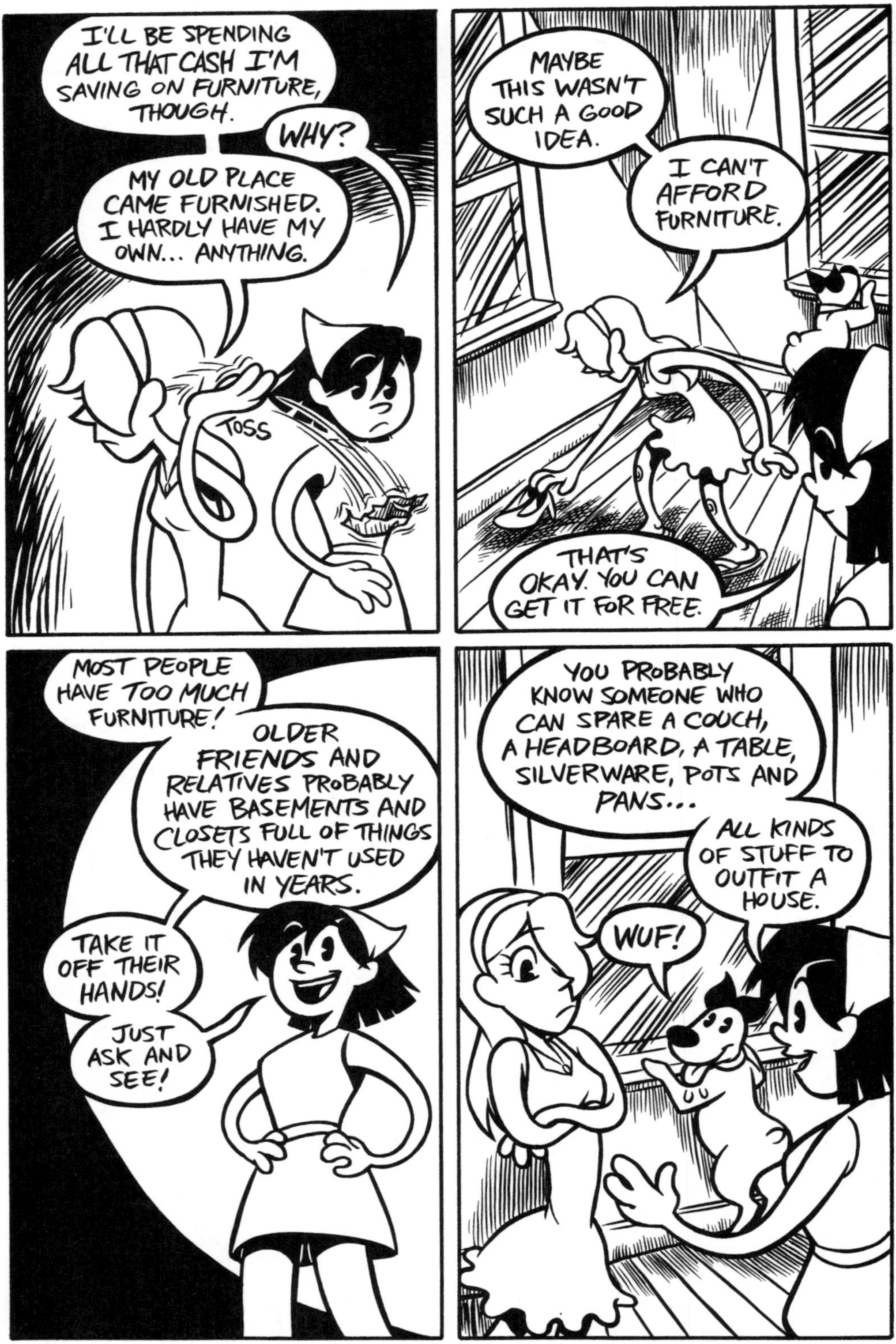
I'LL BE SPENDING ALL THAT CASH I'M SAVING ON FURNITURE, THOUGH.
WHY?
MY OLD PLACE CAME FURNISHED. I HARDLY HAVE MY OWN... ANYTHING.
TOSS
MAYBE THIS WASN'T SUCH A GOOD IDEA.
I CAN'T AFFORD FURNITURE.
THAT'S OKAY. YOU CAN GET IT FOR FREE.
MOST PEOPLE HAVE TOO MUCH FURNITURE!
OLDER FRIENDS AND RELATIVES PROBABLY HAVE BASEMENTS AND CLOSETS FULL OF THINGS THEY HAVEN'T USED IN YEARS.
TAKE IT OFF THEIR HANDS!
JUST ASK AND SEE!
YOU PROBABLY KNOW SOMEONE WHO CAN SPARE A COUCH, A HEADBOARD, A TABLE, SILVERWARE, POTS AND PANS...
ALL KINDS OF STUFF TO OUTFIT A HOUSE.
WUF!

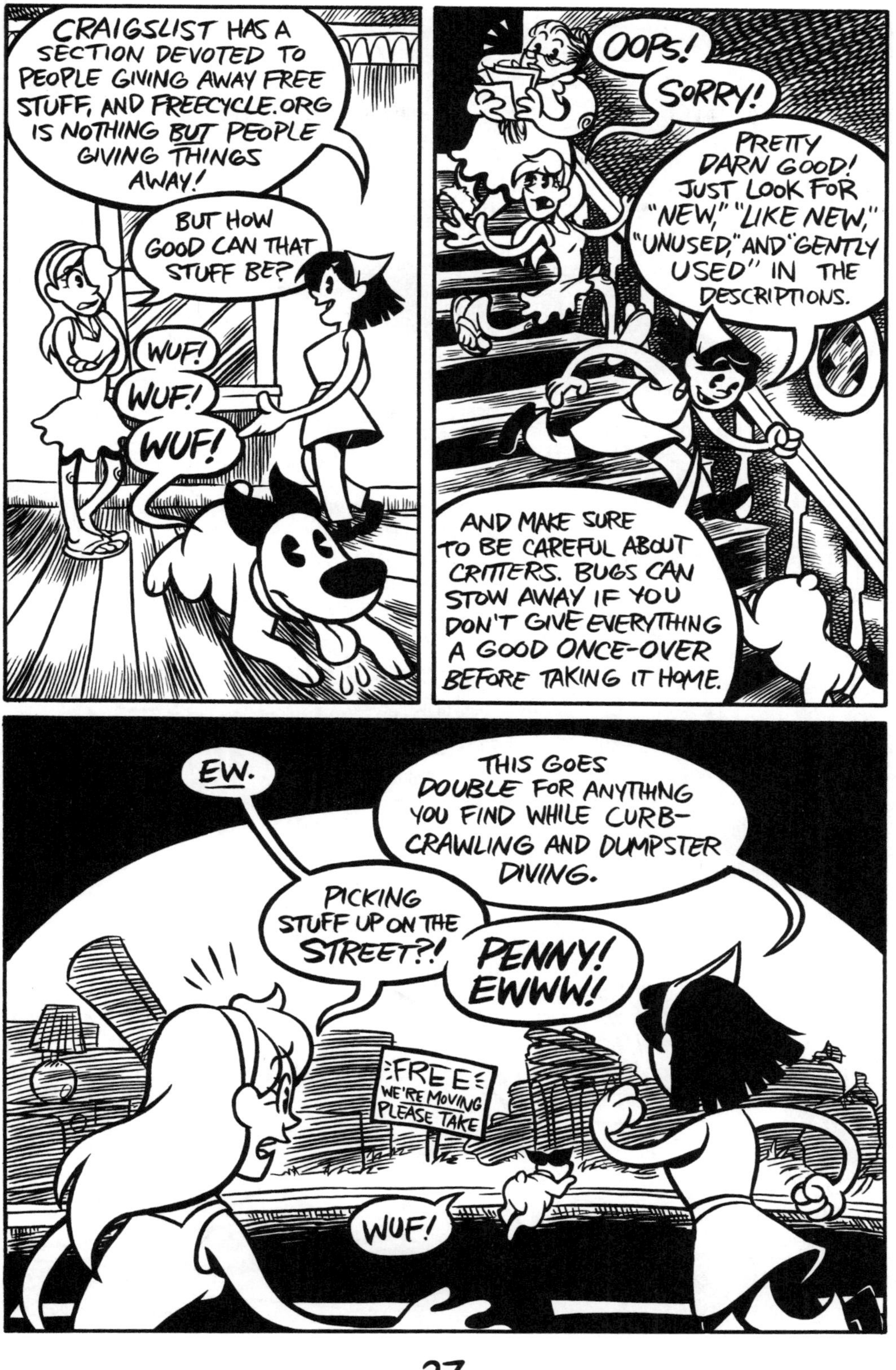
CRAIGSLIST HAS A SECTION DEVOTED TO PEOPLE GIVING AWAY FREE STUFF, AND FREECYCLE.ORG IS NOTHING BUT PEOPLE GIVING THINGS AWAY!
BUT HOW GOOD CAN THAT STUFF BE?
WUF!
WUF!
WUF!
OOPS!
SORRY!
PRETTY DARN GOOD! JUST LOOK FOR "NEW," "LIKE NEW," "UNUSED," AND "GENTLY USED" IN THE DESCRIPTIONS.
AND MAKE SURE TO BE CAREFUL ABOUT CRITTERS. BUGS CAN STOW AWAY IF YOU DON'T GIVE EVERYTHING A GOOD ONCE-OVER BEFORE TAKING IT HOME.
EW.
THIS GOES DOUBLE FOR ANYTHING YOU FIND WHILE CURB-CRAWLING AND DUMPSTER DIVING.
PICKING STUFF UP ON THE STREET?!
PENNY! EWWW!
FREE WE'RE MOVING PLEASE TAKE
WUF!

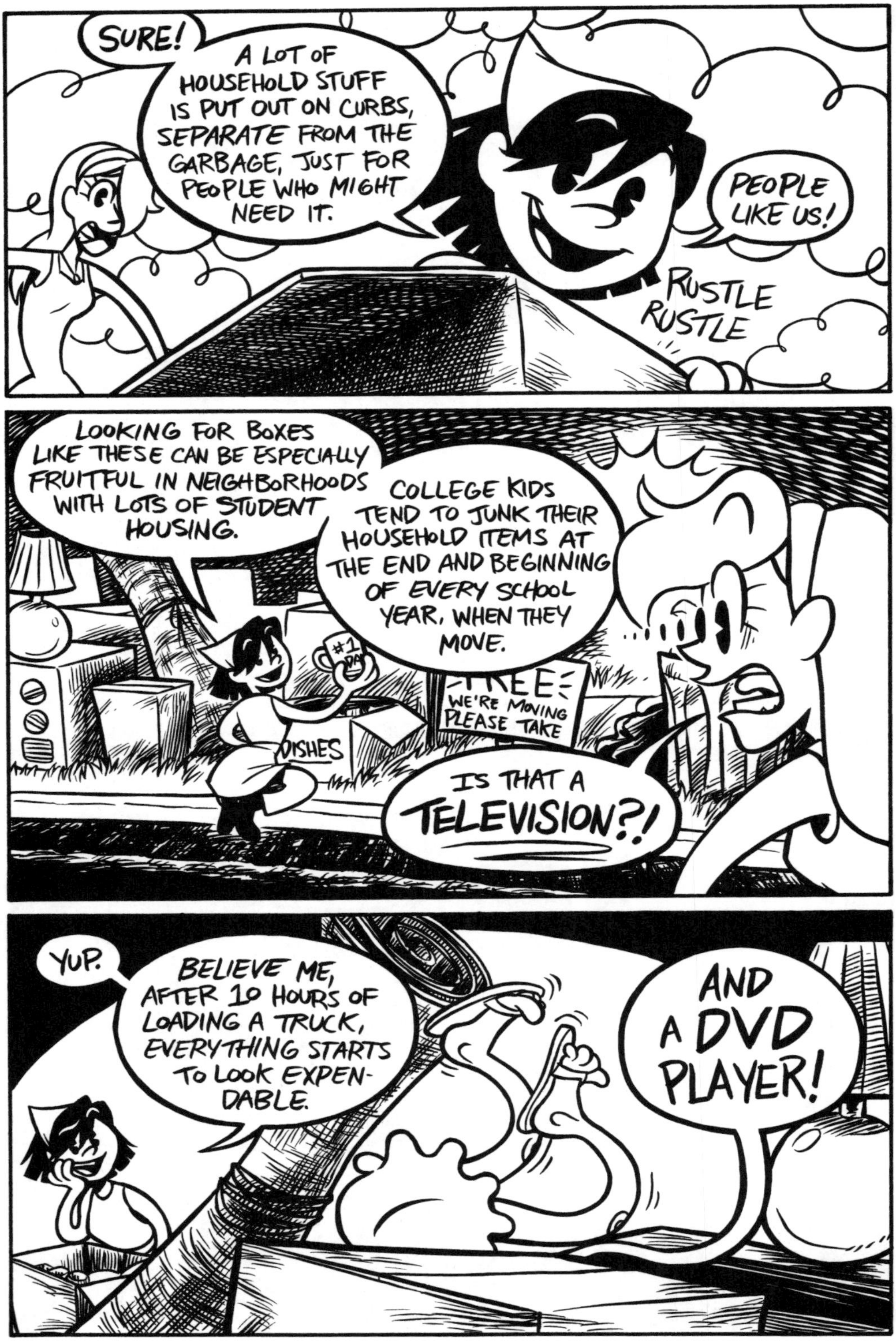
SURE!
A LOT OF HOUSEHOLD STUFF IS PUT OUT ON CURBS, SEPARATE FROM THE GARBAGE, JUST FOR PEOPLE WHO MIGHT NEED IT.
PEOPLE LIKE US!
RUSTLE RUSTLE
LOOKING FOR BOXES LIKE THESE CAN BE ESPECIALLY FRUITFUL IN NEIGHBORHOODS WITH LOTS OF STUDENT HOUSING.
COLLEGE KIDS TEND TO JUNK THEIR HOUSEHOLD ITEMS AT THE END AND BEGINNING OF EVERY SCHOOL YEAR, WHEN THEY MOVE.
FREE WE'RE MOVING PLEASE TAKE
DISHES
IS THAT A TELEVISION?!
YUP.
BELIEVE ME, AFTER 10 HOURS OF LOADING A TRUCK, EVERYTHING STARTS TO LOOK EXPENDABLE.
AND A DVD PLAYER!

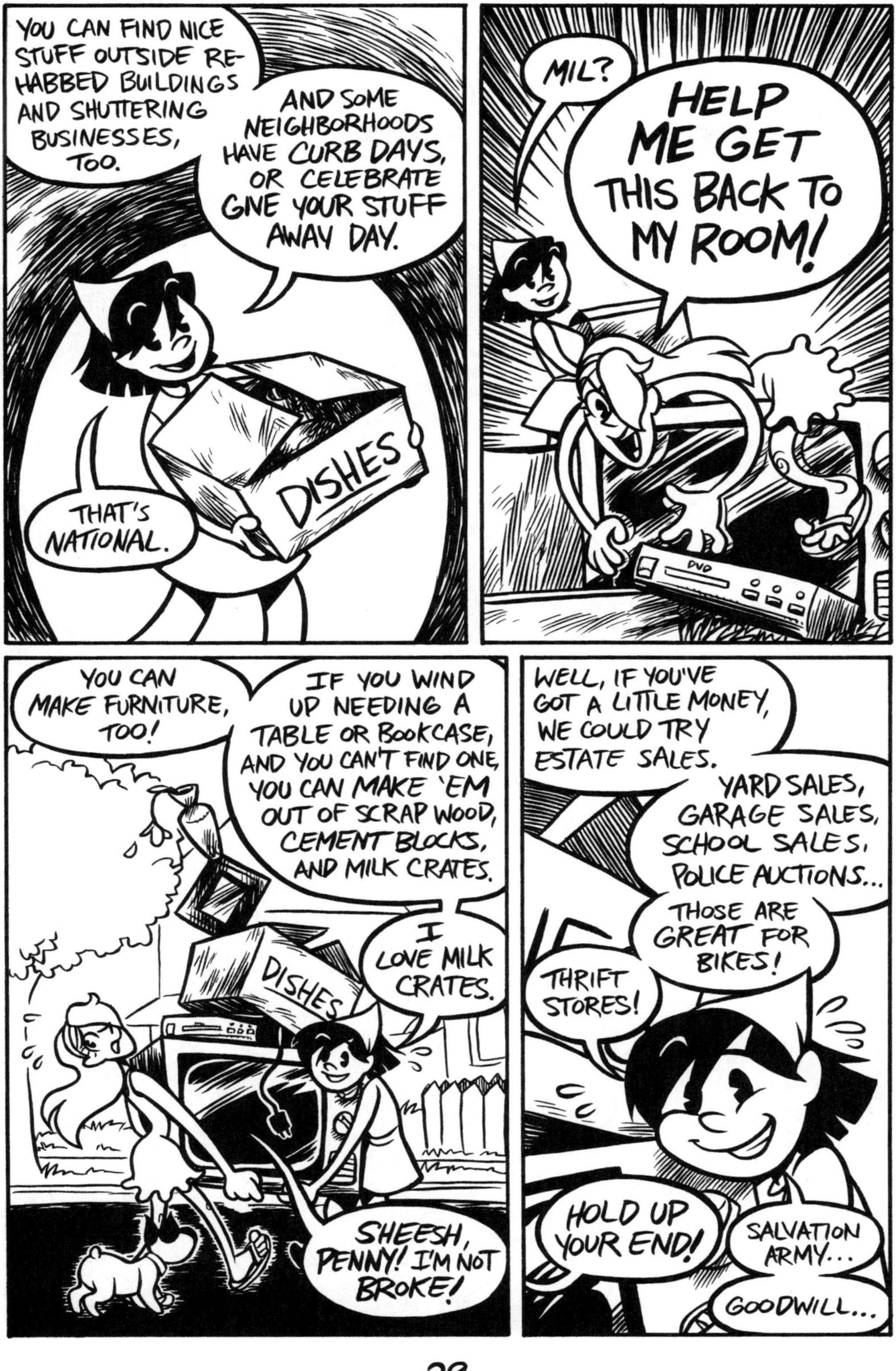
YOU CAN FIND NICE STUFF OUTSIDE RE-HABBED BUILDINGS AND SHUTTERING BUSINESSES, TOO.
AND SOME NEIGHBORHOODS HAVE CURB DAYS, OR CELEBRATE GIVE YOUR STUFF AWAY DAY.
THAT'S NATIONAL.
DISHES
MIL?
HELP ME GET THIS BACK TO MY ROOM!
DVD
YOU CAN MAKE FURNITURE, TOO!
IF YOU WIND UP NEEDING A TABLE OR BOOKCASE, AND YOU CAN'T FIND ONE, YOU CAN MAKE 'EM OUT OF SCRAP WOOD, CEMENT BLOCKS, AND MILK CRATES.
I LOVE MILK CRATES.
DISHES
SHEESH, PENNY! I'M NOT BROKE!
WELL, IF YOU'VE GOT A LITTLE MONEY, WE COULD TRY ESTATE SALES.
YARD SALES, GARAGE SALES, SCHOOL SALES, POLICE AUCTIONS...
THOSE ARE GREAT FOR BIKES!
THRIFT STORES!
HOLD UP YOUR END!
SALVATION ARMY...
GOODWILL...

4: Moving What You've Got

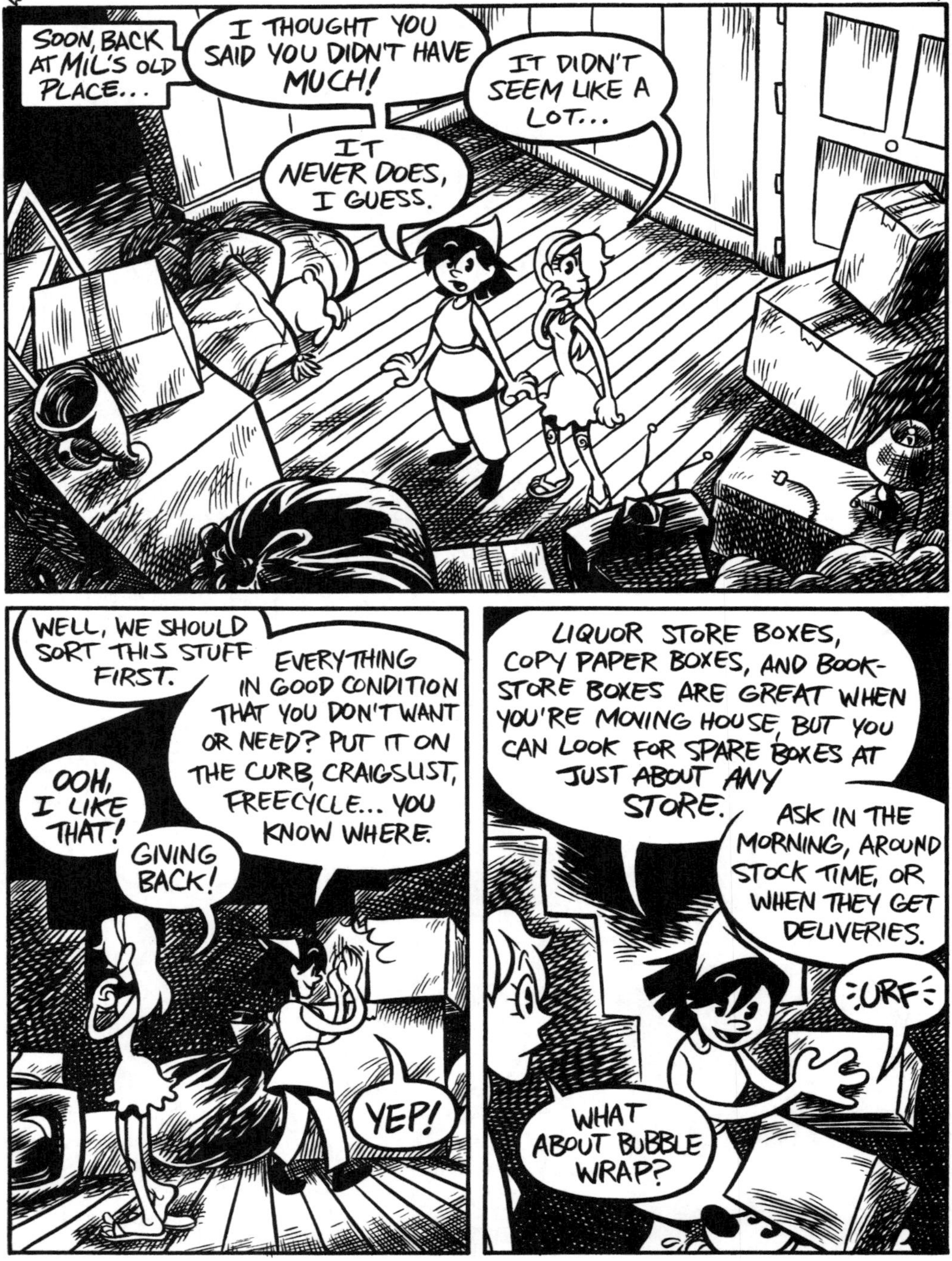

SOON, BACK AT MIL'S OLD PLACE...
I THOUGHT YOU SAID YOU DIDN'T HAVE MUCH!
IT DIDN'T SEEM LIKE A LOT...
IT NEVER DOES, I GUESS.
WELL, WE SHOULD SORT THIS STUFF FIRST.
EVERYTHING IN GOOD CONDITION THAT YOU DON'T WANT OR NEED? PUT IT ON THE CURB, CRAIGSLIST, FREECYCLE... YOU KNOW WHERE.
OOH, I LIKE THAT!
GIVING BACK!
YEP!
LIQUOR STORE BOXES, COPY PAPER BOXES, AND BOOK-STORE BOXES ARE GREAT WHEN YOU'RE MOVING HOUSE, BUT YOU CAN LOOK FOR SPARE BOXES AT JUST ABOUT ANY STORE.
ASK IN THE MORNING, AROUND STOCK TIME, OR WHEN THEY GET DELIVERIES.
URF
WHAT ABOUT BUBBLE WRAP?

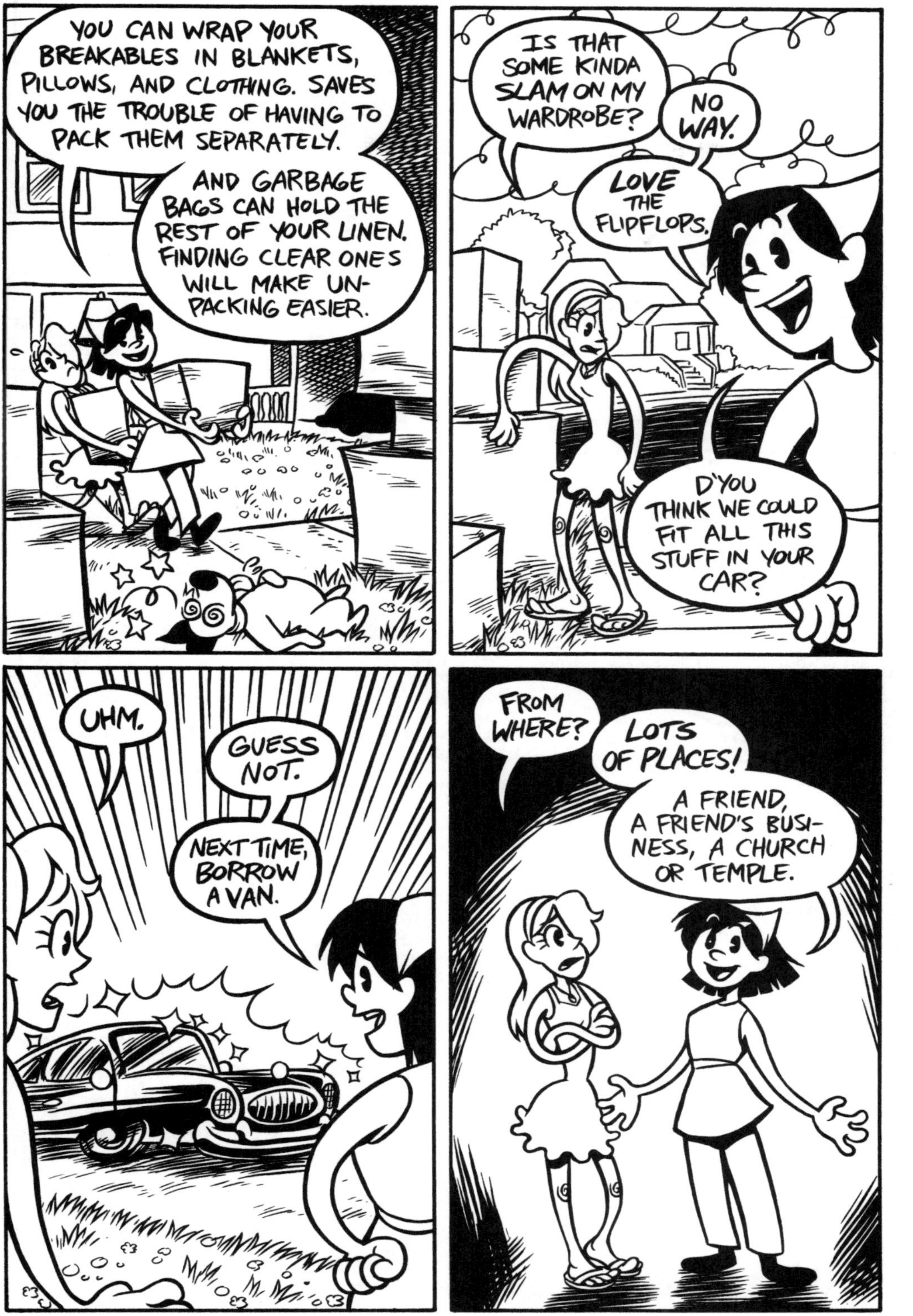
YOU CAN WRAP YOUR BREAKABLES IN BLANKETS, PILLOWS, AND CLOTHING. SAVES YOU THE TROUBLE OF HAVING TO PACK THEM SEPARATELY.
AND GARBAGE BAGS CAN HOLD THE REST OF YOUR LINEN. FINDING CLEAR ONES WILL MAKE UN-PACKING EASIER.
IS THAT SOME KINDA SLAM ON MY WARDROBE?
NO WAY.
LOVE THE FLIPFLOPS.
D'YOU THINK WE COULD FIT ALL THIS STUFF IN YOUR CAR?
UHM.
GUESS NOT.
NEXT TIME, BORROW A VAN.
FROM WHERE?
LOTS OF PLACES!
A FRIEND, A FRIEND'S BUSI-NESS, A CHURCH OR TEMPLE.

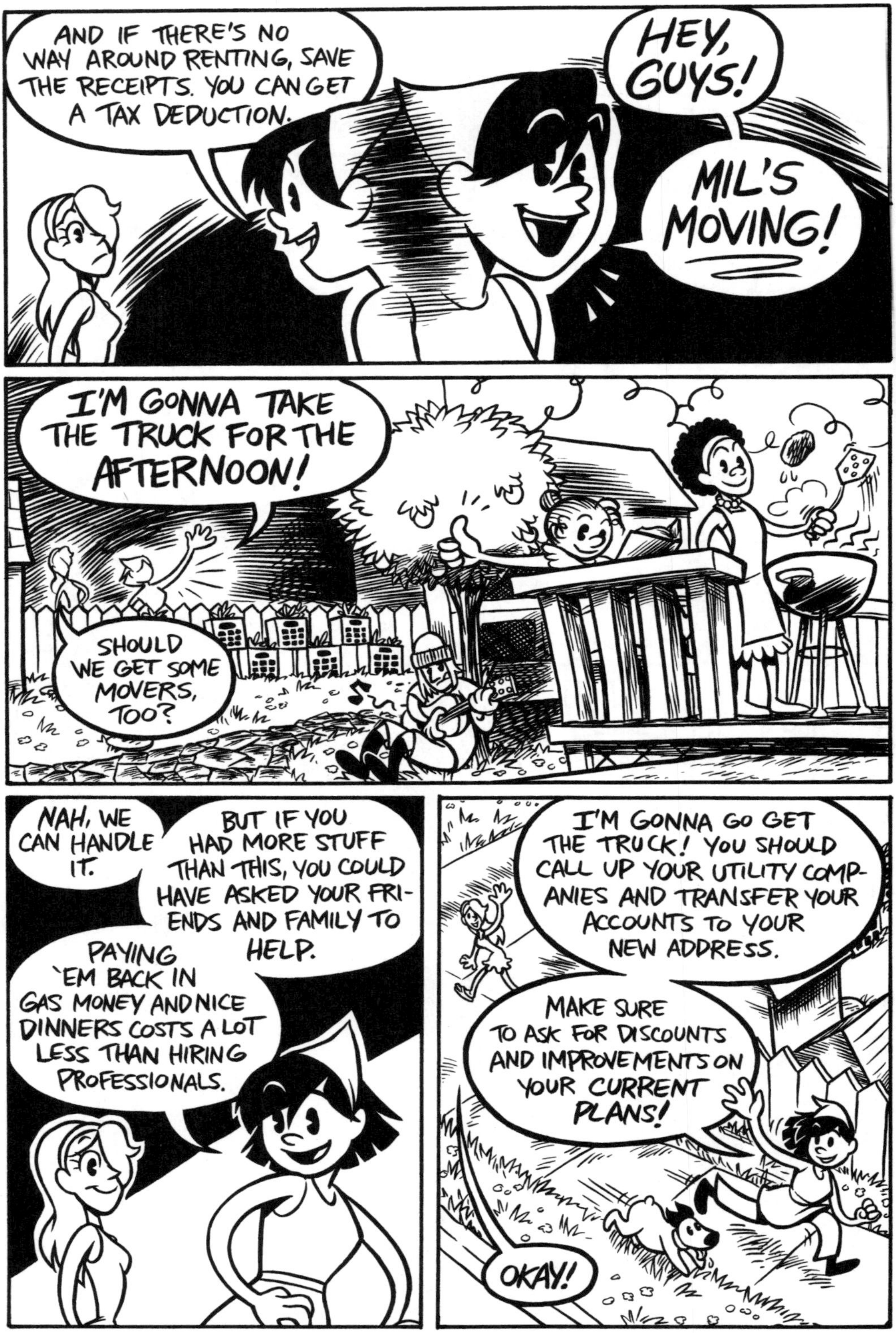

AND IF THERE'S NO WAY AROUND RENTING, SAVE THE RECEIPTS. YOU CAN GET A TAX DEDUCTION.
HEY, GUYS!
MIL'S MOVING!
I'M GONNA TAKE THE TRUCK FOR THE AFTERNOON!
SHOULD WE GET SOME MOVERS, TOO?
NAH, WE CAN HANDLE IT.
BUT IF YOU HAD MORE STUFF THAN THIS, YOU COULD HAVE ASKED YOUR FRIENDS AND FAMILY TO HELP.
PAYING `EM BACK IN GAS MONEY AND NICE DINNERS COSTS A LOT LESS THAN HIRING PROFESSIONALS.
I'M GONNA GO GET THE TRUCK! YOU SHOULD CALL UP YOUR UTILITY COMPANIES AND TRANSFER YOUR ACCOUNTS TO YOUR NEW ADDRESS.
MAKE SURE TO ASK FOR DISCOUNTS AND IMPROVEMENTS ON YOUR CURRENT PLANS!
OKAY!

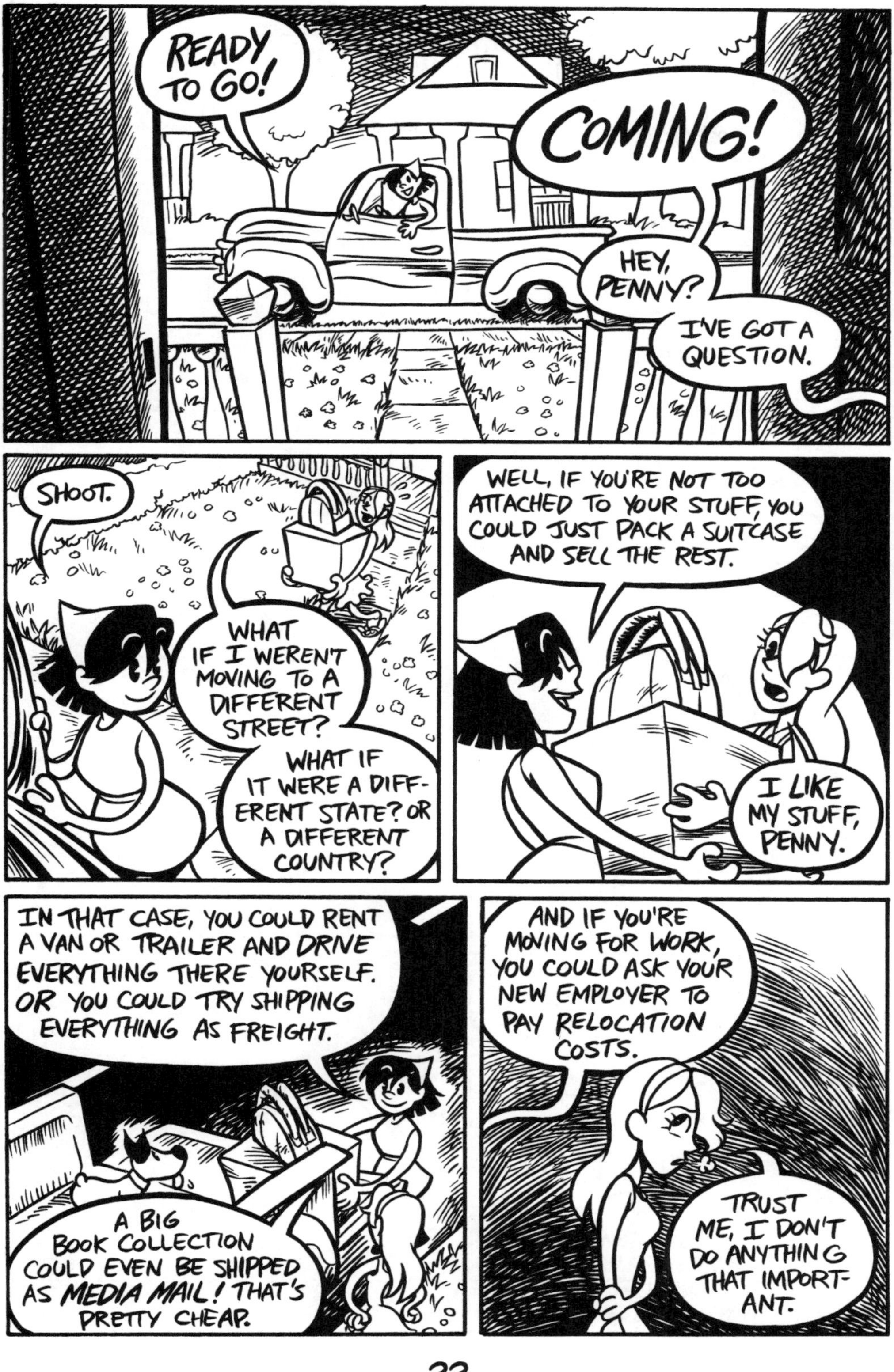
READY TO GO!
COMING!
HEY, PENNY?
I'VE GOT A QUESTION.
SHOOT.
WHAT IF I WEREN'T MOVING TO A DIFFERENT STREET?
WHAT IF IT WERE A DIFF-ERENT STATE? OR A DIFFERENT COUNTRY?
WELL, IF YOU'RE NOT TOO ATTACHED TO YOUR STUFF, YOU COULD JUST PACK A SUITCASE AND SELL THE REST.
I LIKE MY STUFF, PENNY.
IN THAT CASE, YOU COULD RENT A VAN OR TRAILER AND DRIVE EVERYTHING THERE YOURSELF. OR YOU COULD TRY SHIPPING EVERYTHING AS FREIGHT.
A BIG BOOK COLLECTION COULD EVEN BE SHIPPED AS MEDIA MAIL! THAT'S PRETTY CHEAP.
AND IF YOU'RE MOVING FOR WORK, YOU COULD ASK YOUR NEW EMPLOYER TO PAY RELOCATION COSTS.
TRUST ME, I DON'T DO ANYTHING THAT IMPORT-ANT.

5: HOUSEKEEPING

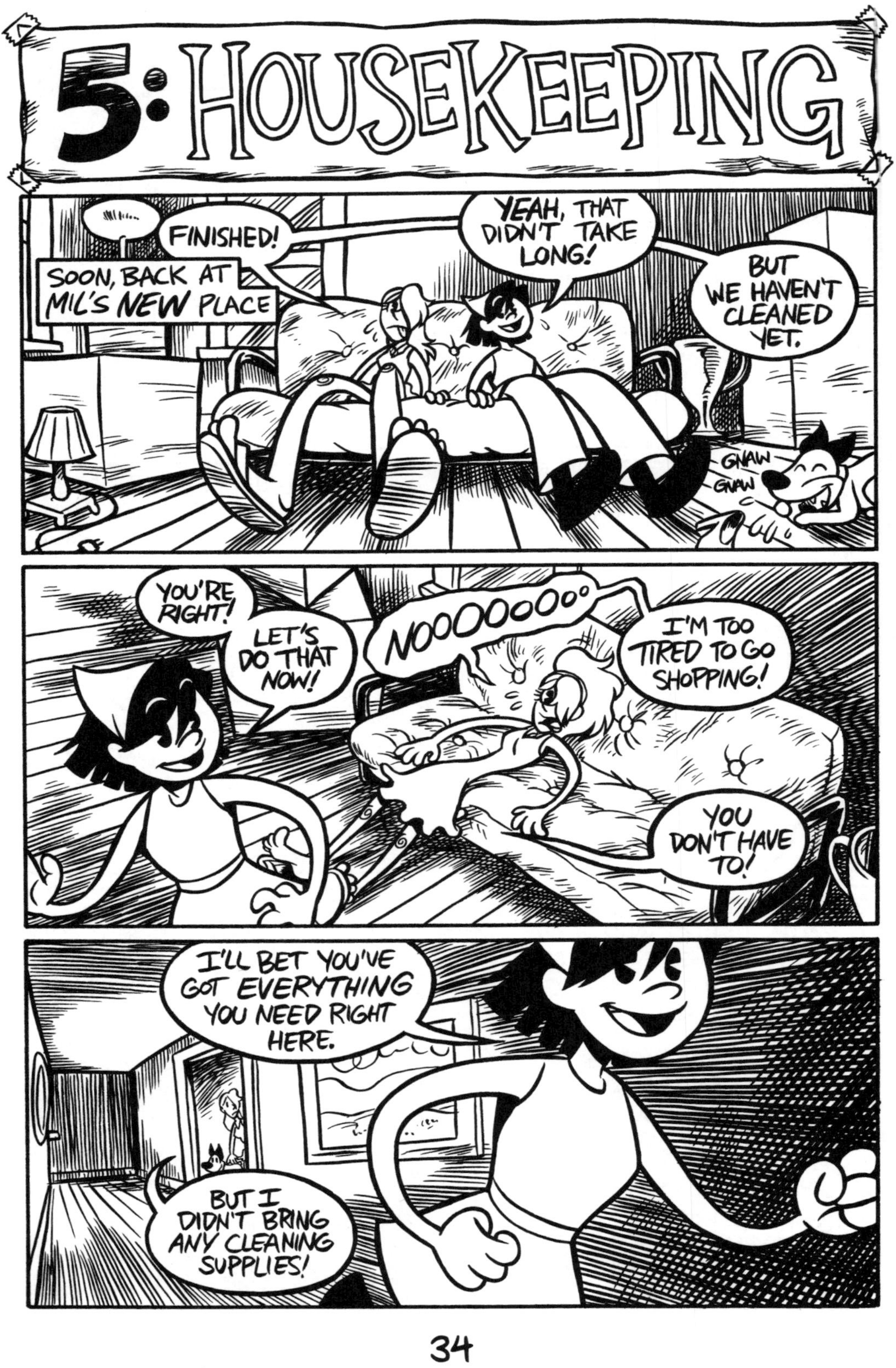
SOON, BACK AT MIL'S NEW PLACE
FINISHED!
YEAH, THAT DIDN'T TAKE LONG!
BUT WE HAVEN'T CLEANED YET.
GNAW GNAW
YOU'RE RIGHT!
LET'S DO THAT NOW!
NOOOOOOOOo
I'M TOO TIRED TO GO SHOPPING!
YOU DON'T HAVE TO!
I'LL BET YOU'VE GOT EVERYTHING YOU NEED RIGHT HERE.
BUT I DIDN'T BRING ANY CLEANING SUPPLIES!

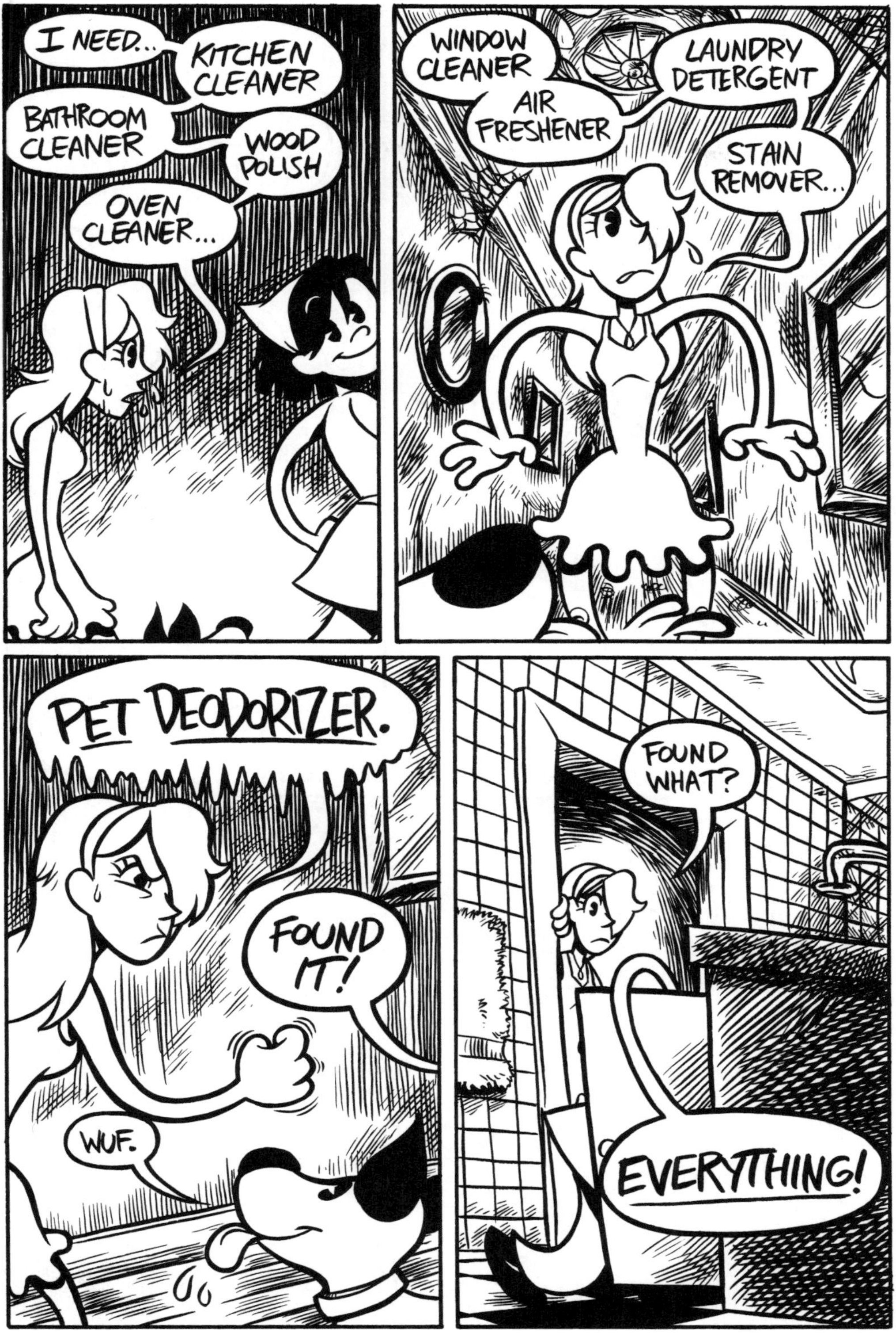
I NEED...
KITCHEN CLEANER
BATHROOM CLEANER
WOOD POLISH
OVEN CLEANER...
WINDOW CLEANER
AIR FRESHENER
LAUNDRY DETERGENT
STAIN REMOVER...
PET DEODORIZER.
FOUND IT!
WUF.
FOUND WHAT?
EVERYTHING!

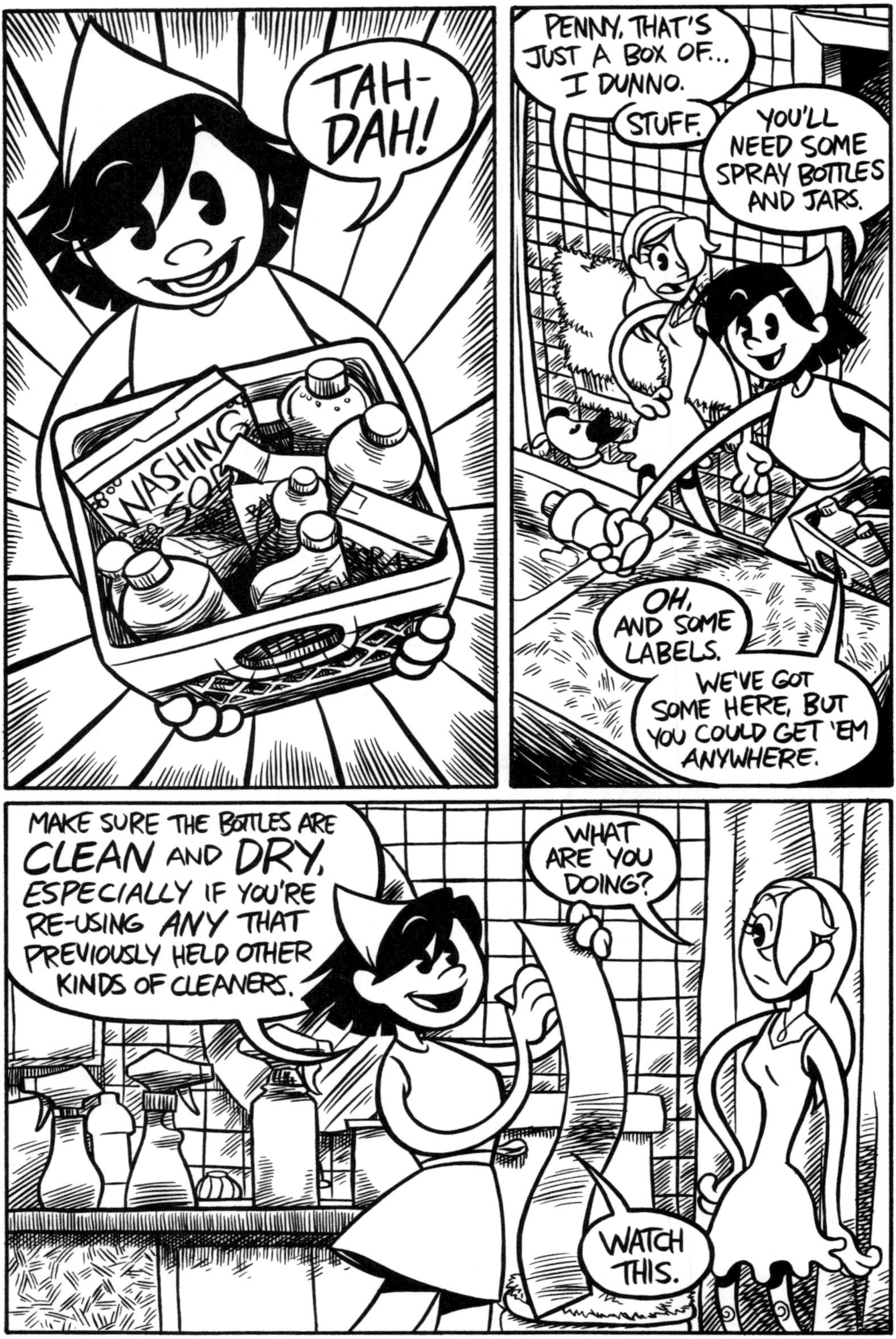
TAH-DAH!
WASHING SOAP
PENNY, THAT'S JUST A BOX OF... I DUNNO.
STUFF.
YOU'LL NEED SOME SPRAY BOTTLES AND JARS.
OH, AND SOME LABELS.
WE'VE GOT SOME HERE, BUT YOU COULD GET 'EM ANYWHERE.
MAKE SURE THE BOTTLES ARE CLEAN AND DRY, ESPECIALLY IF YOU'RE RE-USING ANY THAT PREVIOUSLY HELD OTHER KINDS OF CLEANERS.
WHAT ARE YOU DOING?
WATCH THIS.

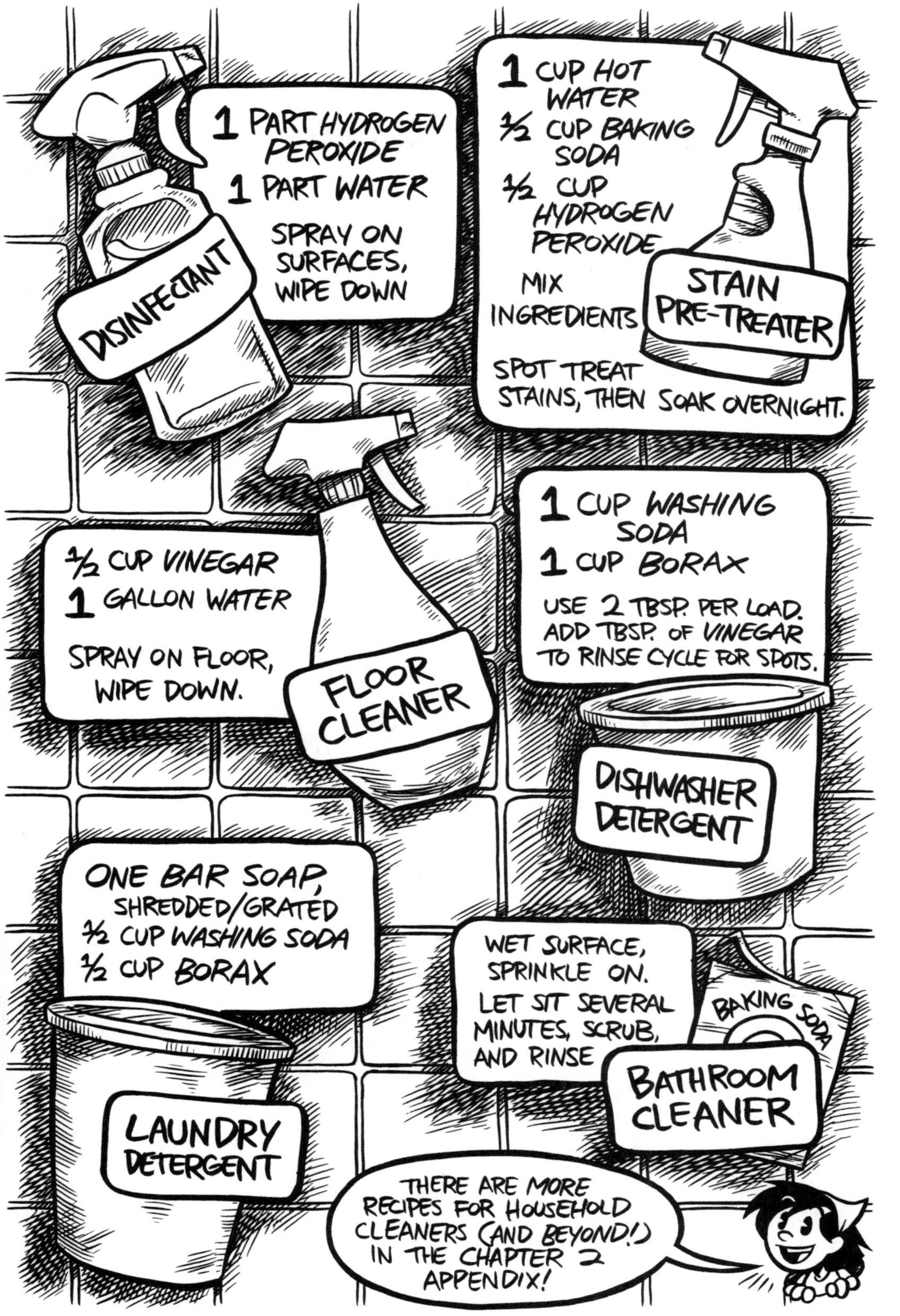
DISINFECTANT
1 PART HYDROGEN PEROXIDE
1 PART WATER
SPRAY ON SURFACES, WIPE DOWN
STAIN PRE-TREATER
1 CUP HOT WATER
1/2 CUP BAKING SODA
1/2 CUP HYDROGEN PEROXIDE
MIX INGREDIENTS
SPOT TREAT STAINS, THEN SOAK OVERNIGHT.
FLOOR CLEANER
1/2 CUP VINEGAR
1 GALLON WATER
SPRAY ON FLOOR, WIPE DOWN.
DISHWASHER DETERGENT
1 CUP WASHING SODA
1 CUP BORAX
USE 2 TBSP. PER LOAD. ADD TBSP. OF VINEGAR TO RINSE CYCLE FOR SPOTS.
LAUNDRY DETERGENT
ONE BAR SOAP, SHREDDED/GRATED
1/2 CUP WASHING SODA
1/2 CUP BORAX
BATHROOM CLEANER
BAKING SODA
WET SURFACE, SPRINKLE ON.
LET SIT SEVERAL MINUTES, SCRUB, AND RINSE
THERE ARE MORE RECIPES FOR HOUSEHOLD CLEANERS (AND BEYOND!) IN THE CHAPTER 2 APPENDIX!

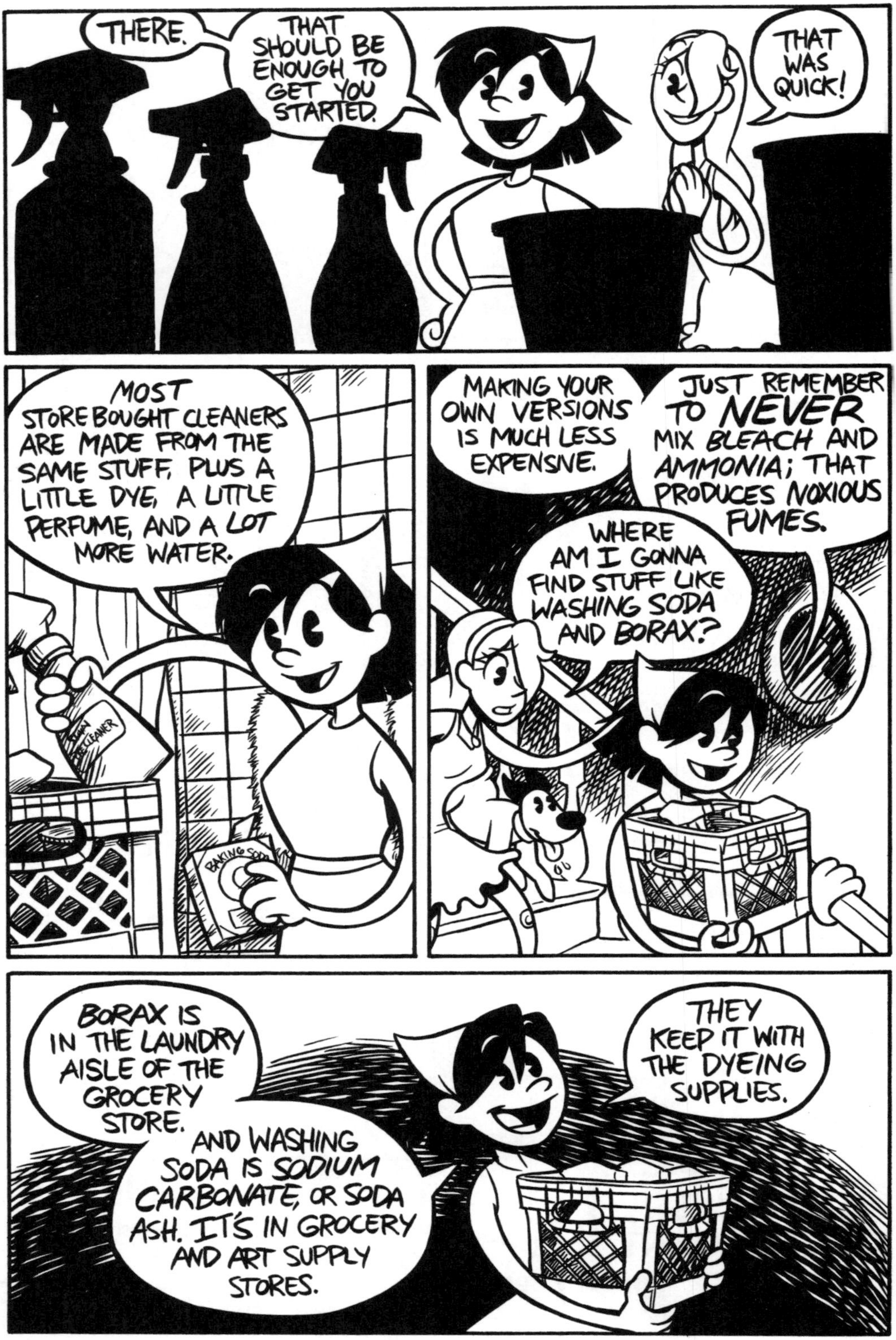
THERE.
THAT SHOULD BE ENOUGH TO GET YOU STARTED.
THAT WAS QUICK!
MOST STORE BOUGHT CLEANERS ARE MADE FROM THE SAME STUFF, PLUS A LITTLE DYE, A LITTLE PERFUME, AND A LOT MORE WATER.
BAKING SODA
MAKING YOUR OWN VERSIONS IS MUCH LESS EXPENSIVE.
JUST REMEMBER TO NEVER MIX BLEACH AND AMMONIA; THAT PRODUCES NOXIOUS FUMES.
WHERE AM I GONNA FIND STUFF LIKE WASHING SODA AND BORAX?
BORAX IS IN THE LAUNDRY AISLE OF THE GROCERY STORE.
AND WASHING SODA IS SODIUM CARBONATE, OR SODA ASH. IT'S IN GROCERY AND ART SUPPLY STORES.
THEY KEEP IT WITH THE DYEING SUPPLIES.

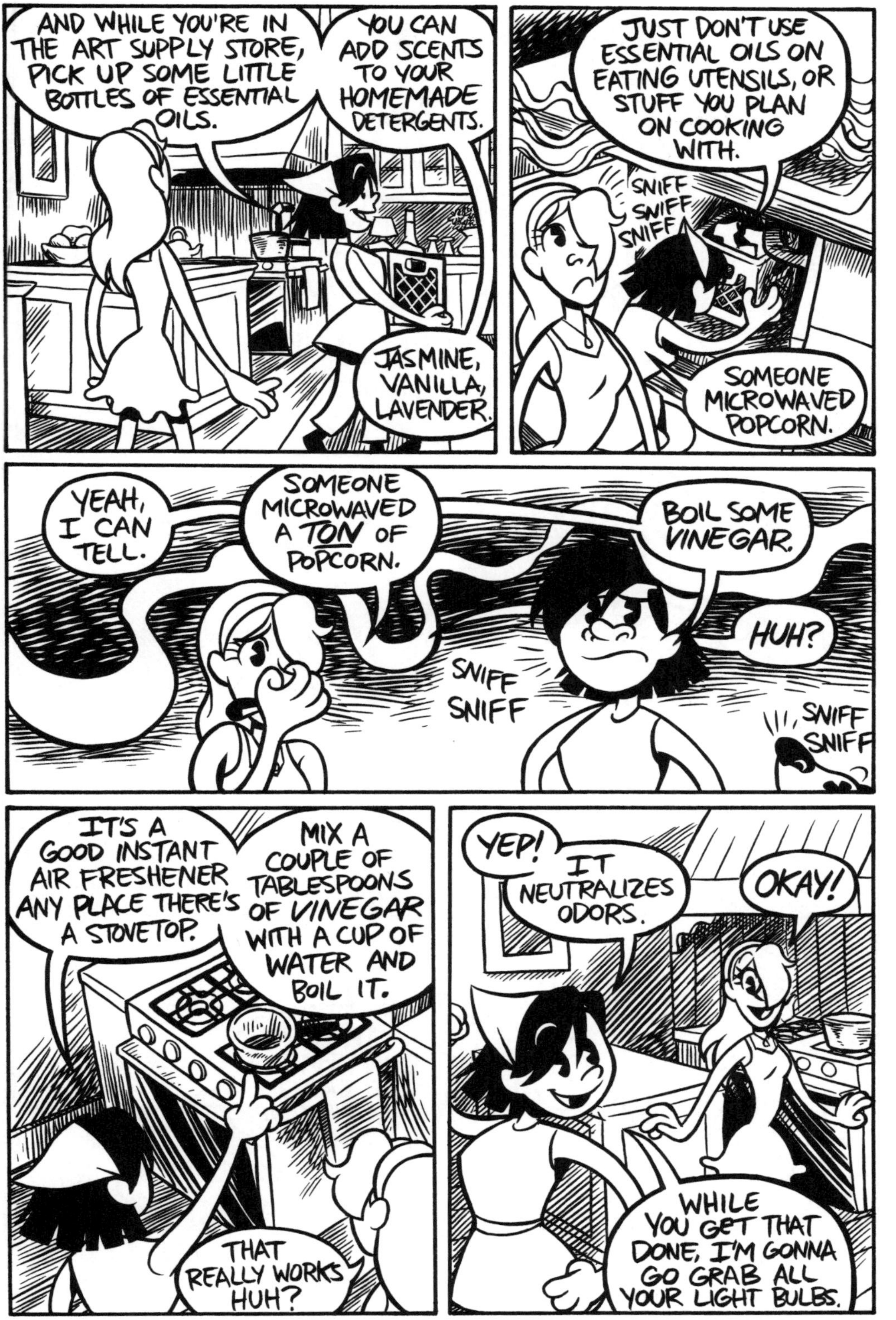
AND WHILE YOU'RE IN THE ART SUPPLY STORE, PICK UP SOME LITTLE BOTTLES OF ESSENTIAL OILS.
YOU CAN ADD SCENTS TO YOUR HOMEMADE DETERGENTS.
JASMINE, VANILLA, LAVENDER.
JUST DON'T USE ESSENTIAL OILS ON EATING UTENSILS, OR STUFF YOU PLAN ON COOKING WITH.
SNIFF SNIFF SNIFF
SOMEONE MICROWAVED POPCORN.
YEAH, I CAN TELL.
SOMEONE MICROWAVED A TON OF POPCORN.
BOIL SOME VINEGAR.
HUH?
SNIFF SNIFF
SNIFF SNIFF
IT'S A GOOD INSTANT AIR FRESHENER ANY PLACE THERE'S A STOVETOP.
MIX A COUPLE OF TABLESPOONS OF VINEGAR WITH A CUP OF WATER AND BOIL IT.
THAT REALLY WORKS HUH?
YEP!
IT NEUTRALIZES ODORS.
OKAY!
WHILE YOU GET THAT DONE, I'M GONNA GO GRAB ALL YOUR LIGHT BULBS.

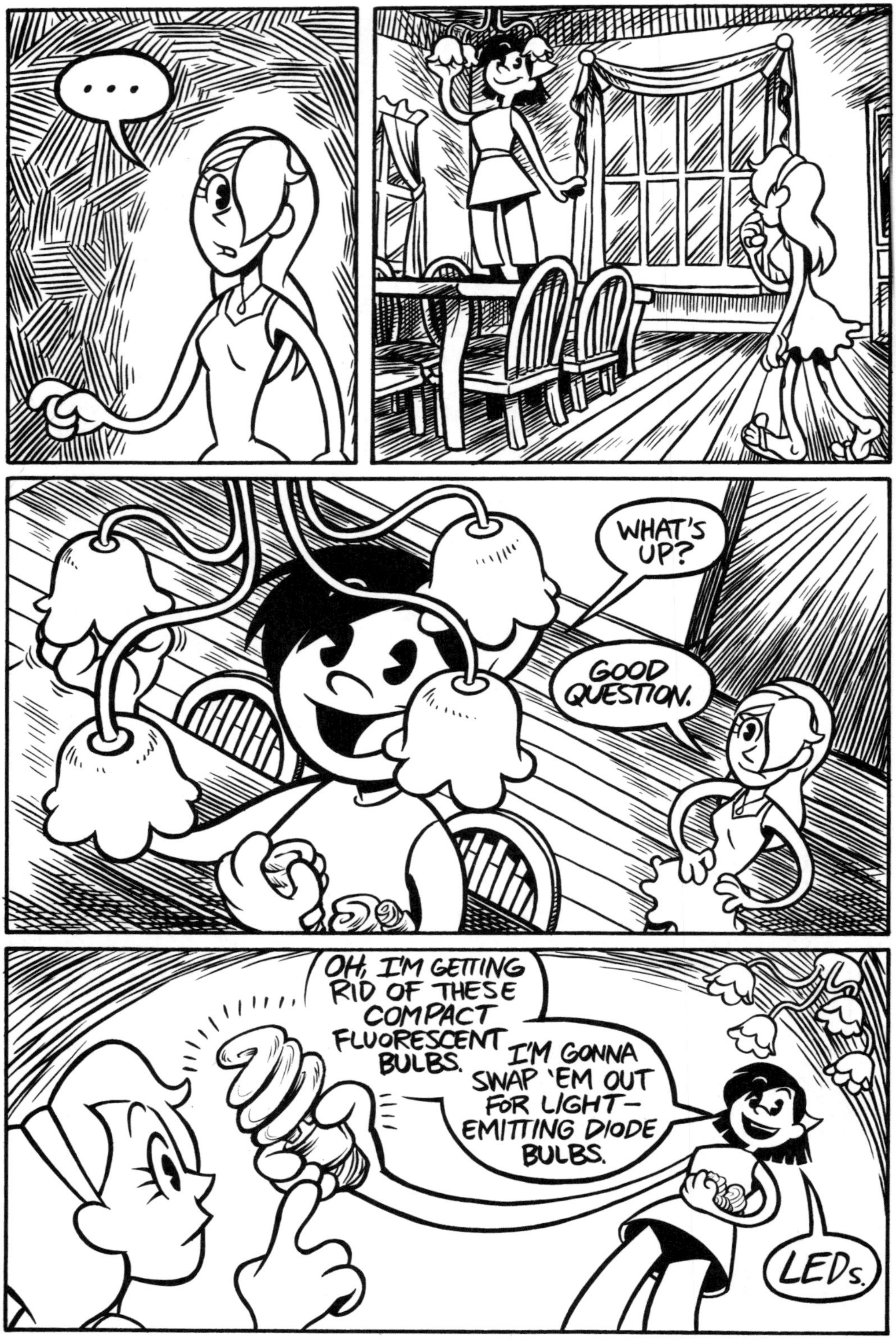
...
WHAT'S UP?
GOOD QUESTION.
OH, I'M GETTING RID OF THESE COMPACT FLUORESCENT BULBS.
I'M GONNA SWAP 'EM OUT FOR LIGHT-EMITTING DIODE BULBS.
LEDs.

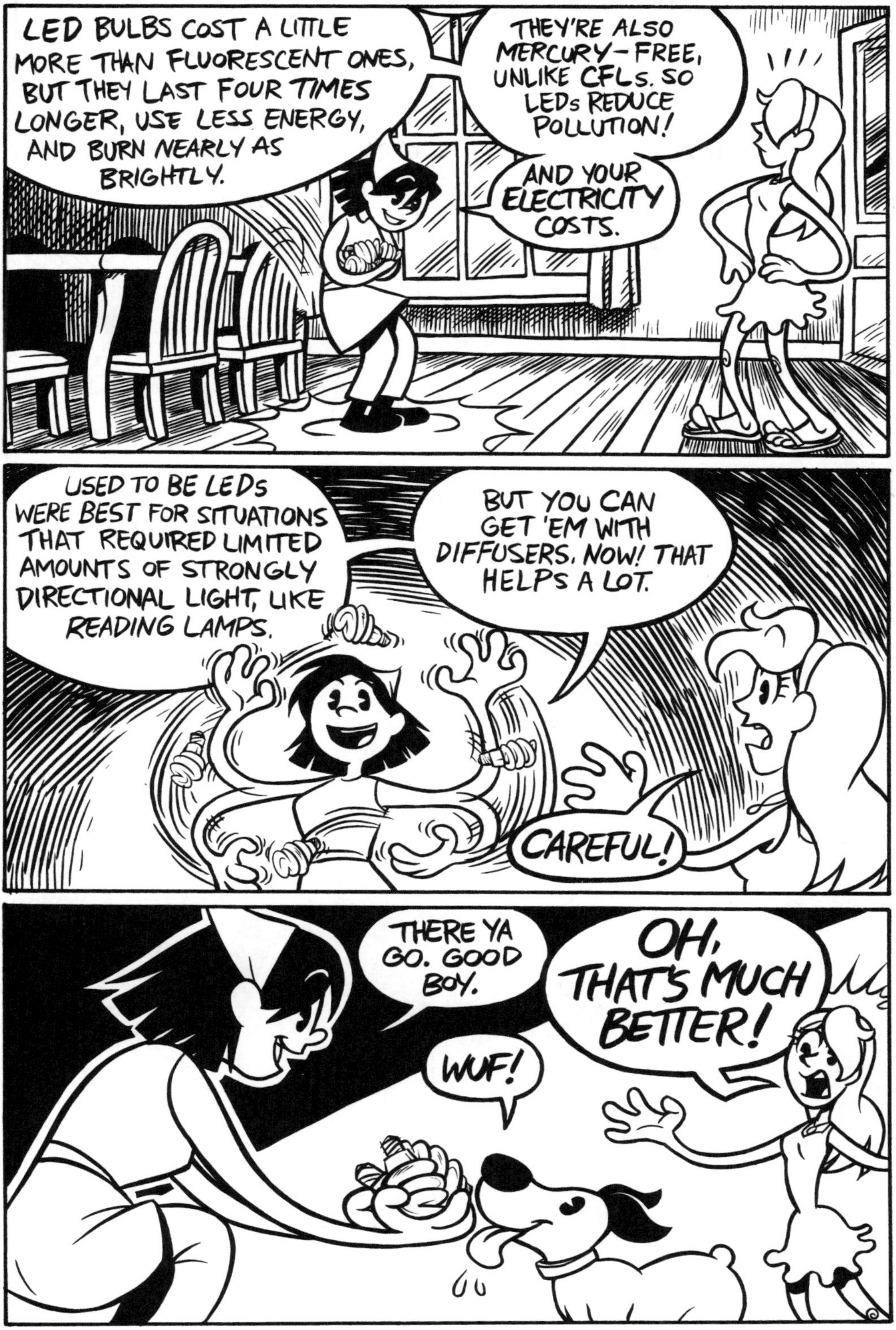

LED BULBS COST A LITTLE MORE THAN FLUORESCENT ONES, BUT THEY LAST FOUR TIMES LONGER, USE LESS ENERGY, AND BURN NEARLY AS BRIGHTLY.
THEY'RE ALSO MERCURY-FREE, UNLIKE CFLs. SO LEDs REDUCE POLLUTION!
AND YOUR ELECTRICITY COSTS.
USED TO BE LEDs WERE BEST FOR SITUATIONS THAT REQUIRED LIMITED AMOUNTS OF STRONGLY DIRECTIONAL LIGHT, LIKE READING LAMPS.
BUT YOU CAN GET 'EM WITH DIFFUSERS, NOW! THAT HELPS A LOT.
CAREFUL!
THERE YA GO. GOOD BOY.
OH, THAT'S MUCH BETTER!
WUF!

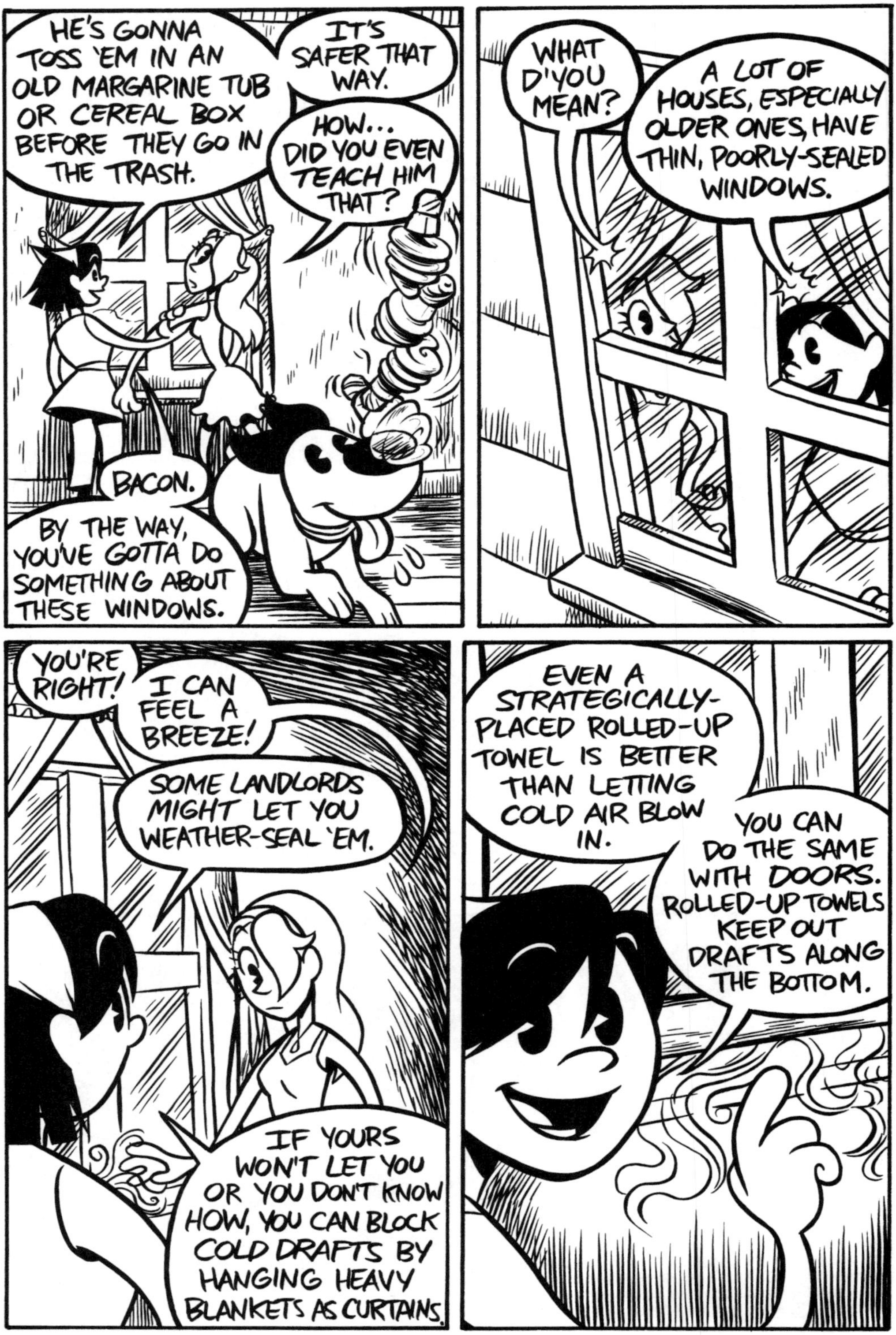
HE'S GONNA TOSS 'EM IN AN OLD MARGARINE TUB OR CEREAL BOX BEFORE THEY GO IN THE TRASH.
IT'S SAFER THAT WAY.
HOW... DID YOU EVEN TEACH HIM THAT?
BACON.
BY THE WAY, YOU'VE GOTTA DO SOMETHING ABOUT THESE WINDOWS.
WHAT D'YOU MEAN?
A LOT OF HOUSES, ESPECIALLY OLDER ONES, HAVE THIN, POORLY-SEALED WINDOWS.
YOU'RE RIGHT!
I CAN FEEL A BREEZE!
SOME LANDLORDS MIGHT LET YOU WEATHER-SEAL 'EM.
IF YOURS WON'T LET YOU OR YOU DON'T KNOW HOW, YOU CAN BLOCK COLD DRAFTS BY HANGING HEAVY BLANKETS AS CURTAINS.
EVEN A STRATEGICALLY-PLACED ROLLED-UP TOWEL IS BETTER THAN LETTING COLD AIR BLOW IN.
YOU CAN DO THE SAME WITH DOORS. ROLLED-UP TOWELS KEEP OUT DRAFTS ALONG THE BOTTOM.

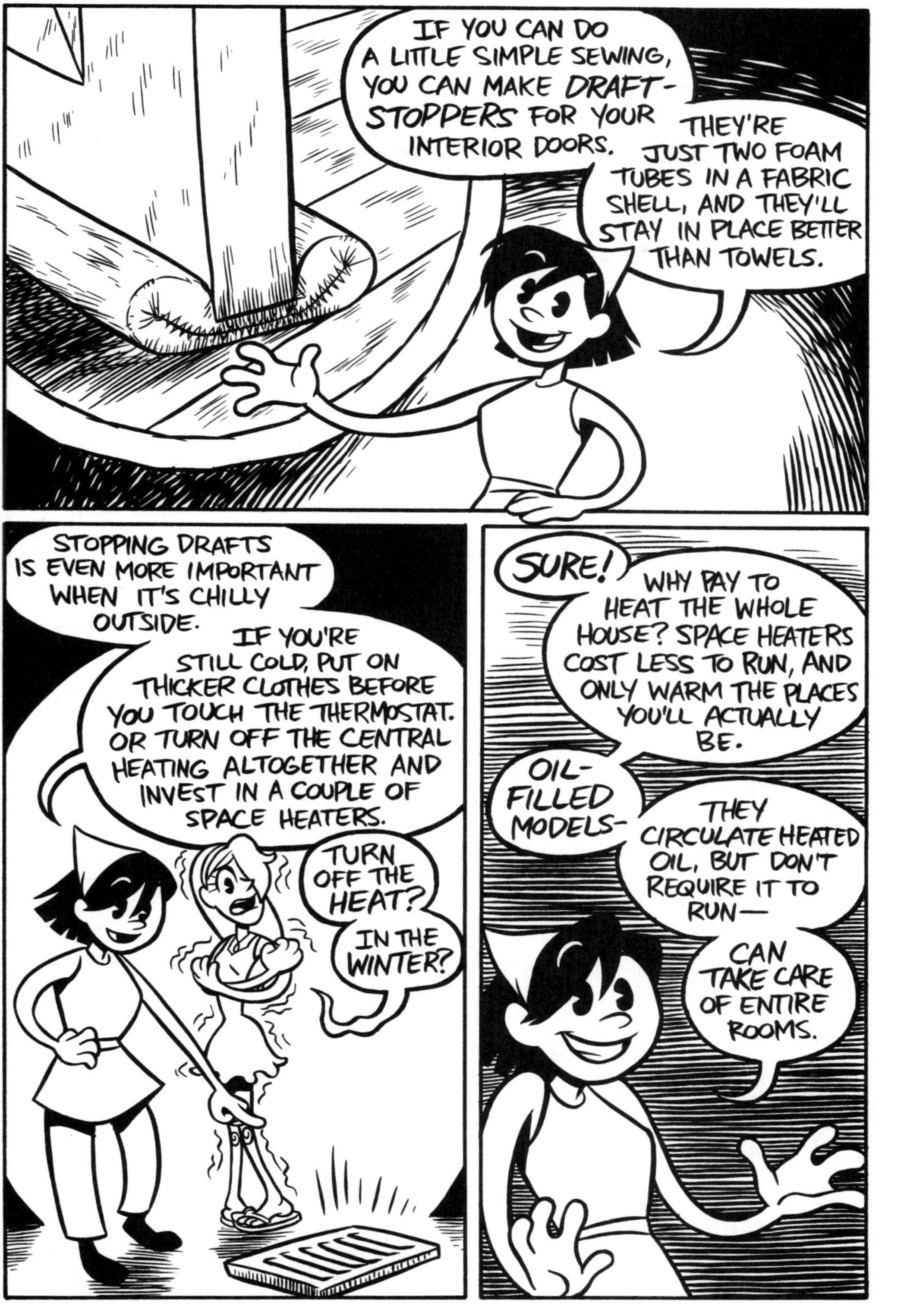
IF YOU CAN DO A LITTLE SIMPLE SEWING, YOU CAN MAKE DRAFT-STOPPERS FOR YOUR INTERIOR DOORS.
THEY'RE JUST TWO FOAM TUBES IN A FABRIC SHELL, AND THEY'LL STAY IN PLACE BETTER THAN TOWELS.
STOPPING DRAFTS IS EVEN MORE IMPORTANT WHEN IT'S CHILLY OUTSIDE.
IF YOU'RE STILL COLD, PUT ON THICKER CLOTHES BEFORE YOU TOUCH THE THERMOSTAT. OR TURN OFF THE CENTRAL HEATING ALTOGETHER AND INVEST IN A COUPLE OF SPACE HEATERS.
TURN OFF THE HEAT?
IN THE WINTER?
SURE!
WHY PAY TO HEAT THE WHOLE HOUSE? SPACE HEATERS COST LESS TO RUN, AND ONLY WARM THE PLACES YOU'LL ACTUALLY BE.
OIL-FILLED MODELS-
THEY CIRCULATE HEATED OIL, BUT DON'T REQUIRE IT TO RUN—
CAN TAKE CARE OF ENTIRE ROOMS.

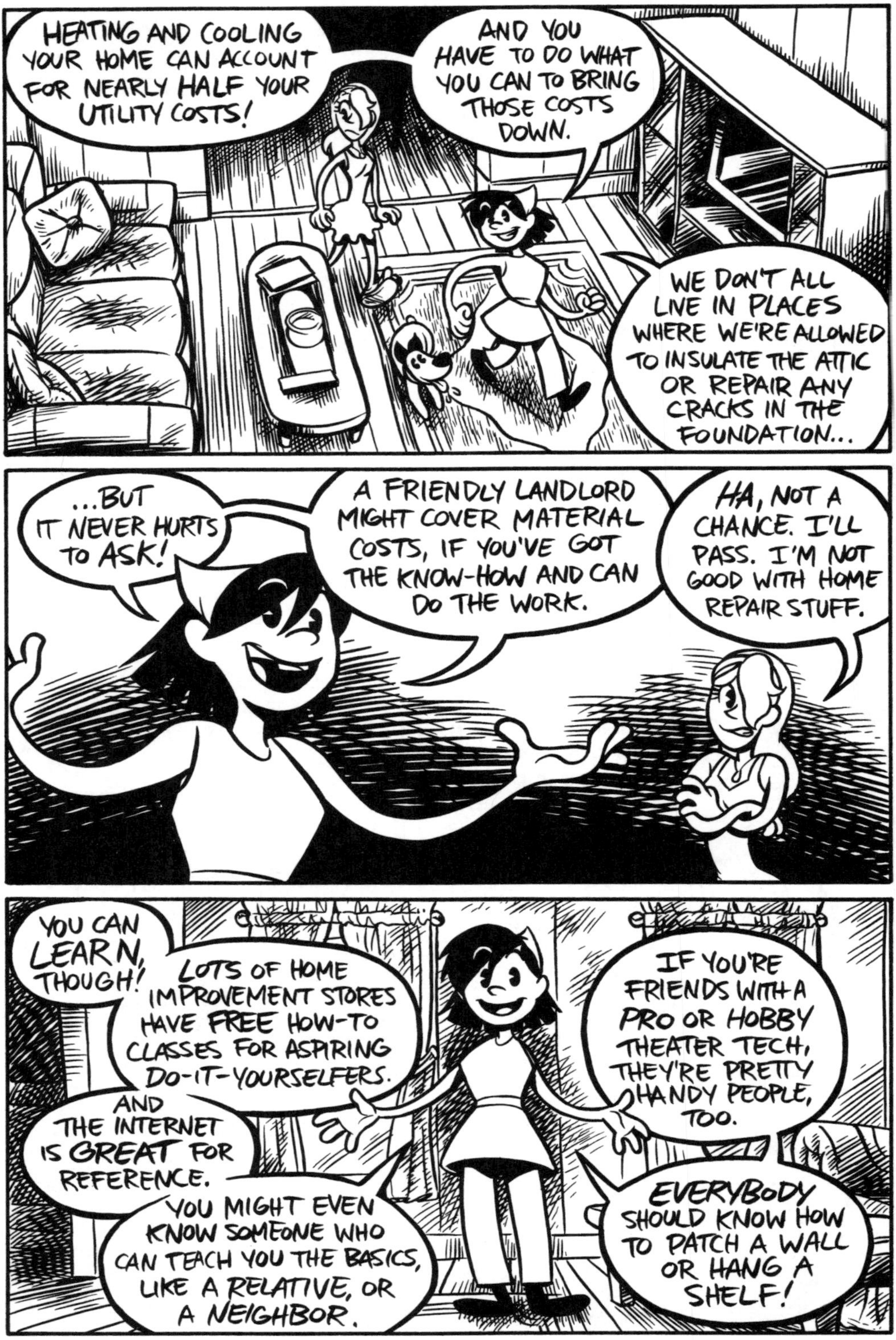
HEATING AND COOLING YOUR HOME CAN ACCOUNT FOR NEARLY HALF YOUR UTILITY COSTS!
AND YOU HAVE TO DO WHAT YOU CAN TO BRING THOSE COSTS DOWN.
WE DON'T ALL LIVE IN PLACES WHERE WE'RE ALLOWED TO INSULATE THE ATTIC OR REPAIR ANY CRACKS IN THE FOUNDATION...
...BUT IT NEVER HURTS TO ASK!
A FRIENDLY LANDLORD MIGHT COVER MATERIAL COSTS, IF YOU'VE GOT THE KNOW-HOW AND CAN DO THE WORK.
HA, NOT A CHANCE. I'LL PASS. I'M NOT GOOD WITH HOME REPAIR STUFF.
YOU CAN LEARN, THOUGH!
LOTS OF HOME IMPROVEMENT STORES HAVE FREE HOW-TO CLASSES FOR ASPIRING DO-IT-YOURSELFERS.
AND THE INTERNET IS GREAT FOR REFERENCE.
YOU MIGHT EVEN KNOW SOMEONE WHO CAN TEACH YOU THE BASICS, LIKE A RELATIVE, OR A NEIGHBOR.
IF YOU'RE FRIENDS WITH A PRO OR HOBBY THEATER TECH, THEY'RE PRETTY HANDY PEOPLE, TOO.
EVERYBODY SHOULD KNOW HOW TO PATCH A WALL OR HANG A SHELF!

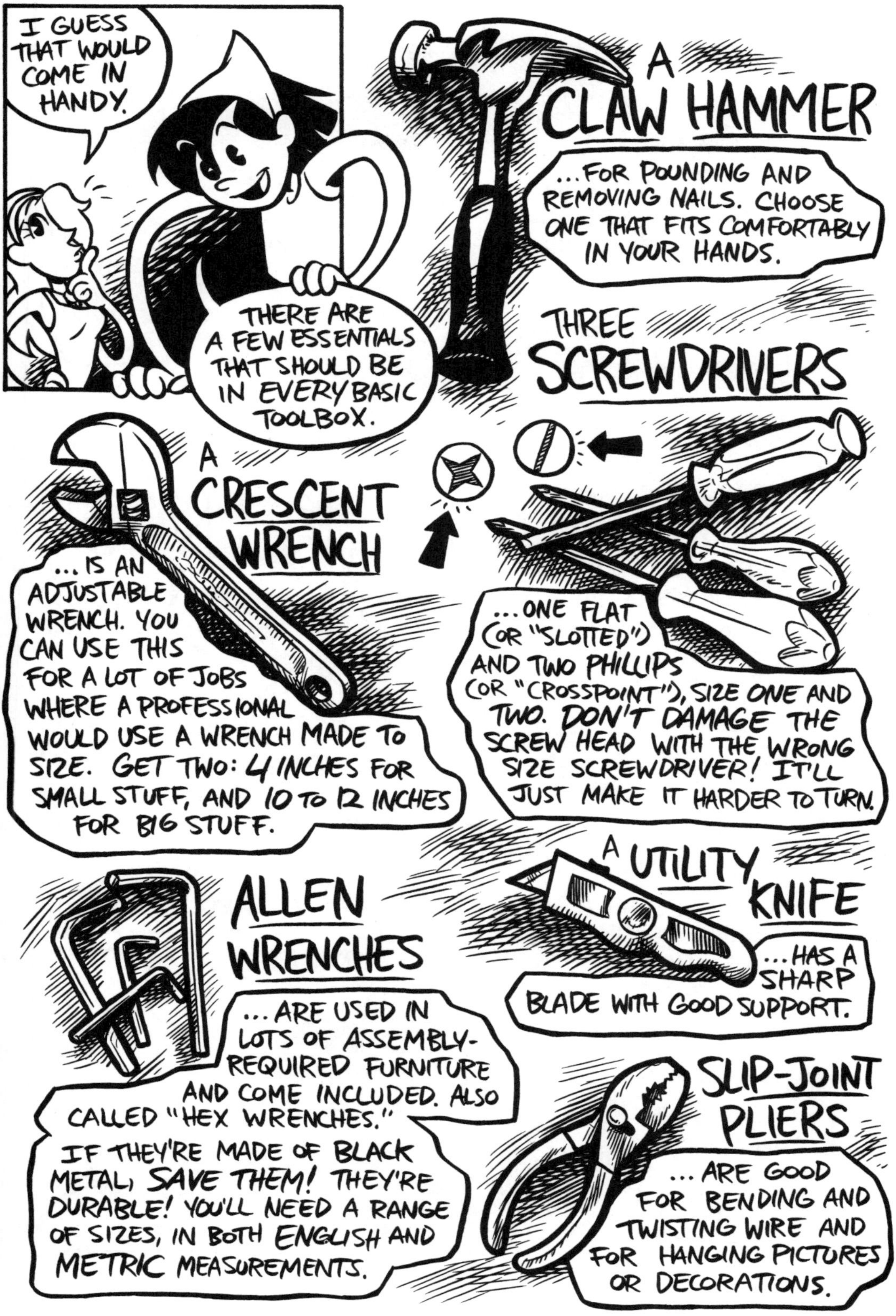
I GUESS THAT WOULD COME IN HANDY.
THERE ARE A FEW ESSENTIALS THAT SHOULD BE IN EVERY BASIC TOOLBOX.
A CLAW HAMMER
...FOR POUNDING AND REMOVING NAILS. CHOOSE ONE THAT FITS COMFORTABLY IN YOUR HANDS.
THREE SCREWDRIVERS
...ONE FLAT (OR "SLOTTED") AND TWO PHILLIPS (OR "CROSSPOINT"), SIZE ONE AND TWO. DON'T DAMAGE THE SCREW HEAD WITH THE WRONG SIZE SCREWDRIVER! IT'LL JUST MAKE IT HARDER TO TURN.
A CRESCENT WRENCH
...IS AN ADJUSTABLE WRENCH. YOU CAN USE THIS FOR A LOT OF JOBS WHERE A PROFESSIONAL WOULD USE A WRENCH MADE TO SIZE. GET TWO: 4 INCHES FOR SMALL STUFF, AND 10 TO 12 INCHES FOR BIG STUFF.
A UTILITY KNIFE
...HAS A SHARP BLADE WITH GOOD SUPPORT.
ALLEN WRENCHES
...ARE USED IN LOTS OF ASSEMBLY-REQUIRED FURNITURE AND COME INCLUDED. ALSO CALLED "HEX WRENCHES."
IF THEY'RE MADE OF BLACK METAL, SAVE THEM! THEY'RE DURABLE! YOU'LL NEED A RANGE OF SIZES, IN BOTH ENGLISH AND METRIC MEASUREMENTS.
SLIP-JOINT PLIERS
...ARE GOOD FOR BENDING AND TWISTING WIRE AND FOR HANGING PICTURES OR DECORATIONS.

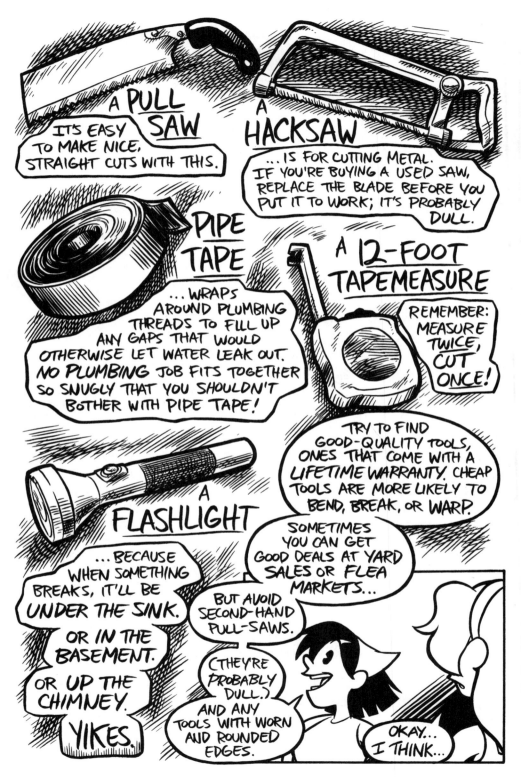

A **PULL** <u>SAW</u>

IT'S EASY TO MAKE NICE, STRAIGHT CUTS WITH THIS.

A **HACKSAW**

...IS FOR CUTTING METAL. IF YOU'RE BUYING A USED SAW, REPLACE THE BLADE BEFORE YOU PUT IT TO WORK; IT'S PROBABLY DULL.

PIPE <u>TAPE</u>

...WRAPS AROUND PLUMBING THREADS TO FILL UP ANY GAPS THAT WOULD OTHERWISE LET WATER LEAK OUT. *NO PLUMBING* JOB FITS TOGETHER SO SNUGLY THAT YOU SHOULDN'T BOTHER WITH PIPE TAPE!

A **12-FOOT** **TAPEMEASURE**

REMEMBER: MEASURE TWICE, CUT ONCE!

TRY TO FIND GOOD-QUALITY TOOLS, ONES THAT COME WITH A *LIFETIME WARRANTY*. CHEAP TOOLS ARE MORE LIKELY TO BEND, BREAK, OR WARP.

A **FLASHLIGHT**

...BECAUSE WHEN SOMETHING BREAKS, IT'LL BE *UNDER THE SINK.* OR IN THE BASEMENT. OR UP THE CHIMNEY. *YIKES.*

SOMETIMES YOU CAN GET GOOD DEALS AT YARD SALES OR *FLEA MARKETS...*

BUT AVOID SECOND-HAND PULL-SAWS.

(THEY'RE PROBABLY DULL.) AND ANY TOOLS WITH WORN AND ROUNDED EDGES.

OKAY... I THINK...

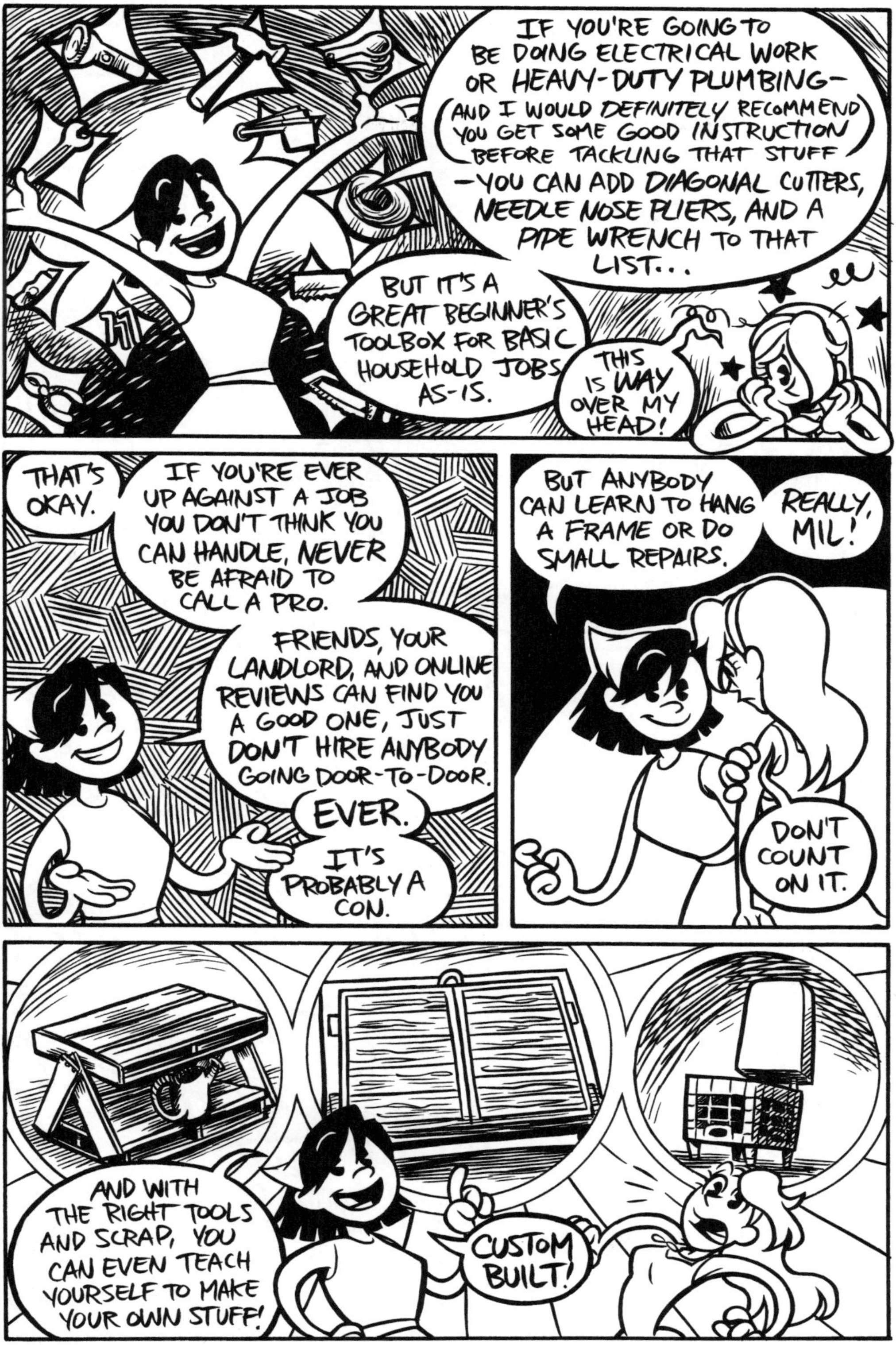
IF YOU'RE GOING TO BE DOING ELECTRICAL WORK OR HEAVY-DUTY PLUMBING—
(AND I WOULD DEFINITELY RECOMMEND YOU GET SOME GOOD INSTRUCTION BEFORE TACKLING THAT STUFF)
—YOU CAN ADD DIAGONAL CUTTERS, NEEDLE NOSE PLIERS, AND A PIPE WRENCH TO THAT LIST...
BUT IT'S A GREAT BEGINNER'S TOOLBOX FOR BASIC HOUSEHOLD JOBS AS-IS.
THIS IS WAY OVER MY HEAD!
THAT'S OKAY.
IF YOU'RE EVER UP AGAINST A JOB YOU DON'T THINK YOU CAN HANDLE, NEVER BE AFRAID TO CALL A PRO.
FRIENDS, YOUR LANDLORD, AND ONLINE REVIEWS CAN FIND YOU A GOOD ONE, JUST DON'T HIRE ANYBODY GOING DOOR-TO-DOOR.
EVER.
IT'S PROBABLY A CON.
BUT ANYBODY CAN LEARN TO HANG A FRAME OR DO SMALL REPAIRS.
REALLY, MIL!
DON'T COUNT ON IT.
AND WITH THE RIGHT TOOLS AND SCRAP, YOU CAN EVEN TEACH YOURSELF TO MAKE YOUR OWN STUFF!
CUSTOM BUILT!

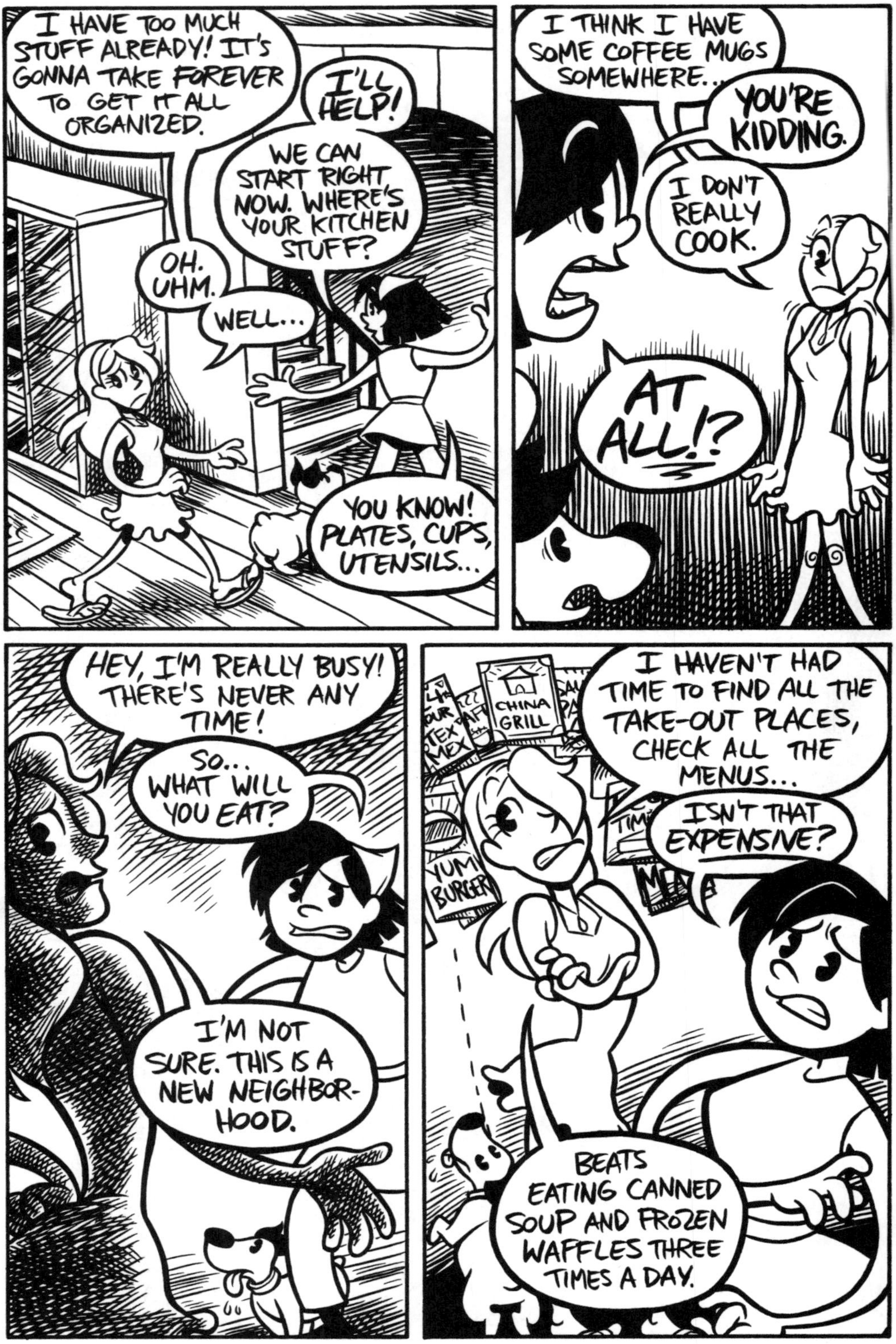
I HAVE TOO MUCH STUFF ALREADY! IT'S GONNA TAKE FOREVER TO GET IT ALL ORGANIZED.
I'LL HELP!
WE CAN START RIGHT NOW. WHERE'S YOUR KITCHEN STUFF?
OH. UHM.
WELL...
YOU KNOW! PLATES, CUPS, UTENSILS...
I THINK I HAVE SOME COFFEE MUGS SOMEWHERE...
YOU'RE KIDDING.
I DON'T REALLY COOK.
AT ALL!?
HEY, I'M REALLY BUSY! THERE'S NEVER ANY TIME!
SO... WHAT WILL YOU EAT?
I'M NOT SURE. THIS IS A NEW NEIGHBOR-HOOD.
CHINA GRILL
TEX MEX
YUM BURGER
I HAVEN'T HAD TIME TO FIND ALL THE TAKE-OUT PLACES, CHECK ALL THE MENUS...
ISN'T THAT EXPENSIVE?
BEATS EATING CANNED SOUP AND FROZEN WAFFLES THREE TIMES A DAY.

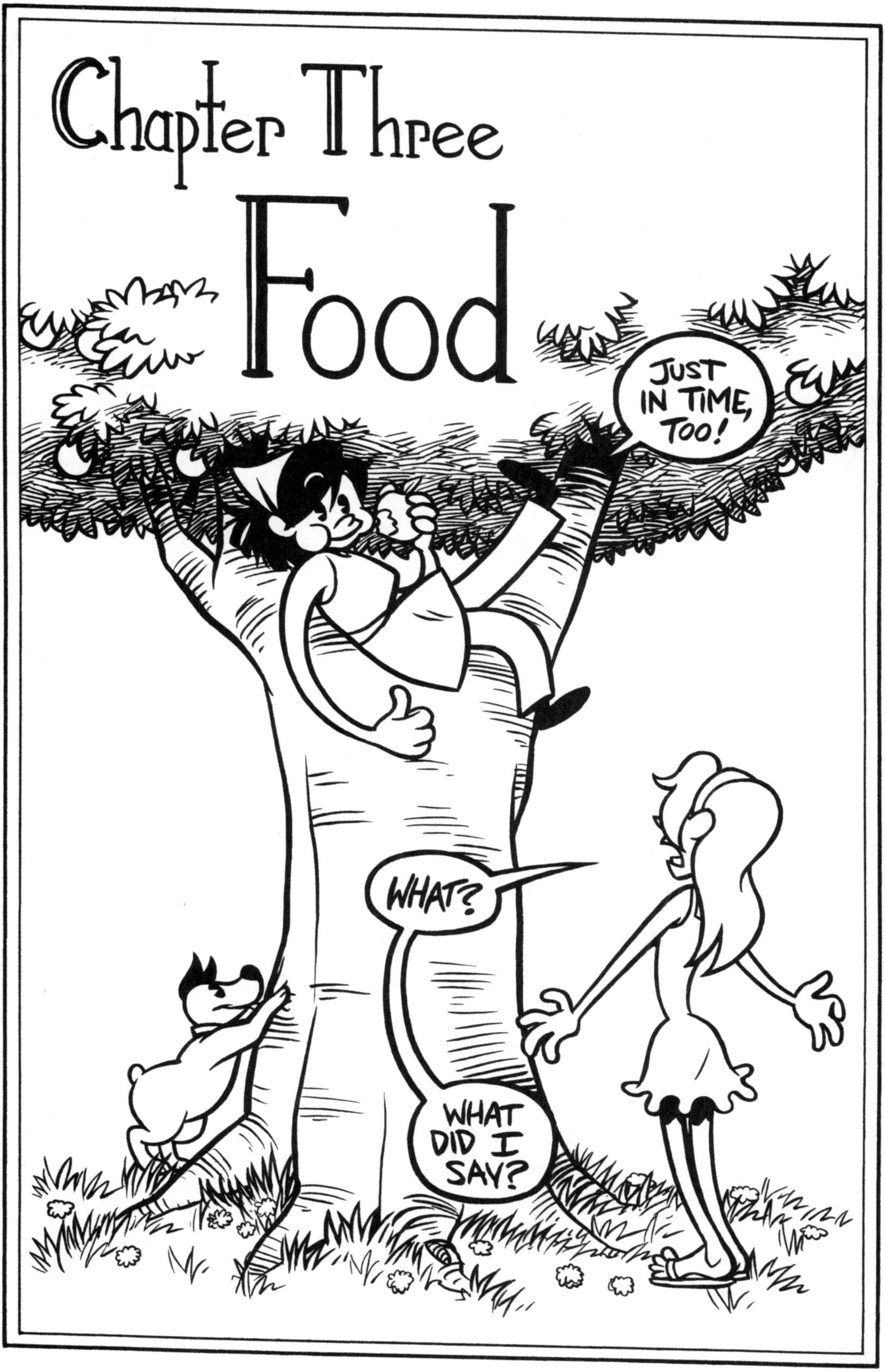
Chapter Three
Food
JUST IN TIME, TOO!
WHAT?
WHAT DID I SAY?

1: FOOD 101: KITCHENWARE

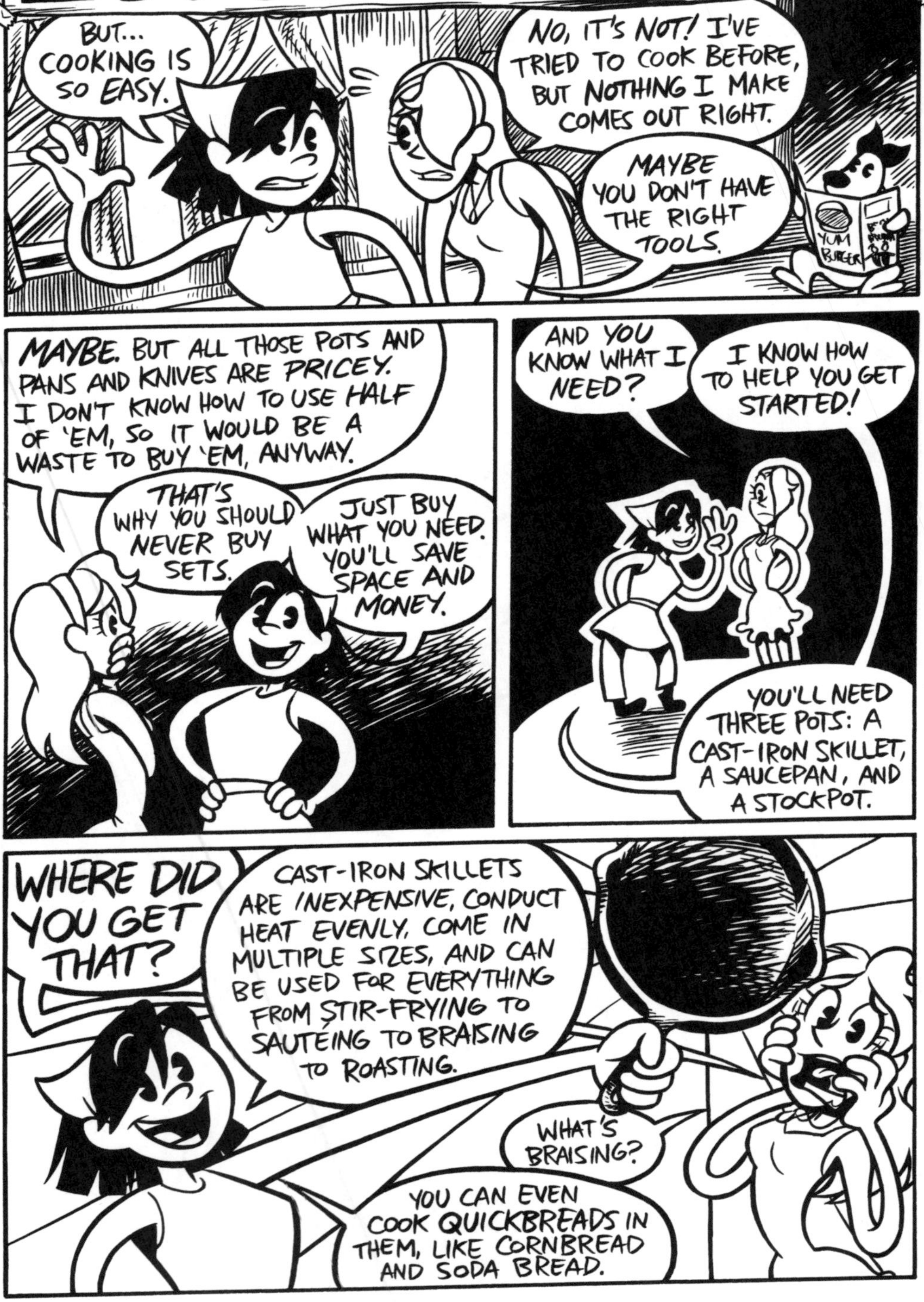
BUT... COOKING IS SO *EASY*.
NO, IT'S *NOT*! I'VE TRIED TO COOK BEFORE, BUT **NOTHING** I MAKE COMES OUT RIGHT.
MAYBE YOU DON'T HAVE THE RIGHT TOOLS.
YUM BURGER
MAYBE. BUT ALL THOSE POTS AND PANS AND KNIVES ARE *PRICEY*. I DON'T KNOW HOW TO USE *HALF* OF 'EM, SO IT WOULD BE A WASTE TO BUY 'EM, ANYWAY.
THAT'S WHY YOU SHOULD *NEVER* BUY SETS.
JUST BUY WHAT YOU NEED. YOU'LL SAVE SPACE AND MONEY.
AND YOU KNOW WHAT I *NEED*?
I KNOW HOW TO HELP YOU GET STARTED!
YOU'LL NEED THREE POTS: A CAST-IRON SKILLET, A SAUCEPAN, AND A STOCKPOT.
WHERE DID YOU GET THAT?
CAST-IRON SKILLETS ARE *INEXPENSIVE*, CONDUCT HEAT EVENLY, COME IN MULTIPLE SIZES, AND CAN BE USED FOR EVERYTHING FROM STIR-FRYING TO SAUTÉING TO BRAISING TO ROASTING.
WHAT'S BRAISING?
YOU CAN EVEN COOK **QUICKBREADS** IN THEM, LIKE CORNBREAD AND SODA BREAD.

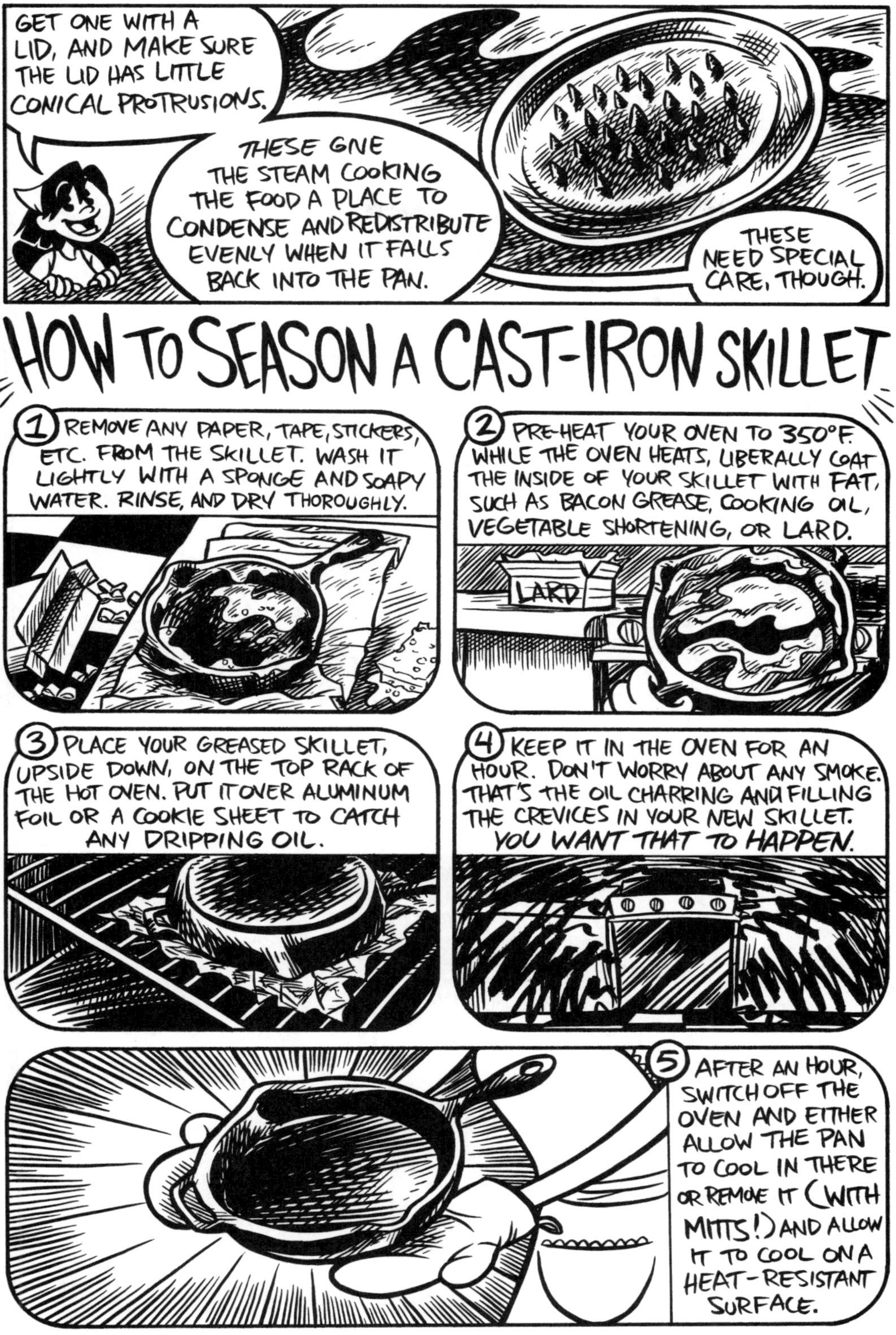
GET ONE WITH A LID, AND MAKE SURE THE LID HAS LITTLE CONICAL PROTRUSIONS.
THESE GIVE THE STEAM COOKING THE FOOD A PLACE TO CONDENSE AND REDISTRIBUTE EVENLY WHEN IT FALLS BACK INTO THE PAN.
THESE NEED SPECIAL CARE, THOUGH.
HOW TO SEASON A CAST-IRON SKILLET
1 REMOVE ANY PAPER, TAPE, STICKERS, ETC. FROM THE SKILLET. WASH IT LIGHTLY WITH A SPONGE AND SOAPY WATER. RINSE, AND DRY THOROUGHLY.
2 PRE-HEAT YOUR OVEN TO 350°F. WHILE THE OVEN HEATS, LIBERALLY COAT THE INSIDE OF YOUR SKILLET WITH FAT, SUCH AS BACON GREASE, COOKING OIL, VEGETABLE SHORTENING, OR LARD.
LARD
3 PLACE YOUR GREASED SKILLET, UPSIDE DOWN, ON THE TOP RACK OF THE HOT OVEN. PUT IT OVER ALUMINUM FOIL OR A COOKIE SHEET TO CATCH ANY DRIPPING OIL.
4 KEEP IT IN THE OVEN FOR AN HOUR. DON'T WORRY ABOUT ANY SMOKE. THAT'S THE OIL CHARRING AND FILLING THE CREVICES IN YOUR NEW SKILLET. YOU WANT THAT TO HAPPEN.
5 AFTER AN HOUR, SWITCH OFF THE OVEN AND EITHER ALLOW THE PAN TO COOL IN THERE OR REMOVE IT (WITH MITTS!) AND ALLOW IT TO COOL ON A HEAT-RESISTANT SURFACE.

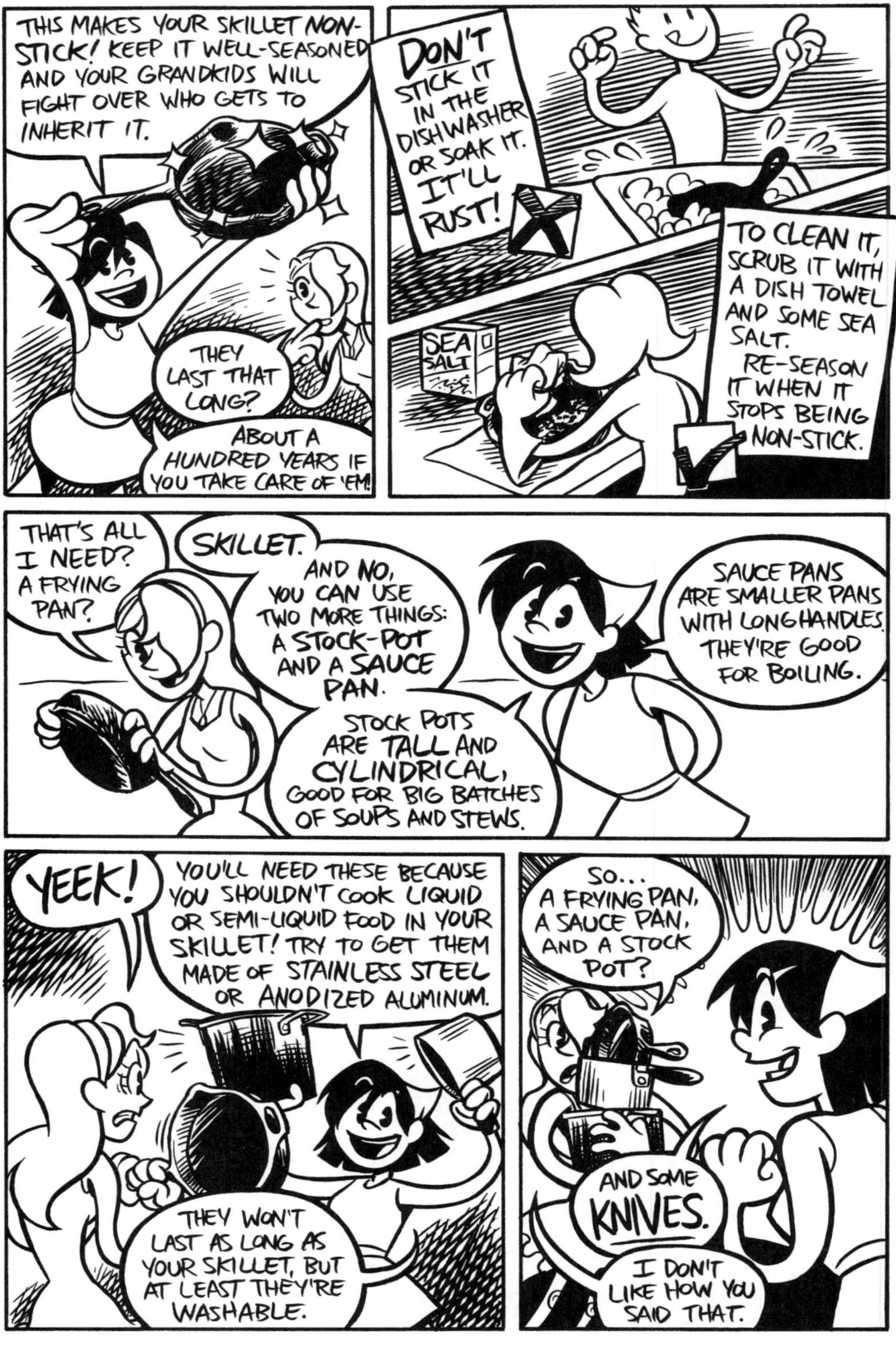

THIS MAKES YOUR SKILLET NON-STICK! KEEP IT WELL-SEASONED AND YOUR GRANDKIDS WILL FIGHT OVER WHO GETS TO INHERIT IT.
THEY LAST THAT LONG?
ABOUT A HUNDRED YEARS IF YOU TAKE CARE OF 'EM!
DON'T STICK IT IN THE DISHWASHER OR SOAK IT. IT'LL RUST!
TO CLEAN IT, SCRUB IT WITH A DISH TOWEL AND SOME SEA SALT.
RE-SEASON IT WHEN IT STOPS BEING NON-STICK.
SEA SALT
THAT'S ALL I NEED? A FRYING PAN?
SKILLET.
AND NO, YOU CAN USE TWO MORE THINGS: A STOCK-POT AND A SAUCE PAN.
STOCK POTS ARE TALL AND CYLINDRICAL, GOOD FOR BIG BATCHES OF SOUPS AND STEWS.
SAUCE PANS ARE SMALLER PANS WITH LONG HANDLES. THEY'RE GOOD FOR BOILING.
YEEK!
YOU'LL NEED THESE BECAUSE YOU SHOULDN'T COOK LIQUID OR SEMI-LIQUID FOOD IN YOUR SKILLET! TRY TO GET THEM MADE OF STAINLESS STEEL OR ANODIZED ALUMINUM.
THEY WON'T LAST AS LONG AS YOUR SKILLET, BUT AT LEAST THEY'RE WASHABLE.
SO... A FRYING PAN, A SAUCE PAN, AND A STOCK POT?
AND SOME KNIVES.
I DON'T LIKE HOW YOU SAID THAT.

BASIC KNIFE ANATOMY

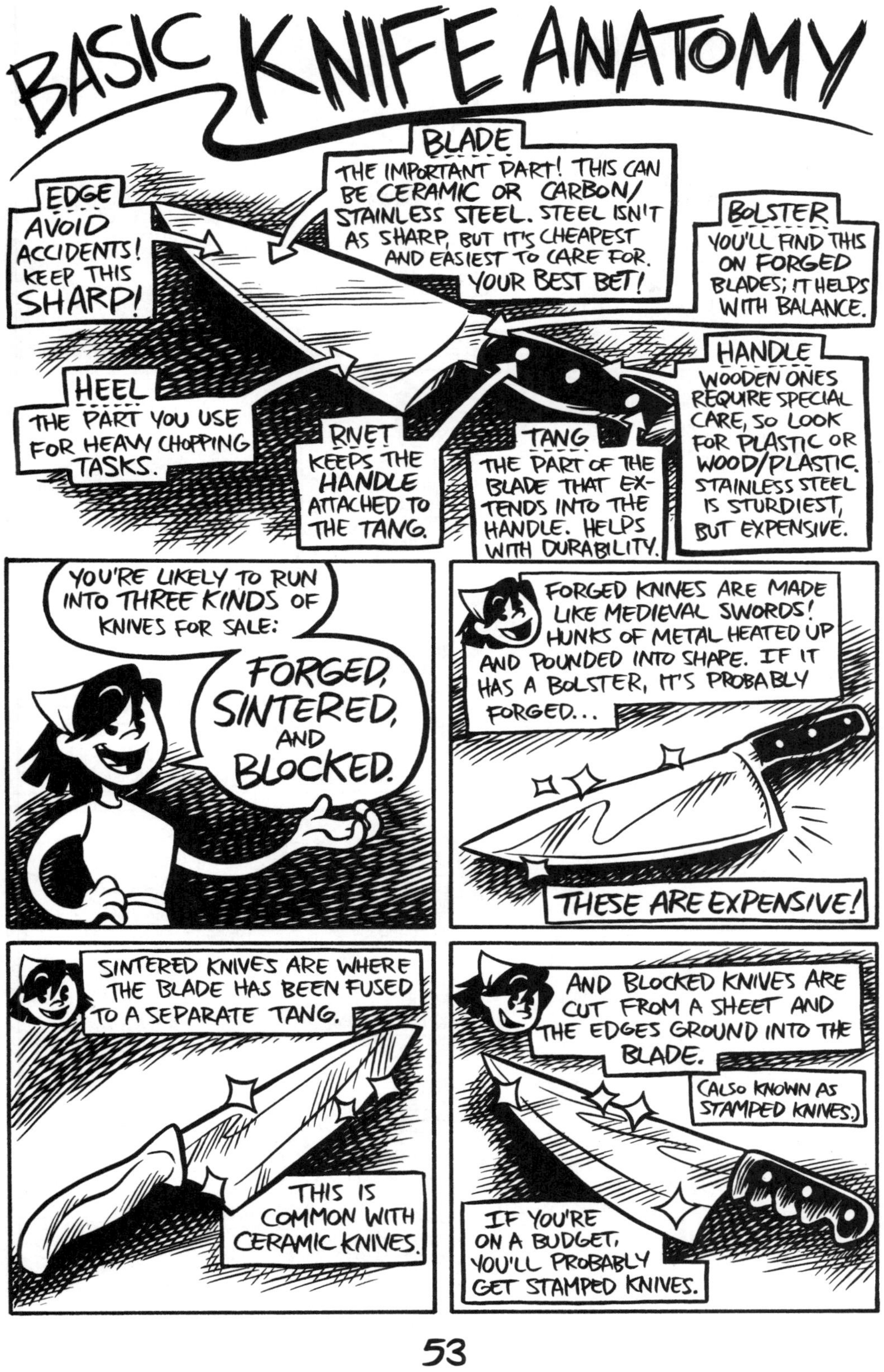

BLADE
THE IMPORTANT PART! THIS CAN BE CERAMIC OR CARBON/ STAINLESS STEEL. STEEL ISN'T AS SHARP, BUT IT'S CHEAPEST AND EASIEST TO CARE FOR. YOUR BEST BET!
EDGE
AVOID ACCIDENTS! KEEP THIS SHARP!
BOLSTER
YOU'LL FIND THIS ON FORGED BLADES; IT HELPS WITH BALANCE.
HEEL
THE PART YOU USE FOR HEAVY CHOPPING TASKS.
RIVET
KEEPS THE HANDLE ATTACHED TO THE TANG.
TANG
THE PART OF THE BLADE THAT EX-TENDS INTO THE HANDLE. HELPS WITH DURABILITY.
HANDLE
WOODEN ONES REQUIRE SPECIAL CARE, SO LOOK FOR PLASTIC OR WOOD/PLASTIC. STAINLESS STEEL IS STURDIEST, BUT EXPENSIVE.
YOU'RE LIKELY TO RUN INTO THREE KINDS OF KNIVES FOR SALE:
FORGED, SINTERED, AND BLOCKED.
FORGED KNIVES ARE MADE LIKE MEDIEVAL SWORDS! HUNKS OF METAL HEATED UP AND POUNDED INTO SHAPE. IF IT HAS A BOLSTER, IT'S PROBABLY FORGED...
THESE ARE EXPENSIVE!
SINTERED KNIVES ARE WHERE THE BLADE HAS BEEN FUSED TO A SEPARATE TANG.
THIS IS COMMON WITH CERAMIC KNIVES.
AND BLOCKED KNIVES ARE CUT FROM A SHEET AND THE EDGES GROUND INTO THE BLADE.
(ALSO KNOWN AS STAMPED KNIVES.)
IF YOU'RE ON A BUDGET, YOU'LL PROBABLY GET STAMPED KNIVES.

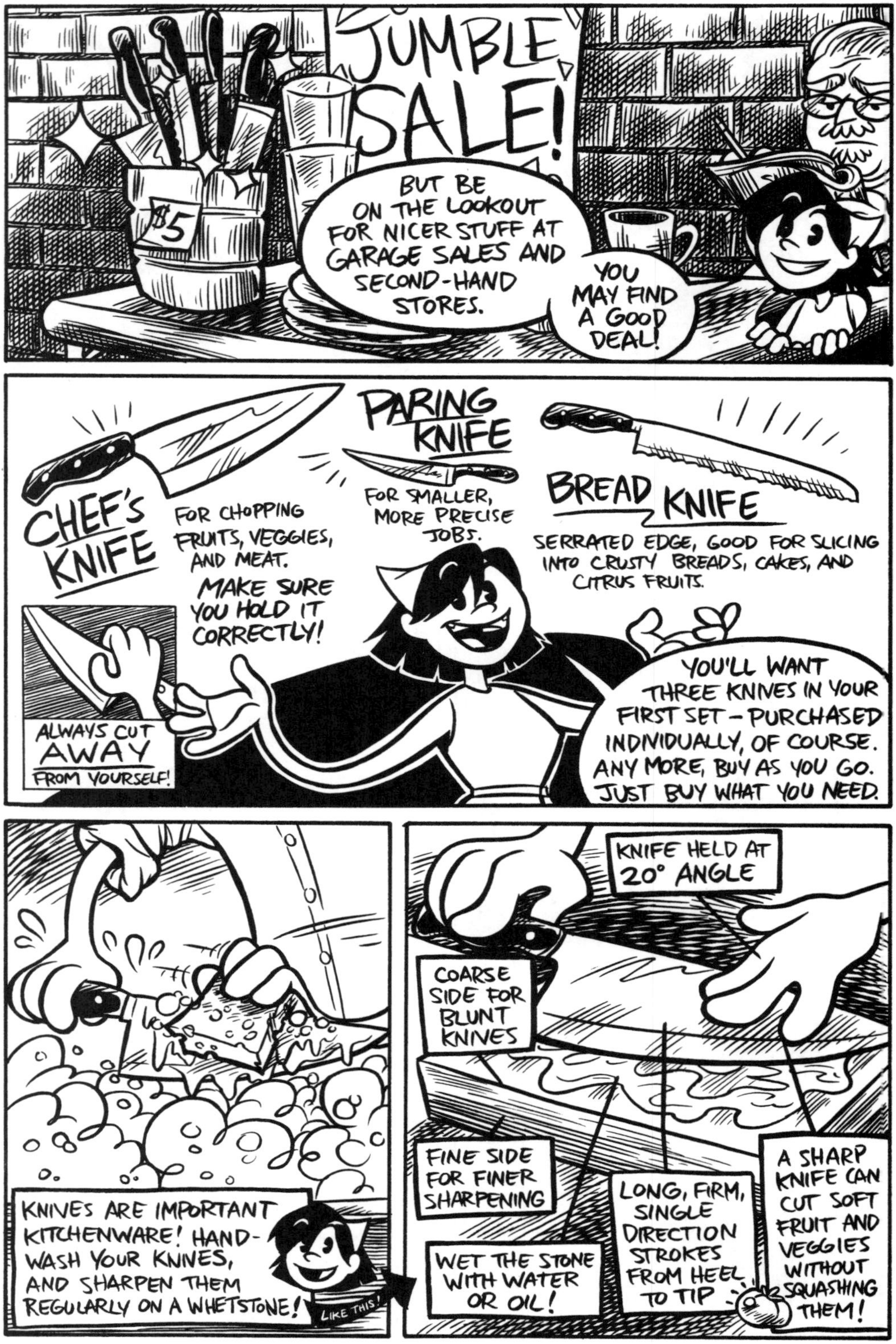
JUMBLE SALE!
$5
BUT BE ON THE LOOKOUT FOR NICER STUFF AT GARAGE SALES AND SECOND-HAND STORES.
YOU MAY FIND A GOOD DEAL!
PARING KNIFE
FOR SMALLER, MORE PRECISE JOBS.
CHEF'S KNIFE
FOR CHOPPING FRUITS, VEGGIES, AND MEAT.
MAKE SURE YOU HOLD IT CORRECTLY!
ALWAYS CUT AWAY FROM YOURSELF!
BREAD KNIFE
SERRATED EDGE, GOOD FOR SLICING INTO CRUSTY BREADS, CAKES, AND CITRUS FRUITS.
YOU'LL WANT THREE KNIVES IN YOUR FIRST SET – PURCHASED INDIVIDUALLY, OF COURSE. ANY MORE, BUY AS YOU GO. JUST BUY WHAT YOU NEED.
KNIVES ARE IMPORTANT KITCHENWARE! HAND-WASH YOUR KNIVES, AND SHARPEN THEM REGULARLY ON A WHETSTONE!
LIKE THIS!
KNIFE HELD AT 20° ANGLE
COARSE SIDE FOR BLUNT KNIVES
FINE SIDE FOR FINER SHARPENING
WET THE STONE WITH WATER OR OIL!
LONG, FIRM, SINGLE DIRECTION STROKES FROM HEEL TO TIP
A SHARP KNIFE CAN CUT SOFT FRUIT AND VEGGIES WITHOUT SQUASHING THEM!

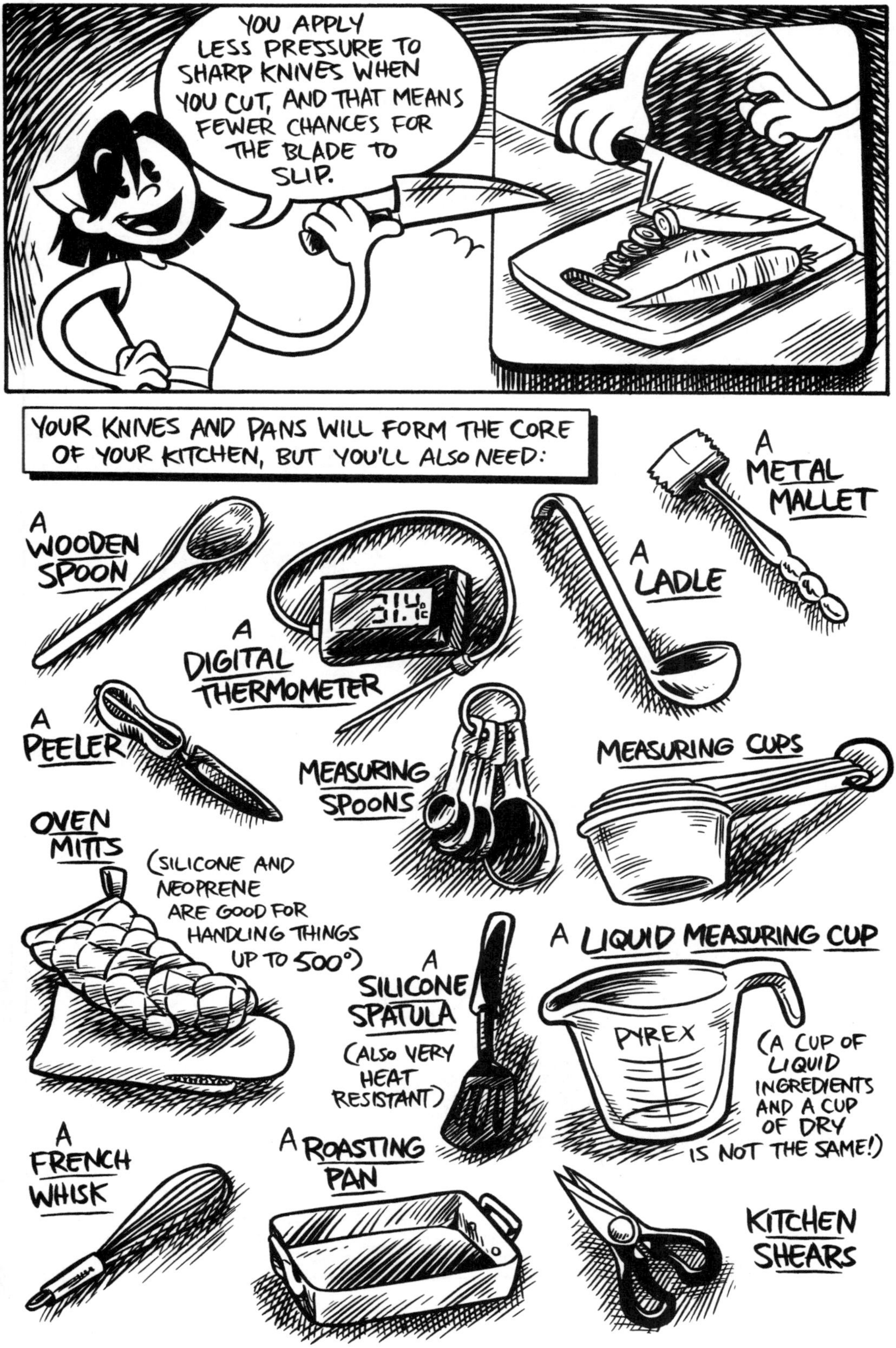

YOU APPLY LESS PRESSURE TO SHARP KNIVES WHEN YOU CUT, AND THAT MEANS FEWER CHANCES FOR THE BLADE TO SLIP.
YOUR KNIVES AND PANS WILL FORM THE CORE OF YOUR KITCHEN, BUT YOU'LL ALSO NEED:
A WOODEN SPOON
A DIGITAL THERMOMETER
A LADLE
A METAL MALLET
A PEELER
MEASURING SPOONS
MEASURING CUPS
OVEN MITTS
(SILICONE AND NEOPRENE ARE GOOD FOR HANDLING THINGS UP TO 500°)
A SILICONE SPATULA
(ALSO VERY HEAT RESISTANT)
A LIQUID MEASURING CUP
PYREX
(A CUP OF LIQUID INGREDIENTS AND A CUP OF DRY IS NOT THE SAME!)
A FRENCH WHISK
A ROASTING PAN
KITCHEN SHEARS

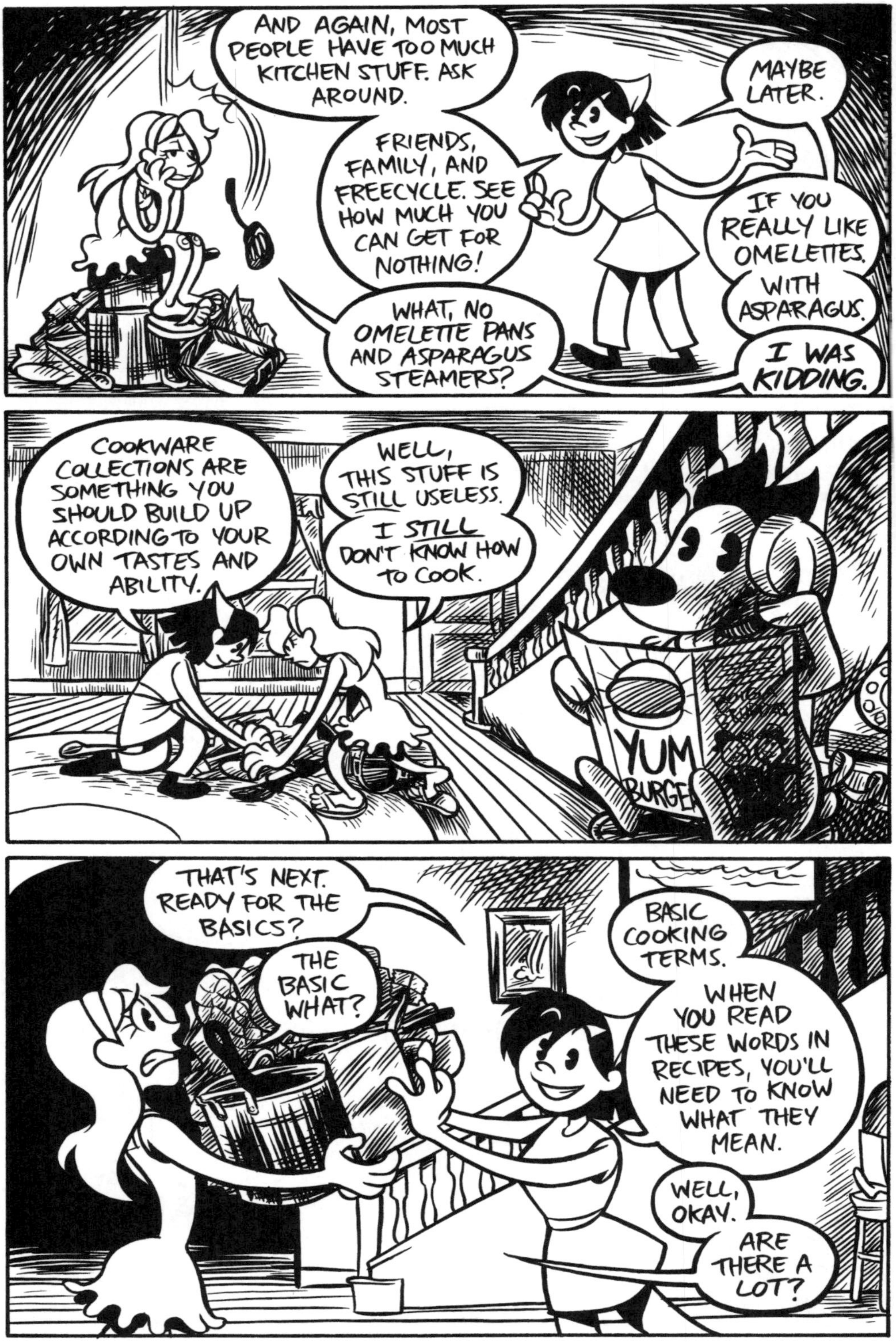
AND AGAIN, MOST PEOPLE HAVE TOO MUCH KITCHEN STUFF. ASK AROUND.
FRIENDS, FAMILY, AND FREECYCLE. SEE HOW MUCH YOU CAN GET FOR NOTHING!
WHAT, NO OMELETTE PANS AND ASPARAGUS STEAMERS?
MAYBE LATER.
IF YOU REALLY LIKE OMELETTES.
WITH ASPARAGUS.
I WAS KIDDING.
COOKWARE COLLECTIONS ARE SOMETHING YOU SHOULD BUILD UP ACCORDING TO YOUR OWN TASTES AND ABILITY.
WELL, THIS STUFF IS STILL USELESS.
I STILL DON'T KNOW HOW TO COOK.
YUM BURGER
THAT'S NEXT. READY FOR THE BASICS?
THE BASIC WHAT?
BASIC COOKING TERMS.
WHEN YOU READ THESE WORDS IN RECIPES, YOU'LL NEED TO KNOW WHAT THEY MEAN.
WELL, OKAY.
ARE THERE A LOT?

FOOD 101: THE GLOSSARY

BAKE – TO COOK IN THE DRY HEAT OF THE OVEN

BARBEQUE – TO COOK MEAT SLOWLY, OFTEN OVER COALS WHILE BASTING IT FREQUENTLY WITH A HEAVILY-SPICED SAUCE

BLANCH – TO SUBMERGE A FOOD INTO BOILING WATER FOR A BRIEF TIME, THEN SUBMERGE THE SAME FOOD IN ICE WATER TO QUICKLY STOP THE COOKING PROCESS

BOIL – TO COOK IN A LIQUID OVER A VERY HIGH HEAT, WHERE BUBBLES ARE VIGOROUSLY BREAKING THE SURFACE

BRAISE – TO SEAR (OR BROWN) FOOD IN HOT FAT ON THE STOVE, THEN CONTINUE COOKING SLOWLY IN A SMALL AMOUNT OF LIQUID IN THE OVEN

DEEP-FRY – TO COOK FOOD BY COMPLETELY IMMERSING IT IN HOT FAT

FRY – TO COOK FOOD IN A SMALL AMOUNT OF FAT ON THE STOVE WITH LIMITED STIRRING OR TURNING; ALSO CALLED *PAN-FRYING*

GRILL – TO QUICKLY COOK FOOD OVER HIGH HEAT

POACH – TO GENTLY COOK FRAGILE FOOD – LIKE EGGS, FISH, OR FRUIT – IN A LIQUID KEPT BELOW THE BOILING POINT

REDUCE – TO EVAPORATE SOME OF THE WATER FROM LIQUID OR SEMI-LIQUID FOOD BY BOILING OR SIMMERING IT IN AN UNCOVERED PAN

ROAST – A LOT LIKE BAKING, BUT THE TERM IS USED FOR MEAT OR VEGETABLES; TO COOK FOOD, UNCOVERED, WITH DRY, INDIRECT HEAT

SAUTÉ – TO QUICKLY SEAR (OR BROWN) SMALL PIECES OF MEAT OR VEGETABLES IN HOT FAT, STIRRING FREQUENTLY; A VERY QUICK METHOD!

SIMMER – TO COOK IN A LIQUID THAT IS KEPT JUST BELOW THE BOILING POINT; LIKE POACHING, BUT FOR LESS DELICATE FOODS THAT NEED LONGER

STEAM – TO COOK FOOD OVER A SMALL AMOUNT OF BOILING WATER; THE WATER AND FOOD ARE KEPT SEPARATE BY A RACK IN THE POT; A HEALTHY METHOD OF COOKING THAT USES NO ADDED FAT

SWEAT – TO GENTLY HEAT VEGETABLES IN A SMALL AMOUNT OF FAT, STIRRING FREQUENTLY AND NOT ALLOWING THE FOOD TO BROWN

STEW – TO SIMMER A MIXTURE OF SOLID FOODS IN A LIQUID

STIR-FRY – A TRADITIONAL CHINESE COOKING TECHNIQUE, SIMILAR TO SAUTÉING; BITE-SIZED FOOD COOKING VERY QUICKLY IN A VERY HOT PAN; VERY LITTLE OIL IS ADDED, AND THE FOOD IS VERY FREQUENTLY STIRRED

PARBOIL – TO PARTIALLY BOIL FOOD, AS PREPARATION FOR LATER COOKING; INSTANT RICE IS PARBOILED!

AT LEAST NOW YOU KNOW WHAT *BRAISING* IS.

HEY, WANNA GET SOME PRACTICE IN? THERE'S A MARKET DOWN THE STREET!

AUUGH!

FOOD 101: SHOPPING

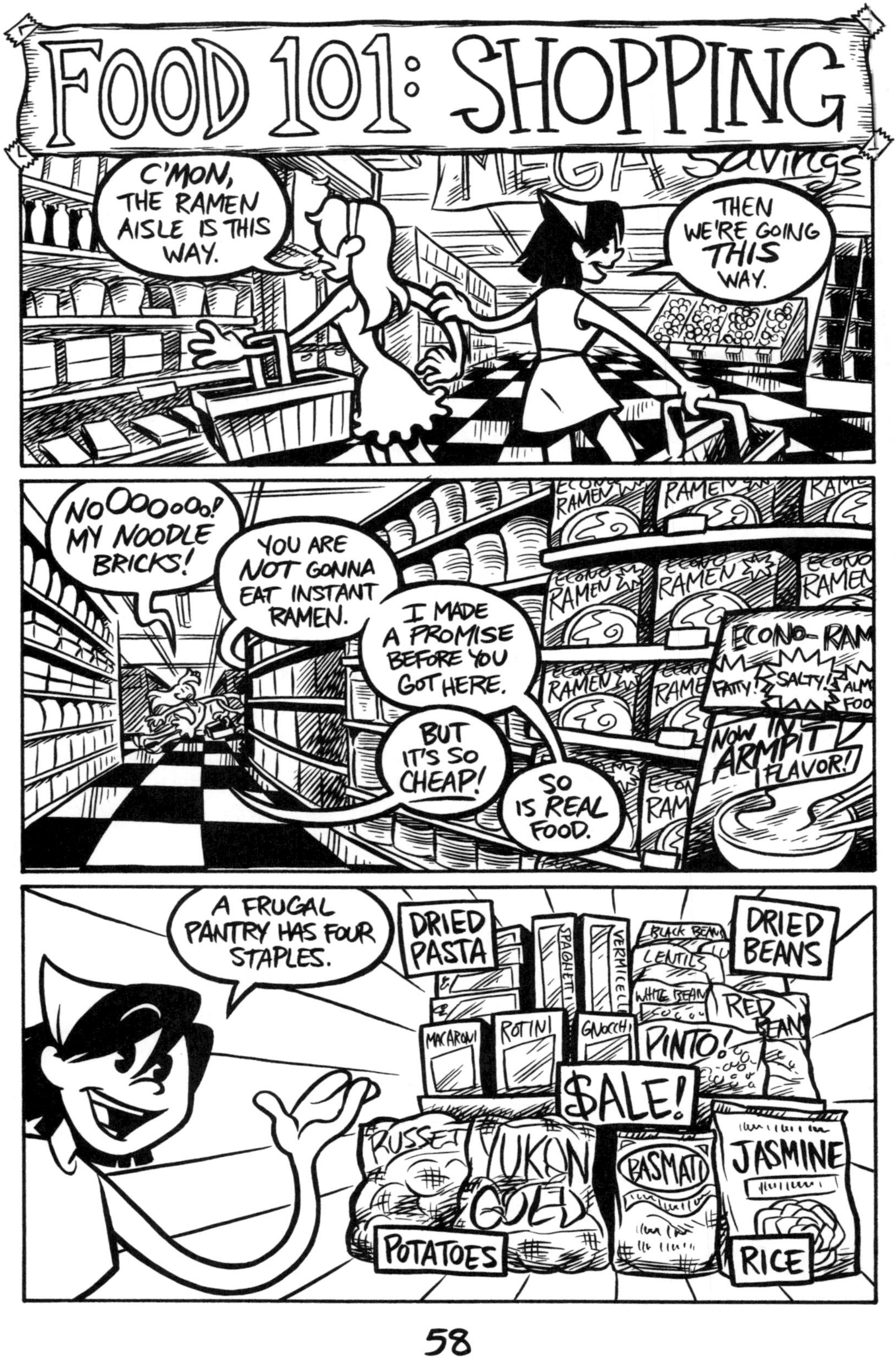

MEGA savings
C'MON, THE RAMEN AISLE IS THIS WAY.
THEN WE'RE GOING THIS WAY.
NoOOOooo! MY NOODLE BRICKS!
YOU ARE NOT GONNA EAT INSTANT RAMEN.
I MADE A PROMISE BEFORE YOU GOT HERE.
BUT IT'S SO CHEAP!
SO IS REAL FOOD.
ECONO RAMEN
ECONO-RAM
FATTY!
SALTY!
NOW IN ARMPIT FLAVOR!
A FRUGAL PANTRY HAS FOUR STAPLES.
DRIED PASTA
SPAGHETTI
VERMICELLI
MACARONI
ROTINI
GNOCCHI
DRIED BEANS
BLACK BEANS
LENTILS
WHITE BEAN
RED BEAN
PINTO!
$ALE!
RUSSET
YUKON GOLD
POTATOES
BASMATI
JASMINE
RICE

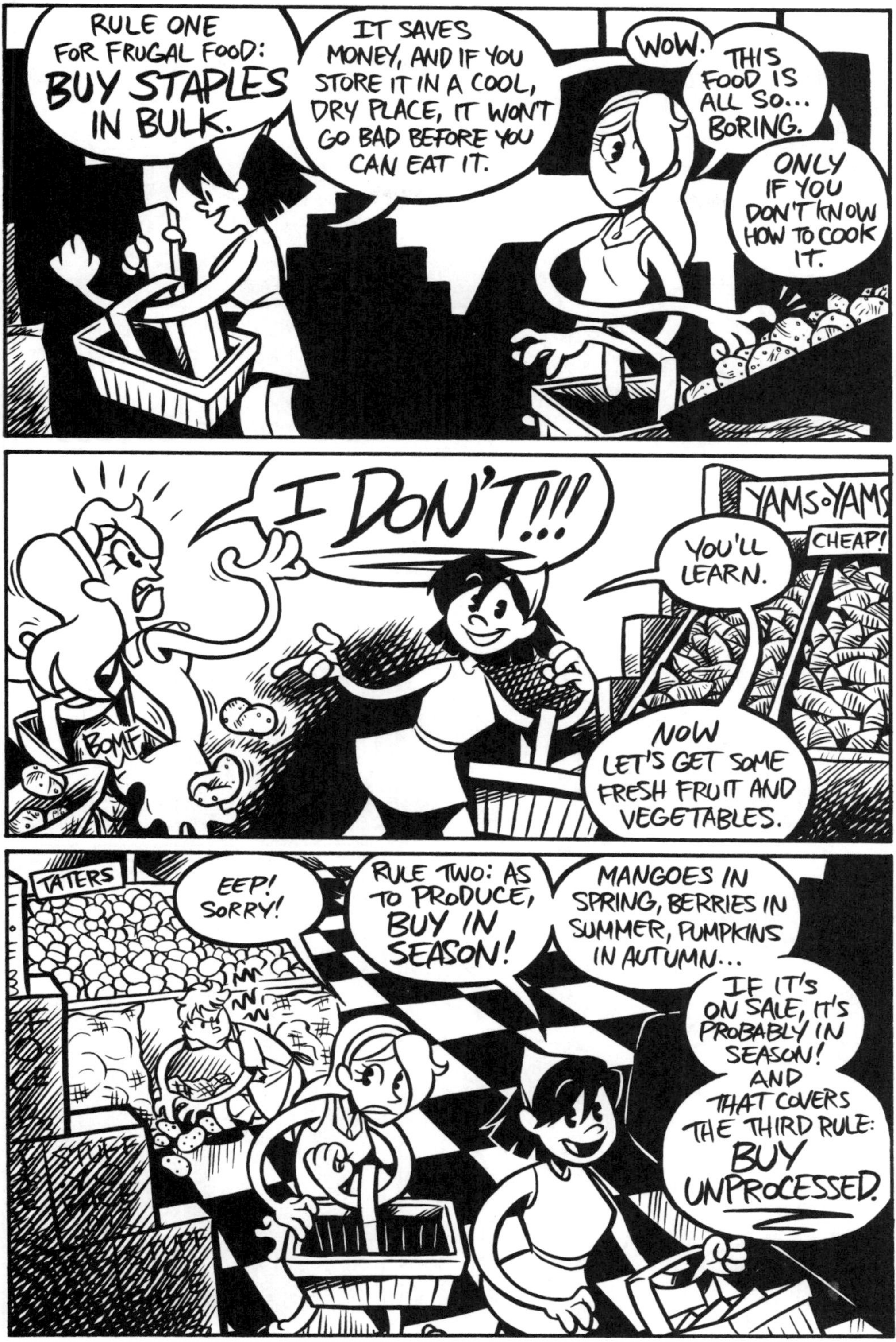
RULE ONE FOR FRUGAL FOOD: BUY STAPLES IN BULK.
IT SAVES MONEY, AND IF YOU STORE IT IN A COOL, DRY PLACE, IT WON'T GO BAD BEFORE YOU CAN EAT IT.
WOW.
THIS FOOD IS ALL SO... BORING.
ONLY IF YOU DON'T KNOW HOW TO COOK IT.
I DON'T!!!
YAMS YAMS
CHEAP!
YOU'LL LEARN.
BOMF
NOW LET'S GET SOME FRESH FRUIT AND VEGETABLES.
TATERS
EEP! SORRY!
RULE TWO: AS TO PRODUCE, BUY IN SEASON!
MANGOES IN SPRING, BERRIES IN SUMMER, PUMPKINS IN AUTUMN...
IF IT'S ON SALE, IT'S PROBABLY IN SEASON! AND THAT COVERS THE THIRD RULE: BUY UNPROCESSED.

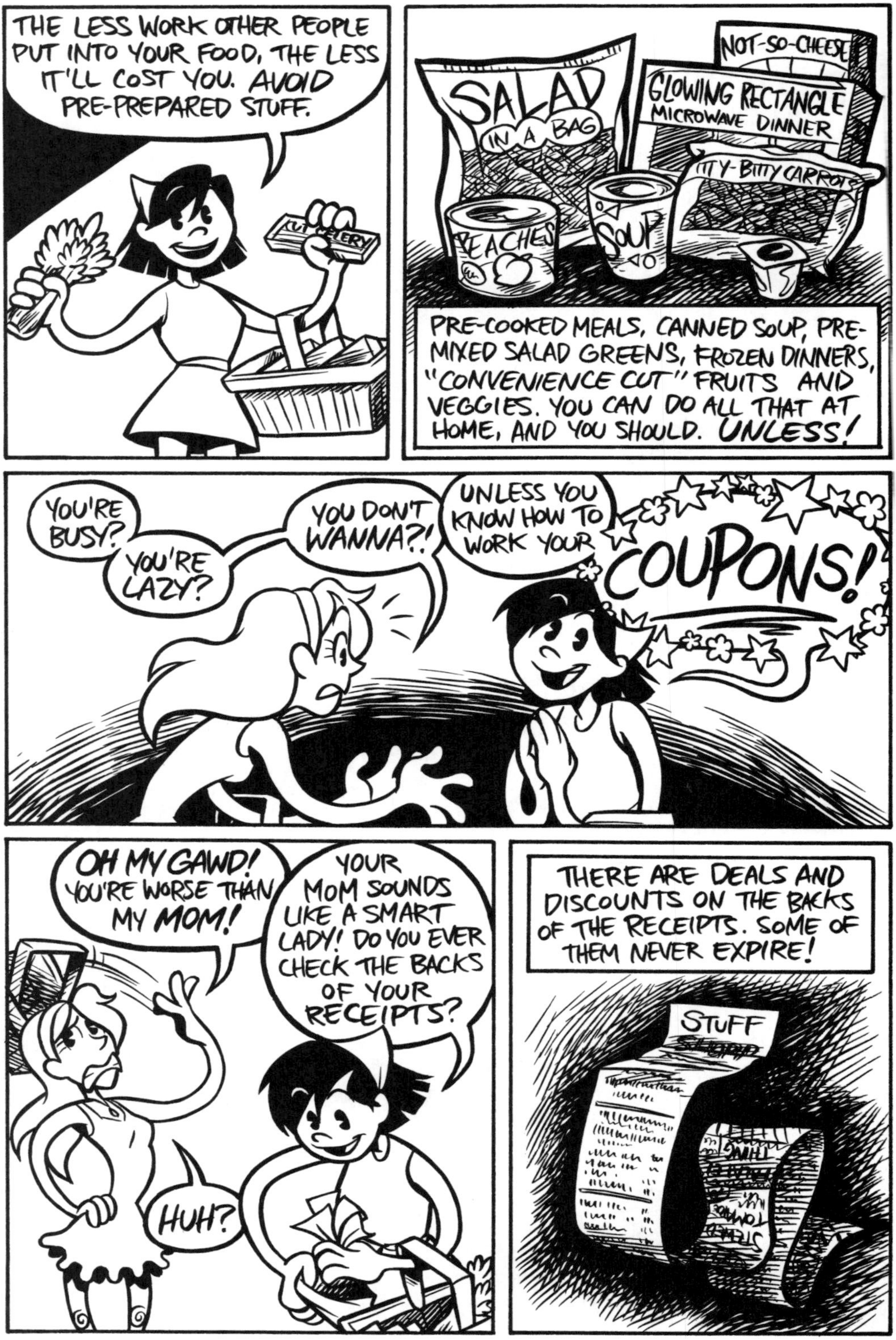
THE LESS WORK OTHER PEOPLE PUT INTO YOUR FOOD, THE LESS IT'LL COST YOU. AVOID PRE-PREPARED STUFF.
CUT CELERY
NOT-SO-CHEESE
SALAD IN A BAG
GLOWING RECTANGLE MICROWAVE DINNER
ITTY-BITTY CARROTS
PEACHES
SOUP
PRE-COOKED MEALS, CANNED SOUP, PRE-MIXED SALAD GREENS, FROZEN DINNERS, "CONVENIENCE CUT" FRUITS AND VEGGIES. YOU CAN DO ALL THAT AT HOME, AND YOU SHOULD. UNLESS!
YOU'RE BUSY?
YOU'RE LAZY?
YOU DON'T WANNA?!
UNLESS YOU KNOW HOW TO WORK YOUR COUPONS!
OH MY GAWD! YOU'RE WORSE THAN MY MOM!
YOUR MOM SOUNDS LIKE A SMART LADY! DO YOU EVER CHECK THE BACKS OF YOUR RECEIPTS?
HUH?
THERE ARE DEALS AND DISCOUNTS ON THE BACKS OF THE RECEIPTS. SOME OF THEM NEVER EXPIRE!
STUFF

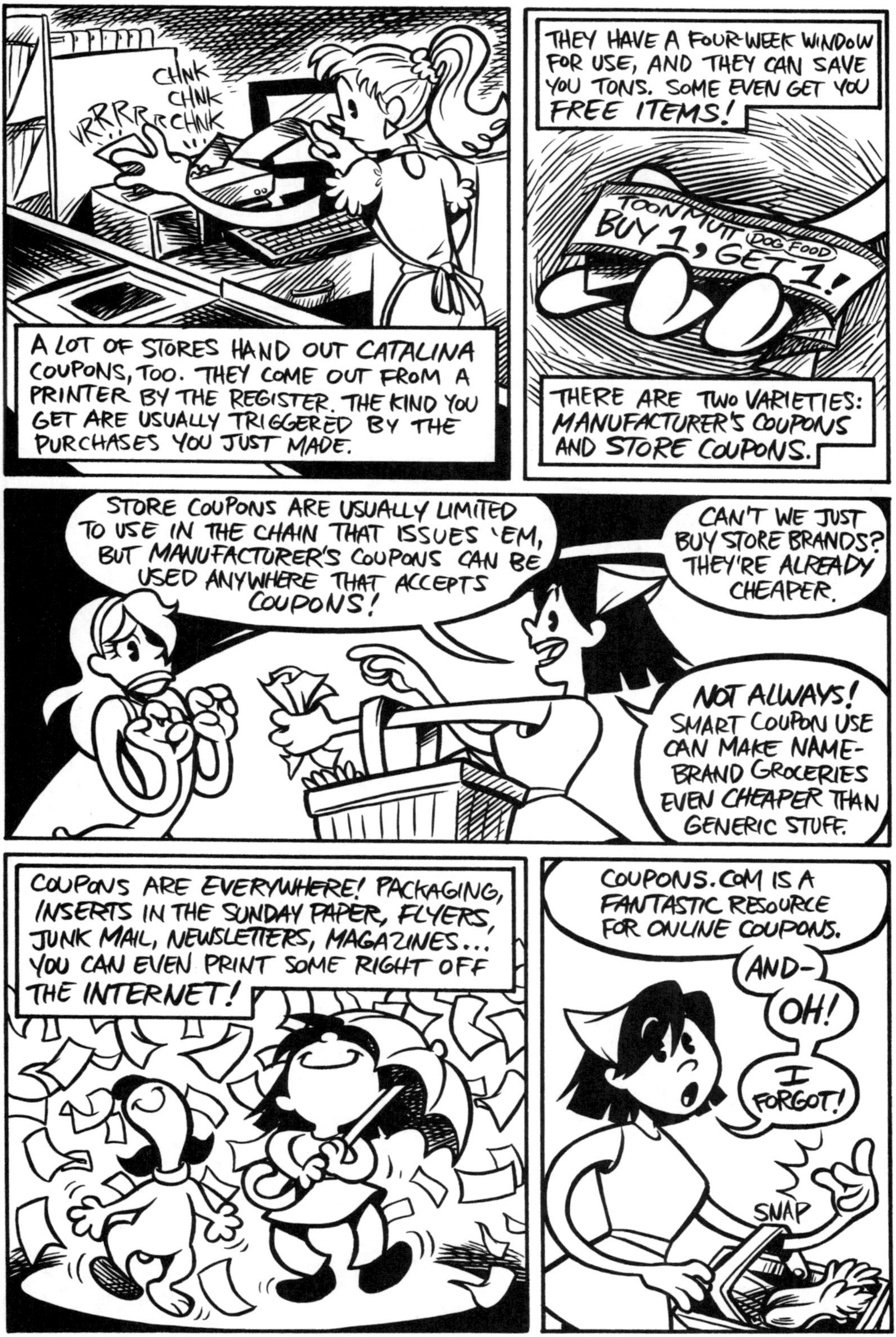
CHNK
CHNK
VRRRRrrCHNK
A LOT OF STORES HAND OUT CATALINA COUPONS, TOO. THEY COME OUT FROM A PRINTER BY THE REGISTER. THE KIND YOU GET ARE USUALLY TRIGGERED BY THE PURCHASES YOU JUST MADE.
THEY HAVE A FOUR-WEEK WINDOW FOR USE, AND THEY CAN SAVE YOU TONS. SOME EVEN GET YOU FREE ITEMS!
TOONMUT BUY 1, GET 1! DOG FOOD
THERE ARE TWO VARIETIES: MANUFACTURER'S COUPONS AND STORE COUPONS.
STORE COUPONS ARE USUALLY LIMITED TO USE IN THE CHAIN THAT ISSUES 'EM, BUT MANUFACTURER'S COUPONS CAN BE USED ANYWHERE THAT ACCEPTS COUPONS!
CAN'T WE JUST BUY STORE BRANDS? THEY'RE ALREADY CHEAPER.
NOT ALWAYS! SMART COUPON USE CAN MAKE NAME-BRAND GROCERIES EVEN CHEAPER THAN GENERIC STUFF.
COUPONS ARE EVERYWHERE! PACKAGING, INSERTS IN THE SUNDAY PAPER, FLYERS, JUNK MAIL, NEWSLETTERS, MAGAZINES... YOU CAN EVEN PRINT SOME RIGHT OFF THE INTERNET!
COUPONS.COM IS A FANTASTIC RESOURCE FOR ONLINE COUPONS.
AND-
OH!
I FORGOT!
SNAP

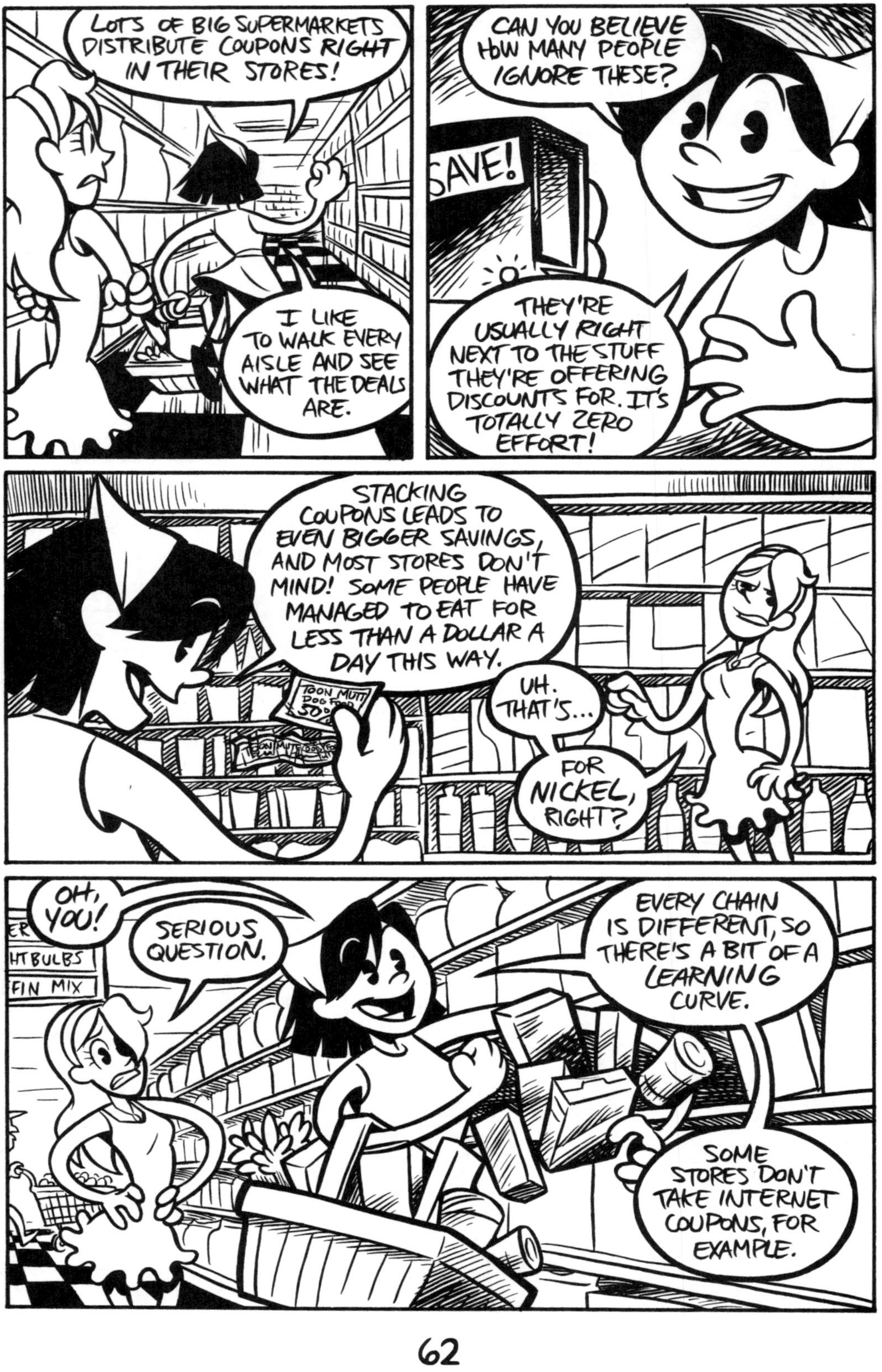
LOTS OF BIG SUPERMARKETS DISTRIBUTE COUPONS RIGHT IN THEIR STORES!
I LIKE TO WALK EVERY AISLE AND SEE WHAT THE DEALS ARE.
CAN YOU BELIEVE HOW MANY PEOPLE IGNORE THESE?
SAVE!
THEY'RE USUALLY RIGHT NEXT TO THE STUFF THEY'RE OFFERING DISCOUNTS FOR. IT'S TOTALLY ZERO EFFORT!
STACKING COUPONS LEADS TO EVEN BIGGER SAVINGS, AND MOST STORES DON'T MIND! SOME PEOPLE HAVE MANAGED TO EAT FOR LESS THAN A DOLLAR A DAY THIS WAY.
TOON MUTT DOG FOOD 50¢
UH. THAT'S...
FOR NICKEL, RIGHT?
OH, YOU!
SERIOUS QUESTION.
EVERY CHAIN IS DIFFERENT, SO THERE'S A BIT OF A LEARNING CURVE.
SOME STORES DON'T TAKE INTERNET COUPONS, FOR EXAMPLE.

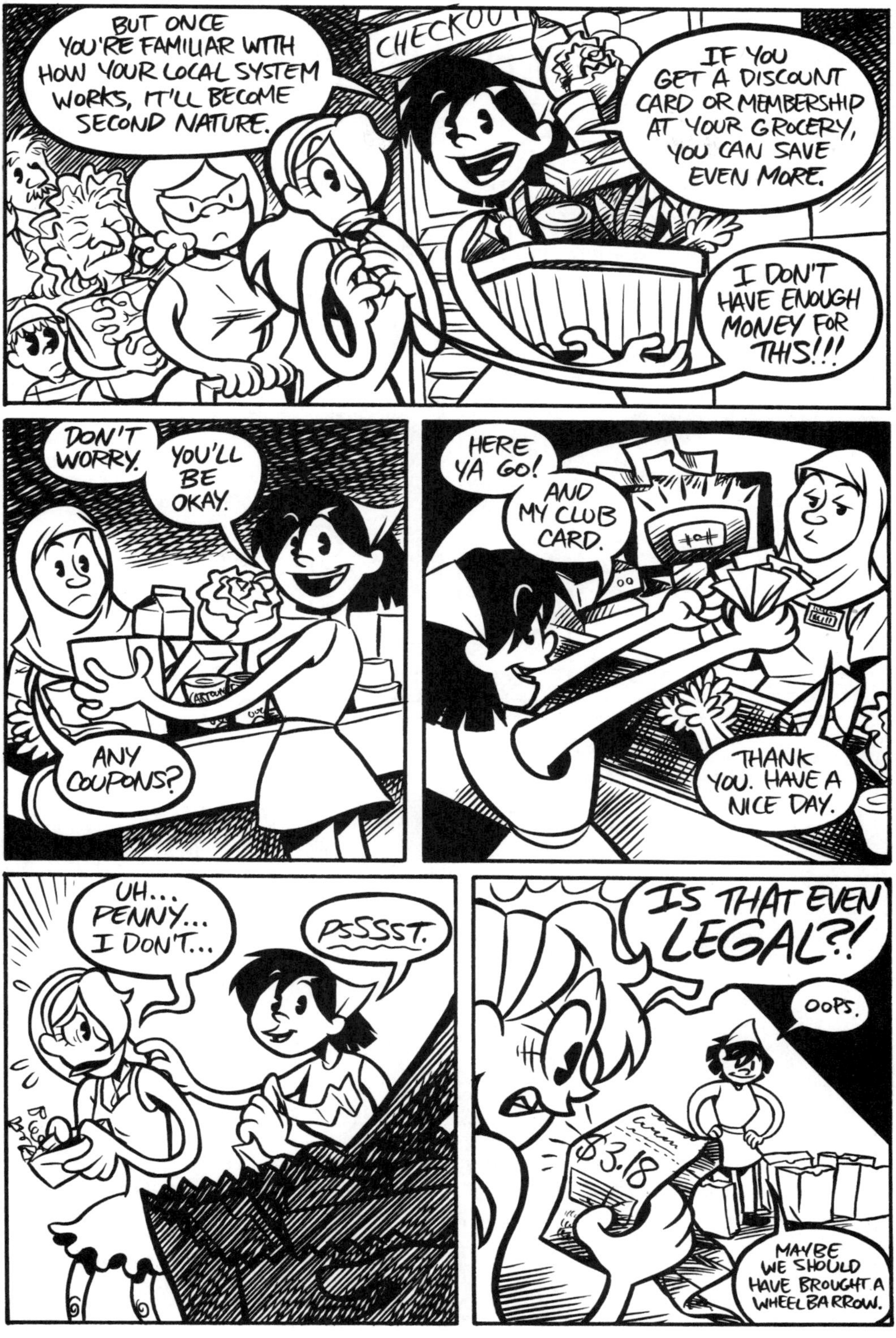

BUT ONCE YOU'RE FAMILIAR WITH HOW YOUR LOCAL SYSTEM WORKS, IT'LL BECOME SECOND NATURE.
CHECKOUT
IF YOU GET A DISCOUNT CARD OR MEMBERSHIP AT YOUR GROCERY, YOU CAN SAVE EVEN MORE.
I DON'T HAVE ENOUGH MONEY FOR THIS!!!
DON'T WORRY.
YOU'LL BE OKAY.
ANY COUPONS?
HERE YA GO!
AND MY CLUB CARD.
THANK YOU. HAVE A NICE DAY.
UH... PENNY... I DON'T...
PSSSST.
IS THAT EVEN LEGAL?!
OOPS.
$3.18
MAYBE WE SHOULD HAVE BROUGHT A WHEELBARROW.

FOOD 101: FORAGING AND GARDENING

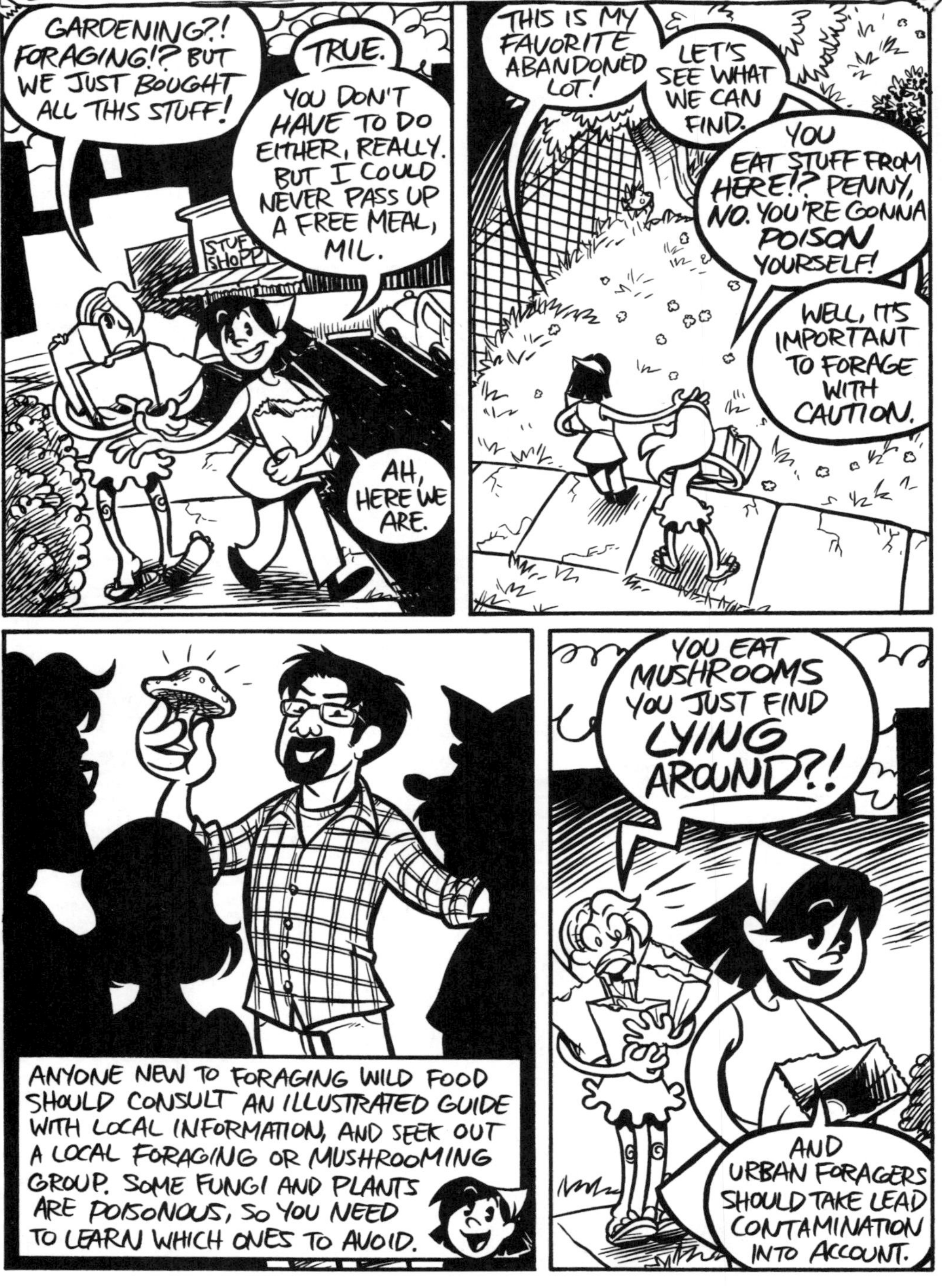
GARDENING?! FORAGING!? BUT WE JUST BOUGHT ALL THIS STUFF!
TRUE.
YOU DON'T HAVE TO DO EITHER, REALLY. BUT I COULD NEVER PASS UP A FREE MEAL, MIL.
AH, HERE WE ARE.
THIS IS MY FAVORITE ABANDONED LOT!
LET'S SEE WHAT WE CAN FIND.
YOU EAT STUFF FROM HERE!? PENNY, NO. YOU'RE GONNA POISON YOURSELF!
WELL, IT'S IMPORTANT TO FORAGE WITH CAUTION.
ANYONE NEW TO FORAGING WILD FOOD SHOULD CONSULT AN ILLUSTRATED GUIDE WITH LOCAL INFORMATION, AND SEEK OUT A LOCAL FORAGING OR MUSHROOMING GROUP. SOME FUNGI AND PLANTS ARE POISONOUS, SO YOU NEED TO LEARN WHICH ONES TO AVOID.
YOU EAT MUSHROOMS YOU JUST FIND LYING AROUND?!
AND URBAN FORAGERS SHOULD TAKE LEAD CONTAMINATION INTO ACCOUNT.

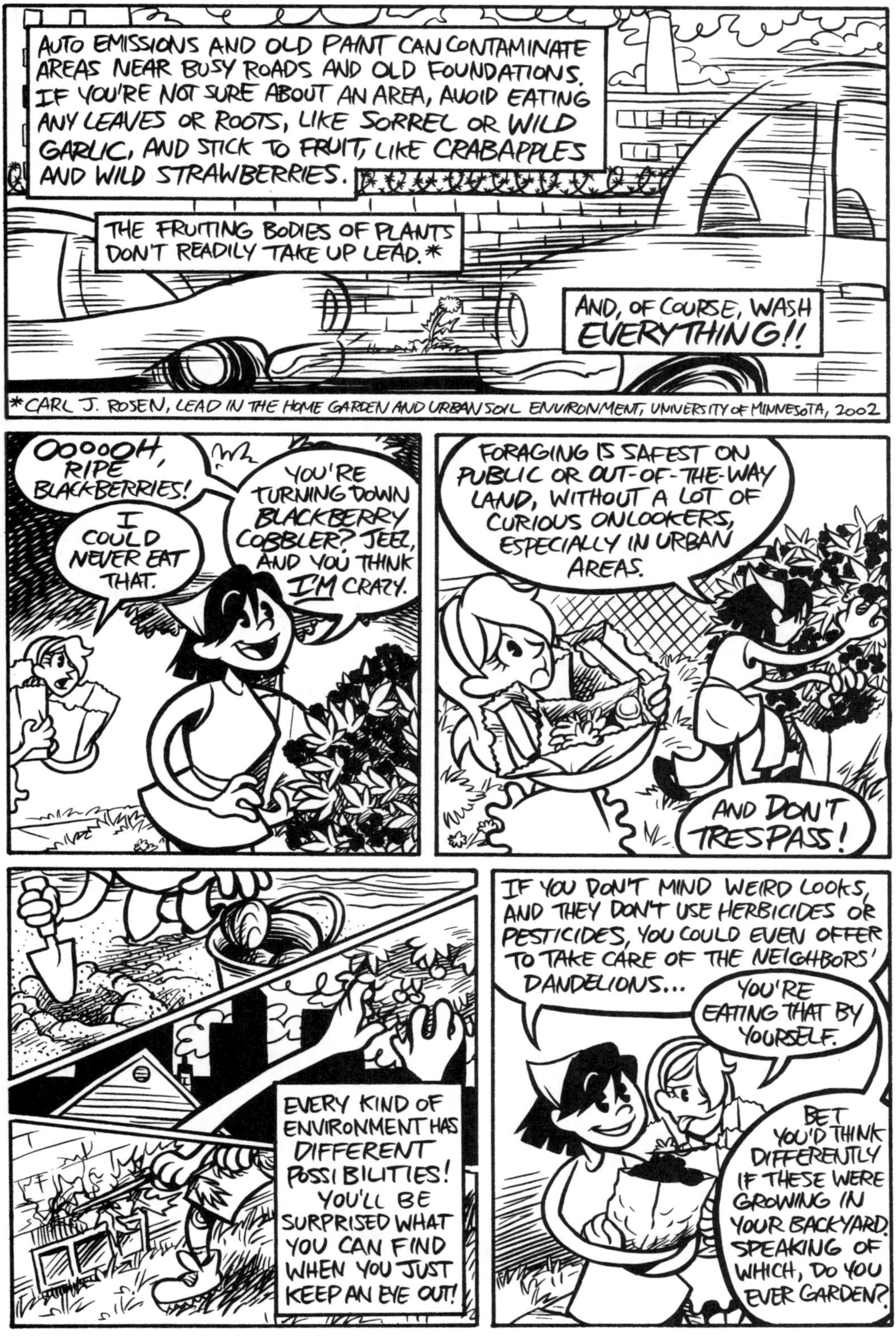
AUTO EMISSIONS AND OLD PAINT CAN CONTAMINATE AREAS NEAR BUSY ROADS AND OLD FOUNDATIONS. IF YOU'RE NOT SURE ABOUT AN AREA, AVOID EATING ANY LEAVES OR ROOTS, LIKE SORREL OR WILD GARLIC, AND STICK TO FRUIT, LIKE CRABAPPLES AND WILD STRAWBERRIES.
THE FRUITING BODIES OF PLANTS DON'T READILY TAKE UP LEAD.*
AND, OF COURSE, WASH EVERYTHING!!
*CARL J. ROSEN, LEAD IN THE HOME GARDEN AND URBAN SOIL ENVIRONMENT, UNIVERSITY OF MINNESOTA, 2002
OOOOOOH, RIPE BLACKBERRIES!
I COULD NEVER EAT THAT.
YOU'RE TURNING DOWN BLACKBERRY COBBLER? JEEZ, AND YOU THINK I'M CRAZY.
FORAGING IS SAFEST ON PUBLIC OR OUT-OF-THE-WAY LAND, WITHOUT A LOT OF CURIOUS ONLOOKERS, ESPECIALLY IN URBAN AREAS.
AND DON'T TRESPASS!
EVERY KIND OF ENVIRONMENT HAS DIFFERENT POSSIBILITIES! YOU'LL BE SURPRISED WHAT YOU CAN FIND WHEN YOU JUST KEEP AN EYE OUT!
IF YOU DON'T MIND WEIRD LOOKS, AND THEY DON'T USE HERBICIDES OR PESTICIDES, YOU COULD EVEN OFFER TO TAKE CARE OF THE NEIGHBORS' DANDELIONS...
YOU'RE EATING THAT BY YOURSELF.
BET YOU'D THINK DIFFERENTLY IF THESE WERE GROWING IN YOUR BACKYARD. SPEAKING OF WHICH, DO YOU EVER GARDEN?

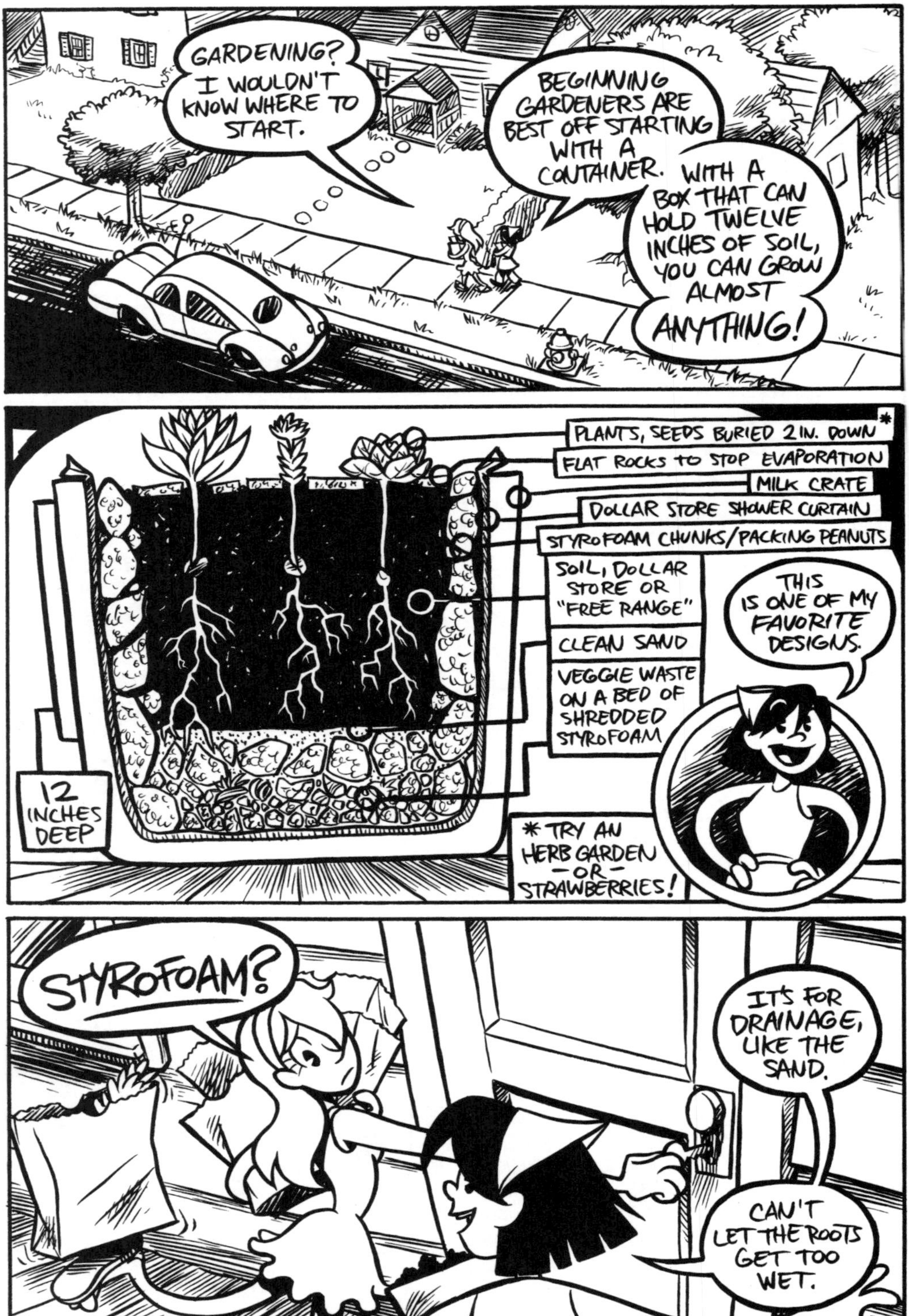
GARDENING? I WOULDN'T KNOW WHERE TO START.
BEGINNING GARDENERS ARE BEST OFF STARTING WITH A CONTAINER.
WITH A BOX THAT CAN HOLD TWELVE INCHES OF SOIL, YOU CAN GROW ALMOST ANYTHING!
PLANTS, SEEDS BURIED 2 IN. DOWN*
FLAT ROCKS TO STOP EVAPORATION
MILK CRATE
DOLLAR STORE SHOWER CURTAIN
STYROFOAM CHUNKS/PACKING PEANUTS
SOIL, DOLLAR STORE OR "FREE RANGE"
CLEAN SAND
VEGGIE WASTE ON A BED OF SHREDDED STYROFOAM
12 INCHES DEEP
* TRY AN HERB GARDEN —OR— STRAWBERRIES!
THIS IS ONE OF MY FAVORITE DESIGNS.
STYROFOAM?
IT'S FOR DRAINAGE, LIKE THE SAND.
CAN'T LET THE ROOTS GET TOO WET.

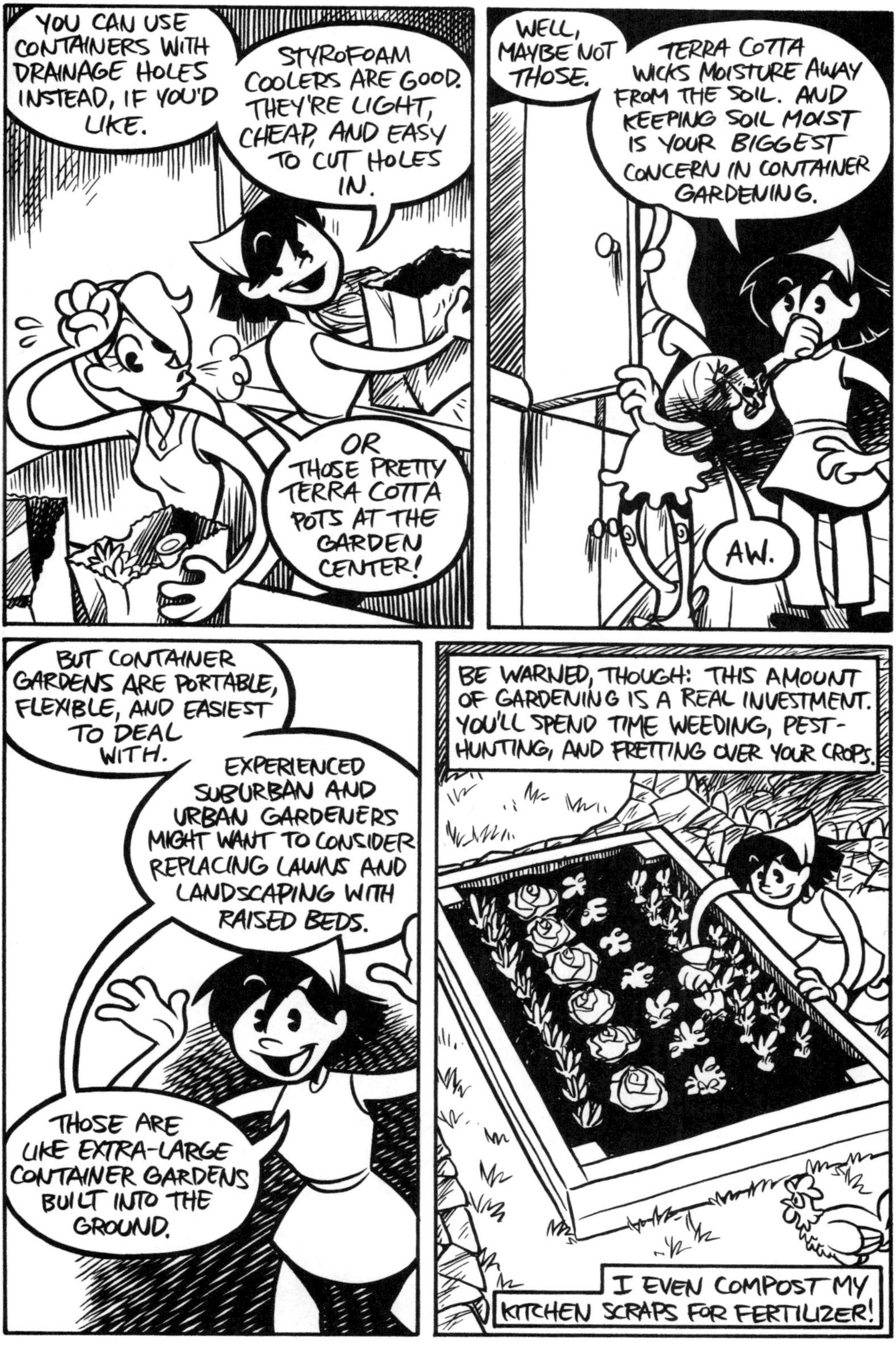
YOU CAN USE CONTAINERS WITH DRAINAGE HOLES INSTEAD, IF YOU'D LIKE.
STYROFOAM COOLERS ARE GOOD. THEY'RE LIGHT, CHEAP, AND EASY TO CUT HOLES IN.
OR THOSE PRETTY TERRA COTTA POTS AT THE GARDEN CENTER!
WELL, MAYBE NOT THOSE.
TERRA COTTA WICKS MOISTURE AWAY FROM THE SOIL. AND KEEPING SOIL MOIST IS YOUR BIGGEST CONCERN IN CONTAINER GARDENING.
AW.
BUT CONTAINER GARDENS ARE PORTABLE, FLEXIBLE, AND EASIEST TO DEAL WITH.
EXPERIENCED SUBURBAN AND URBAN GARDENERS MIGHT WANT TO CONSIDER REPLACING LAWNS AND LANDSCAPING WITH RAISED BEDS.
THOSE ARE LIKE EXTRA-LARGE CONTAINER GARDENS BUILT INTO THE GROUND.
BE WARNED, THOUGH: THIS AMOUNT OF GARDENING IS A REAL INVESTMENT. YOU'LL SPEND TIME WEEDING, PEST-HUNTING, AND FRETTING OVER YOUR CROPS.
I EVEN COMPOST MY KITCHEN SCRAPS FOR FERTILIZER!

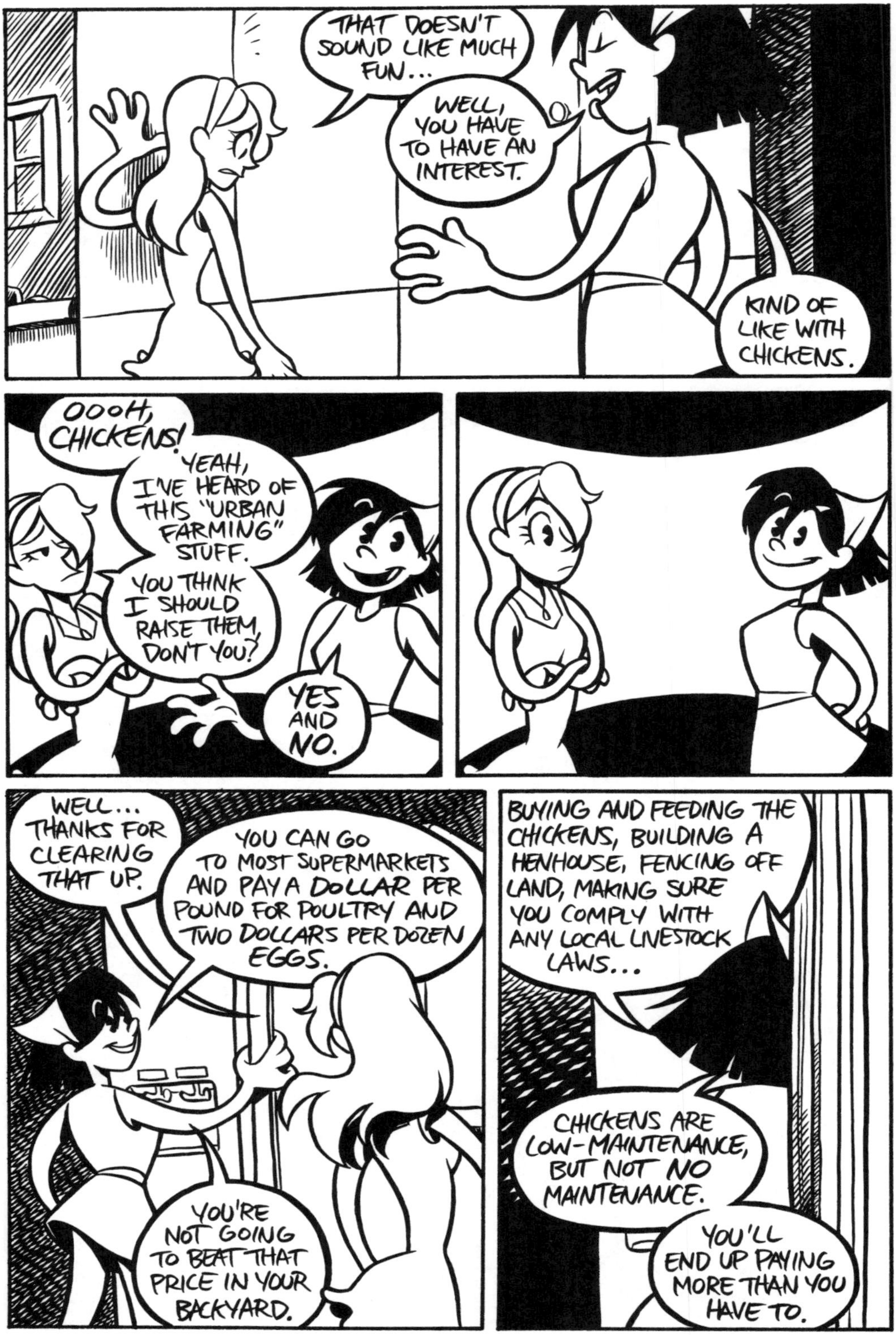
THAT DOESN'T SOUND LIKE MUCH FUN...
WELL, YOU HAVE TO HAVE AN INTEREST.
KIND OF LIKE WITH CHICKENS.
OOOH, CHICKENS!
YEAH, I'VE HEARD OF THIS "URBAN FARMING" STUFF.
YOU THINK I SHOULD RAISE THEM, DON'T YOU?
YES AND NO.
WELL... THANKS FOR CLEARING THAT UP.
YOU CAN GO TO MOST SUPERMARKETS AND PAY A DOLLAR PER POUND FOR POULTRY AND TWO DOLLARS PER DOZEN EGGS.
YOU'RE NOT GOING TO BEAT THAT PRICE IN YOUR BACKYARD.
BUYING AND FEEDING THE CHICKENS, BUILDING A HENHOUSE, FENCING OFF LAND, MAKING SURE YOU COMPLY WITH ANY LOCAL LIVESTOCK LAWS...
CHICKENS ARE LOW-MAINTENANCE, BUT NOT NO MAINTENANCE.
YOU'LL END UP PAYING MORE THAN YOU HAVE TO.

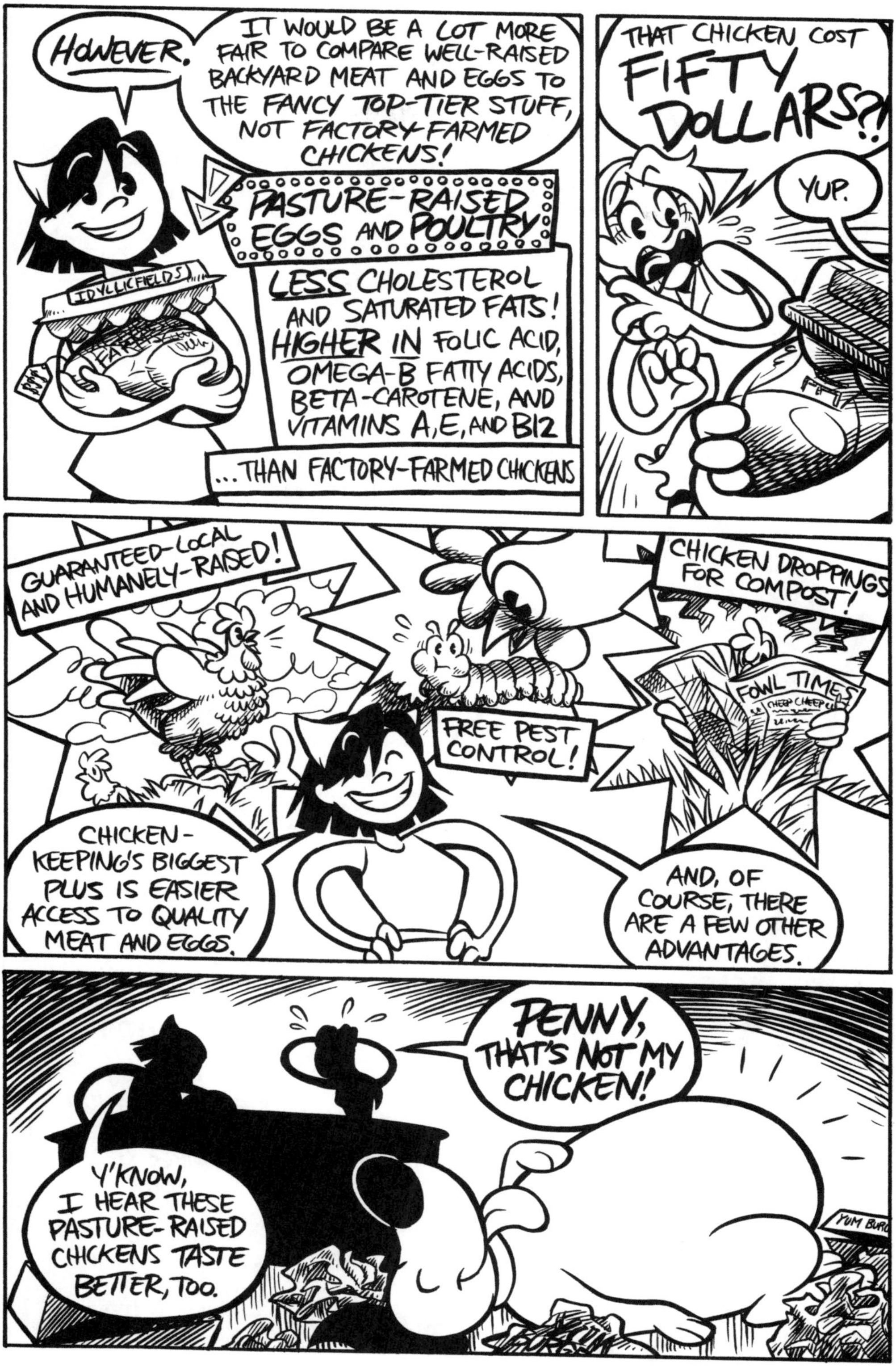
HOWEVER.
IT WOULD BE A LOT MORE FAIR TO COMPARE WELL-RAISED BACKYARD MEAT AND EGGS TO THE FANCY TOP-TIER STUFF, NOT FACTORY-FARMED CHICKENS!
PASTURE-RAISED EGGS AND POULTRY
LESS CHOLESTEROL AND SATURATED FATS! HIGHER IN FOLIC ACID, OMEGA-B FATTY ACIDS, BETA-CAROTENE, AND VITAMINS A, E, AND B12
...THAN FACTORY-FARMED CHICKENS
IDYLLIC FIELDS
THAT CHICKEN COST FIFTY DOLLARS?!
YUP.
GUARANTEED-LOCAL AND HUMANELY-RAISED!
CHICKEN DROPPINGS FOR COMPOST!
FOWL TIMES
CHEEP CHEEP
FREE PEST CONTROL!
CHICKEN-KEEPING'S BIGGEST PLUS IS EASIER ACCESS TO QUALITY MEAT AND EGGS.
AND, OF COURSE, THERE ARE A FEW OTHER ADVANTAGES.
PENNY, THAT'S NOT MY CHICKEN!
Y'KNOW, I HEAR THESE PASTURE-RAISED CHICKENS TASTE BETTER, TOO.

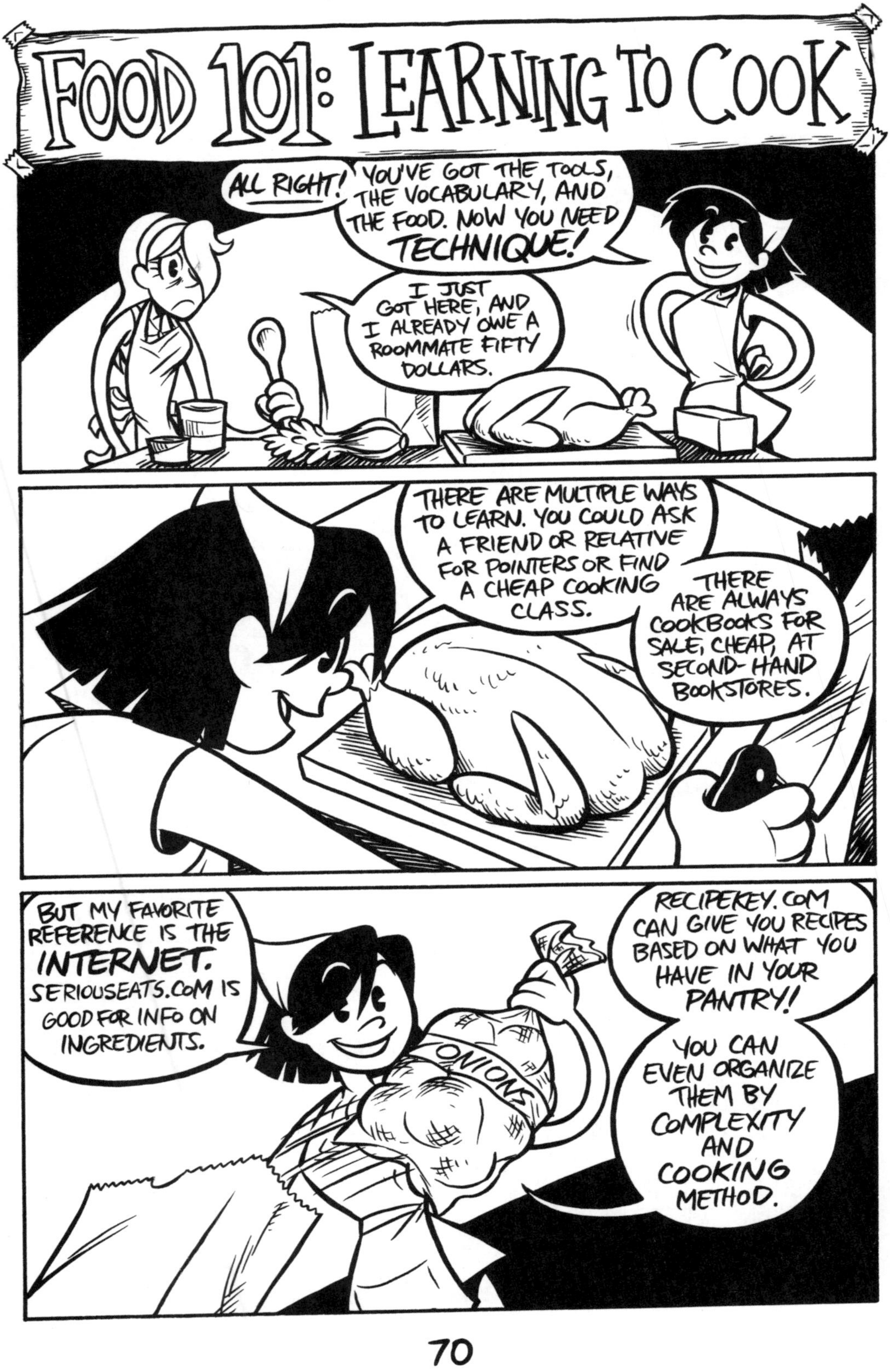
FOOD 101: LEARNING TO COOK
ALL RIGHT!
YOU'VE GOT THE TOOLS, THE VOCABULARY, AND THE FOOD. NOW YOU NEED TECHNIQUE!
I JUST GOT HERE, AND I ALREADY OWE A ROOMMATE FIFTY DOLLARS.
THERE ARE MULTIPLE WAYS TO LEARN. YOU COULD ASK A FRIEND OR RELATIVE FOR POINTERS OR FIND A CHEAP COOKING CLASS.
THERE ARE ALWAYS COOKBOOKS FOR SALE, CHEAP, AT SECOND-HAND BOOKSTORES.
BUT MY FAVORITE REFERENCE IS THE INTERNET. SERIOUSEATS.COM IS GOOD FOR INFO ON INGREDIENTS.
ONIONS
RECIPEKEY.COM CAN GIVE YOU RECIPES BASED ON WHAT YOU HAVE IN YOUR PANTRY!
YOU CAN EVEN ORGANIZE THEM BY COMPLEXITY AND COOKING METHOD.

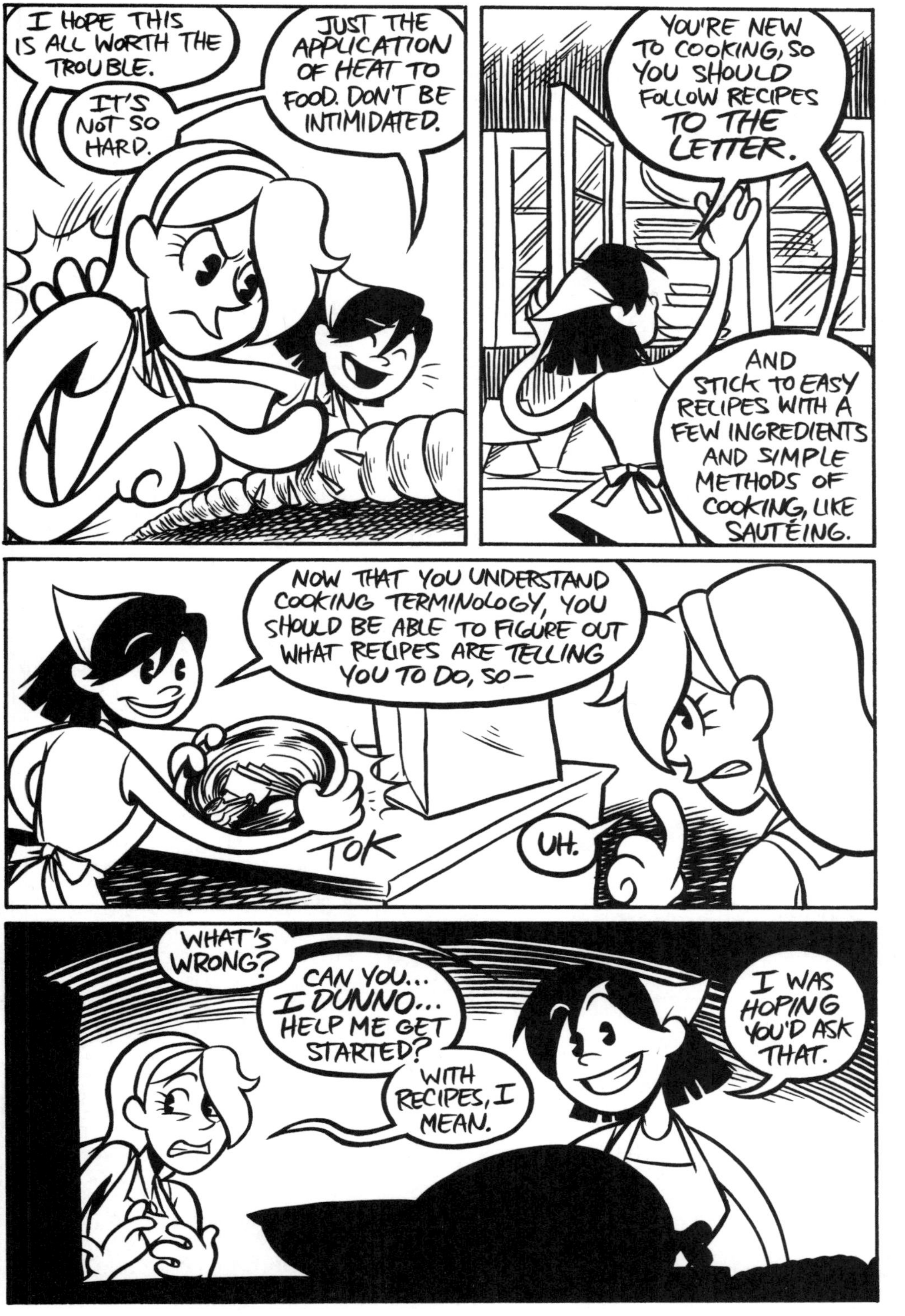
I HOPE THIS IS ALL WORTH THE TROUBLE.
IT'S NOT SO HARD.
JUST THE APPLICATION OF HEAT TO FOOD. DON'T BE INTIMIDATED.
YOU'RE NEW TO COOKING, SO YOU SHOULD FOLLOW RECIPES TO THE LETTER.
AND STICK TO EASY RECIPES WITH A FEW INGREDIENTS AND SIMPLE METHODS OF COOKING, LIKE SAUTÉING.
NOW THAT YOU UNDERSTAND COOKING TERMINOLOGY, YOU SHOULD BE ABLE TO FIGURE OUT WHAT RECIPES ARE TELLING YOU TO DO, SO–
TOK
UH.
WHAT'S WRONG?
CAN YOU... I DUNNO... HELP ME GET STARTED?
WITH RECIPES, I MEAN.
I WAS HOPING YOU'D ASK THAT.

YOUR FRIEND, THE POTATO

WORLD'S MOST FORGIVING CARBOHYDRATE

IT'S HARD TO MESS ME UP.

BAKED POTATO
▷ SERVES ONE ◁

1 RUSSET POTATO
VEGETABLE OR CANOLA OIL
SALT + SEASONINGS

- WASH THE POTATO
- RUB POTATO SKIN WITH OIL UNTIL SHINY BUT NOT DRIPPING
- SPRINKLE SKIN LIGHTLY WITH SALT
- PLACE POTATO DIRECTLY ON OVEN RACK @ 350°F FOR ONE HOUR

THE POTATO IS DONE WHEN THE SKIN IS DRY AND PAPERY AND THE FLESH IS SOFT. EAT IT WITH SALT, PEPPER, CHEESE, SOUR CREAM, CHIVES, BACON, BUTTER...

OVEN-FRIED POTATOES
▷ SERVES TWO ◁

2 RUSSET OR YUKON GOLD POTATOES
CANOLA OIL   PEPPER
SALT   PAPRIKA

- POUR SHALLOW POOL OF OIL INTO ROASTING PAN; PUT IN 350°F OVEN
- WASH POTATOES AND SLICE LENGTH-WISE; SLICE EACH HALF INTO THREE LONG, EQUAL PIECES
- COVER POTATOES WITH WATER IN STOCK POT OVER HIGH HEAT; ADD LID
- BOIL FOR 10 MIN.; DRAIN; PUT IN MIXING BOWL AND SPRINKLE WITH SALT, PEPPER, AND PAPRIKA
- TOSS POTATOES IN BOWL
- GENTLY PLACE POTATOES IN HOT ROASTING PAN
- ROAST 40 MIN.; FLIP HALFWAY

POTATO SOUP
▷ SERVES TWO ◁

2 RUSSET POTATOES   MILK
1 LARGE ONION   SALT + PEPPER
  WATER   BUTTER

- WASH AND PEEL THE POTATOES
- CHOP POTATOES INTO ½-INCH PIECES
- SLICE ONION IN HALF LENGTHWISE; DICE CUT-SIDE DOWN INTO EVEN SQUARES
- MELT A TBSP. OF BUTTER IN FRYING PAN OVER MEDIUM HEAT; WHEN PAN IS HOT, POUR IN DICED ONION AND STIR WITH WOODEN SPOON UNTIL TRANSLUCENT (ABOUT 5-8 MINUTES)
- REMOVE ONIONS FROM HEAT, PUT CHOPPED POTATOES IN STOCK POT, COVER WITH WATER, AND ADD LID OVER HIGH HEAT
- BOIL POTATOES FOR 40 MINUTES OR UNTIL SOFT; TURN OFF HEAT AND DRAIN HALF THE WATER; REPLACE WATER WITH MILK + MASHED POTATOES
- MIX IN ONIONS AND BUTTER FROM PAN
- ADD SALT AND PEPPER TO TASTE

ADD EXTRA BUTTER, COOKED BACON OR HAM, COOKED MUSHROOMS, OR REPLACE MILK WITH CREAM OR HALF + HALF FOR RICHER SOUP!

MASHED POTATOES
▷ SERVES FOUR ◁

10 RED POTATOES
GARLIC
MILK
BUTTER
SALT
PEPPER

- WASH POTATOES AND CHOP EACH INTO FOUR EQUAL PIECES
- CRUSH 2 GARLIC CLOVES
- PUT POTATOES AND GARLIC IN POT, COVER WITH WATER, ADD LID, PUT OVER HIGH HEAT
- BOIL UNTIL SOFT (40 MIN.)
- DRAIN AND MASH IN BOWL WITH FORK; MELT IN 2 TBSP. OF BUTTER
- POUR IN ⅓ TO ½ CUP MILK
- MIX UP AND ADD SALT + PEPPER

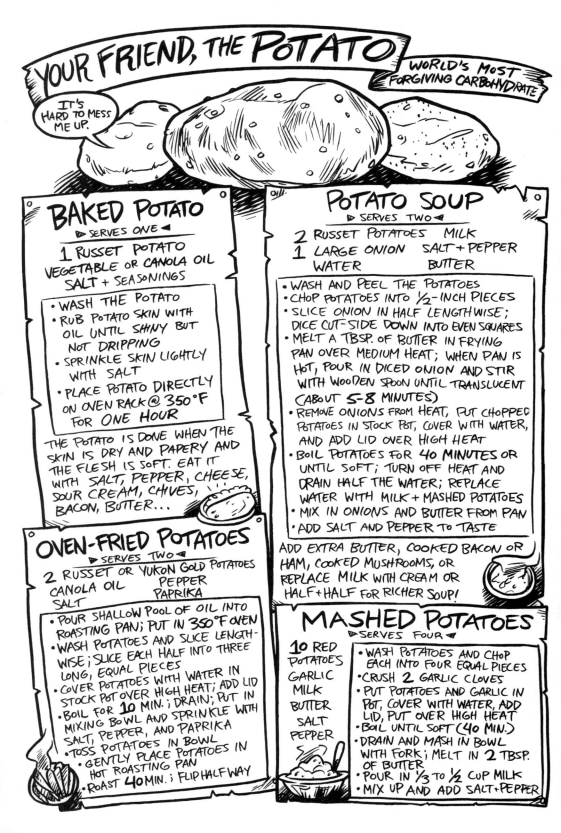

BEANS! CHEAP 'N' TASTY PROTEIN!

AND SOMETIMES EMBARRASSING!

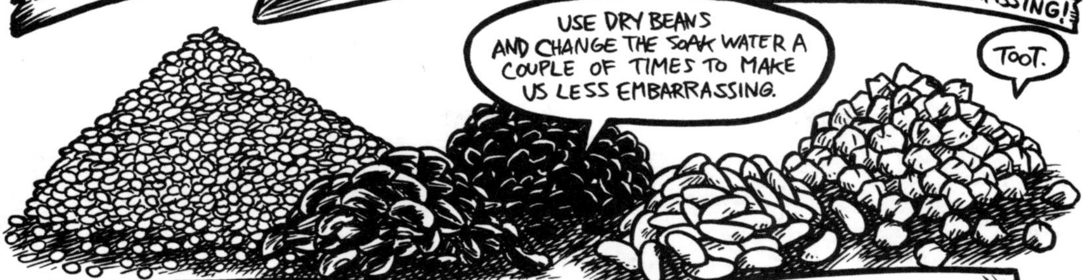
USE DRY BEANS AND CHANGE THE SOAK WATER A COUPLE OF TIMES TO MAKE US LESS EMBARRASSING.
TOOT.

RICE + BEANS

SERVES 6–8

1 LB. BAG OF DRIED BEANS (ANY KIND)
1½ CUPS LONG GRAIN WHITE RICE
5 SLICES OF BACON CAYENNE PEPPER
2 BELL PEPPERS 2 ONIONS
3 GARLIC CLOVES 2 BAY LEAVES
CUMIN SALT + PEPPER WATER

- WASH BEANS AND POUR INTO BOWL; COVER WITH *LOTS* OF WATER AND SALT GENEROUSLY
- SOAK FOR 4 HOURS; DRAIN + REPLACE WITH FRESH SALT WATER; SOAK AGAIN
- BAKE BACON IN OVEN AT 400°F FOR 15–20 MINUTES, UNTIL CRISPY
- PEEL + DICE ONIONS; CRUSH + DICE GARLIC
- WASH, REMOVE PITH, DICE BELL PEPPERS
- DRAIN BACON; KEEP BACON FAT
- COOK ONIONS IN BACON FAT OVER MED HEAT FOR 5–8 MINUTES; STIR OCCASIONALLY
- ADD GARLIC; COOK 1 MINUTE
- ADD BELL PEPPERS; COOK 3–5 MIN.
- DRAIN BEANS + ADD TO SKILLET; POUR IN AMOUNT OF FRESH WATER TO COVER THE SKILLET CONTENTS
- ADD BAY LEAVES AND 2 TSP. OF CUMIN
- TURN HEAT TO HIGH + BRING TO BOIL
- ONCE BOILING, TURN HEAT TO MED-LOW, PUT ON LID, AND SIMMER FOR 1½ HRS.
- WASH RICE IN MIXING BOWL; CHANGE WATER UNTIL CLEAR; DRAIN + PUT IN A SAUCEPAN; ADD 3 CUPS OF WATER
- COVER PAN WITH LID; HIGH HEAT; BOIL
- COOK RICE ON LOW FOR 20 MINUTES
- LET SIT COVERED FOR 5 MIN. AFTER
- FLUFF RICE + TASTE FOR DONENESS
- WHEN BEANS ARE READY, SALT + PEPPER TO TASTE; DISH RICE, ADD BEANS, + CRUMBLE BACON ON TOP

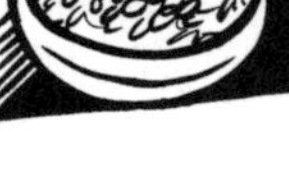

CRUNCHY ROASTED CHICKPEAS

SERVES TWO (PREFERABLY IN FRONT OF A T.V.)

1 CAN OF CHICKPEAS, IN WATER
OLIVE OIL SALT

- DRAIN LIQUID FROM THE CAN OF CHICKPEAS; POUR CHICKPEAS ONTO PAPER TOWEL AND PAT THEM DRY WITH ANOTHER
- POUR CHICKPEAS INTO MIXING BOWL; TOSS WITH ENOUGH OIL TO LIGHTLY COAT THEM; SPRINKLE WITH SALT
- POUR CHICKPEAS INTO ROASTING PAN IN A SINGLE LAYER
- ROAST IN 400°F OVEN FOR 20 MINUTES OR UNTIL BROWN 'N' CRUNCHY

... TRY ADDING CURRY POWDER, SOY SAUCE, ONION SALT, GARLIC...

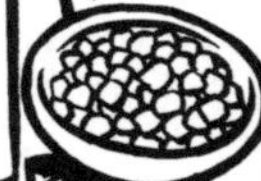

LENTIL SOUP

SERVES 6

1 LB. BAG OF DRY LENTILS OLIVE OIL
1 ONION 1 CARROT 1 CELERY RIB
2 GARLIC CLOVES 2 QT. VEG/CHICKEN STOCK
2 BAY LEAVES SALT + PEPPER CUMIN
1 14 OZ. CAN, CRUSHED TOMATOES

- PICK PEBBLES + DEBRIS FROM LENTILS
- PEEL + DICE ONION; WASH, PEEL, AND CUT CARROT INTO COINS; CUT EACH COIN INTO EQUAL QUARTERS
- DISCARD LEAFY PART OF CELERY; CLEAN AND CHOP INTO ½-INCH PIECES
- CRUSH + CHOP GARLIC; DICE FINELY
- PUT 2 TBSP. OF OIL IN STOCK POT OVER MED. HEAT; POUR IN ONION, CARROT, CELERY; STIR UNTIL ONION IS TRANSLUCENT
- ADD GARLIC, BAY LEAVES, ½ TSP. CUMIN
- COOK 1 MIN.; PUT IN LENTILS, TOMATOES, STOCK ON HIGH HEAT
- BRING TO BOIL; LOW HEAT FOR 40 MINUTES; SALT + PEPPER

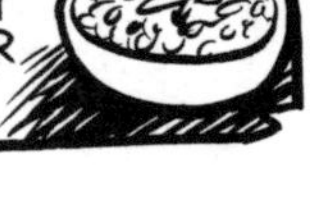

PASTA! AT LEAST AS GOOD AS THE STUFF IN THE CANS!

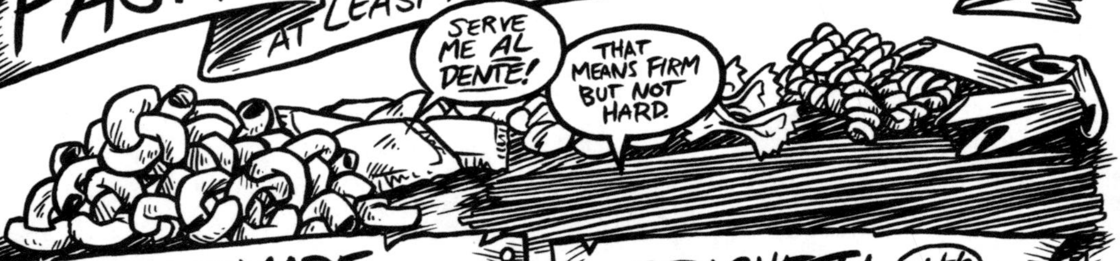
SERVE ME AL DENTE!
THAT MEANS FIRM BUT NOT HARD.

HOMEMADE MACARONI + CHEESE

▶SERVES 8◀

1 16 OZ. PACKAGE DRIED ELBOW MACARONI
VEGETABLE OR CANOLA OIL 1 STICK BUTTER
1/3 CUP FLOUR 4 CUPS MILK
1 LARGE ONION 2 LARGE EGGS
1/2 CUP OF YOUR FAVORITE CHEESE
BREAD OR CRACKER CRUMBS
BAY LEAVES SALT + PEPPER

- FILL STOCK POT HALFWAY WITH WATER; SALT GENEROUSLY; BOIL OVER HIGH HEAT
- ADD 1 TBSP. OIL + THE MACARONI; COOK 8-10 MIN.; TURN OFF HEAT; DRAIN
- PEEL AND DICE ONION
- IN SAUCEPAN, MELT BUTTER OVER MED. HEAT; STIR IN FLOUR, MILK, ONION
- ADD 1 BAY LEAF; SIMMER 10 MIN.
- TAKE OFF HEAT; DISCARD BAY LEAF
- BREAK EGGS INTO MIXING BOWL; MIX WITH FORK; SLOWLY ADD IN MILK; MIX
- STIR IN MACARONI
- POUR MIXTURE INTO ROASTING PAN; TOP WITH BREAD/CRUMBS + CHEESE
- BAKE @ 350°F FOR 35 MINUTES OR UNTIL IT'S BUBBLY AT THE EDGES

SPAGHETTI (with) HOMEMADE TOMATO SAUCE

▶SERVES 6-8◀

5 LB. RIPE TOMATOES 2 ONIONS
2 ANCHOVY TINS in OLIVE OIL GARLIC
WHITE SUGAR THYME BASIL OLIVE OIL
BAY LEAVES SALT + PEPPER DRY SPAGHETTI

- WASH TOMATOES; CUT OFF STEMS
- CHOP IN HALF; PLACE IN STOCK POT; PUT ON LID; BRING TO BOIL OVER MED-HIGH HEAT; SIMMER ON MED-LOW FOR 10-15 MINUTES; PEEL + DICE ONION; CRUSH, PEEL, DICE GARLIC
- REMOVE LID WHEN TOMATOES LOOK WRINKLED; CRUSH + STIR WITH SPOON
- ADD ONIONS, GARLIC, ANCHOVIES (WITH OLIVE OIL); THEN, 2 BAY LEAVES, TSP. OF THYME, TSP. OF BASIL, TBSP. OF WHITE SUGAR; STIR UNTIL MIXED
- SIMMER ON MED-HIGH UNTIL THICKENED
- SALT + PEPPER TO TASTE
- WHILE MAKING SAUCE, HALFWAY FILL SAUCEPAN WITH WATER; SALT GENEROUSLY
- BOIL ON HIGH + ADD A FISTFUL OF DRY SPAGHETTI; TURN TO MED-HIGH
- BOIL UNCOVERED FOR 8-10 MINUTES
- DRAIN + SERVE WITH TOMATO SAUCE

PASTA (with) ROASTED VEGGIES

▶SERVES 8-10◀

1 LB. DRY PENNE PASTA
2 RED PEPPERS
2 ZUCCHINI
2 CARROTS
10 WHITE MUSHROOMS
1 GARLIC CLOVE
1 ONION
1 CUP FROZEN PEAS
1/4 CUP OLIVE OIL
BASIL + THYME + OREGANO
1 CUP MOZZARELLA
3 CUPS TOMATO SAUCE
BUTTER SALT + PEPPER

- WASH PEPPERS, ZUCCHINI, MUSHROOMS; CORE AND SLICE PEPPERS INTO 1-INCH STRIPS; CUT ZUCCHINI INTO 1-INCH CUBES; HALVE MUSHROOMS
- CRUSH + PEEL GARLIC; PEEL + CUT CARROTS AND ONION INTO 1/2-INCH SLICES
- TOSS ALL WITH OLIVE OIL; 1/2 TSP. EACH OF BASIL, PEPPER, THYME, OREGANO
- POUR INTO ROASTING PAN; ROAST 15 MIN. @ 450°F
- FILL STOCK POT WITH WATER; ADD SALT
- BOIL ON HIGH; COOK PENNE FOR 8-10 MIN.
- DRAIN PASTA + MIX WITH SAUCE, PEAS, MOZZARELLA; SALT + PEPPER TO TASTE
- POUR INTO BAKING PAN; TOP WITH 2 TBSP. BUTTER + MOZZARELLA; ROAST 15-20 MIN.

RICE! THE WORLD'S MOST IMPORTANT FOOD! SERIOUSLY!

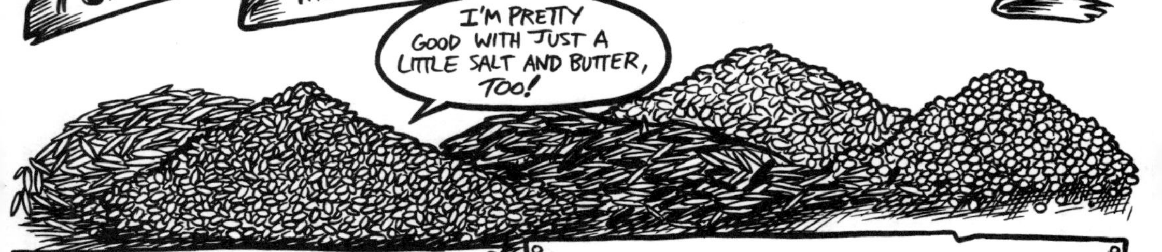
I'M PRETTY GOOD WITH JUST A LITTLE SALT AND BUTTER, TOO!

VERY BASIC RISOTTO

SERVES TWO

4 CUPS CHICKEN OR VEGGIE STOCK
1 CUP ARBORIO RICE SALT + PEPPER
2 TBSP. OLIVE OIL 2 TBSP. BUTTER
1 ONION 1 CUP FROZEN PEAS

- PEEL + DICE ONION; ADD OLIVE OIL TO SAUCEPAN OVER MED. HEAT; ADD BUTTER; ADD ONION AND COOK 5-8 MIN., STIRRING OCCASIONALLY
- ADD RICE; CONTINUE STIRRING 2 MIN.
- POUR IN STOCK; STIR OCCASIONALLY AND ALLOW RICE TO ABSORB IT UNTIL IT HAS CONSISTENCY OF PORRIDGE
- TASTE; IF GRAINS ARE STILL HARD, ADD 1/4 CUP WATER + COOK 5 MIN.
- WHEN COOKED, ADD PEAS; TAKE PAN OFF HEAT TO LET PEAS WARM
- SALT + PEPPER TO TASTE

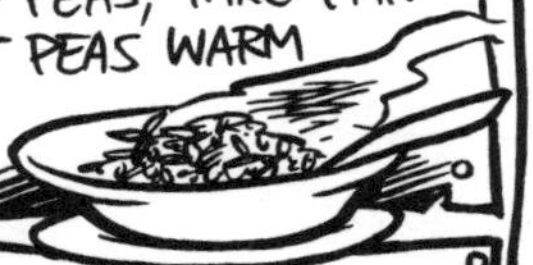

CONGEE (RICE PORRIDGE)

SERVES 6

1 CUP UNCOOKED LONG-GRAIN WHITE RICE
9 CUPS WATER/STOCK/BROTH (ANY KIND)
SALT + PEPPER

- POUR RICE INTO STOCK POT; ADD WATER, STOCK, OR BROTH; PUT ON LID + BRING TO A BOIL OVER HIGH HEAT
- ONCE BOILING, TURN DOWN TO LOW; TILT LID TO ALLOW STEAM TO ESCAPE
- STIR OCCASIONALLY AND COOK UNTIL RICE IS VERY SOFT + GRAINS ARE BROKEN, ABOUT 1-1½ HOURS
- ADD MORE LIQUID OR ALLOW LIQUID TO BOIL AWAY, DEPENDING ON DESIRED CONSISTENCY (SOUP-LIKE VS. PORRIDGE-LIKE)
- SERVE WITH SALT AND GARNISH TO TASTE; BE CREATIVE!

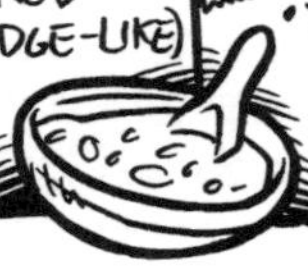

CLEAN-THE-FRIDGE FRIED RICE

SERVES 4

LEFTOVER COOKED RICE, WHITE OR BROWN
1 ONION EGGS SOY SAUCE
5 TBSP. VEGETABLE OR CANOLA OIL
1½ CUPS FRESH/FROZEN MIXED VEG.
½ CUP LEFTOVER MEAT/MEAT SUBSTITUTE
SALT + PEPPER

- MIX 2 OR 3 EGGS IN MIXING BOWL; PEEL AND DICE ONION; IF FRESH, WASH, PEEL, + DICE VEGGIES; DICE MEAT/SUBSTITUTE
- ADD 2 TBSP. OF OIL TO SKILLET OVER MED. HEAT; WHEN HOT, POUR IN EGGS + STIR WITH SPOON UNTIL SCRAMBLED; REMOVE EGGS
- ADD 2 TBSP. OF OIL TO SKILLET; POUR IN ONION AND COOK 5-8 MIN.; STIR OCCASIONALLY
- POUR IN MEAT + VEGGIES; COOK + STIR UNTIL TENDER OR DEFROSTED; PUT WITH EGGS
- ADD 1 TBSP. OF OIL TO SKILLET + 1½-3 CUPS RICE; BREAK UP AND STIR WITH SPOON, COVER EVENLY WITH OIL; ADD 1 TBSP. SOY SAUCE, STOP STIRRING + COOK 2-3 MIN.
- WHEN RICE IS CRISPY, ADD EGGS, VEGGIES, MEAT, STIR IN, REMOVE FROM HEAT
- SALT + PEPPER TO TASTE

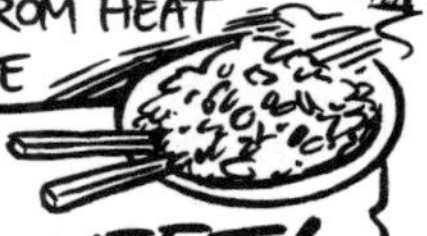

CONGEE Garnishes...

SAVORY!

(FOR THINNER CONGEE)

- COOKED EGGS
- SPRING ONIONS
- CHICKEN, SEAFOOD, BEEF, OR PORK
- MEATBALLS OR SAUSAGE
- SARDINES
- SOY, FISH, OR OYSTER SAUCE
- CHILI PASTE
- GINGER + CILANTRO

SWEET!

(FOR THICKER CONGEE)

- HONEY OR MAPLE SYRUP
- BROWN/WHITE SUGAR
- DRIED/FRESH FRUIT
- NUT BUTTERS
- NUTS AND SEEDS
- BUTTER
- CINNAMON

FRUITS 'N' VEGETABLES!

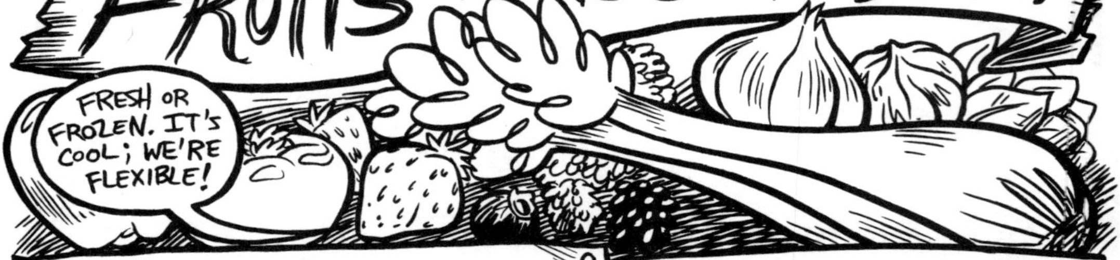
FRESH OR FROZEN. IT'S COOL; WE'RE FLEXIBLE!

VEGETARIAN STIR-FRY

SERVES 4–6

1 TBSP. CANOLA OIL 2 GARLIC CLOVES
2 CARROTS ½ CUP MUSHROOMS 1 BELL PEPPER
1 CUP CAULIFLOWER 1 CUP BROCCOLI
2 CUPS CABBAGE 1 ONION ½ CUP SNOW PEAS
SOY SAUCE LEMON JUICE GINGER CHILI POWDER

- WASH CARROTS, MUSHROOMS, BELL PEPPER, CAULIFLOWER, BROCCOLI, CABBAGE, PEAS
- PEEL + SLICE ONION INTO ½-INCH STRIPS; CRUSH, PEEL, MINCE GARLIC; CORE + SLICE PEPPERS INTO STRIPS; HALVE MUSHROOMS; PEEL + CUT CARROTS INTO STRIPS; CHOP CAULIFLOWER + BROCCOLI INTO BITE-SIZED CHUNKS; SHRED CABBAGE INTO ½-INCH STRIPS
- HEAT OIL IN SKILLET OVER MED-HIGH HEAT
- ADD ONION; COOK + STIR FOR 5–8 MIN.
- ADD GARLIC; COOK + STIR FOR 1 MIN.
- ADD CAULIFLOWER, BROCCOLI, CABBAGE, AND CARROTS; COOK + STIR FOR 5–7 MIN.
- ADD PEPPERS + PEAS; COOK UNTIL VEGGIES ARE TENDER, BUT NOT SOFT
- ADD SOY SAUCE, LEMON JUICE, GINGER, CHILI POWDER TO TASTE; SERVE OVER RICE

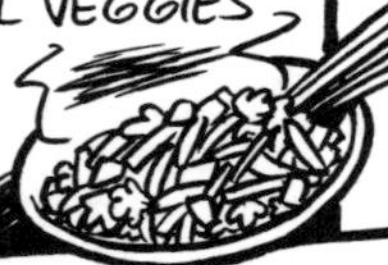

FRUIT COMPOTE

SERVES 6

3 CUPS FRESH/FROZEN FRUIT, LIKE VARIOUS BERRIES, PEACHES, APPLES...
3 TBSP. WATER SUGAR LEMON JUICE

- WASH ANY FRESH FRUIT AND SKIN ANY APPLES; DICE IF NECESSARY
- POUR INTO SAUCEPAN; ADD WATER
- BRING TO BOIL OVER MED-HIGH HEAT; PUT ON LID; REDUCE TO MED-LOW
- SIMMER; STIR OCCASIONALLY FOR 10 MIN.
- TASTE FOR SWEETNESS; ADD SUGAR TO TASTE; ADD LEMON JUICE TO ADJUST TARTNESS
- COOK UNTIL IT REACHES DESIRED SOFTNESS; REMOVE FROM HEAT
- ONCE COOL, SERVE WITH ICE CREAM, TOAST, YOGURT, CAKE, OR BY ITSELF!

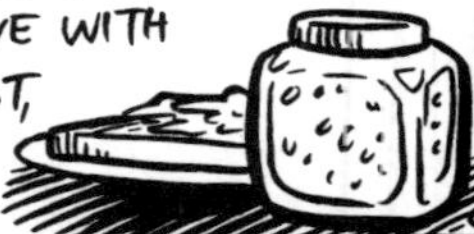

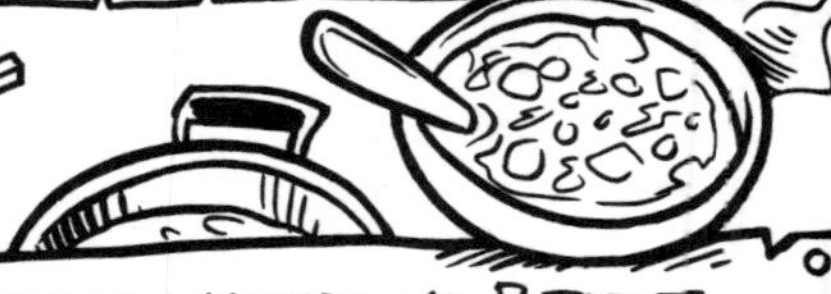

VEGETABLE STEW

SERVES 6

2 TBSP. OLIVE OIL 1 ONION
6 GARLIC CLOVES 3 CARROTS
2 CELERY RIBS 2 BAY LEAVES
2 RED OR YUKON GOLD POTATOES
3 CUPS WHOLE WHITE MUSHROOMS
3 CUPS WHOLE WHITE MUSHROOMS
1 LB. CAN OF WHOLE TOMATOES
1 LB. CAN OF GARBANZO BEANS
¼ TSP. DRIED THYME
1 CUP DRY RED WINE SALT
1 TBSP. FLOUR PEPPER
2 CUPS OF WATER

- WASH CARROTS, CELERY, MUSHROOMS, POTATOES,
- PEEL GARLIC + ONION; QUARTER ONION; CHOP CELERY INTO 2-INCH PIECES; PEEL + QUARTER POTATOES; HALVE MUSHROOMS; PEEL + CHOP CARROTS
- QUARTER CANNED TOMATOES; SAVE JUICE IN CAN
- HEAT OIL IN STOCK POT OVER MED. HEAT; ADD ONIONS, GARLIC, MUSHROOMS, THYME, BAY LEAVES; STIR OCCASIONALLY ABOUT 10–15 MINUTES
- ADD CARROTS, CELERY, POTATOES; STIR + COOK FOR 5 MIN.; TURN HEAT ON HIGH + ADD WINE
- STIR + SIMMER UNTIL LIQUID IS HALVED; 10 MIN.
- ADD WATER, TOMATOES, TOMATO JUICE, FLOUR; STIR WELL; REDUCE HEAT TO LOW + COVER
- SIMMER 20–25 MIN., UNTIL VEGGIES ARE TENDER
- ADD GARBANZO BEANS; SIMMER 5 MINUTES
- ADD SALT + PEPPER TO TASTE

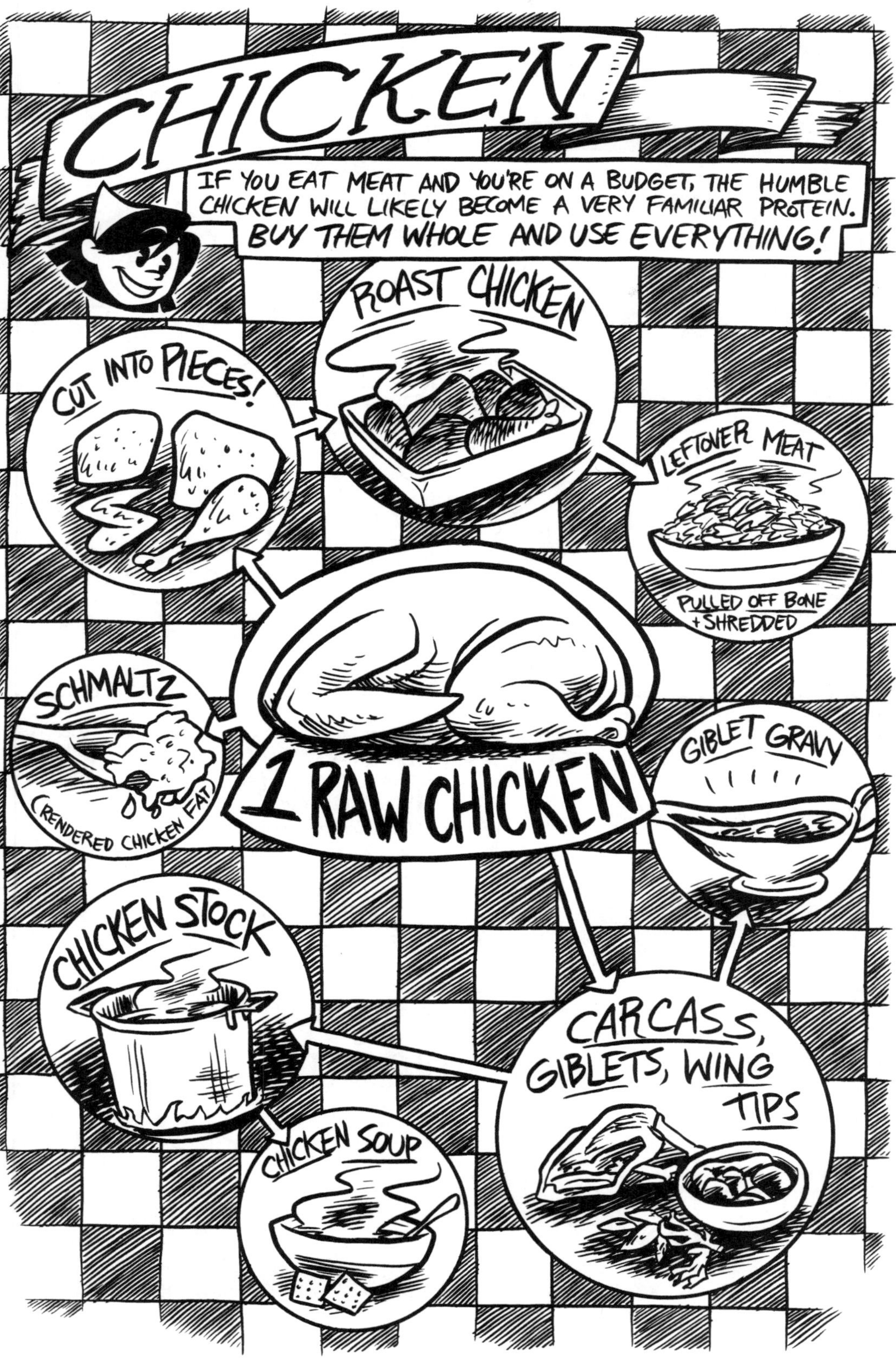
CHICKEN
IF YOU EAT MEAT AND YOU'RE ON A BUDGET, THE HUMBLE CHICKEN WILL LIKELY BECOME A VERY FAMILIAR PROTEIN.
BUY THEM WHOLE AND USE EVERYTHING!
ROAST CHICKEN
CUT INTO PIECES!
LEFTOVER MEAT
PULLED OFF BONE + SHREDDED
SCHMALTZ
(RENDERED CHICKEN FAT)
1 RAW CHICKEN
GIBLET GRAVY
CHICKEN STOCK
CARCASS, GIBLETS, WING TIPS
CHICKEN SOUP

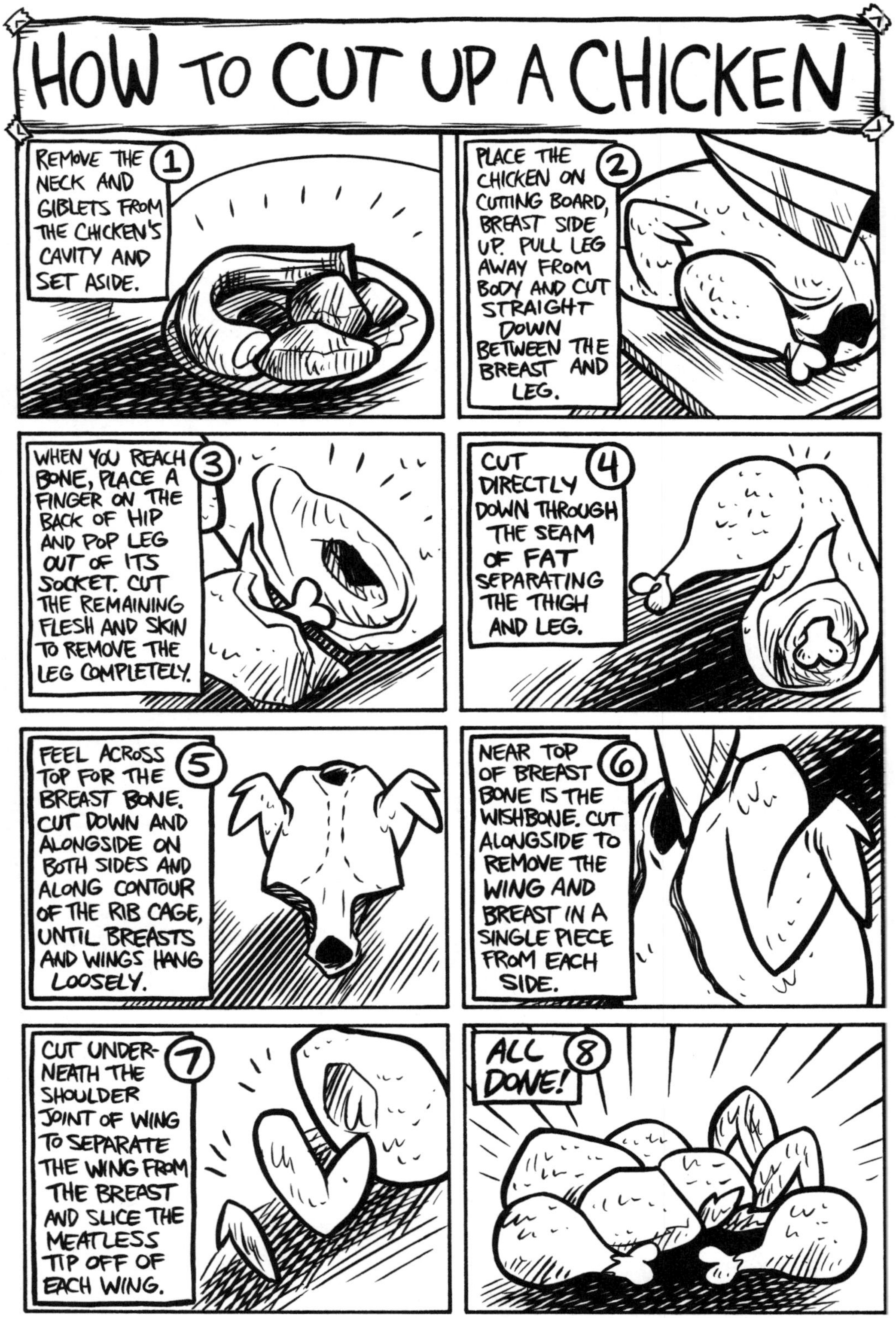
HOW TO CUT UP A CHICKEN
1
REMOVE THE NECK AND GIBLETS FROM THE CHICKEN'S CAVITY AND SET ASIDE.
2
PLACE THE CHICKEN ON CUTTING BOARD, BREAST SIDE UP. PULL LEG AWAY FROM BODY AND CUT STRAIGHT DOWN BETWEEN THE BREAST AND LEG.
3
WHEN YOU REACH BONE, PLACE A FINGER ON THE BACK OF HIP AND POP LEG OUT OF ITS SOCKET. CUT THE REMAINING FLESH AND SKIN TO REMOVE THE LEG COMPLETELY.
4
CUT DIRECTLY DOWN THROUGH THE SEAM OF FAT SEPARATING THE THIGH AND LEG.
5
FEEL ACROSS TOP FOR THE BREAST BONE. CUT DOWN AND ALONGSIDE ON BOTH SIDES AND ALONG CONTOUR OF THE RIB CAGE, UNTIL BREASTS AND WINGS HANG LOOSELY.
6
NEAR TOP OF BREAST BONE IS THE WISHBONE. CUT ALONGSIDE TO REMOVE THE WING AND BREAST IN A SINGLE PIECE FROM EACH SIDE.
7
CUT UNDER-NEATH THE SHOULDER JOINT OF WING TO SEPARATE THE WING FROM THE BREAST AND SLICE THE MEATLESS TIP OFF OF EACH WING.
8
ALL DONE!

HOW TO COOK A CHICKEN

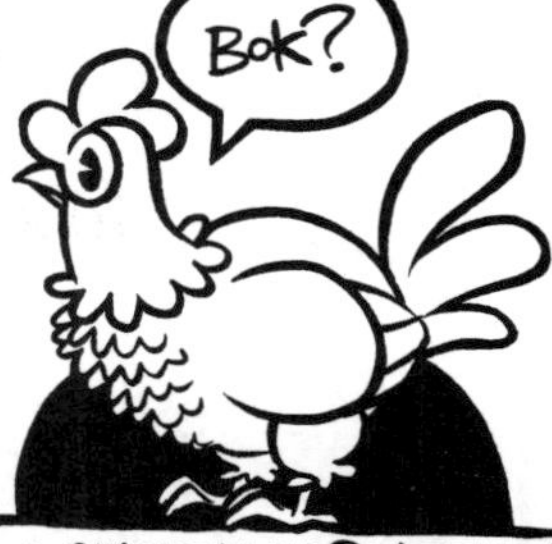
BOK?

ROAST CHICKEN

WITH THE CRISPIEST SKIN. EXPERTS AGREE!*

1 CHICKEN, CUT INTO PARTS 1 TBSP SALT
1 TSP BAKING POWDER ½ TSP PEPPER

- LOOSEN THE SKIN ON THE BREASTS, LEGS, AND THIGHS WITH YOUR FINGERS; SEPARATE IT FROM THE UNDERLYING MEAT
- WITH A SKEWER/TOOTHPICK, POKE MULTIPLE HOLES IN THE SKIN OVER FAT DEPOSITS
- MIX SALT + PEPPER AND BAKING POWDER; COAT CHICKEN'S SKIN
- COOL CHICKEN ON RACK IN FRIDGE FOR AT LEAST 12 HOURS (24 FOR BEST RESULTS.)

*SERIOUS EATS, AMERICA'S TEST KITCHEN, COOKS ILLUSTRATED

- PLACE RACK + CHICKEN IN ROASTING PAN WITH TINFOIL LINING
- ROAST IN OVEN @450°F FOR 30-40 MINUTES, FLIPPING PIECES HALFWAY THROUGH
- WHEN CHICKEN IS LIGHTLY BROWNED, TURN HEAT UP TO 500°F AND COOK FOR A FURTHER 8-10 MIN.
- CHICKEN IS DONE WHEN ITS JUICE RUNS CLEAR; WHITE MEAT (BREAST) MAY FINISH BEFORE DARK; IF SO, REMOVE THEM AND ALLOW THE REST TO CONTINUE COOKING
- REMOVE CHICKEN FROM THE PAN; ALLOW IT TO REST FOR 10 MINUTES.

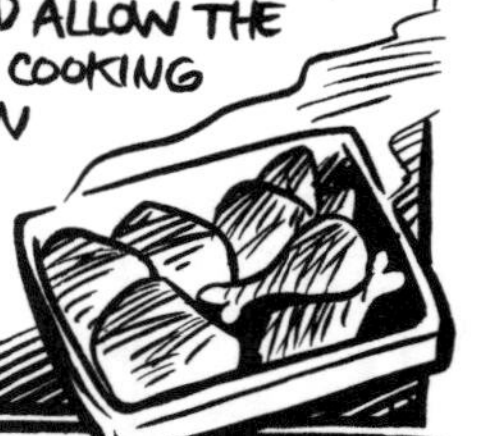

GIBLET GRAVY

TIME THIS RIGHT, AND YOU CAN FINISH THE GRAVY WHILE THE CHICKEN IS RESTING.

NECK + GIBLETS FROM 1 CHICKEN ½ ONION
1 STALK CELERY 4 CUPS OF COLD WATER
PAN DRIPPINGS WHITE FLOUR

- WASH NECK + GIBLETS; ROUGHLY CHOP CELERY + ONION INTO QUARTERS; PLACE ALL IN SAUCEPAN WITH 2 CUPS OF COLD WATER; SIMMER ON MED-LOW, COVERED, FOR TWO HOURS
- GENTLY SCRAPE BAKED-ON DRIPPINGS OFF OF TINFOIL; REMOVE TINFOIL + RETURN DRIPPINGS TO ROASTING PAN
- ADD FLOUR, 1 TBSP AT A TIME, UNTIL THE DRIPPINGS THICKEN INTO A PASTE (ROUX)
- PLACE PAN WITH ROUX ON STOVE ON MED-HIGH HEAT; WHEN ROUX BUBBLES, ADD 2 CUPS WATER + GIBLET STOCK.
- TURN HEAT TO MED-LOW; STIR OCCASIONALLY FOR 10 MIN
- SEASON! SALT, PEPPER, ONION POWDER, WORCESTERSHIRE...

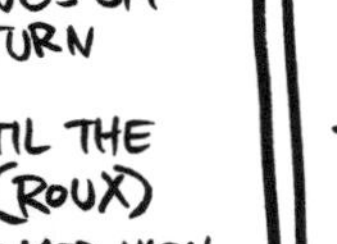

CHICKEN STOCK

2-3 CHICKEN CARCASSES 4-6 WING TIPS
COLD WATER 2 STALKS CELERY
2 CARROTS 1 ONION 1 BAY LEAF
3 CLOVES GARLIC SALT + PEPPER
¼ TSP THYME ¼ TSP PARSLEY

- WASH CELERY + CARROTS; CHOP CELERY, CARROTS, + ONION IN HALF WITHOUT PEELING ONION; CRUSH GARLIC, WITHOUT PEELING
- PLACE VEGGIES, WING TIPS, + CARCASSES INTO STOCK POT; COVER IN COLD WATER; ADD GARLIC, BAY LEAF, THYME, AND PARSLEY
- BRING STOCK TO A BOIL; SKIM ANY SCUM OFF THE SURFACE
- REDUCE HEAT TO MED-LOW; SIMMER UNCOVERED FOR THREE HOURS
- STRAIN INTO CONTAINER IN SINK FULL OF ICE WATER TO COOL RAPIDLY
- REFRIDGERATE STOCK; SKIM FAT OFF TOP AND SAVE AS SCHMALTZ

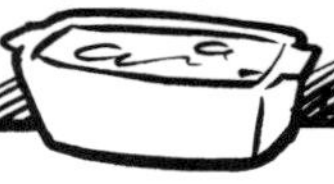

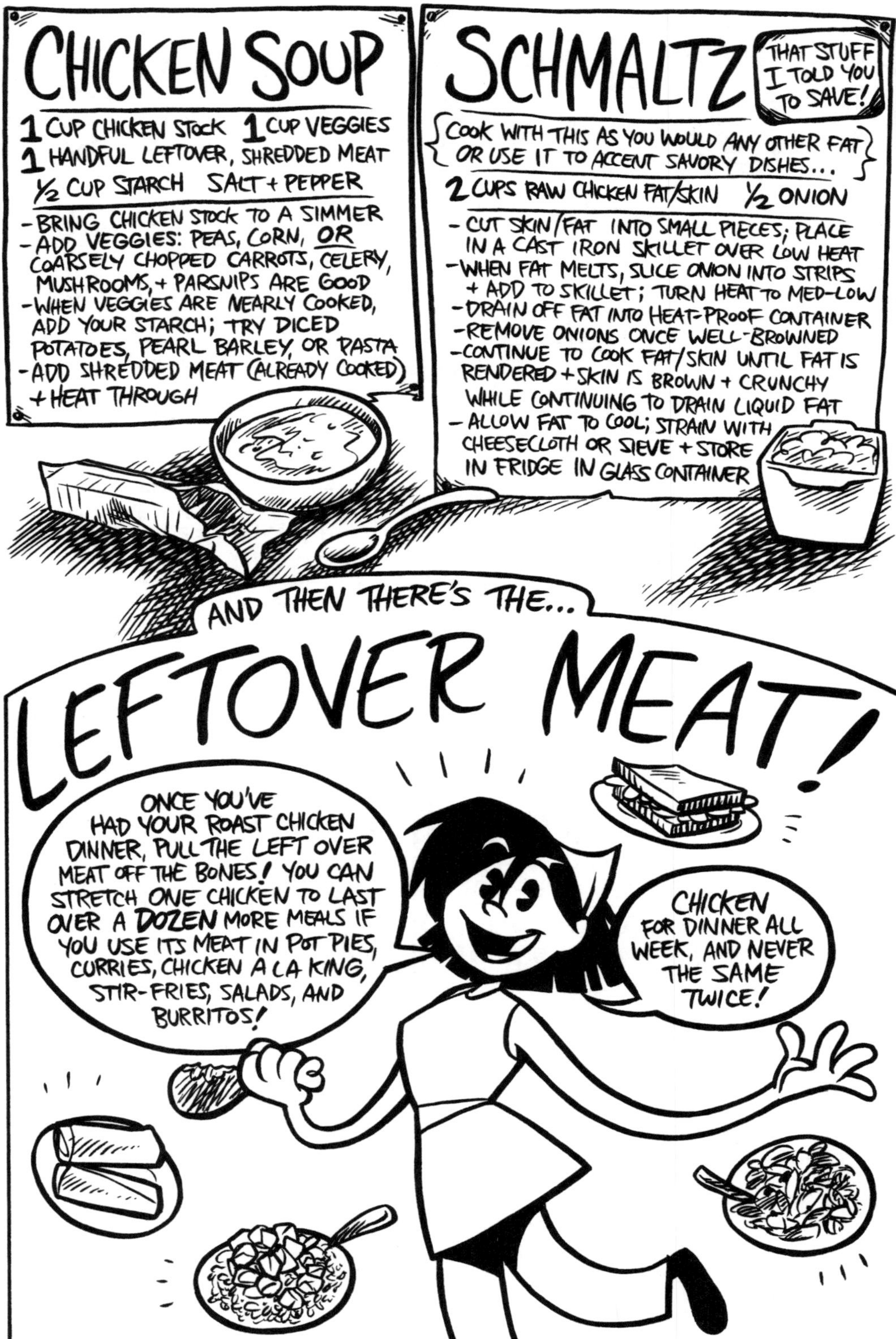
CHICKEN SOUP
1 CUP CHICKEN STOCK 1 CUP VEGGIES
1 HANDFUL LEFTOVER, SHREDDED MEAT
½ CUP STARCH SALT + PEPPER
- BRING CHICKEN STOCK TO A SIMMER
- ADD VEGGIES: PEAS, CORN, OR COARSELY CHOPPED CARROTS, CELERY, MUSHROOMS, + PARSNIPS ARE GOOD
- WHEN VEGGIES ARE NEARLY COOKED, ADD YOUR STARCH; TRY DICED POTATOES, PEARL BARLEY, OR PASTA
- ADD SHREDDED MEAT (ALREADY COOKED) + HEAT THROUGH
SCHMALTZ
THAT STUFF I TOLD YOU TO SAVE!
{COOK WITH THIS AS YOU WOULD ANY OTHER FAT OR USE IT TO ACCENT SAVORY DISHES...}
2 CUPS RAW CHICKEN FAT/SKIN ½ ONION
- CUT SKIN/FAT INTO SMALL PIECES; PLACE IN A CAST IRON SKILLET OVER LOW HEAT
- WHEN FAT MELTS, SLICE ONION INTO STRIPS + ADD TO SKILLET; TURN HEAT TO MED-LOW
- DRAIN OFF FAT INTO HEAT-PROOF CONTAINER
- REMOVE ONIONS ONCE WELL-BROWNED
- CONTINUE TO COOK FAT/SKIN UNTIL FAT IS RENDERED + SKIN IS BROWN + CRUNCHY WHILE CONTINUING TO DRAIN LIQUID FAT
- ALLOW FAT TO COOL; STRAIN WITH CHEESECLOTH OR SIEVE + STORE IN FRIDGE IN GLASS CONTAINER
AND THEN THERE'S THE...
LEFTOVER MEAT!
ONCE YOU'VE HAD YOUR ROAST CHICKEN DINNER, PULL THE LEFT OVER MEAT OFF THE BONES! YOU CAN STRETCH ONE CHICKEN TO LAST OVER A DOZEN MORE MEALS IF YOU USE ITS MEAT IN POT PIES, CURRIES, CHICKEN A LA KING, STIR-FRIES, SALADS, AND BURRITOS!
CHICKEN FOR DINNER ALL WEEK, AND NEVER THE SAME TWICE!

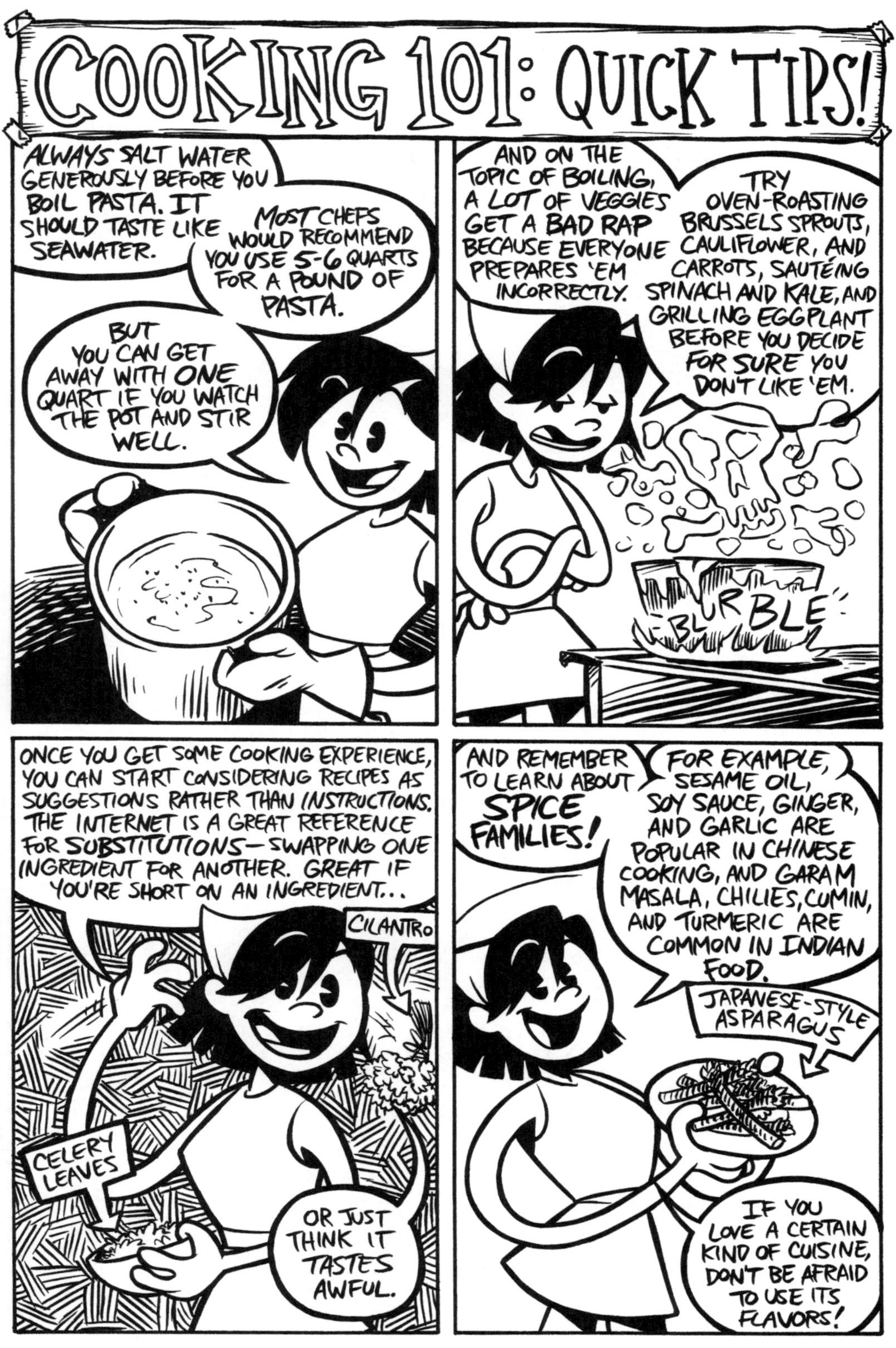
COOKING 101: QUICK TIPS!
ALWAYS SALT WATER GENEROUSLY BEFORE YOU BOIL PASTA. IT SHOULD TASTE LIKE SEAWATER.
MOST CHEFS WOULD RECOMMEND YOU USE 5-6 QUARTS FOR A POUND OF PASTA.
BUT YOU CAN GET AWAY WITH ONE QUART IF YOU WATCH THE POT AND STIR WELL.
AND ON THE TOPIC OF BOILING, A LOT OF VEGGIES GET A BAD RAP BECAUSE EVERYONE PREPARES 'EM INCORRECTLY.
TRY OVEN-ROASTING BRUSSELS SPROUTS, CAULIFLOWER, AND CARROTS, SAUTÉING SPINACH AND KALE, AND GRILLING EGGPLANT BEFORE YOU DECIDE FOR SURE YOU DON'T LIKE 'EM.
BLURBLE
ONCE YOU GET SOME COOKING EXPERIENCE, YOU CAN START CONSIDERING RECIPES AS SUGGESTIONS RATHER THAN INSTRUCTIONS. THE INTERNET IS A GREAT REFERENCE FOR SUBSTITUTIONS— SWAPPING ONE INGREDIENT FOR ANOTHER. GREAT IF YOU'RE SHORT ON AN INGREDIENT...
CILANTRO
CELERY LEAVES
OR JUST THINK IT TASTES AWFUL.
AND REMEMBER TO LEARN ABOUT SPICE FAMILIES!
FOR EXAMPLE, SESAME OIL, SOY SAUCE, GINGER, AND GARLIC ARE POPULAR IN CHINESE COOKING, AND GARAM MASALA, CHILIES, CUMIN, AND TURMERIC ARE COMMON IN INDIAN FOOD.
JAPANESE-STYLE ASPARAGUS
IF YOU LOVE A CERTAIN KIND OF CUISINE, DON'T BE AFRAID TO USE ITS FLAVORS!

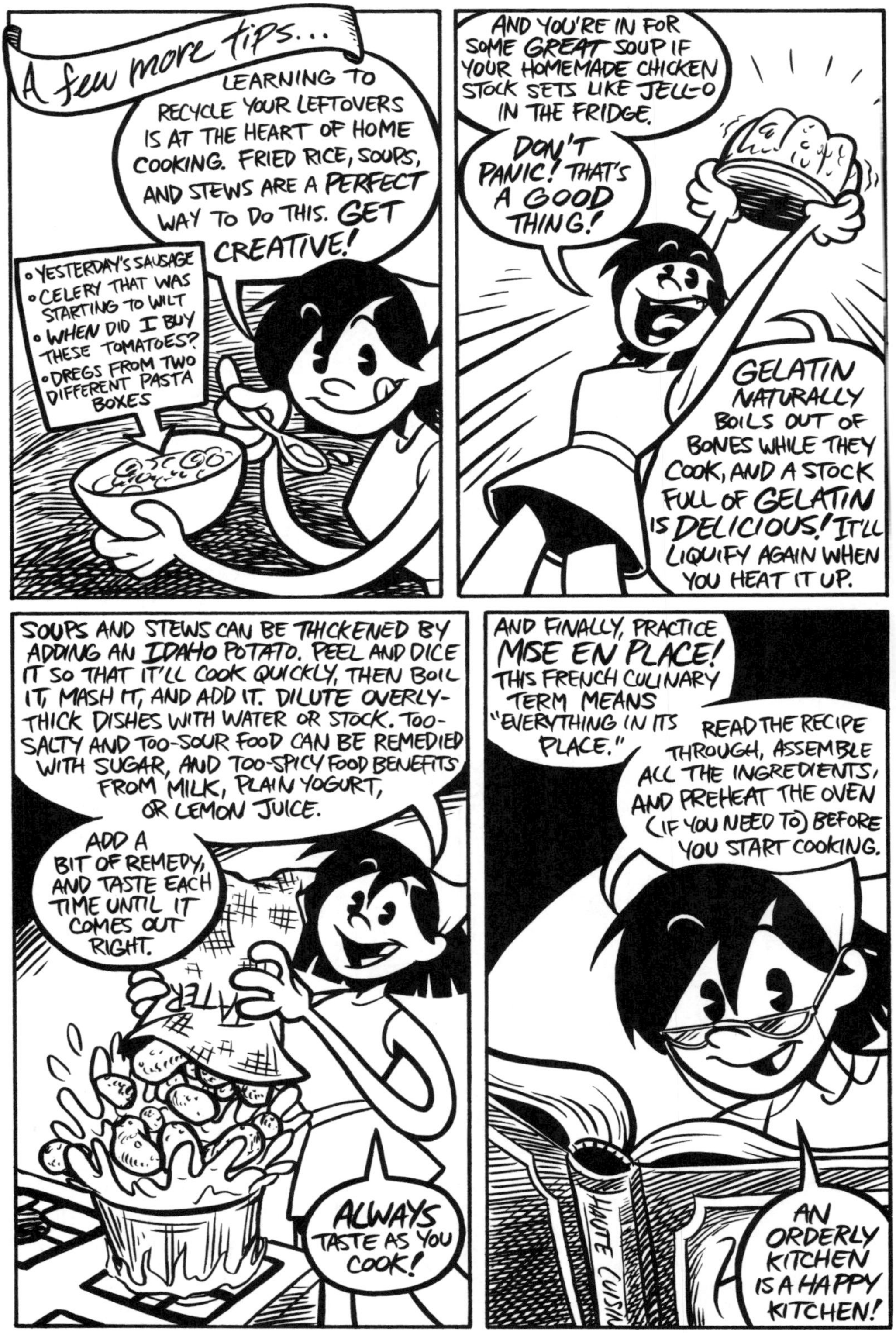
A few more tips...
LEARNING TO RECYCLE YOUR LEFTOVERS IS AT THE HEART OF HOME COOKING. FRIED RICE, SOUPS, AND STEWS ARE A PERFECT WAY TO DO THIS. GET CREATIVE!
• YESTERDAY'S SAUSAGE • CELERY THAT WAS STARTING TO WILT • WHEN DID I BUY THESE TOMATOES? • DREGS FROM TWO DIFFERENT PASTA BOXES
AND YOU'RE IN FOR SOME GREAT SOUP IF YOUR HOMEMADE CHICKEN STOCK SETS LIKE JELL-O IN THE FRIDGE.
DON'T PANIC! THAT'S A GOOD THING!
GELATIN NATURALLY BOILS OUT OF BONES WHILE THEY COOK, AND A STOCK FULL OF GELATIN IS DELICIOUS! IT'LL LIQUIFY AGAIN WHEN YOU HEAT IT UP.
SOUPS AND STEWS CAN BE THICKENED BY ADDING AN IDAHO POTATO. PEEL AND DICE IT SO THAT IT'LL COOK QUICKLY, THEN BOIL IT, MASH IT, AND ADD IT. DILUTE OVERLY-THICK DISHES WITH WATER OR STOCK. TOO-SALTY AND TOO-SOUR FOOD CAN BE REMEDIED WITH SUGAR, AND TOO-SPICY FOOD BENEFITS FROM MILK, PLAIN YOGURT, OR LEMON JUICE.
ADD A BIT OF REMEDY, AND TASTE EACH TIME UNTIL IT COMES OUT RIGHT.
ALWAYS TASTE AS YOU COOK!
AND FINALLY, PRACTICE MISE EN PLACE! THIS FRENCH CULINARY TERM MEANS "EVERYTHING IN ITS PLACE."
READ THE RECIPE THROUGH, ASSEMBLE ALL THE INGREDIENTS, AND PREHEAT THE OVEN (IF YOU NEED TO) BEFORE YOU START COOKING.
HAUTE CUISIN
AN ORDERLY KITCHEN IS A HAPPY KITCHEN!

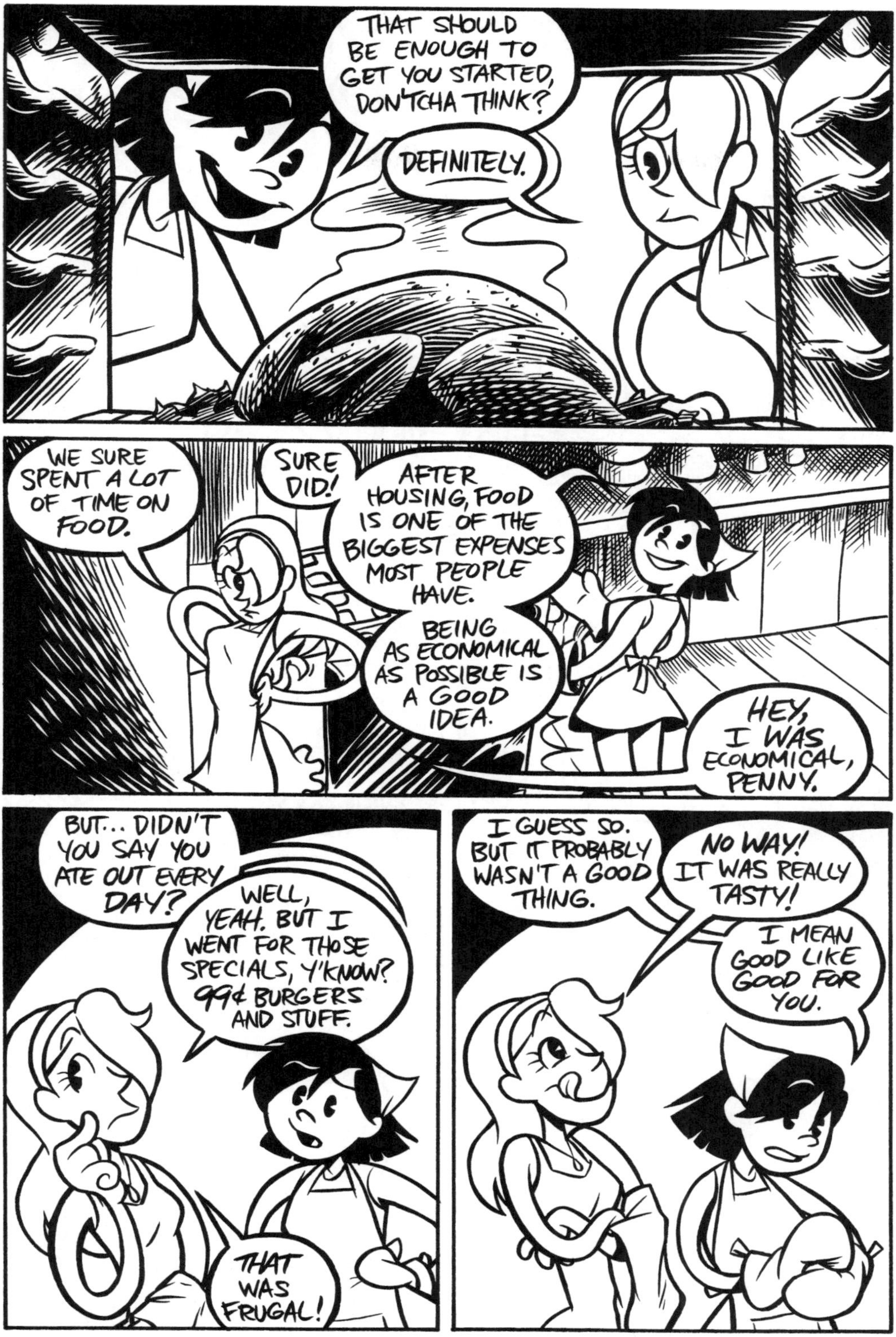
THAT SHOULD BE ENOUGH TO GET YOU STARTED, DON'TCHA THINK?
DEFINITELY.
WE SURE SPENT A LOT OF TIME ON FOOD.
SURE DID!
AFTER HOUSING, FOOD IS ONE OF THE BIGGEST EXPENSES MOST PEOPLE HAVE.
BEING AS ECONOMICAL AS POSSIBLE IS A GOOD IDEA.
HEY, I WAS ECONOMICAL, PENNY.
BUT... DIDN'T YOU SAY YOU ATE OUT EVERY DAY?
WELL, YEAH. BUT I WENT FOR THOSE SPECIALS, Y'KNOW? 99¢ BURGERS AND STUFF.
THAT WAS FRUGAL!
I GUESS SO. BUT IT PROBABLY WASN'T A GOOD THING.
NO WAY! IT WAS REALLY TASTY!
I MEAN GOOD LIKE GOOD FOR YOU.

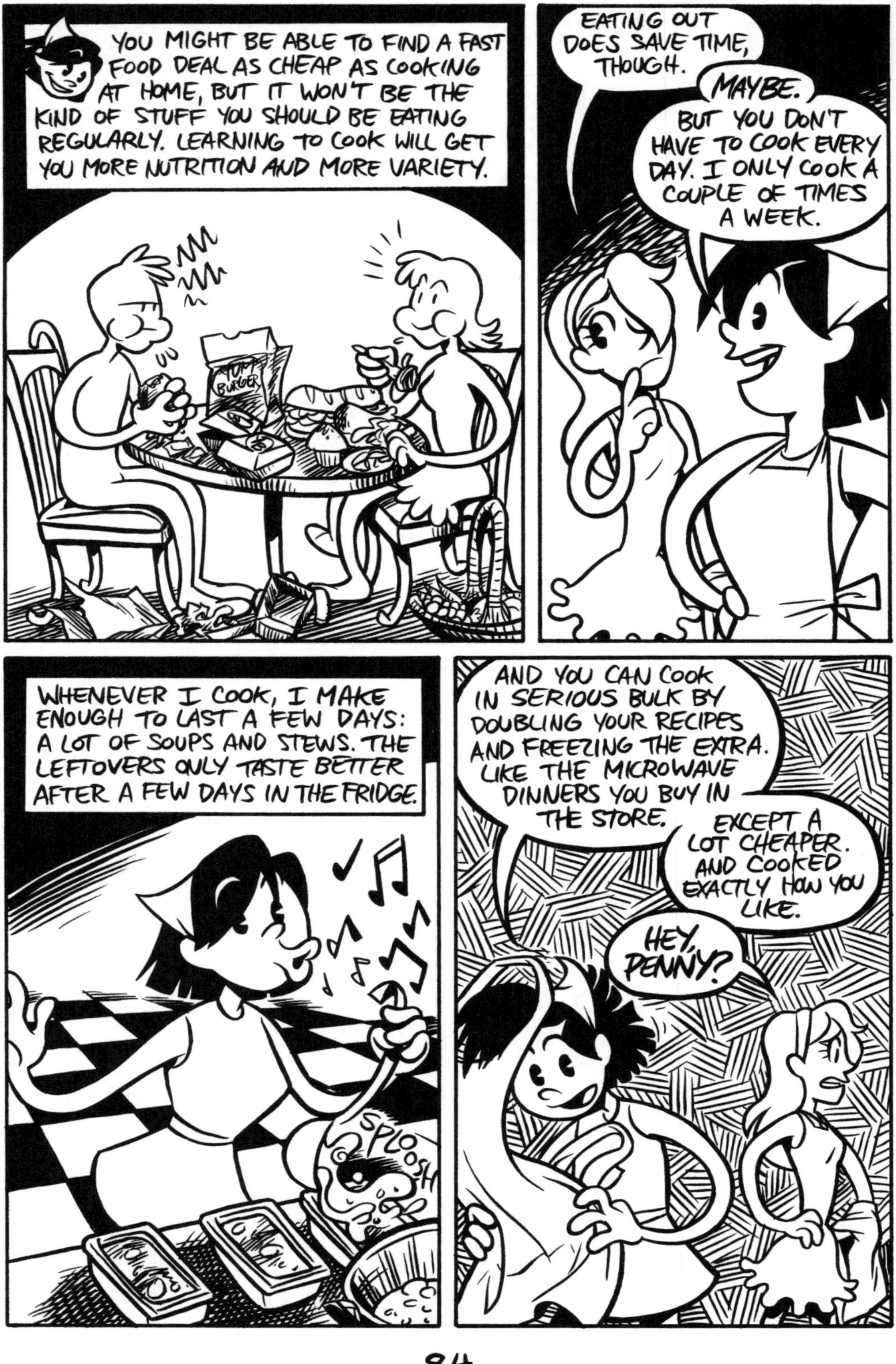
YOU MIGHT BE ABLE TO FIND A FAST FOOD DEAL AS CHEAP AS COOKING AT HOME, BUT IT WON'T BE THE KIND OF STUFF YOU SHOULD BE EATING REGULARLY. LEARNING TO COOK WILL GET YOU MORE NUTRITION AND MORE VARIETY.
BURGER
EATING OUT DOES SAVE TIME, THOUGH.
MAYBE.
BUT YOU DON'T HAVE TO COOK EVERY DAY. I ONLY COOK A COUPLE OF TIMES A WEEK.
WHENEVER I COOK, I MAKE ENOUGH TO LAST A FEW DAYS: A LOT OF SOUPS AND STEWS. THE LEFTOVERS ONLY TASTE BETTER AFTER A FEW DAYS IN THE FRIDGE.
SPLOOSH
AND YOU CAN COOK IN SERIOUS BULK BY DOUBLING YOUR RECIPES AND FREEZING THE EXTRA. LIKE THE MICROWAVE DINNERS YOU BUY IN THE STORE.
EXCEPT A LOT CHEAPER. AND COOKED EXACTLY HOW YOU LIKE.
HEY, PENNY?

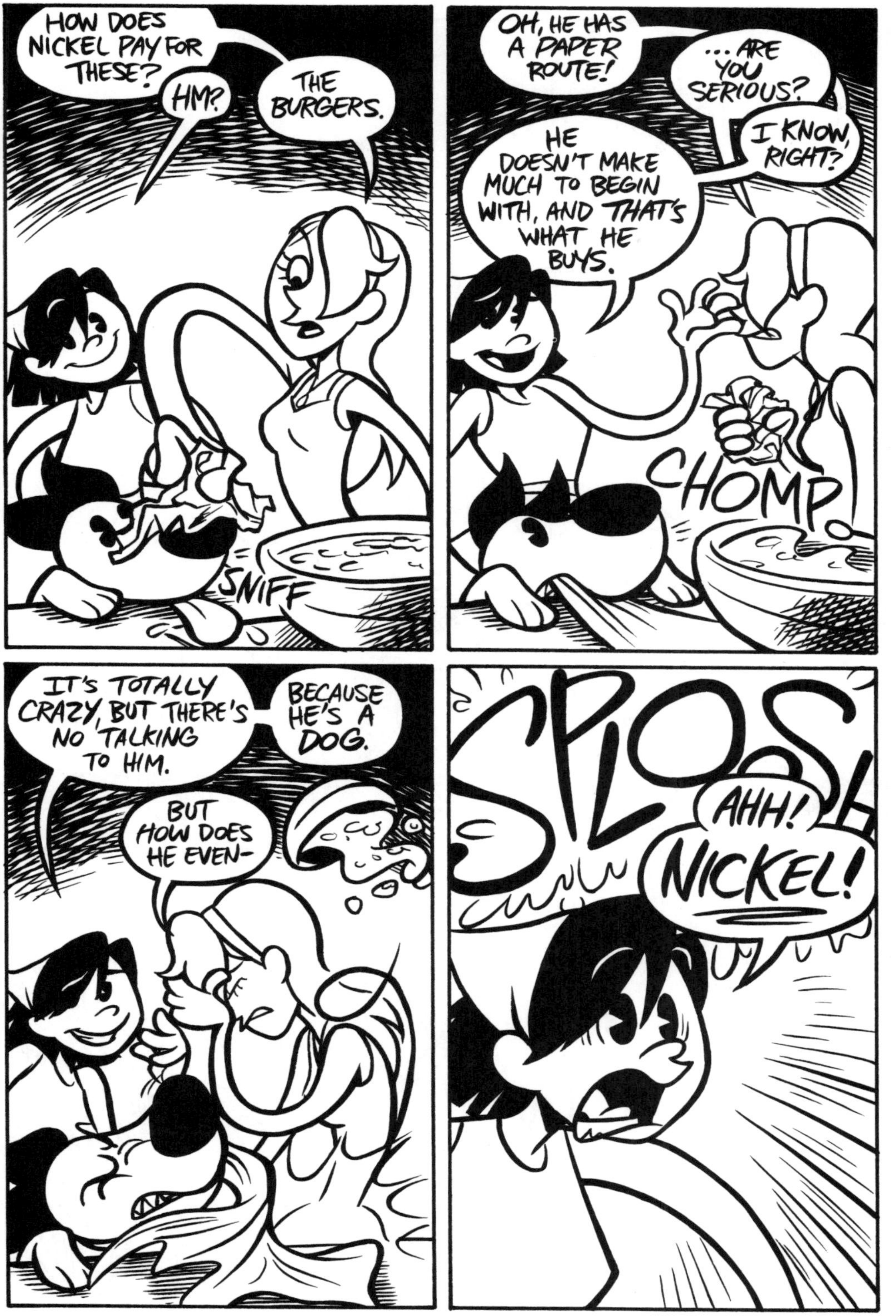
HOW DOES NICKEL PAY FOR THESE?
HM?
THE BURGERS.
SNIFF
OH, HE HAS A PAPER ROUTE!
... ARE YOU SERIOUS?
I KNOW, RIGHT?
HE DOESN'T MAKE MUCH TO BEGIN WITH, AND THAT'S WHAT HE BUYS.
CHOMP
IT'S TOTALLY CRAZY, BUT THERE'S NO TALKING TO HIM.
BECAUSE HE'S A DOG.
BUT HOW DOES HE EVEN-
SPLOOSH
AHH!
NICKEL!

Chapter Four
Fashion

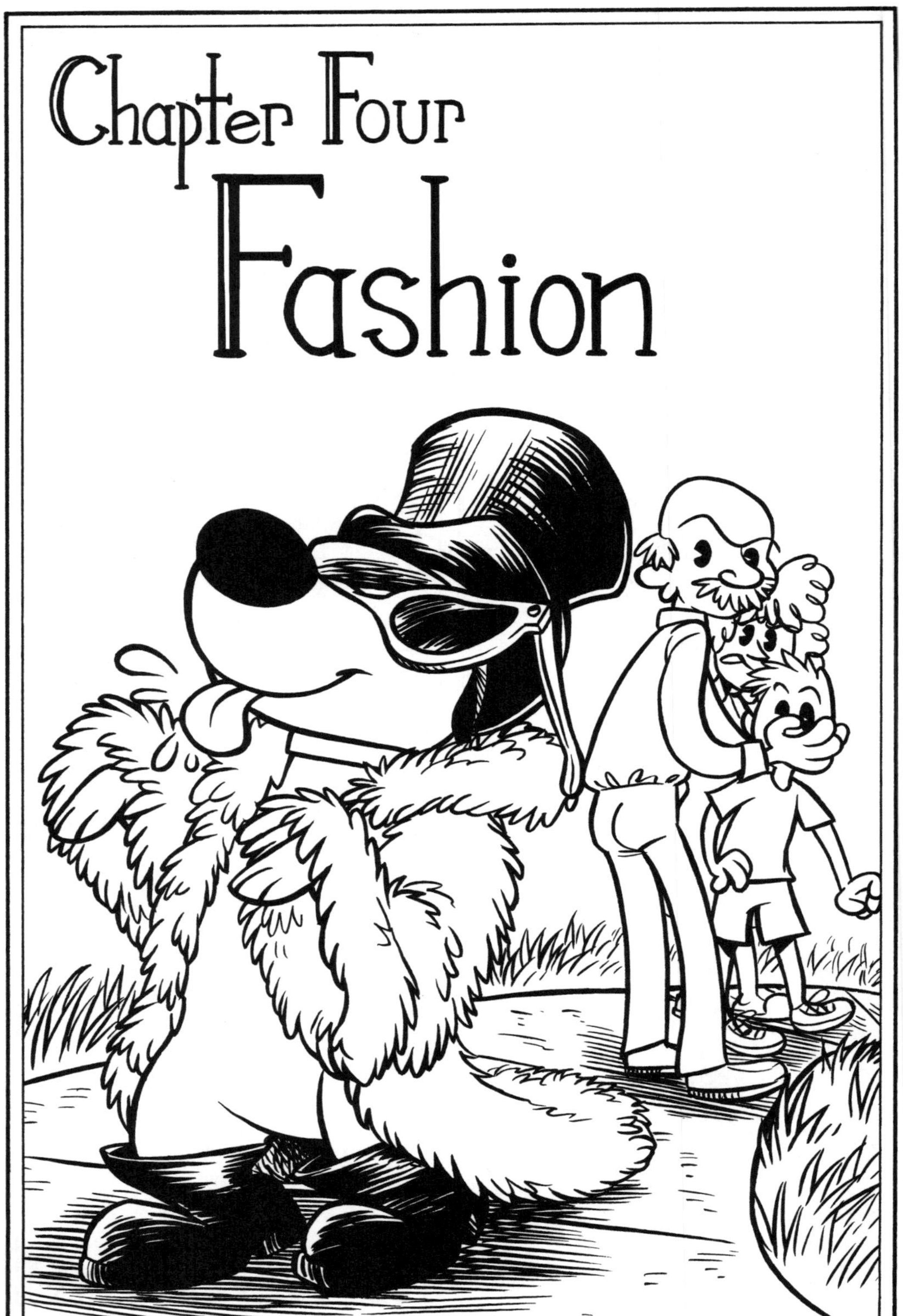

YOU WILL DEFINITELY NEED CLOTHES. (And shoes!)

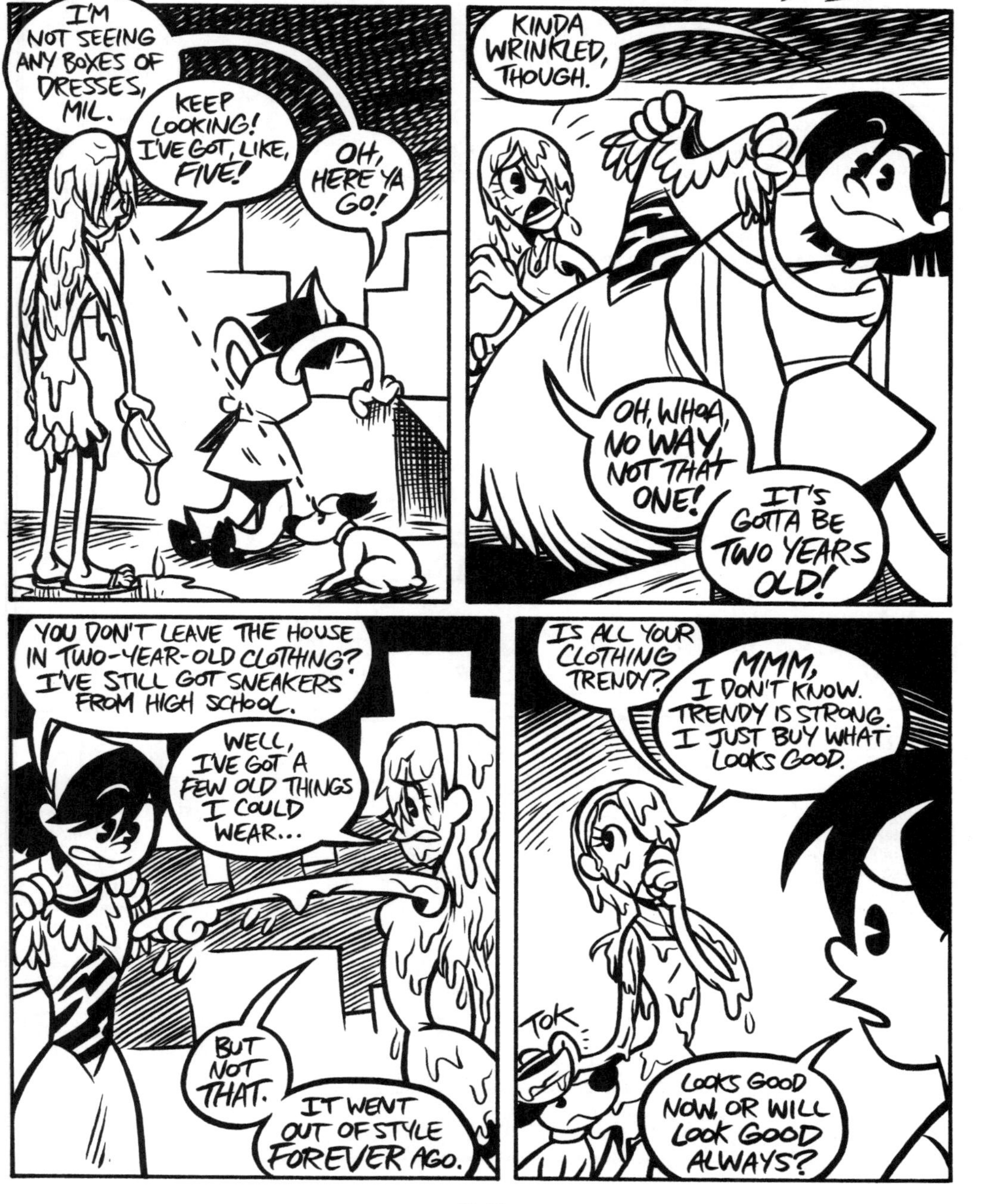

I'M NOT SEEING ANY BOXES OF DRESSES, MIL.
KEEP LOOKING! I'VE GOT, LIKE, FIVE!
OH, HERE YA GO!
KINDA WRINKLED, THOUGH.
OH, WHOA, NO WAY, NOT THAT ONE!
IT'S GOTTA BE TWO YEARS OLD!
YOU DON'T LEAVE THE HOUSE IN TWO-YEAR-OLD CLOTHING? I'VE STILL GOT SNEAKERS FROM HIGH SCHOOL.
WELL, I'VE GOT A FEW OLD THINGS I COULD WEAR...
BUT NOT THAT.
IT WENT OUT OF STYLE FOREVER AGO.
IS ALL YOUR CLOTHING TRENDY?
MMM, I DON'T KNOW. TRENDY IS STRONG. I JUST BUY WHAT LOOKS GOOD.
TOK
LOOKS GOOD NOW, OR WILL LOOK GOOD ALWAYS?

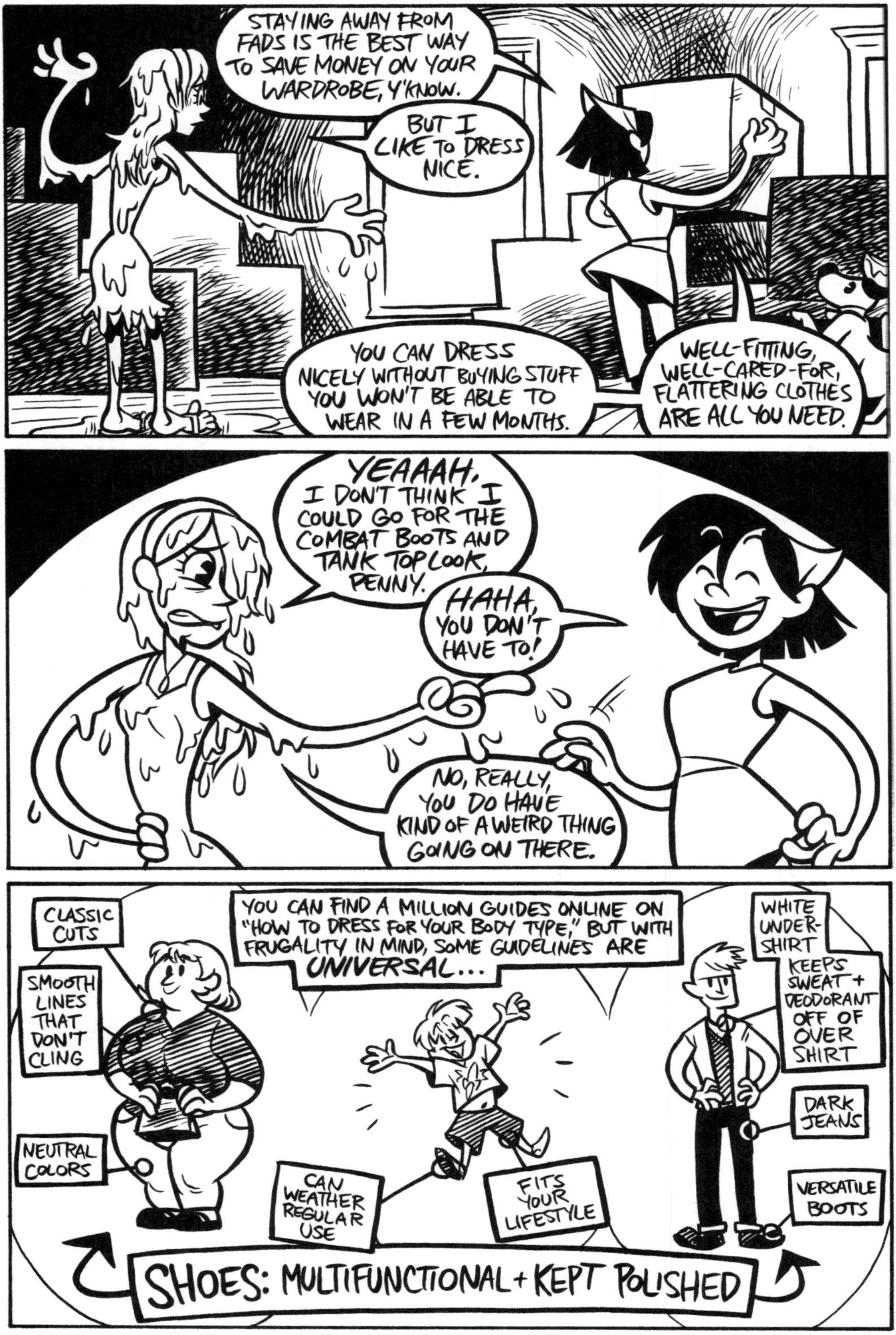
STAYING AWAY FROM FADS IS THE BEST WAY TO SAVE MONEY ON YOUR WARDROBE, Y'KNOW.
BUT I LIKE TO DRESS NICE.
YOU CAN DRESS NICELY WITHOUT BUYING STUFF YOU WON'T BE ABLE TO WEAR IN A FEW MONTHS.
WELL-FITTING, WELL-CARED-FOR, FLATTERING CLOTHES ARE ALL YOU NEED.
YEAAAH, I DON'T THINK I COULD GO FOR THE COMBAT BOOTS AND TANK TOP LOOK, PENNY.
HAHA, YOU DON'T HAVE TO!
NO, REALLY, YOU DO HAVE KIND OF A WEIRD THING GOING ON THERE.
YOU CAN FIND A MILLION GUIDES ONLINE ON "HOW TO DRESS FOR YOUR BODY TYPE," BUT WITH FRUGALITY IN MIND, SOME GUIDELINES ARE UNIVERSAL...
CLASSIC CUTS
SMOOTH LINES THAT DON'T CLING
NEUTRAL COLORS
CAN WEATHER REGULAR USE
FITS YOUR LIFESTYLE
WHITE UNDER-SHIRT KEEPS SWEAT + DEODORANT OFF OF OVER SHIRT
DARK JEANS
VERSATILE BOOTS
SHOES: MULTIFUNCTIONAL + KEPT POLISHED

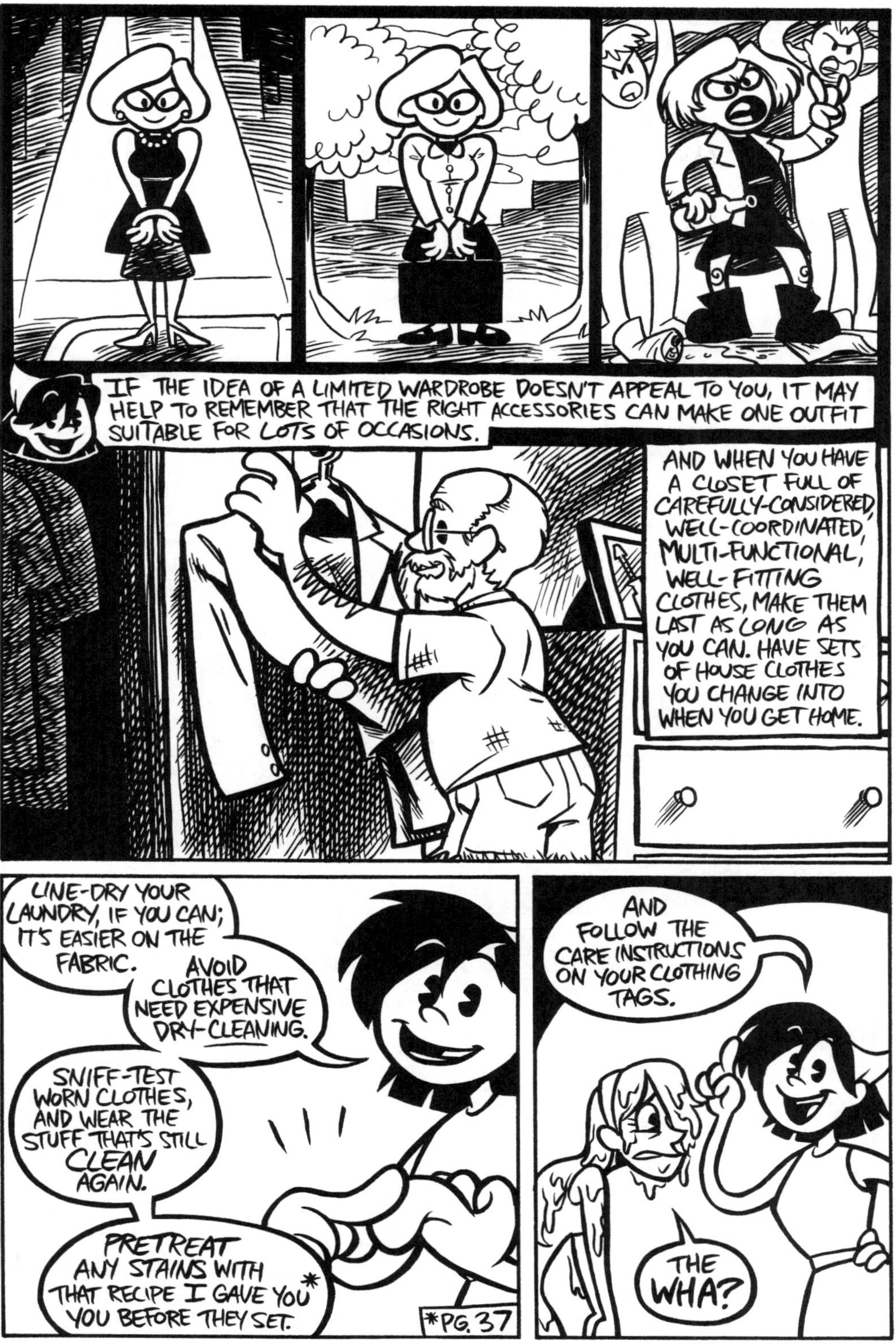
IF THE IDEA OF A LIMITED WARDROBE DOESN'T APPEAL TO YOU, IT MAY HELP TO REMEMBER THAT THE RIGHT ACCESSORIES CAN MAKE ONE OUTFIT SUITABLE FOR LOTS OF OCCASIONS.
AND WHEN YOU HAVE A CLOSET FULL OF CAREFULLY-CONSIDERED, WELL-COORDINATED, MULTI-FUNCTIONAL, WELL-FITTING CLOTHES, MAKE THEM LAST AS LONG AS YOU CAN. HAVE SETS OF HOUSE CLOTHES YOU CHANGE INTO WHEN YOU GET HOME.
LINE-DRY YOUR LAUNDRY, IF YOU CAN; IT'S EASIER ON THE FABRIC.
AVOID CLOTHES THAT NEED EXPENSIVE DRY-CLEANING.
SNIFF-TEST WORN CLOTHES, AND WEAR THE STUFF THAT'S STILL CLEAN AGAIN.
PRETREAT ANY STAINS WITH THAT RECIPE I GAVE YOU* YOU BEFORE THEY SET.
*PG. 37
AND FOLLOW THE CARE INSTRUCTIONS ON YOUR CLOTHING TAGS.
THE WHA?

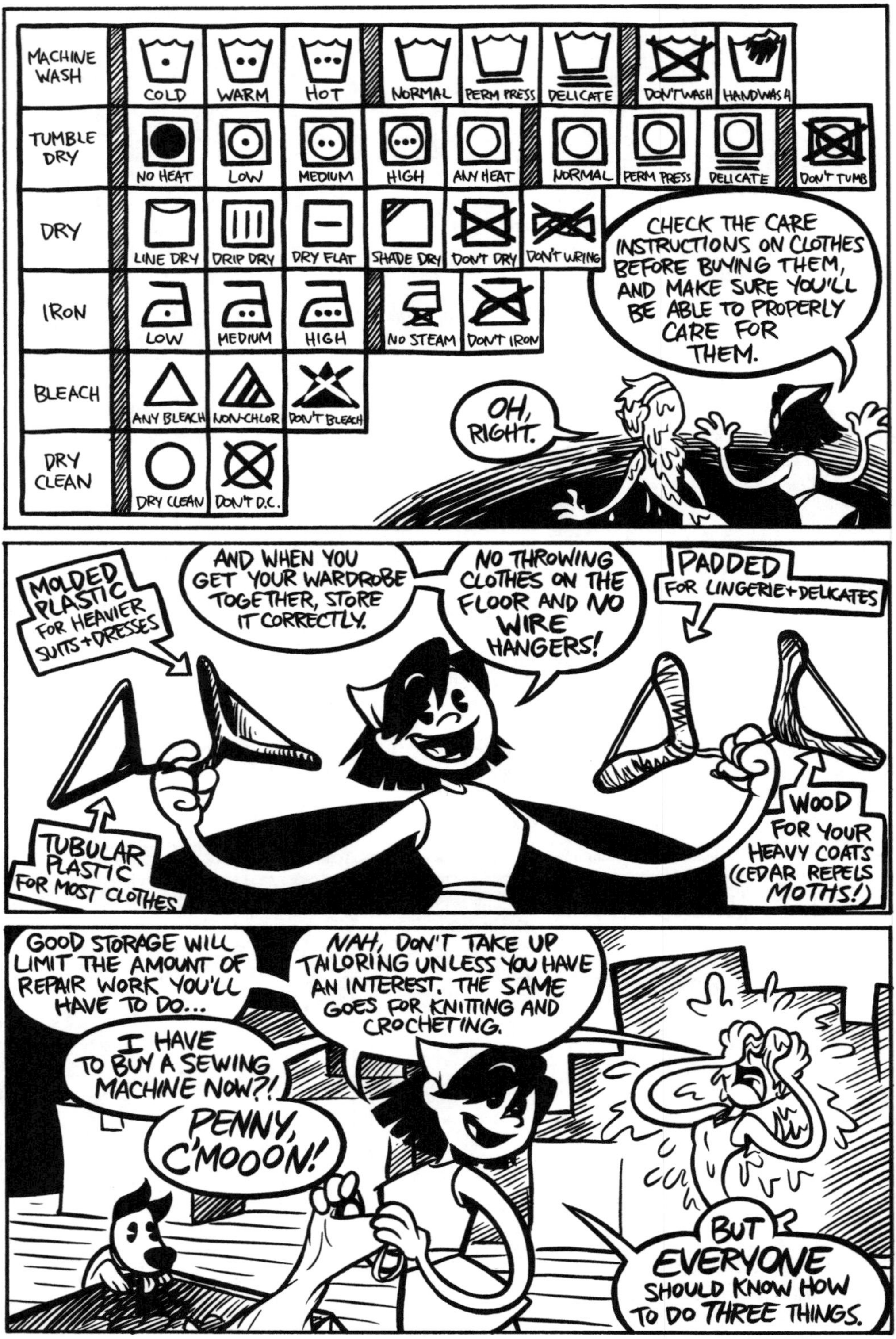
MACHINE WASH
COLD
WARM
HOT
NORMAL
PERM PRESS
DELICATE
DON'T WASH
HANDWASH
TUMBLE DRY
NO HEAT
LOW
MEDIUM
HIGH
ANY HEAT
NORMAL
PERM PRESS
DELICATE
DON'T TUMB
DRY
LINE DRY
DRIP DRY
DRY FLAT
SHADE DRY
DON'T DRY
DON'T WRING
IRON
LOW
MEDIUM
HIGH
NO STEAM
DON'T IRON
BLEACH
ANY BLEACH
NON-CHLOR
DON'T BLEACH
DRY CLEAN
DRY CLEAN
DON'T D.C.
CHECK THE CARE INSTRUCTIONS ON CLOTHES BEFORE BUYING THEM, AND MAKE SURE YOU'LL BE ABLE TO PROPERLY CARE FOR THEM.
OH, RIGHT.
AND WHEN YOU GET YOUR WARDROBE TOGETHER, STORE IT CORRECTLY.
NO THROWING CLOTHES ON THE FLOOR AND NO WIRE HANGERS!
MOLDED PLASTIC FOR HEAVIER SUITS+DRESSES
PADDED FOR LINGERIE+DELICATES
TUBULAR PLASTIC FOR MOST CLOTHES
WOOD FOR YOUR HEAVY COATS (CEDAR REPELS MOTHS!)
GOOD STORAGE WILL LIMIT THE AMOUNT OF REPAIR WORK YOU'LL HAVE TO DO...
I HAVE TO BUY A SEWING MACHINE NOW?!
NAH, DON'T TAKE UP TAILORING UNLESS YOU HAVE AN INTEREST. THE SAME GOES FOR KNITTING AND CROCHETING.
PENNY, C'MOOON!
BUT EVERYONE SHOULD KNOW HOW TO DO THREE THINGS.

FASHION 101: MENDING

SEW ON A BUTTON

YOU'LL NEED...
- THREAD (MATCH IT TO THE GARMENT)
- BUTTON (PREFERABLY THE ORIGINAL)
- NEEDLE
- SCISSORS

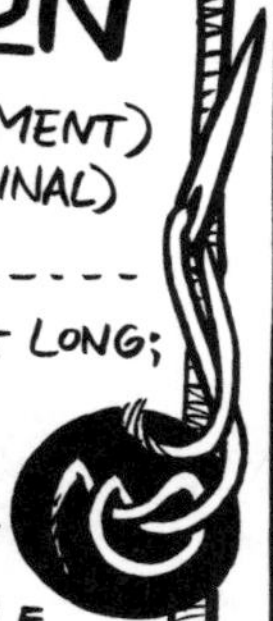

- CUT A LENGTH OF THREAD A FOOT LONG; THREAD YOUR NEEDLE; DOUBLE IT AND THEN DOUBLE-KNOT THE END
- HOLD BUTTON 1/8 INCH ABOVE FABRIC WITH THUMB + FOREFINGER, AND BRING NEEDLE UP THROUGH BUTTONHOLE, THROUGH UNDERSIDE OF SHIRT; THE KNOT SHOULD KEEP IT IN PLACE
- BRING NEEDLE DOWN THROUGH ANOTHER HOLE, MIMICKING THE WAY THE OTHER BUTTONS ARE SEWN
- REPEAT THIS PROCESS FIVE TIMES PER HOLE; TRIM OFF EXTRA + DOUBLE-KNOT ENDS ON UNDERSIDE OF SHIRT

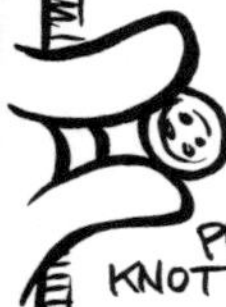

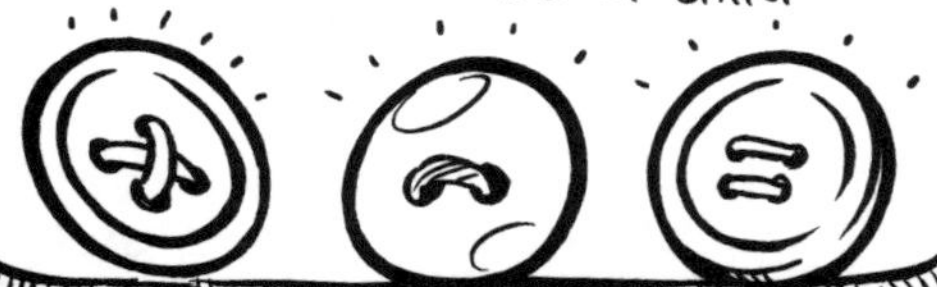

HEM

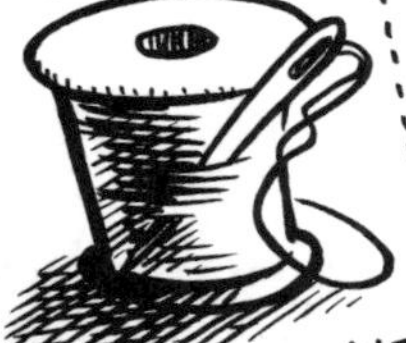

YOU'LL NEED...
- SEAM RIPPER
- IRON
- SEWING PINS
- TAPE MEASURE
- NEEDLE
- THREAD PINS
- SCISSORS

- REMOVE THE EXISTING HEM WITH SEAM RIPPER AND IRON FORMER SEAM FLAT (USE CORRECT IRON SETTING!!)
- PUT ON GARMENT; PICK LOCATION OF HEM; PIN AT TOP + BOTTOM OF FOLD
- REMOVE GARMENT + TURN INSIDE-OUT; MEASURE NEW HEM + PIN IT THROUGHOUT GARMENT
- IRON NEW HEM; CUT LENGTH OF THREAD 6 FT. LONG FOR A PANT LEG (TWICE THAT FOR A SKIRT); DOUBLE IT + DOUBLE-KNOT THE END
- BLIND STITCH NEW HEM IN PLACE + REMOVE PINS AS YOU GO
- TRIM OFF EXTRA THREAD + DOUBLE KNOT ENDS ON UNDERSIDE

PATCH A HOLE

YOU'LL NEED...
- EMBROIDERY FLOSS
- NEEDLE
- SCISSORS

NOT WORTH THE TIME ON SMALL, CHEAP ITEMS LIKE GYM SOCKS, BUT A GREAT WAY TO SAVE OLD LINEN, BLANKETS, SWEATERS, AND PANTS!

- TRIM OFF ANY LOOSE OR RAGGED ENDS AROUND THE HOLE WITH SCISSORS; PLACE ANY LARGE HOLES OVER A SMOOTH, FIRM SURFACE
- CUT A LENGTH OF THREAD LONG ENOUGH TO COVER THE HOLE TWICE; THREAD YOUR NEEDLE WITH IT AND *DOUBLE* IT
- TURN THE CLOTHING INSIDE-OUT; REINFORCE THE EDGES THE HOLE BY SEWING IN A CIRCLE BEYOND THE WEAKENED FABRIC AROUND THE HOLE

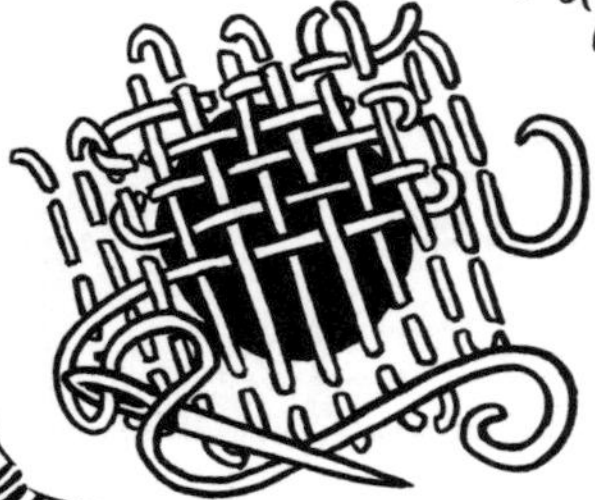

- SPACING YOUR ROWS ONE THICKNESS OF MENDING APART; STITCH IN VERTICAL ROWS OVER THE INSIDE OF THE PREVIOUSLY STITCHED CIRCLE LOOPING BACK WITH EACH END
- STITCH OVER THE VERTICAL MENDING WITH HORIZONTAL ROWS, SEWING OVER AND UNDER ALTERNATING THREADS; DARN ABOUT TWO THREADS OF STITCHING BEYOND THE HOLE, THEN DOUBLE-BACK
- TRIM OFF EXCESS THREAD + TUCK IN LOOSE ENDS

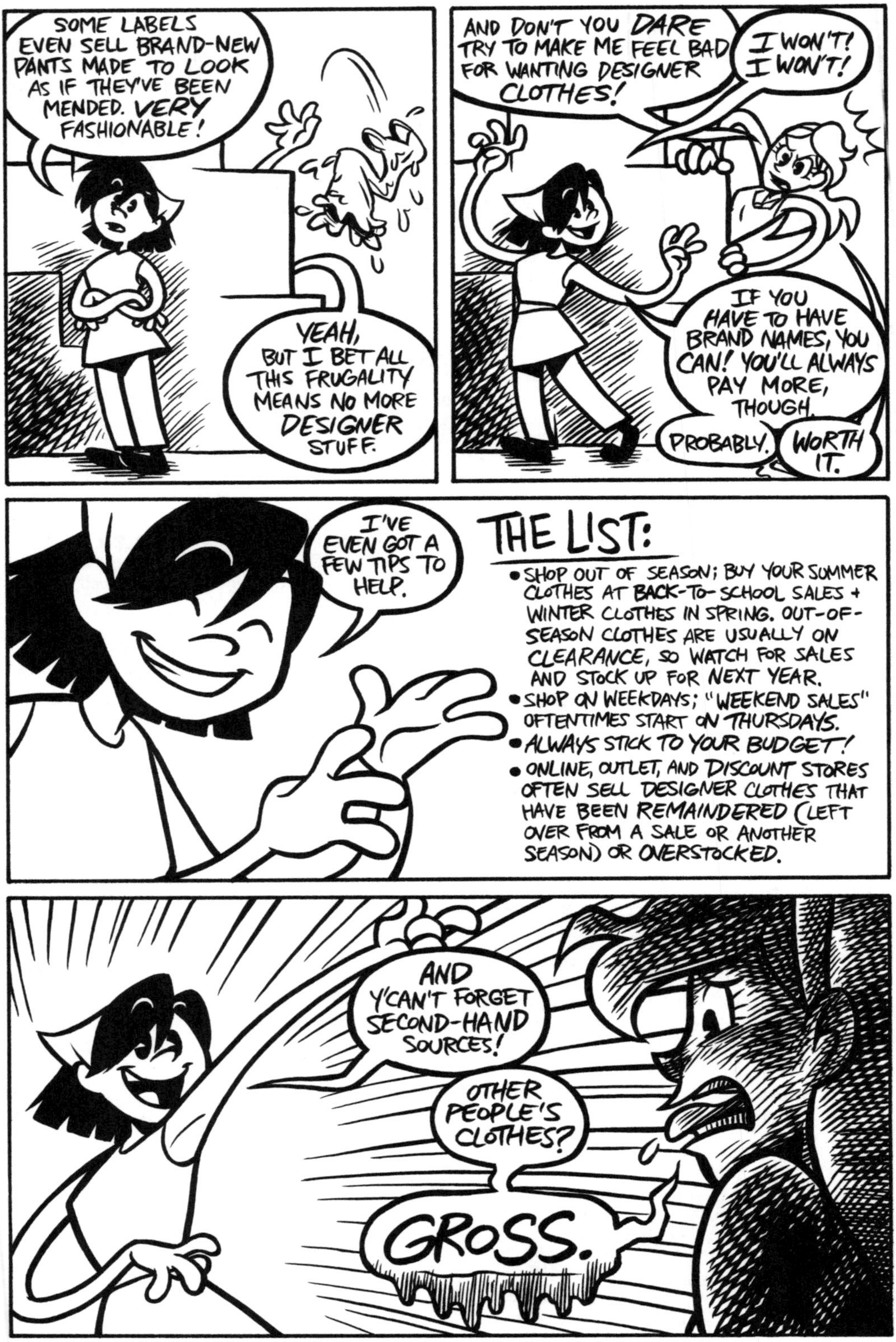
SOME LABELS EVEN SELL BRAND-NEW PANTS MADE TO LOOK AS IF THEY'VE BEEN MENDED. VERY FASHIONABLE!
YEAH, BUT I BET ALL THIS FRUGALITY MEANS NO MORE DESIGNER STUFF.
AND DON'T YOU DARE TRY TO MAKE ME FEEL BAD FOR WANTING DESIGNER CLOTHES!
I WON'T! I WON'T!
IF YOU HAVE TO HAVE BRAND NAMES, YOU CAN! YOU'LL ALWAYS PAY MORE, THOUGH.
PROBABLY.
WORTH IT.
I'VE EVEN GOT A FEW TIPS TO HELP.
THE LIST:
• SHOP OUT OF SEASON; BUY YOUR SUMMER CLOTHES AT BACK-TO-SCHOOL SALES + WINTER CLOTHES IN SPRING. OUT-OF-SEASON CLOTHES ARE USUALLY ON CLEARANCE, SO WATCH FOR SALES AND STOCK UP FOR NEXT YEAR.
• SHOP ON WEEKDAYS; "WEEKEND SALES" OFTENTIMES START ON THURSDAYS.
• ALWAYS STICK TO YOUR BUDGET!
• ONLINE, OUTLET, AND DISCOUNT STORES OFTEN SELL DESIGNER CLOTHES THAT HAVE BEEN REMAINDERED (LEFT OVER FROM A SALE OR ANOTHER SEASON) OR OVERSTOCKED.
AND Y'CAN'T FORGET SECOND-HAND SOURCES!
OTHER PEOPLE'S CLOTHES?
GROSS.

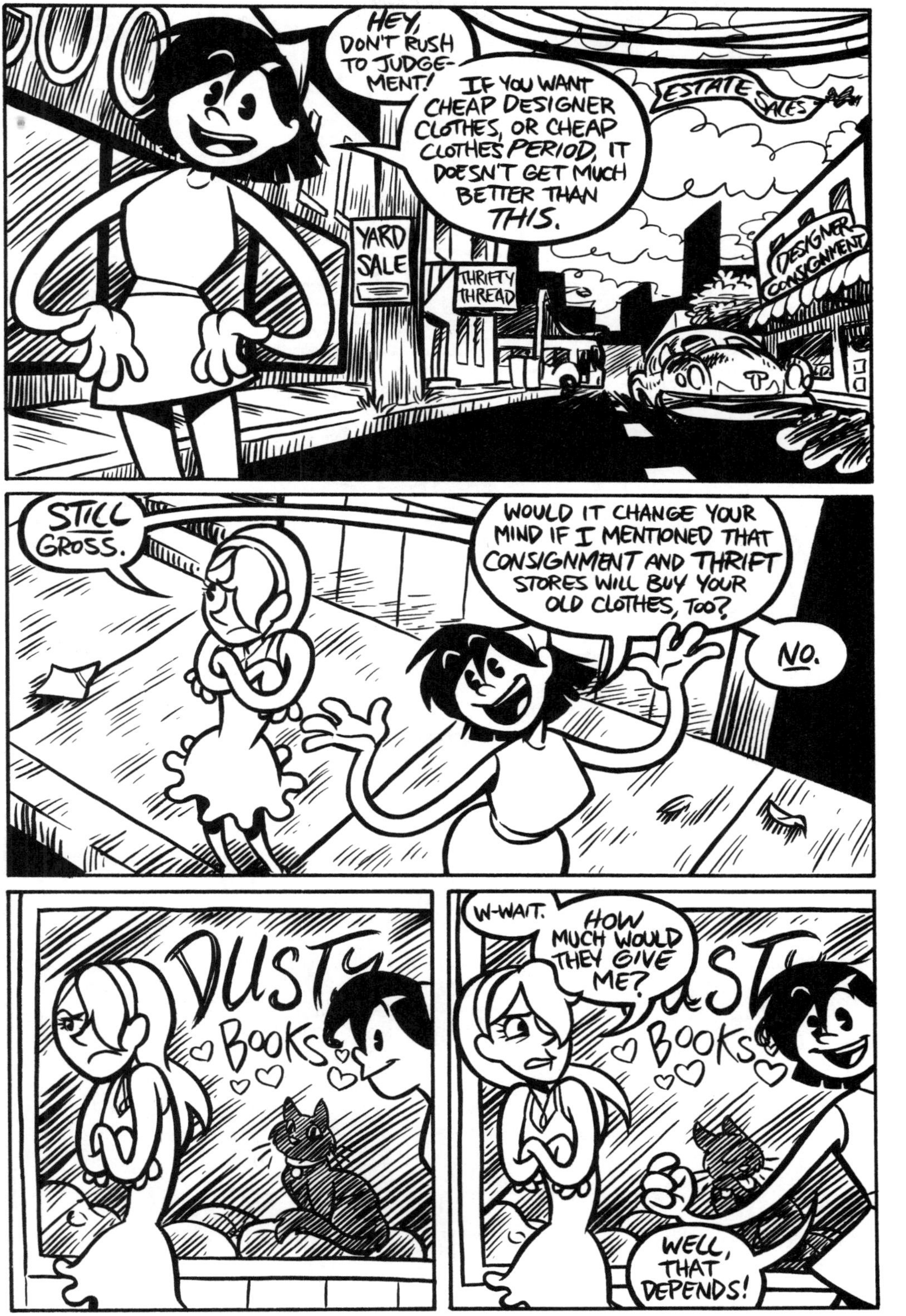
HEY, DON'T RUSH TO JUDGEMENT!
IF YOU WANT CHEAP DESIGNER CLOTHES, OR CHEAP CLOTHES PERIOD, IT DOESN'T GET MUCH BETTER THAN THIS.
ESTATE SALES
YARD SALE
THRIFTY THREAD
DESIGNER CONSIGNMENT
STILL GROSS.
WOULD IT CHANGE YOUR MIND IF I MENTIONED THAT CONSIGNMENT AND THRIFT STORES WILL BUY YOUR OLD CLOTHES, TOO?
NO.
DUSTY BOOKS
W-WAIT.
HOW MUCH WOULD THEY GIVE ME?
WELL, THAT DEPENDS!

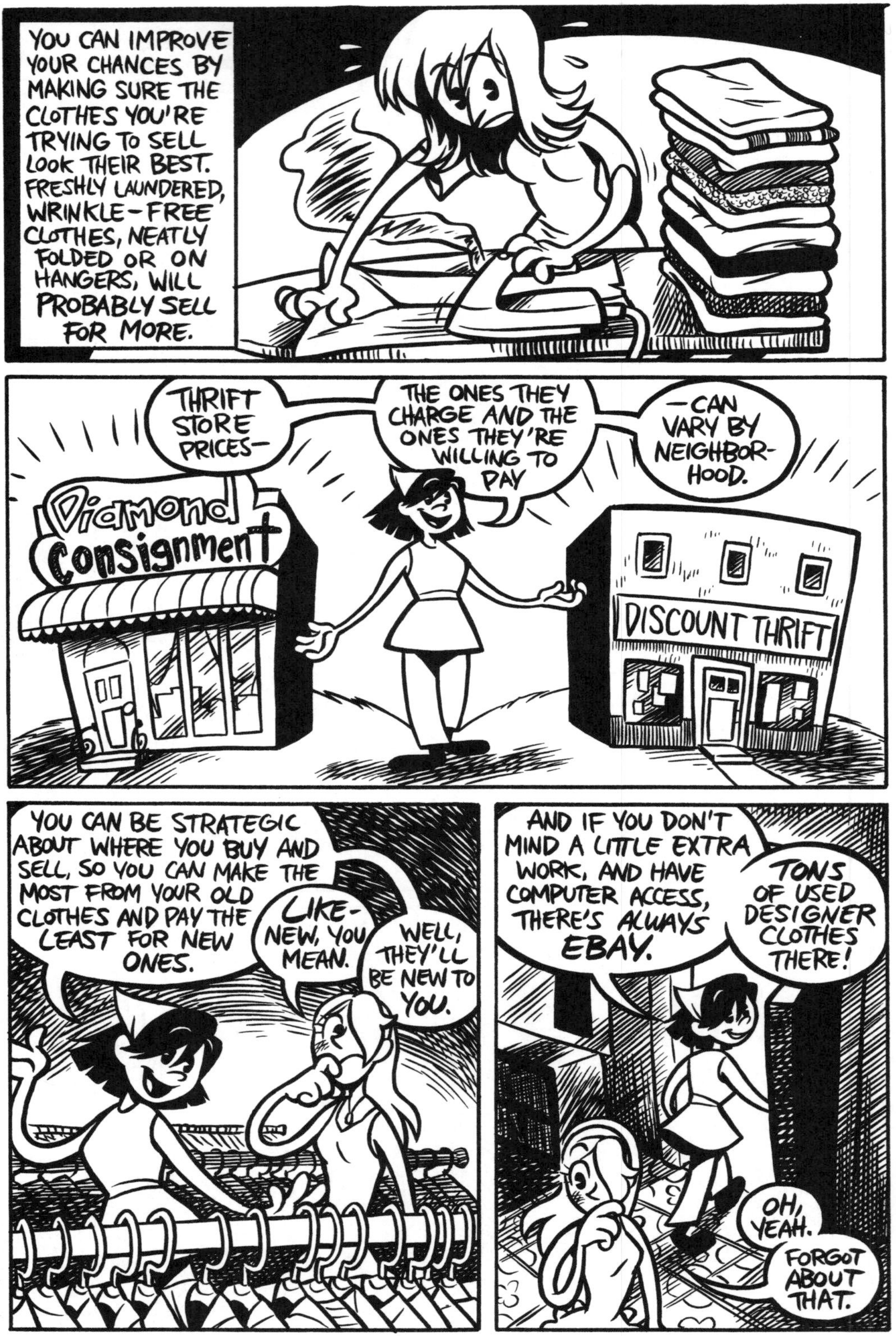
YOU CAN IMPROVE YOUR CHANCES BY MAKING SURE THE CLOTHES YOU'RE TRYING TO SELL LOOK THEIR BEST. FRESHLY LAUNDERED, WRINKLE-FREE CLOTHES, NEATLY FOLDED OR ON HANGERS, WILL PROBABLY SELL FOR MORE.
THRIFT STORE PRICES—
THE ONES THEY CHARGE AND THE ONES THEY'RE WILLING TO PAY
—CAN VARY BY NEIGHBOR-HOOD.
Diamond Consignment
DISCOUNT THRIFT
YOU CAN BE STRATEGIC ABOUT WHERE YOU BUY AND SELL, SO YOU CAN MAKE THE MOST FROM YOUR OLD CLOTHES AND PAY THE LEAST FOR NEW ONES.
LIKE-NEW, YOU MEAN.
WELL, THEY'LL BE NEW TO YOU.
AND IF YOU DON'T MIND A LITTLE EXTRA WORK, AND HAVE COMPUTER ACCESS, THERE'S ALWAYS EBAY.
TONS OF USED DESIGNER CLOTHES THERE!
OH, YEAH.
FORGOT ABOUT THAT.

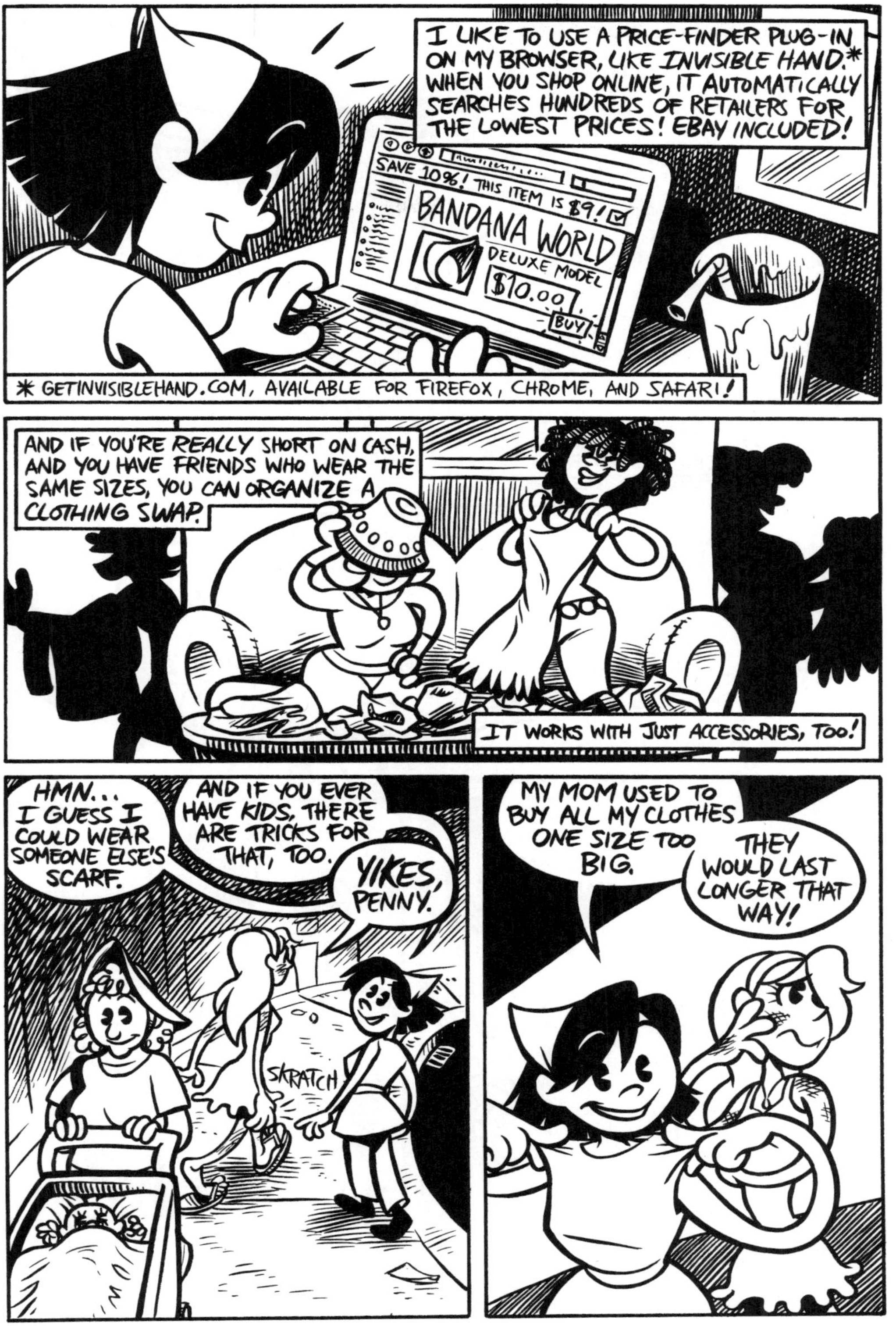
I LIKE TO USE A PRICE-FINDER PLUG-IN ON MY BROWSER, LIKE INVISIBLE HAND.* WHEN YOU SHOP ONLINE, IT AUTOMATICALLY SEARCHES HUNDREDS OF RETAILERS FOR THE LOWEST PRICES! EBAY INCLUDED!
SAVE 10%! THIS ITEM IS $9!
BANDANA WORLD
DELUXE MODEL
$10.00
BUY
* GETINVISIBLEHAND.COM, AVAILABLE FOR FIREFOX, CHROME, AND SAFARI!
AND IF YOU'RE REALLY SHORT ON CASH, AND YOU HAVE FRIENDS WHO WEAR THE SAME SIZES, YOU CAN ORGANIZE A CLOTHING SWAP.
IT WORKS WITH JUST ACCESSORIES, TOO!
HMN... I GUESS I COULD WEAR SOMEONE ELSE'S SCARF.
AND IF YOU EVER HAVE KIDS, THERE ARE TRICKS FOR THAT, TOO.
YIKES, PENNY.
SKRATCH
MY MOM USED TO BUY ALL MY CLOTHES ONE SIZE TOO BIG.
THEY WOULD LAST LONGER THAT WAY!

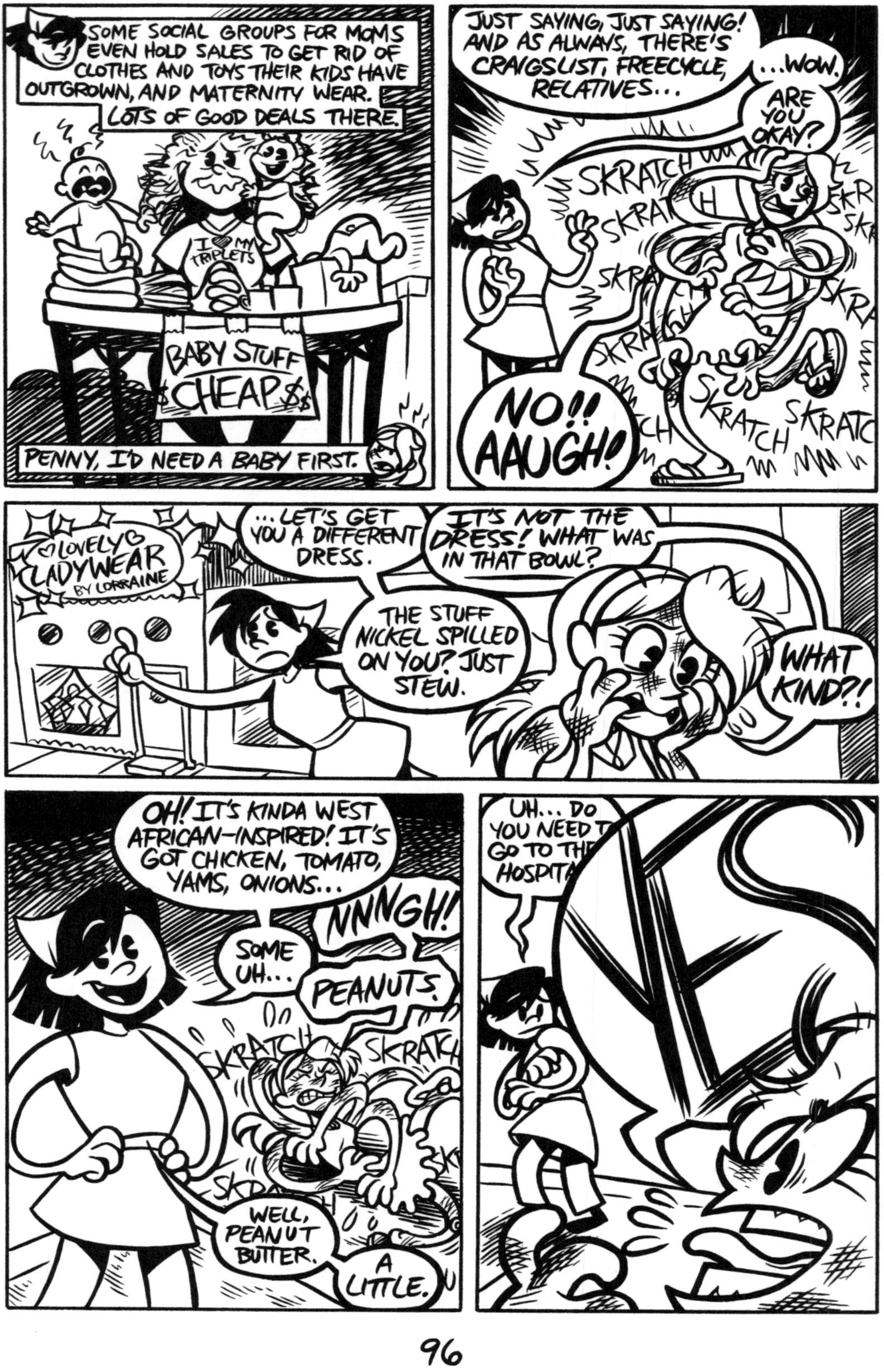
SOME SOCIAL GROUPS FOR MOMS EVEN HOLD SALES TO GET RID OF CLOTHES AND TOYS THEIR KIDS HAVE OUTGROWN, AND MATERNITY WEAR.
LOTS OF GOOD DEALS THERE.
I ♥ MY TRIPLETS
BABY STUFF $CHEAP$$
PENNY, I'D NEED A BABY FIRST.
JUST SAYING, JUST SAYING! AND AS ALWAYS, THERE'S CRAIGSLIST, FREECYCLE, RELATIVES...
...WOW.
ARE YOU OKAY?
SKRATCH
SKRATCH
SKRATCH
SKRATCH
SKRATCH
NO!! AAUGH!
♥LOVELY♥ LADYWEAR BY LORRAINE
...LET'S GET YOU A DIFFERENT DRESS.
IT'S NOT THE DRESS! WHAT WAS IN THAT BOWL?
THE STUFF NICKEL SPILLED ON YOU? JUST STEW.
WHAT KIND?!
OH! IT'S KINDA WEST AFRICAN-INSPIRED! IT'S GOT CHICKEN, TOMATO, YAMS, ONIONS...
NNNGH!
SOME UH...
PEANUTS.
SKRATCH
SKRATCH
WELL, PEANUT BUTTER.
A LITTLE.
UH... DO YOU NEED TO GO TO THE HOSPITAL
YES

Chapter Five
Health

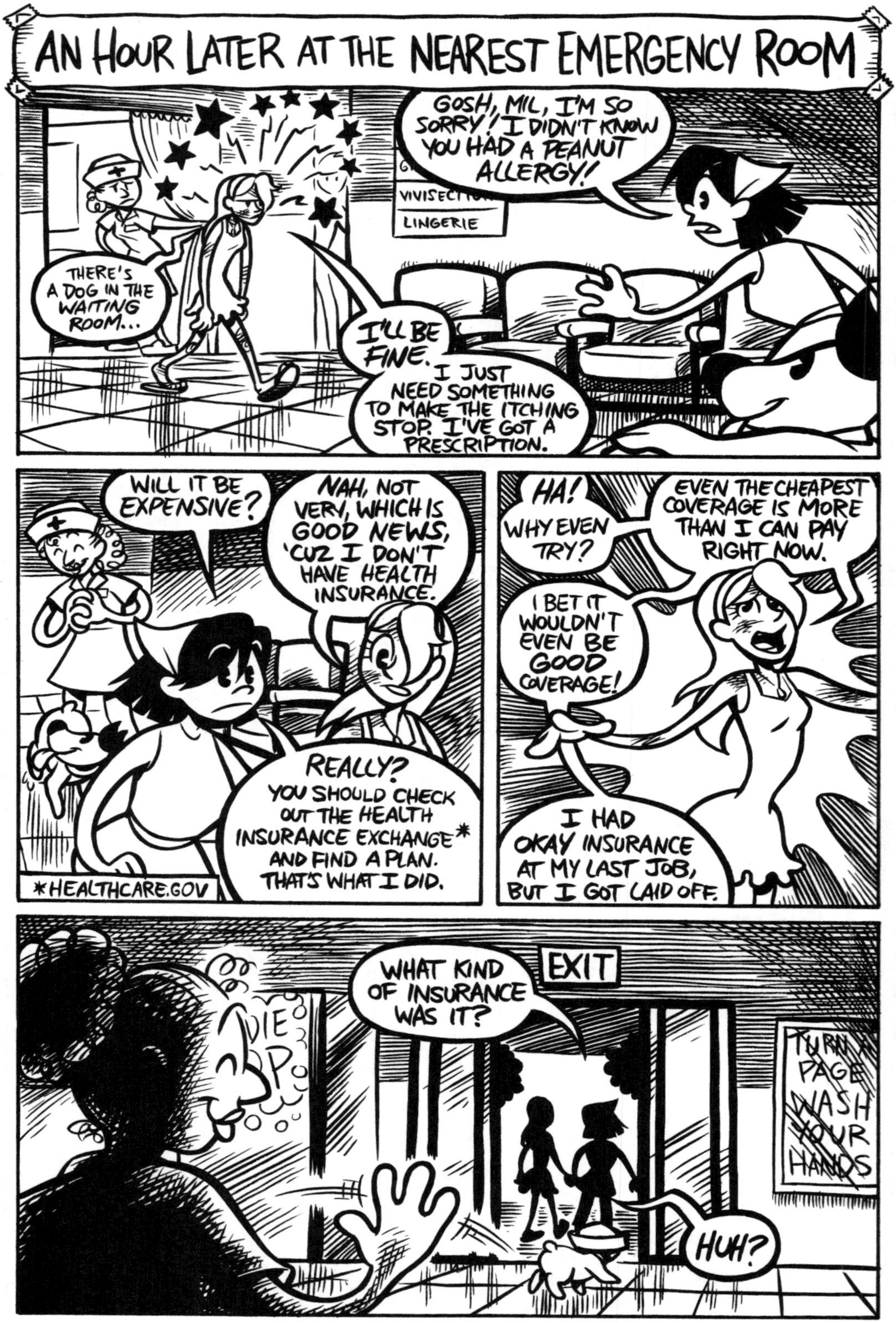
AN HOUR LATER AT THE NEAREST EMERGENCY ROOM
GOSH, MIL, I'M SO SORRY! I DIDN'T KNOW YOU HAD A PEANUT ALLERGY!
LINGERIE
THERE'S A DOG IN THE WAITING ROOM...
I'LL BE FINE. I JUST NEED SOMETHING TO MAKE THE ITCHING STOP. I'VE GOT A PRESCRIPTION.
WILL IT BE EXPENSIVE?
NAH, NOT VERY, WHICH IS GOOD NEWS, 'CUZ I DON'T HAVE HEALTH INSURANCE.
REALLY? YOU SHOULD CHECK OUT THE HEALTH INSURANCE EXCHANGE* AND FIND A PLAN. THAT'S WHAT I DID.
*HEALTHCARE.GOV
HA! WHY EVEN TRY?
EVEN THE CHEAPEST COVERAGE IS MORE THAN I CAN PAY RIGHT NOW.
I BET IT WOULDN'T EVEN BE GOOD COVERAGE!
I HAD OKAY INSURANCE AT MY LAST JOB, BUT I GOT LAID OFF.
WHAT KIND OF INSURANCE WAS IT?
EXIT
TURN PAGE WASH YOUR HANDS
HUH?

HMO – HEALTH MAINTENANCE ORGANIZATIONS ARE THE LEAST EXPENSIVE FORM OF HEALTH INSURANCE, BUT ALSO THE MOST RESTRICTIVE. THEY FEATURE LOW OR NO CO-PAYMENTS – THE SMALL FEE PAID BY AN INSURED PERSON WHENEVER MEDICAL SERVICES ARE MADE USE OF – AND LOW AMOUNTS OF PAPERWORK. HOWEVER, YOU MUST CHOOSE A **PRIMARY CARE PHYSICIAN (PCP)** FROM AN APPROVED LIST OF DOCTORS AND GET A PCP REFERRAL TO SEE A SPECIALIST. YOUR PCP COORDINATES ALL OF YOUR HEALTH CARE. HMOs ARE A GOOD CHOICE IF YOU HAVE MANY DOCTOR'S APPOINTMENTS EVERY MONTH.

- - - - - - - - - -

POS – POINT OF SERVICE PLANS ARE MORE FLEXIBLE THAN HMOs. YOU MAY VISIT A DOCTOR OUTSIDE THE INSURER'S NETWORK OF APPROVED PHYSICIANS AND STILL RECEIVE COVERAGE, BUT NOT AS MUCH AS IF YOU'D STAYED WITHIN IT. YOU MUST STILL CHOOSE A PCP, AS WELL. IF THE PCP DOES NOT PROVIDE A REFERRAL FOR YOUR DOCTORS' VISITS OUTSIDE THE NETWORK, YOU'RE LIKELY TO WIND UP SUBMITTING PAPERWORK FOR THE BILLS TO YOUR INSURER FOR REIMBURSEMENT, WHICH YOU MAY OR MAY NOT RECEIVE.

- - - - - - - - - -

PPO – PREFERRED PROVIDER ORGANIZATIONS ENCOURAGE POLICY-HOLDERS TO STAY WITHIN A NETWORK OF PRACTITIONERS BY OFFERING SIGNIFICANT DISCOUNTS, AND PCP PERMISSION IS NOT NECESSARY FOR SPECIALIST VISITS, AS LONG AS THE SPECIALIST IS PART OF THE NETWORK. IF YOU SEE AN OUT-OF-NETWORK DOCTOR, YOU MAY HAVE TO PAY THE ENTIRE BILL YOURSELF, THEN SUBMIT PAPERWORK FOR REIMBURSEMENT. YOU MAY ALSO HAVE TO PAY A **DEDUCTIBLE** – A MINIMUM AMOUNT A POLICYHOLDER MUST PAY OUT-OF-POCKET BEFORE INSURANCE KICKS IN – IF YOU CHOOSE TO GO OUTSIDE THE NETWORK, OR PAY THE DIFFERENCE BETWEEN WHAT THE NETWORK DOCTORS CHARGE VS. WHAT THE OUT-OF-NETWORK DOCTORS CHARGE.

- - - - - - - - - -

FFS – FEE FOR SERVICE PLANS ARE THE MOST FLEXIBLE KIND OF PLAN. THEY ALLOW POLICYHOLDERS TO CHOOSE THEIR OWN DOCTORS, HOSPITALS, AND SPECIALISTS, IN EXCHANGE FOR HIGHER CO-PAYMENTS, MORE PAPERWORK AND HIGHER DEDUCTIBLES.

EPO – EXCLUSIVE PROVIDER ORGANIZATIONS ONLY COVER SERVICES PROVIDED BY DOCTORS IN THE PLAN'S NETWORK (EXCEPT FOR EMERGENCIES). CHEAP, BUT RESTRICTIVE!

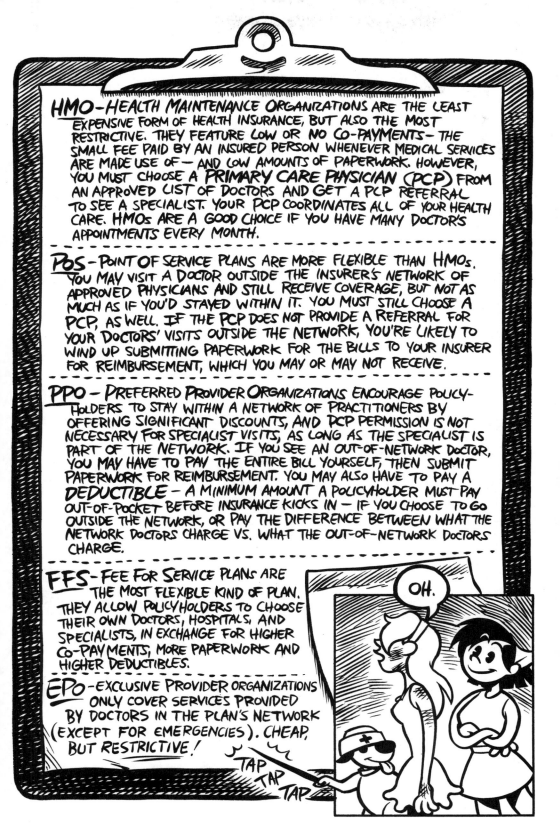

OH.

TAP TAP TAP

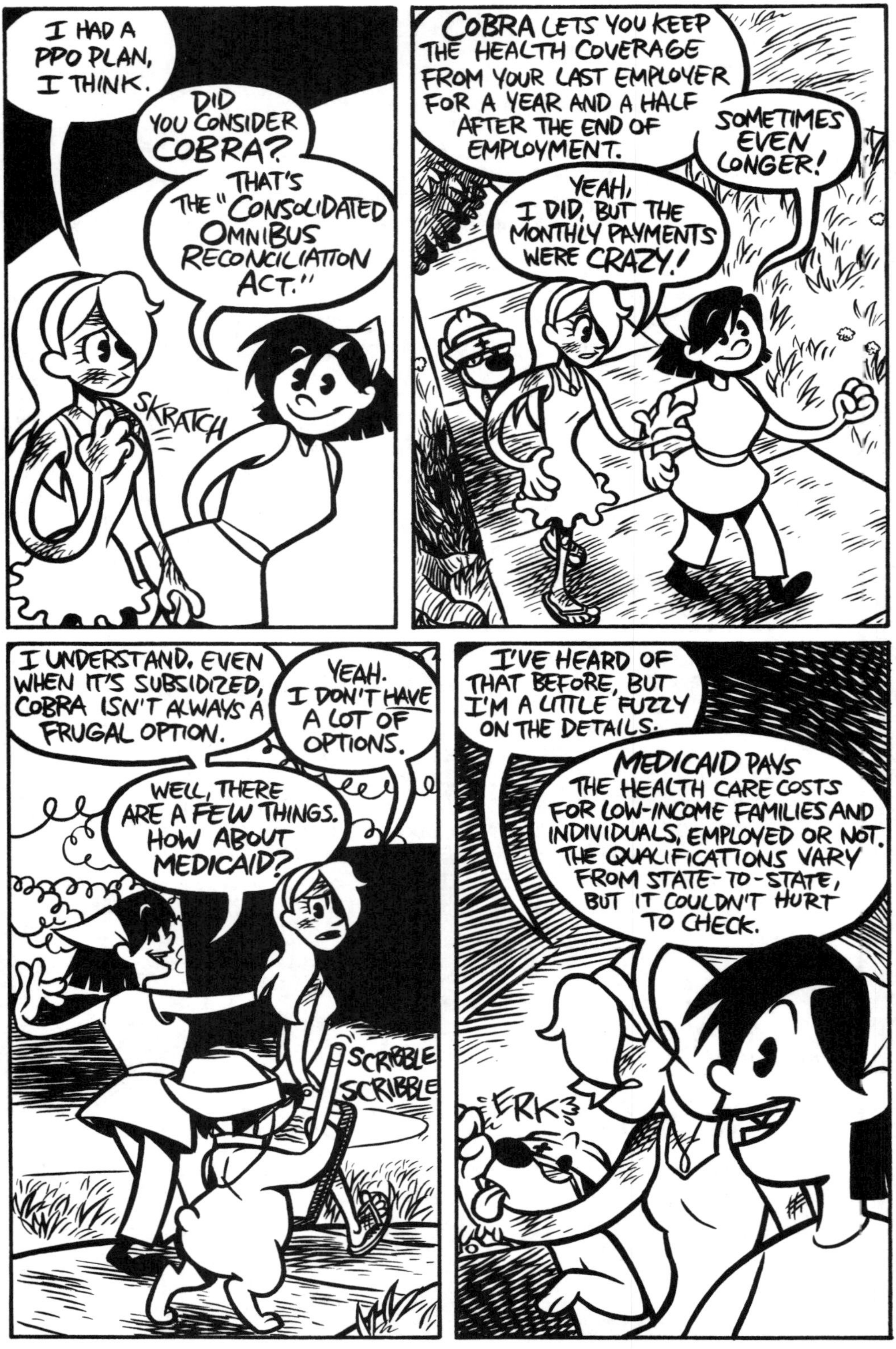
I HAD A PPO PLAN, I THINK.
DID YOU CONSIDER COBRA?
THAT'S THE "CONSOLIDATED OMNIBUS RECONCILIATION ACT."
SKRATCH
COBRA LETS YOU KEEP THE HEALTH COVERAGE FROM YOUR LAST EMPLOYER FOR A YEAR AND A HALF AFTER THE END OF EMPLOYMENT.
SOMETIMES EVEN LONGER!
YEAH, I DID, BUT THE MONTHLY PAYMENTS WERE CRAZY!
I UNDERSTAND. EVEN WHEN IT'S SUBSIDIZED, COBRA ISN'T ALWAYS A FRUGAL OPTION.
YEAH. I DON'T HAVE A LOT OF OPTIONS.
WELL, THERE ARE A FEW THINGS. HOW ABOUT MEDICAID?
SCRIBBLE SCRIBBLE
I'VE HEARD OF THAT BEFORE, BUT I'M A LITTLE FUZZY ON THE DETAILS.
MEDICAID PAYS THE HEALTH CARE COSTS FOR LOW-INCOME FAMILIES AND INDIVIDUALS, EMPLOYED OR NOT. THE QUALIFICATIONS VARY FROM STATE-TO-STATE, BUT IT COULDN'T HURT TO CHECK.
ERK

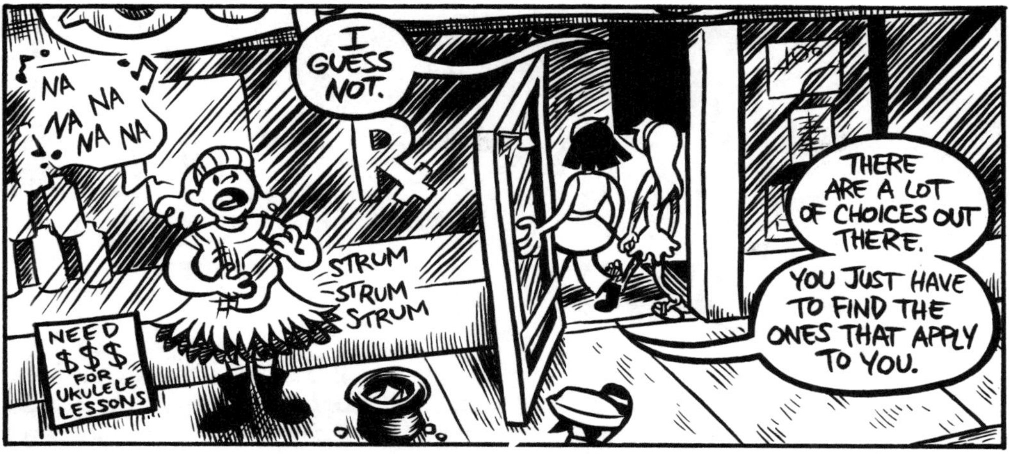
NA NA NA NA NA
I GUESS NOT.
STRUM STRUM STRUM
NEED $$$ FOR UKULELE LESSONS
THERE ARE A LOT OF CHOICES OUT THERE.
YOU JUST HAVE TO FIND THE ONES THAT APPLY TO YOU.

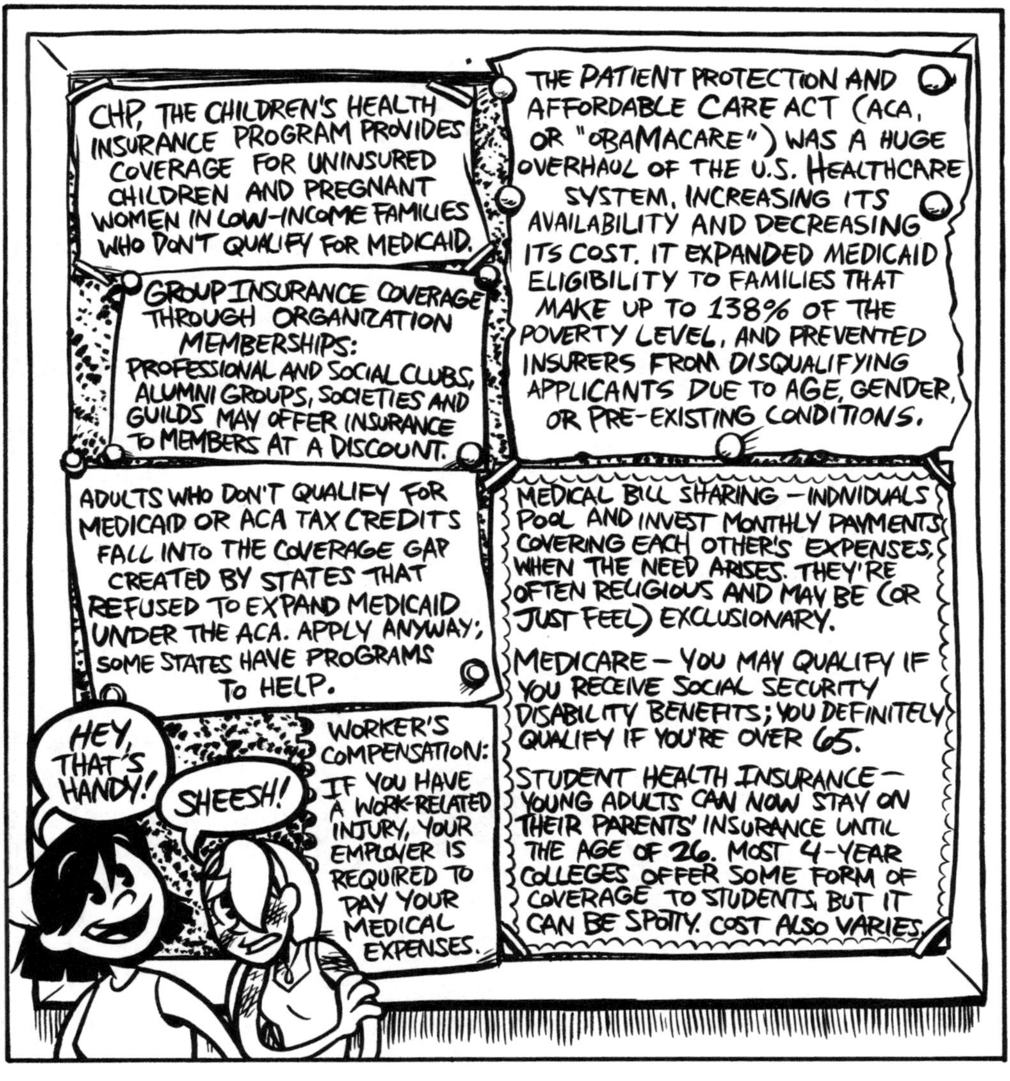
CHP, THE CHILDREN'S HEALTH INSURANCE PROGRAM PROVIDES COVERAGE FOR UNINSURED CHILDREN AND PREGNANT WOMEN IN LOW-INCOME FAMILIES WHO DON'T QUALIFY FOR MEDICAID.
GROUP INSURANCE COVERAGE THROUGH ORGANIZATION MEMBERSHIPS: PROFESSIONAL AND SOCIAL CLUBS, ALUMNI GROUPS, SOCIETIES AND GUILDS MAY OFFER INSURANCE TO MEMBERS AT A DISCOUNT.
THE PATIENT PROTECTION AND AFFORDABLE CARE ACT (ACA, OR "OBAMACARE") WAS A HUGE OVERHAUL OF THE U.S. HEALTHCARE SYSTEM, INCREASING ITS AVAILABILITY AND DECREASING ITS COST. IT EXPANDED MEDICAID ELIGIBILITY TO FAMILIES THAT MAKE UP TO 138% OF THE POVERTY LEVEL, AND PREVENTED INSURERS FROM DISQUALIFYING APPLICANTS DUE TO AGE, GENDER, OR PRE-EXISTING CONDITIONS.
ADULTS WHO DON'T QUALIFY FOR MEDICAID OR ACA TAX CREDITS FALL INTO THE COVERAGE GAP CREATED BY STATES THAT REFUSED TO EXPAND MEDICAID UNDER THE ACA. APPLY ANYWAY; SOME STATES HAVE PROGRAMS TO HELP.
MEDICAL BILL SHARING — INDIVIDUALS POOL AND INVEST MONTHLY PAYMENTS COVERING EACH OTHER'S EXPENSES, WHEN THE NEED ARISES. THEY'RE OFTEN RELIGIOUS AND MAY BE (OR JUST FEEL) EXCLUSIONARY.
MEDICARE — YOU MAY QUALIFY IF YOU RECEIVE SOCIAL SECURITY DISABILITY BENEFITS; YOU DEFINITELY QUALIFY IF YOU'RE OVER 65.
STUDENT HEALTH INSURANCE — YOUNG ADULTS CAN NOW STAY ON THEIR PARENTS' INSURANCE UNTIL THE AGE OF 26. MOST 4-YEAR COLLEGES OFFER SOME FORM OF COVERAGE TO STUDENTS, BUT IT CAN BE SPOTTY. COST ALSO VARIES.
HEY, THAT'S HANDY!
SHEESH!
WORKER'S COMPENSATION: IF YOU HAVE A WORK-RELATED INJURY, YOUR EMPLOYER IS REQUIRED TO PAY YOUR MEDICAL EXPENSES.

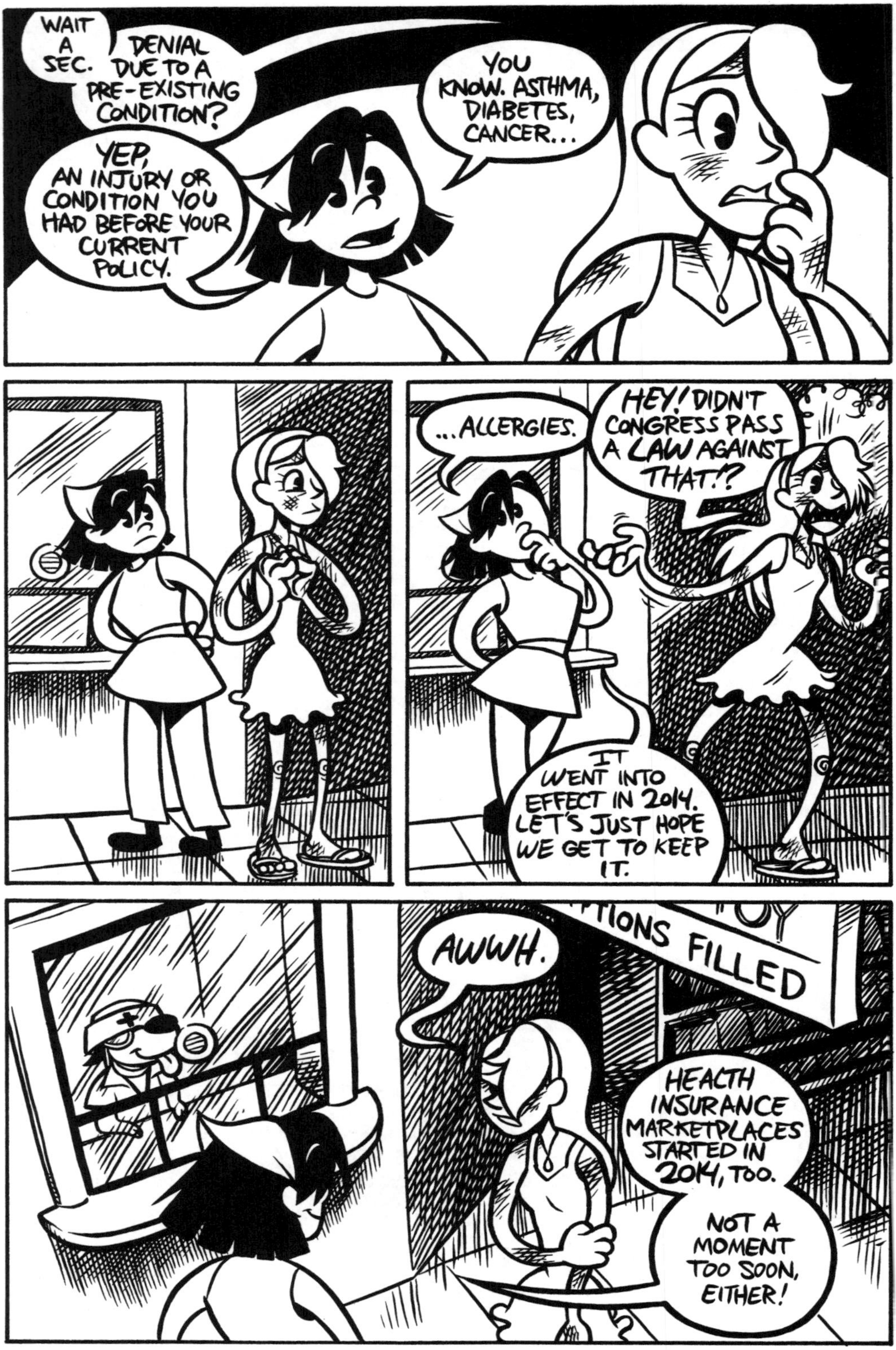
WAIT A SEC.
DENIAL DUE TO A PRE-EXISTING CONDITION?
YEP, AN INJURY OR CONDITION YOU HAD BEFORE YOUR CURRENT POLICY.
YOU KNOW. ASTHMA, DIABETES, CANCER...
...ALLERGIES.
HEY! DIDN'T CONGRESS PASS A LAW AGAINST THAT!?
IT WENT INTO EFFECT IN 2014. LET'S JUST HOPE WE GET TO KEEP IT.
AWWH.
TIONS FILLED
HEACTH INSURANCE MARKETPLACES STARTED IN 2014, TOO.
NOT A MOMENT TOO SOON, EITHER!

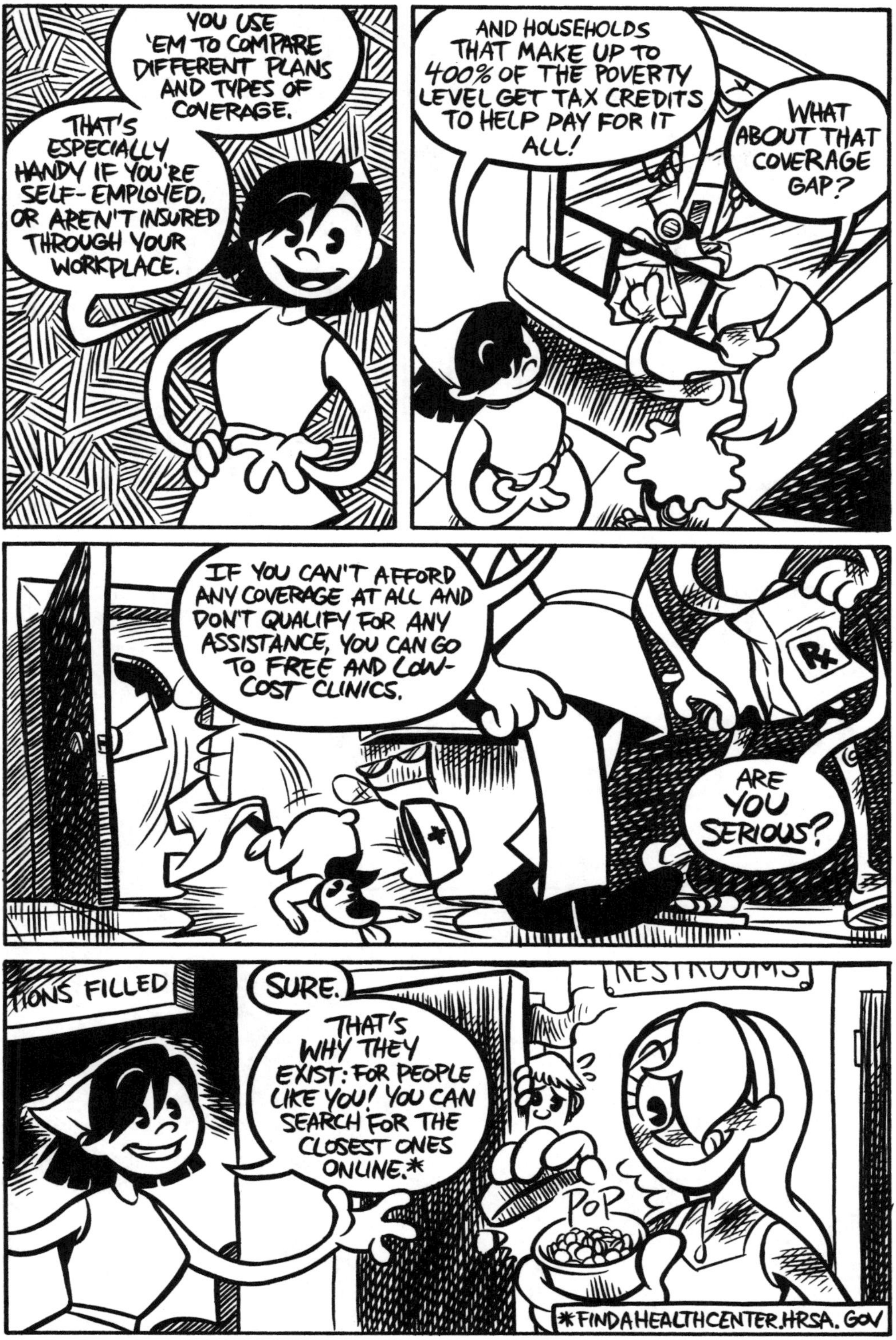
YOU USE 'EM TO COMPARE DIFFERENT PLANS AND TYPES OF COVERAGE.
THAT'S ESPECIALLY HANDY IF YOU'RE SELF-EMPLOYED, OR AREN'T INSURED THROUGH YOUR WORKPLACE.
AND HOUSEHOLDS THAT MAKE UP TO 400% OF THE POVERTY LEVEL GET TAX CREDITS TO HELP PAY FOR IT ALL!
WHAT ABOUT THAT COVERAGE GAP?
IF YOU CAN'T AFFORD ANY COVERAGE AT ALL AND DON'T QUALIFY FOR ANY ASSISTANCE, YOU CAN GO TO FREE AND LOW-COST CLINICS.
Rx
ARE YOU SERIOUS?
TIONS FILLED
RESTROOMS
SURE.
THAT'S WHY THEY EXIST: FOR PEOPLE LIKE YOU! YOU CAN SEARCH FOR THE CLOSEST ONES ONLINE.*
POP
*FINDAHEALTHCENTER.HRSA.GOV

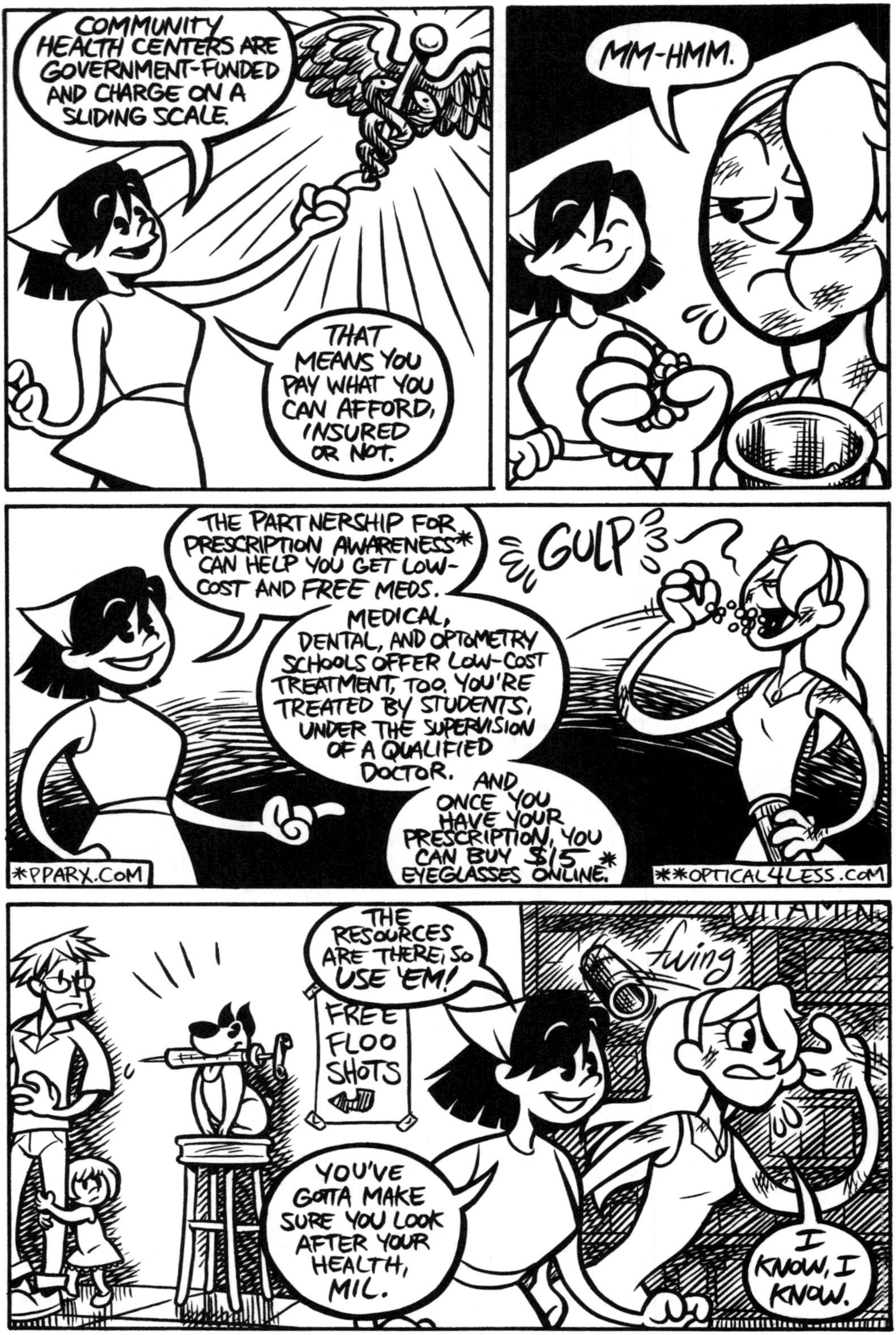
COMMUNITY HEALTH CENTERS ARE GOVERNMENT-FUNDED AND CHARGE ON A SLIDING SCALE.
THAT MEANS YOU PAY WHAT YOU CAN AFFORD, INSURED OR NOT.
MM-HMM.
THE PARTNERSHIP FOR PRESCRIPTION AWARENESS* CAN HELP YOU GET LOW-COST AND FREE MEDS.
GULP
MEDICAL, DENTAL, AND OPTOMETRY SCHOOLS OFFER LOW-COST TREATMENT, TOO. YOU'RE TREATED BY STUDENTS, UNDER THE SUPERVISION OF A QUALIFIED DOCTOR.
AND ONCE YOU HAVE YOUR PRESCRIPTION, YOU CAN BUY $15** EYEGLASSES ONLINE.
*PPARX.COM
**OPTICAL4LESS.COM
THE RESOURCES ARE THERE, SO USE 'EM!
VITAMIN
twing
FREE FLOO SHOTS
YOU'VE GOTTA MAKE SURE YOU LOOK AFTER YOUR HEALTH, MIL.
I KNOW, I KNOW.

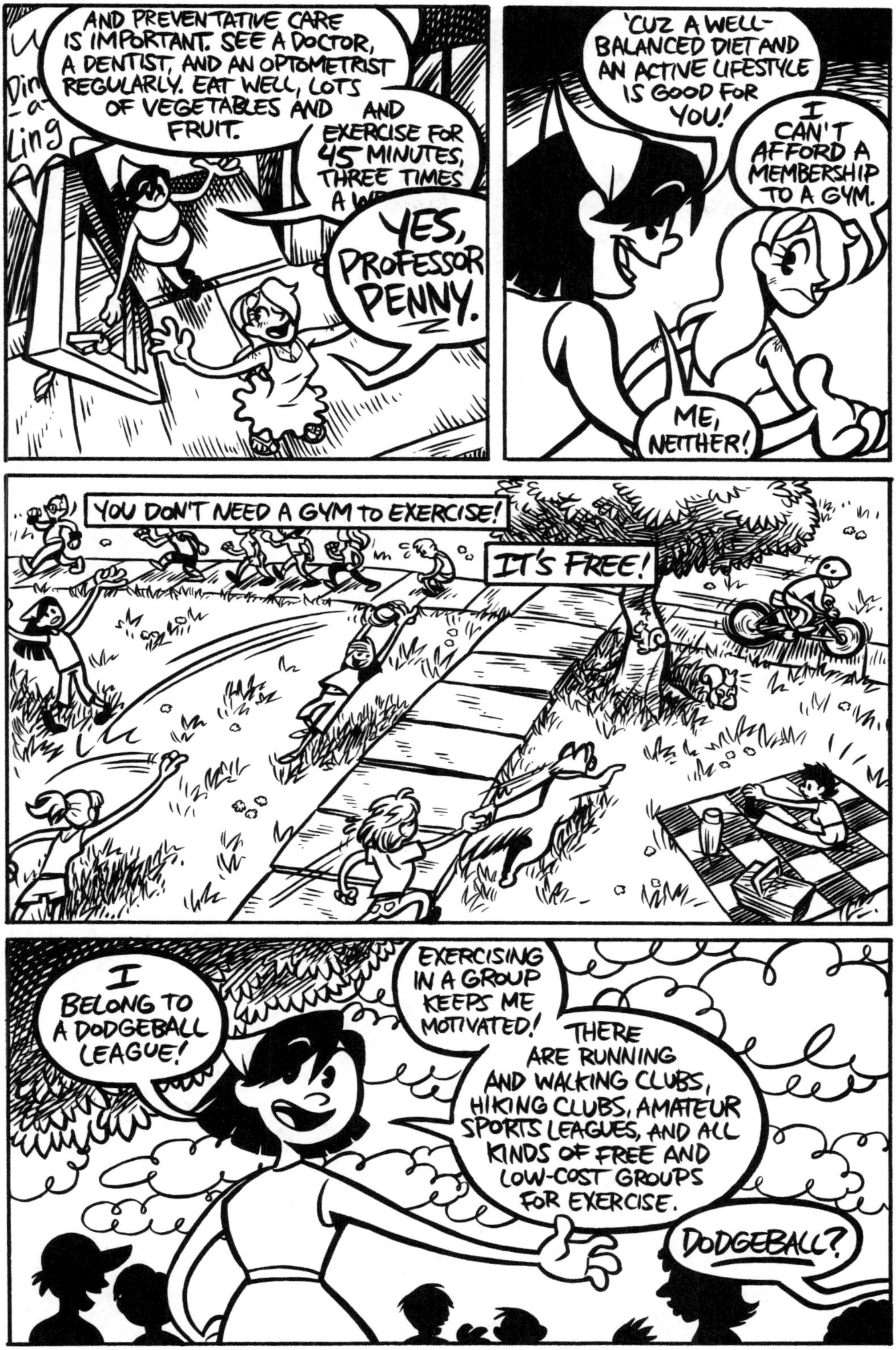
Ding-a-Ling
AND PREVENTATIVE CARE IS IMPORTANT. SEE A DOCTOR, A DENTIST, AND AN OPTOMETRIST REGULARLY. EAT WELL, LOTS OF VEGETABLES AND FRUIT.
AND EXERCISE FOR 45 MINUTES, THREE TIMES A W
YES, PROFESSOR PENNY.
'CUZ A WELL-BALANCED DIET AND AN ACTIVE LIFESTYLE IS GOOD FOR YOU!
I CAN'T AFFORD A MEMBERSHIP TO A GYM.
ME, NEITHER!
YOU DON'T NEED A GYM TO EXERCISE!
IT'S FREE!
I BELONG TO A DODGEBALL LEAGUE!
EXERCISING IN A GROUP KEEPS ME MOTIVATED!
THERE ARE RUNNING AND WALKING CLUBS, HIKING CLUBS, AMATEUR SPORTS LEAGUES, AND ALL KINDS OF FREE AND LOW-COST GROUPS FOR EXERCISE.
DODGEBALL?

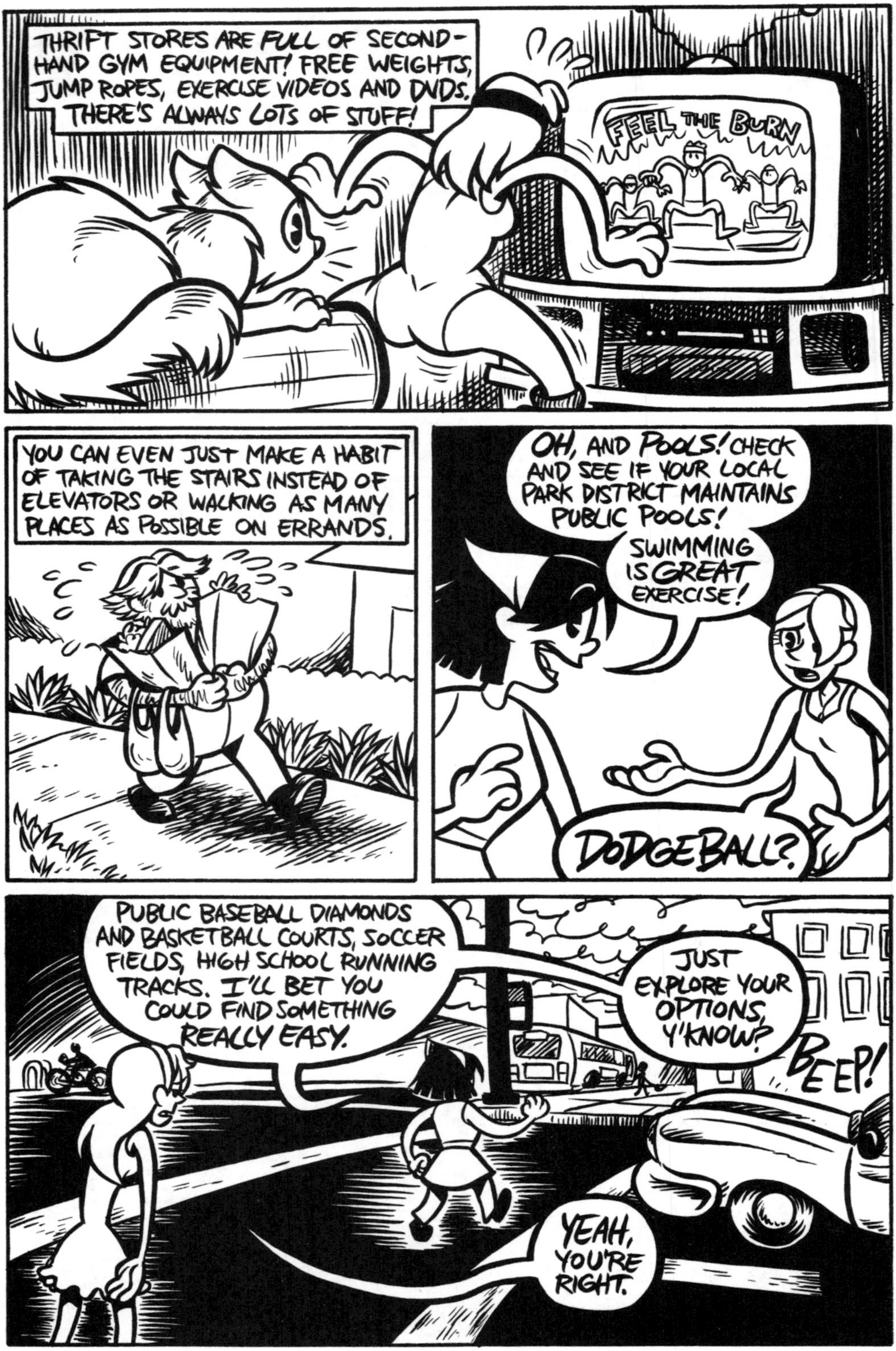
THRIFT STORES ARE FULL OF SECOND-HAND GYM EQUIPMENT! FREE WEIGHTS, JUMP ROPES, EXERCISE VIDEOS AND DVDS. THERE'S ALWAYS LOTS OF STUFF!
FEEL THE BURN
YOU CAN EVEN JUST MAKE A HABIT OF TAKING THE STAIRS INSTEAD OF ELEVATORS OR WALKING AS MANY PLACES AS POSSIBLE ON ERRANDS.
OH, AND POOLS! CHECK AND SEE IF YOUR LOCAL PARK DISTRICT MAINTAINS PUBLIC POOLS!
SWIMMING IS GREAT EXERCISE!
DODGEBALL?
PUBLIC BASEBALL DIAMONDS AND BASKETBALL COURTS, SOCCER FIELDS, HIGH SCHOOL RUNNING TRACKS. I'LL BET YOU COULD FIND SOMETHING REALLY EASY.
JUST EXPLORE YOUR OPTIONS, Y'KNOW?
BEEP!
YEAH, YOU'RE RIGHT.

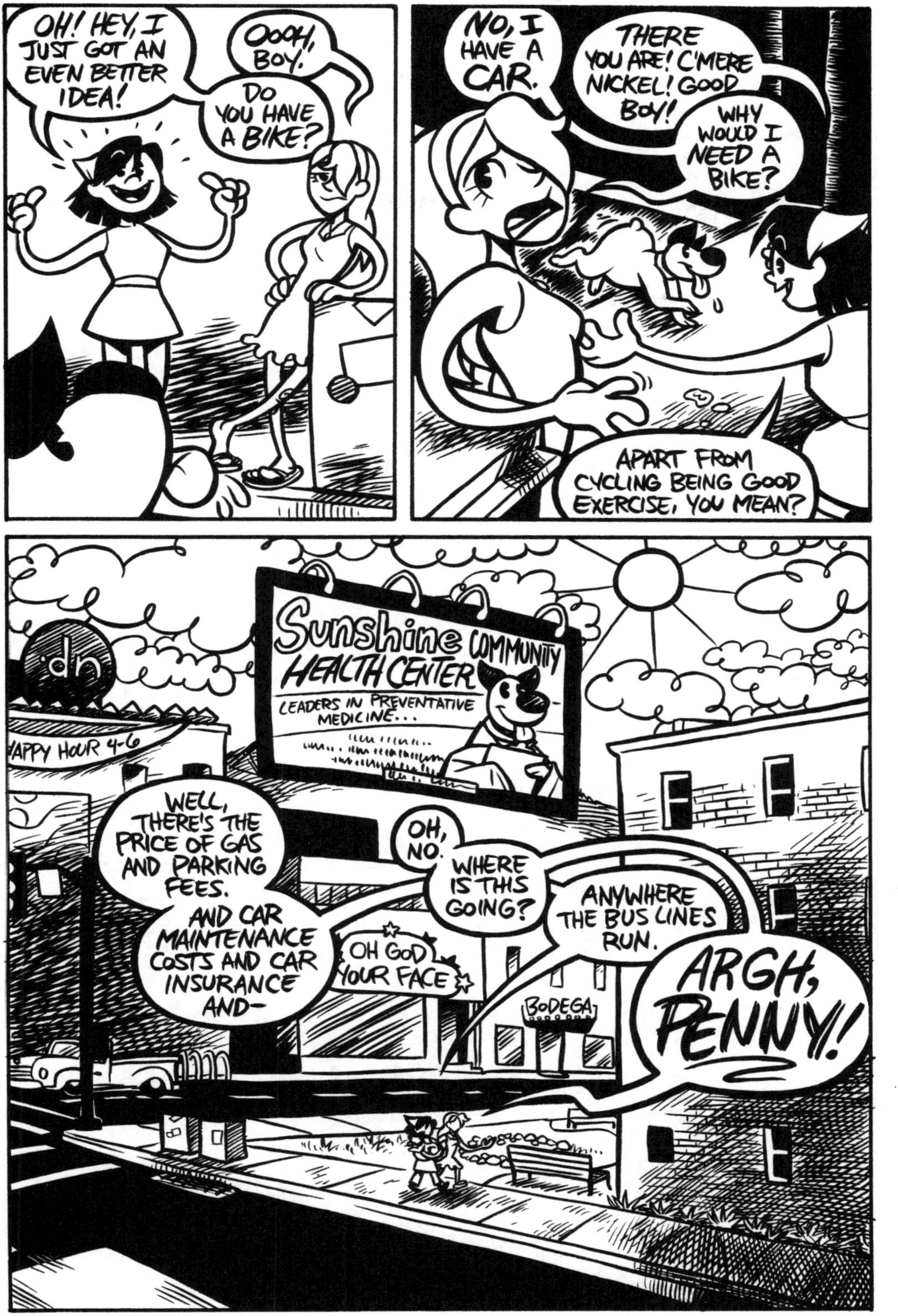
OH! HEY, I JUST GOT AN EVEN BETTER IDEA!
OOOH, BOY.
DO YOU HAVE A BIKE?
NO, I HAVE A CAR.
THERE YOU ARE! C'MERE NICKEL! GOOD BOY!
WHY WOULD I NEED A BIKE?
APART FROM CYCLING BEING GOOD EXERCISE, YOU MEAN?
Sunshine COMMUNITY HEALTH CENTER
LEADERS IN PREVENTATIVE MEDICINE...
HAPPY HOUR 4-6
WELL, THERE'S THE PRICE OF GAS AND PARKING FEES.
AND CAR MAINTENANCE COSTS AND CAR INSURANCE AND-
OH GOD YOUR FACE
OH, NO.
WHERE IS THIS GOING?
ANYWHERE THE BUS LINES RUN.
ARGH, PENNY!
BODEGA

Chapter Six

Transportation

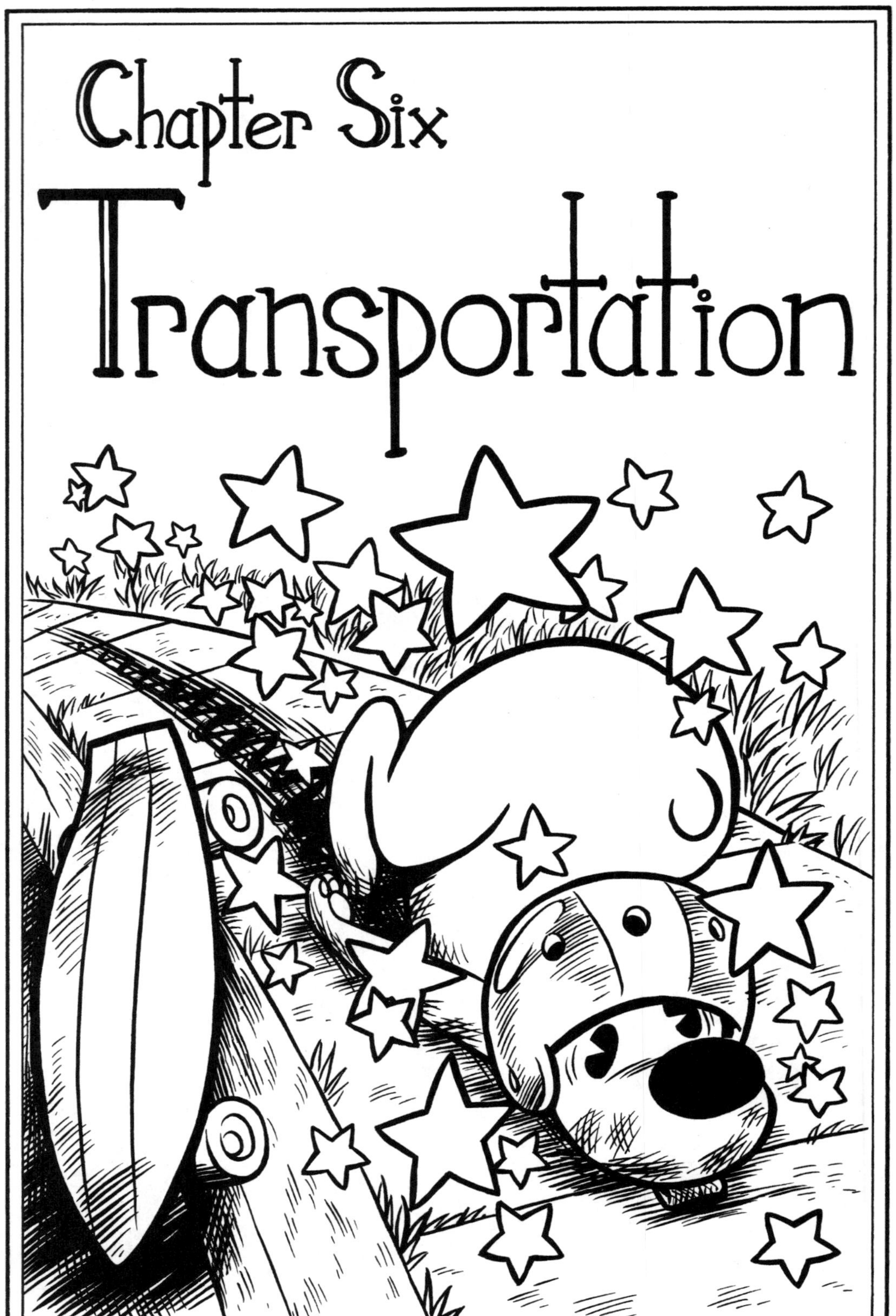

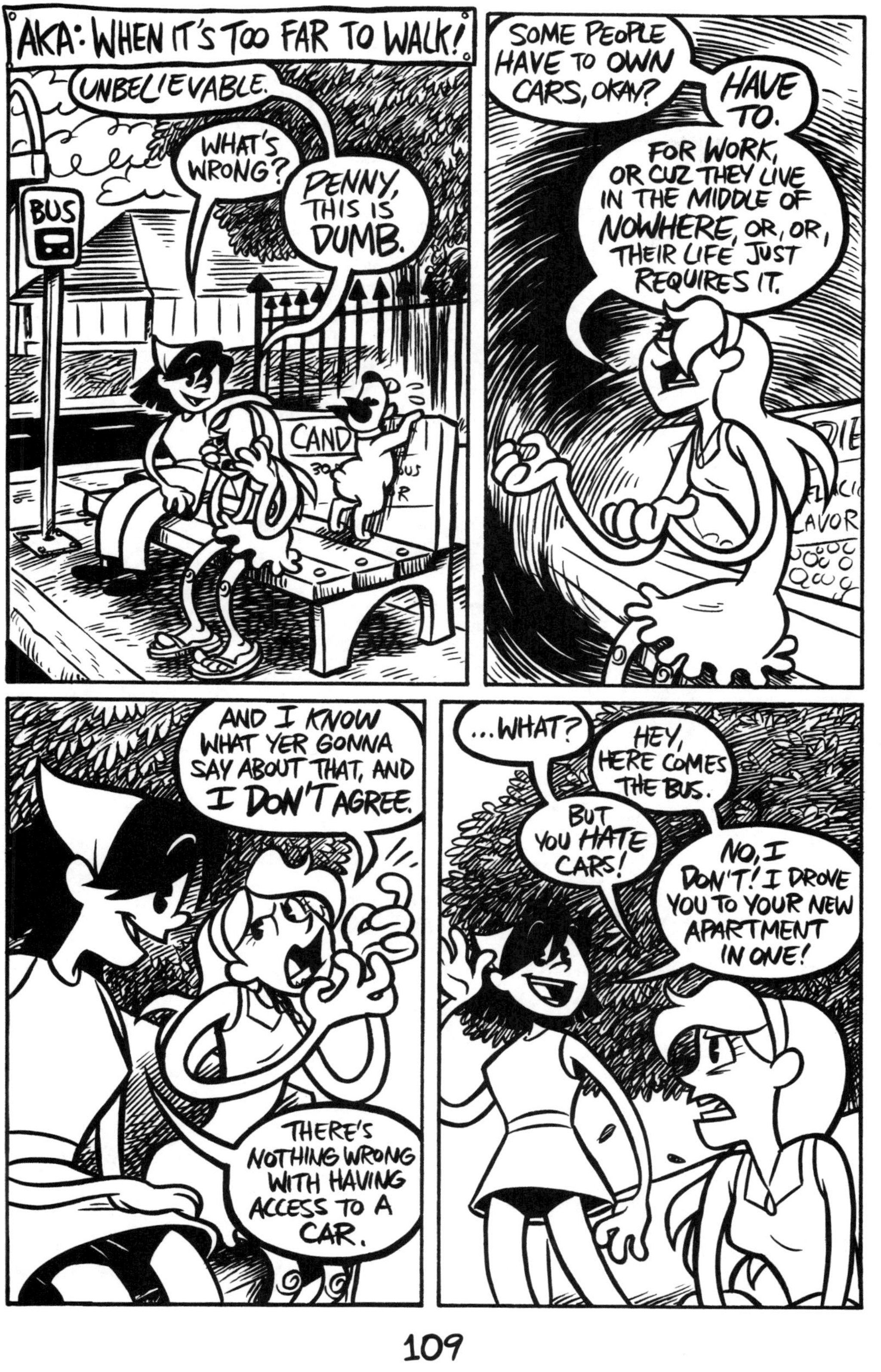
AKA: WHEN IT'S TOO FAR TO WALK!
UNBELIEVABLE.
WHAT'S WRONG?
PENNY, THIS IS DUMB.
CAND
SOME PEOPLE HAVE TO OWN CARS, OKAY?
HAVE TO.
FOR WORK, OR CUZ THEY LIVE IN THE MIDDLE OF NOWHERE, OR, OR, THEIR LIFE JUST REQUIRES IT.
LAVOR
AND I KNOW WHAT YER GONNA SAY ABOUT THAT, AND I DON'T AGREE.
THERE'S NOTHING WRONG WITH HAVING ACCESS TO A CAR.
...WHAT?
HEY, HERE COMES THE BUS.
BUT YOU HATE CARS!
NO, I DON'T! I DROVE YOU TO YOUR NEW APARTMENT IN ONE!

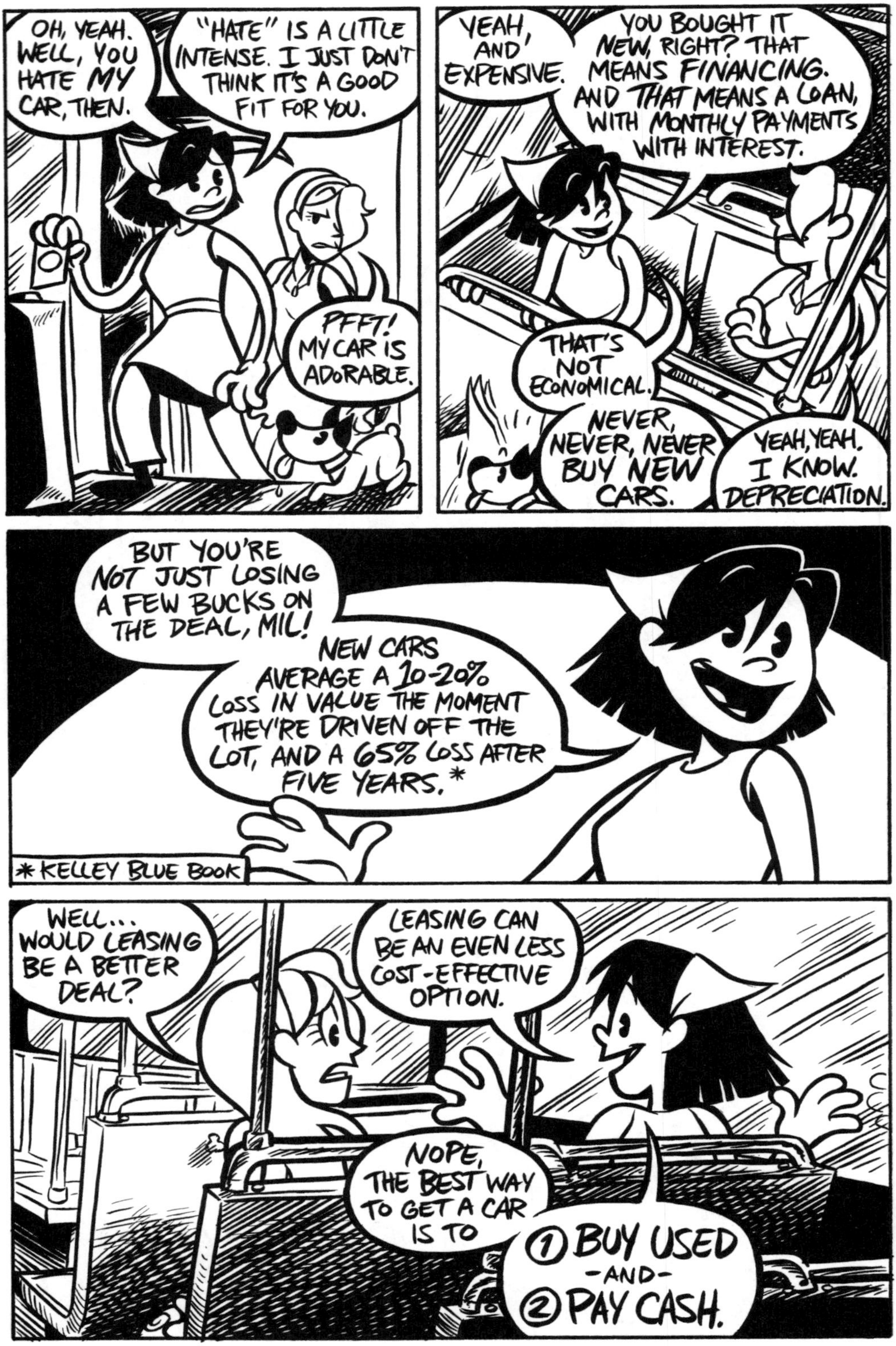
OH, YEAH. WELL, YOU HATE MY CAR, THEN.
"HATE" IS A LITTLE INTENSE. I JUST DON'T THINK IT'S A GOOD FIT FOR YOU.
PFFT! MY CAR IS ADORABLE.
YEAH, AND EXPENSIVE.
YOU BOUGHT IT NEW, RIGHT? THAT MEANS FINANCING. AND THAT MEANS A LOAN, WITH MONTHLY PAYMENTS WITH INTEREST.
THAT'S NOT ECONOMICAL.
NEVER, NEVER, NEVER BUY NEW CARS.
YEAH, YEAH. I KNOW. DEPRECIATION.
BUT YOU'RE NOT JUST LOSING A FEW BUCKS ON THE DEAL, MIL!
NEW CARS AVERAGE A 10-20% LOSS IN VALUE THE MOMENT THEY'RE DRIVEN OFF THE LOT, AND A 65% LOSS AFTER FIVE YEARS.*
* KELLEY BLUE BOOK
WELL... WOULD LEASING BE A BETTER DEAL?
LEASING CAN BE AN EVEN LESS COST-EFFECTIVE OPTION.
NOPE, THE BEST WAY TO GET A CAR IS TO
1 BUY USED -AND- 2 PAY CASH.

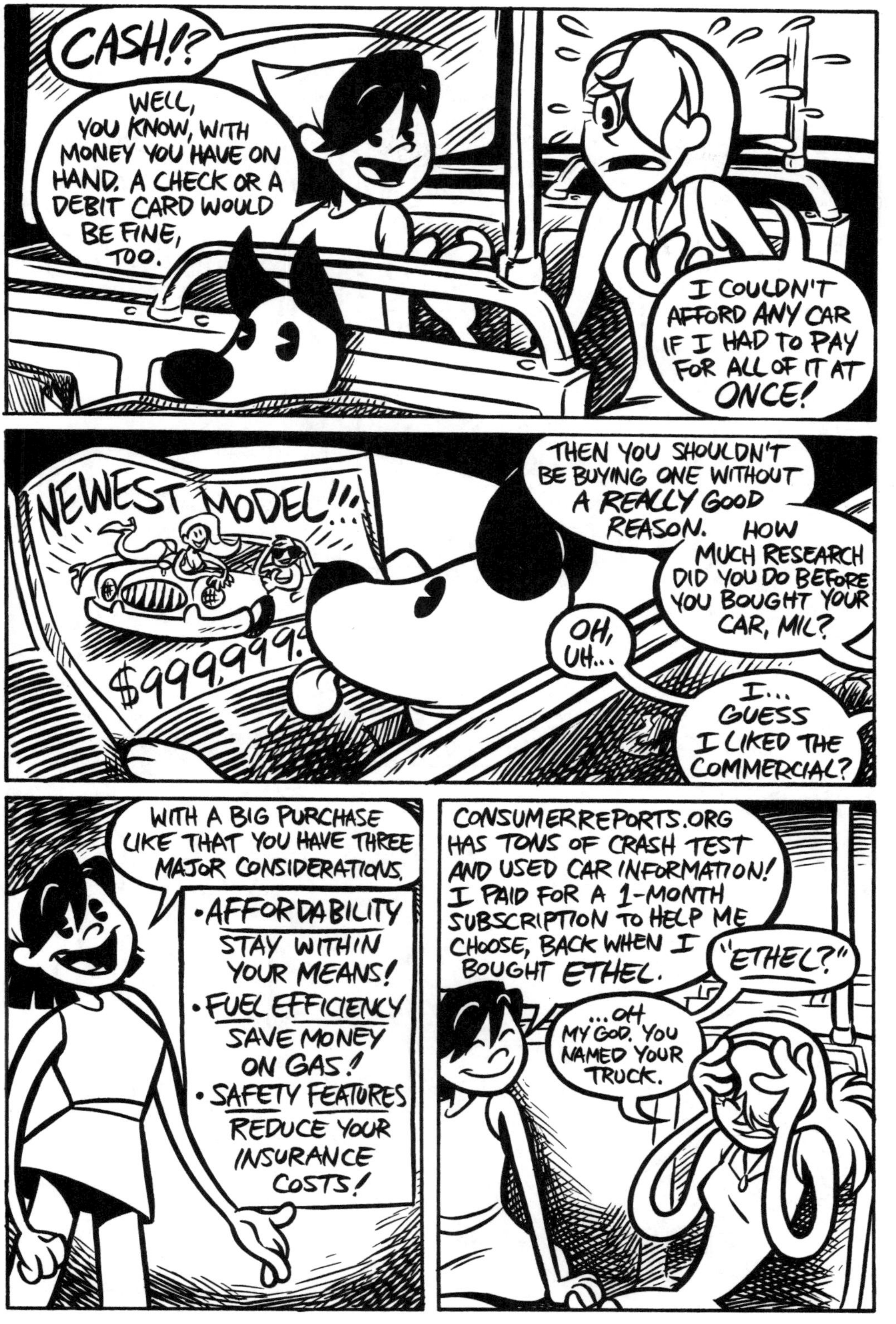
CASH!?
WELL, YOU KNOW, WITH MONEY YOU HAVE ON HAND. A CHECK OR A DEBIT CARD WOULD BE FINE, TOO.
I COULDN'T AFFORD ANY CAR IF I HAD TO PAY FOR ALL OF IT AT ONCE!
NEWEST MODEL!!!
$999,999.
THEN YOU SHOULDN'T BE BUYING ONE WITHOUT A REALLY GOOD REASON. HOW MUCH RESEARCH DID YOU DO BEFORE YOU BOUGHT YOUR CAR, MIL?
OH, UH...
I... GUESS I LIKED THE COMMERCIAL?
WITH A BIG PURCHASE LIKE THAT YOU HAVE THREE MAJOR CONSIDERATIONS.
• AFFORDABILITY STAY WITHIN YOUR MEANS!
• FUEL EFFICIENCY SAVE MONEY ON GAS!
• SAFETY FEATURES REDUCE YOUR INSURANCE COSTS!
CONSUMERREPORTS.ORG HAS TONS OF CRASH TEST AND USED CAR INFORMATION! I PAID FOR A 1-MONTH SUBSCRIPTION TO HELP ME CHOOSE, BACK WHEN I BOUGHT ETHEL.
"ETHEL?"
...OH MY GOD. YOU NAMED YOUR TRUCK.

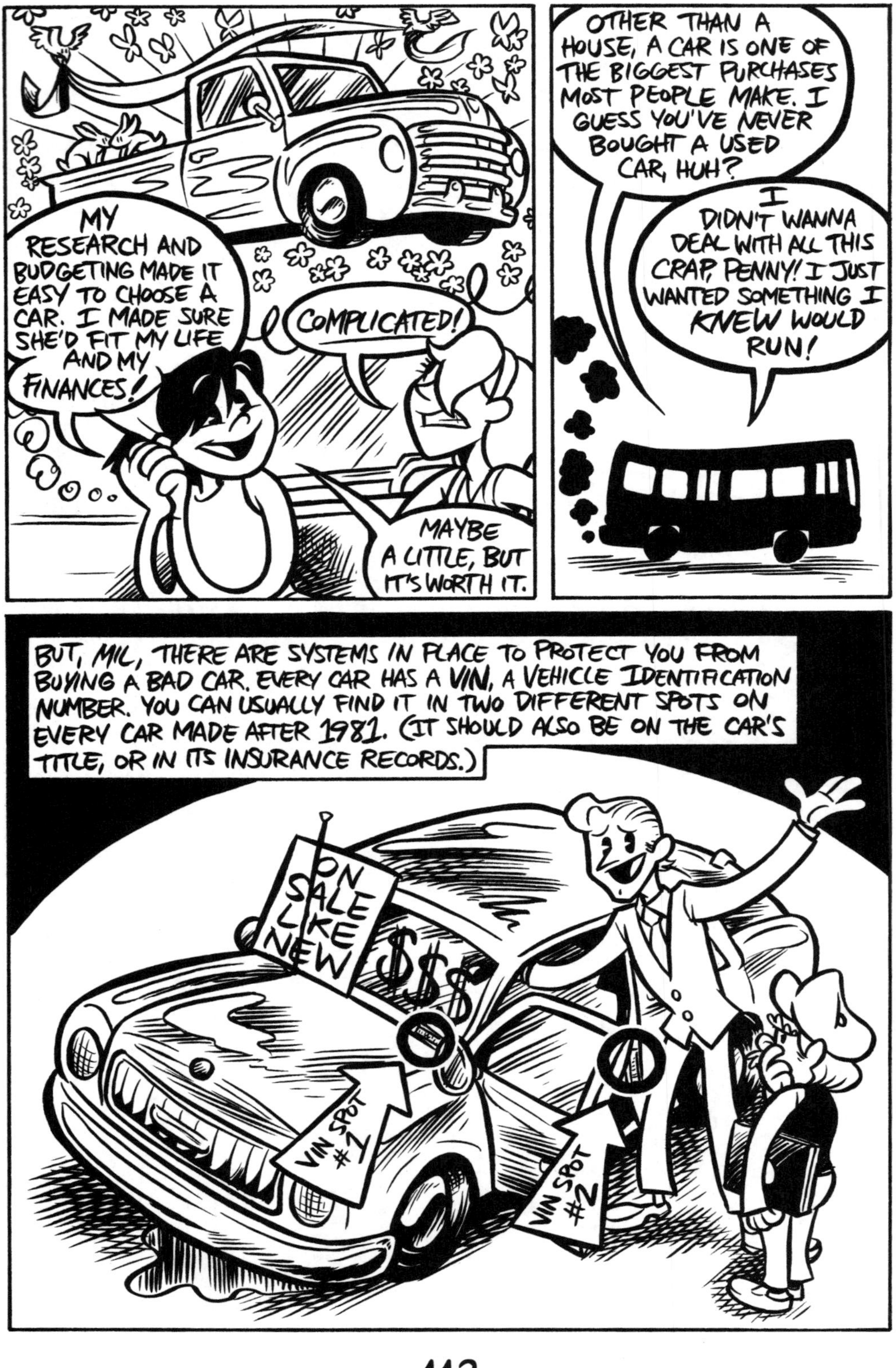
MY RESEARCH AND BUDGETING MADE IT EASY TO CHOOSE A CAR. I MADE SURE SHE'D FIT MY LIFE AND MY FINANCES!
COMPLICATED!
MAYBE A LITTLE, BUT IT'S WORTH IT.
OTHER THAN A HOUSE, A CAR IS ONE OF THE BIGGEST PURCHASES MOST PEOPLE MAKE. I GUESS YOU'VE NEVER BOUGHT A USED CAR, HUH?
I DIDN'T WANNA DEAL WITH ALL THIS CRAP, PENNY! I JUST WANTED SOMETHING I KNEW WOULD RUN!
BUT, MIL, THERE ARE SYSTEMS IN PLACE TO PROTECT YOU FROM BUYING A BAD CAR. EVERY CAR HAS A VIN, A VEHICLE IDENTIFICATION NUMBER. YOU CAN USUALLY FIND IT IN TWO DIFFERENT SPOTS ON EVERY CAR MADE AFTER 1981. (IT SHOULD ALSO BE ON THE CAR'S TITLE, OR IN ITS INSURANCE RECORDS.)
ON SALE LIKE NEW
$$$
VIN SPOT #1
VIN SPOT #2

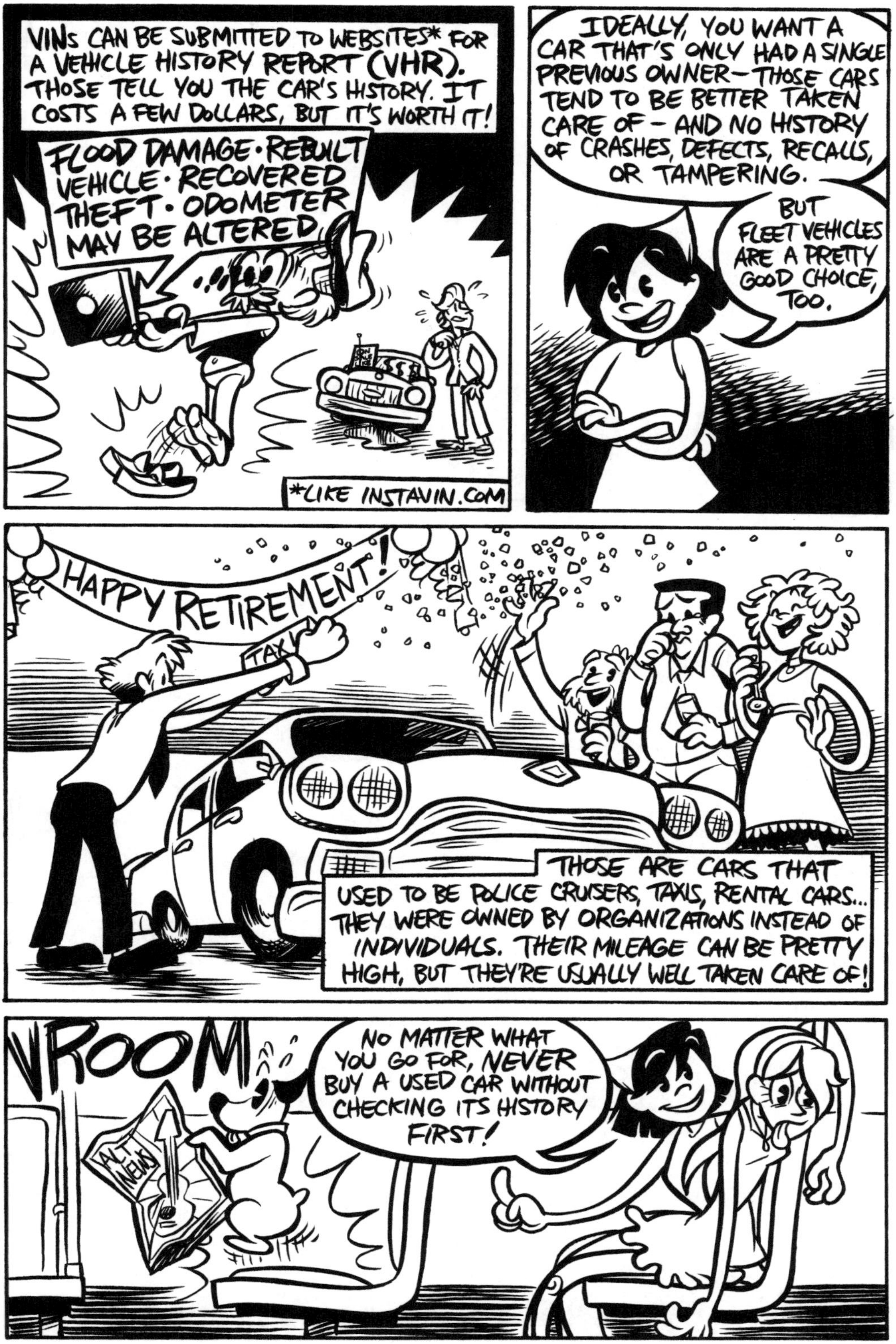
VINs CAN BE SUBMITTED TO WEBSITES* FOR A VEHICLE HISTORY REPORT (VHR). THOSE TELL YOU THE CAR'S HISTORY. IT COSTS A FEW DOLLARS, BUT IT'S WORTH IT!
FLOOD DAMAGE • REBUILT VEHICLE • RECOVERED THEFT • ODOMETER MAY BE ALTERED
*LIKE INSTAVIN.COM
IDEALLY, YOU WANT A CAR THAT'S ONLY HAD A SINGLE PREVIOUS OWNER— THOSE CARS TEND TO BE BETTER TAKEN CARE OF – AND NO HISTORY OF CRASHES, DEFECTS, RECALLS, OR TAMPERING.
BUT FLEET VEHICLES ARE A PRETTY GOOD CHOICE, TOO.
HAPPY RETIREMENT!
TAXI
THOSE ARE CARS THAT USED TO BE POLICE CRUISERS, TAXIS, RENTAL CARS... THEY WERE OWNED BY ORGANIZATIONS INSTEAD OF INDIVIDUALS. THEIR MILEAGE CAN BE PRETTY HIGH, BUT THEY'RE USUALLY WELL TAKEN CARE OF!
VROOM
ALT NEWS
NO MATTER WHAT YOU GO FOR, NEVER BUY A USED CAR WITHOUT CHECKING ITS HISTORY FIRST!

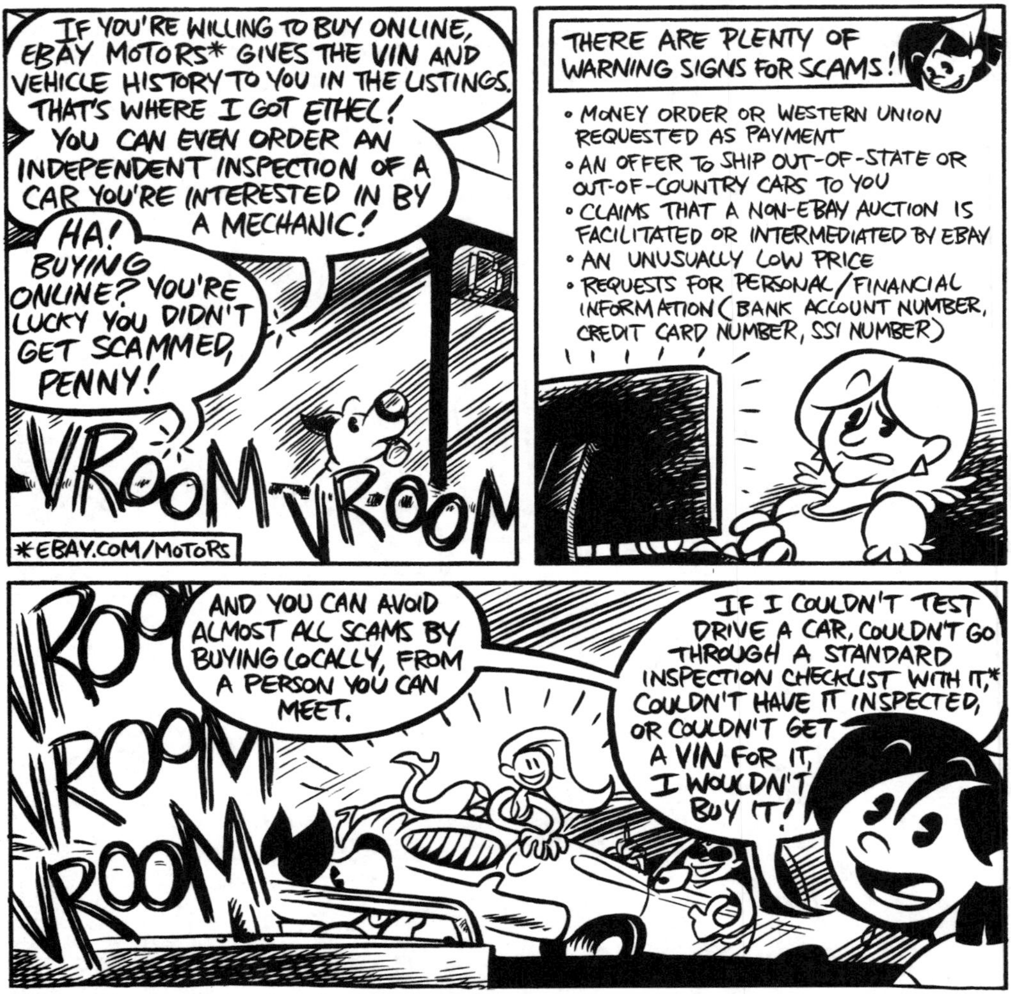
IF YOU'RE WILLING TO BUY ONLINE, EBAY MOTORS* GIVES THE VIN AND VEHICLE HISTORY TO YOU IN THE LISTINGS. THAT'S WHERE I GOT ETHEL! YOU CAN EVEN ORDER AN INDEPENDENT INSPECTION OF A CAR YOU'RE INTERESTED IN BY A MECHANIC!
HA! BUYING ONLINE? YOU'RE LUCKY YOU DIDN'T GET SCAMMED, PENNY!
VROOM VROOM
*EBAY.COM/MOTORS
THERE ARE PLENTY OF WARNING SIGNS FOR SCAMS!
• MONEY ORDER OR WESTERN UNION REQUESTED AS PAYMENT
• AN OFFER TO SHIP OUT-OF-STATE OR OUT-OF-COUNTRY CARS TO YOU
• CLAIMS THAT A NON-EBAY AUCTION IS FACILITATED OR INTERMEDIATED BY EBAY
• AN UNUSUALLY LOW PRICE
• REQUESTS FOR PERSONAL/FINANCIAL INFORMATION (BANK ACCOUNT NUMBER, CREDIT CARD NUMBER, SSI NUMBER)
VROOM VROOM VROOM
AND YOU CAN AVOID ALMOST ALL SCAMS BY BUYING LOCALLY, FROM A PERSON YOU CAN MEET.
IF I COULDN'T TEST DRIVE A CAR, COULDN'T GO THROUGH A STANDARD INSPECTION CHECKLIST WITH IT,* COULDN'T HAVE IT INSPECTED, OR COULDN'T GET A VIN FOR IT, I WOULDN'T BUY IT!

*POPULARMECHANICS.COM/CARS/HOW-TO/a7280/how-to-buy-a-used-car-without-getting-burned

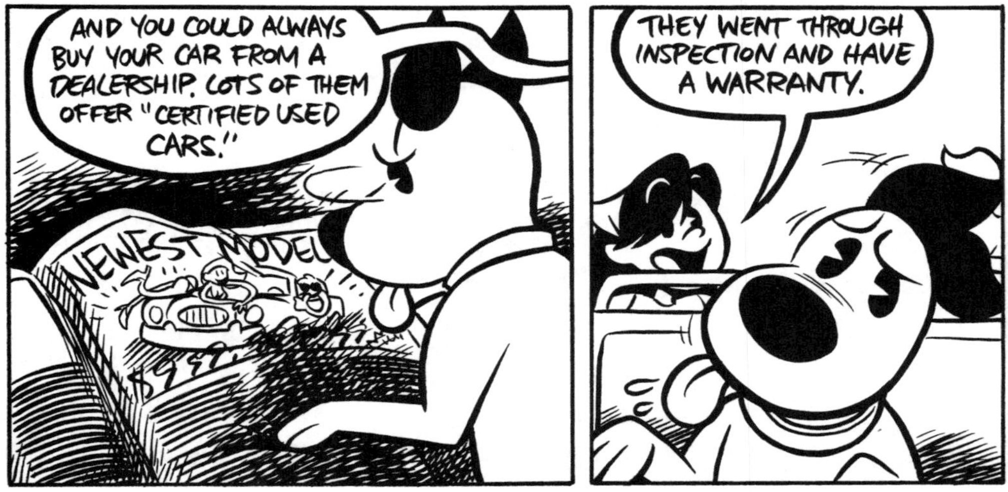
AND YOU COULD ALWAYS BUY YOUR CAR FROM A DEALERSHIP. LOTS OF THEM OFFER "CERTIFIED USED CARS."
NEWEST MODEL
THEY WENT THROUGH INSPECTION AND HAVE A WARRANTY.

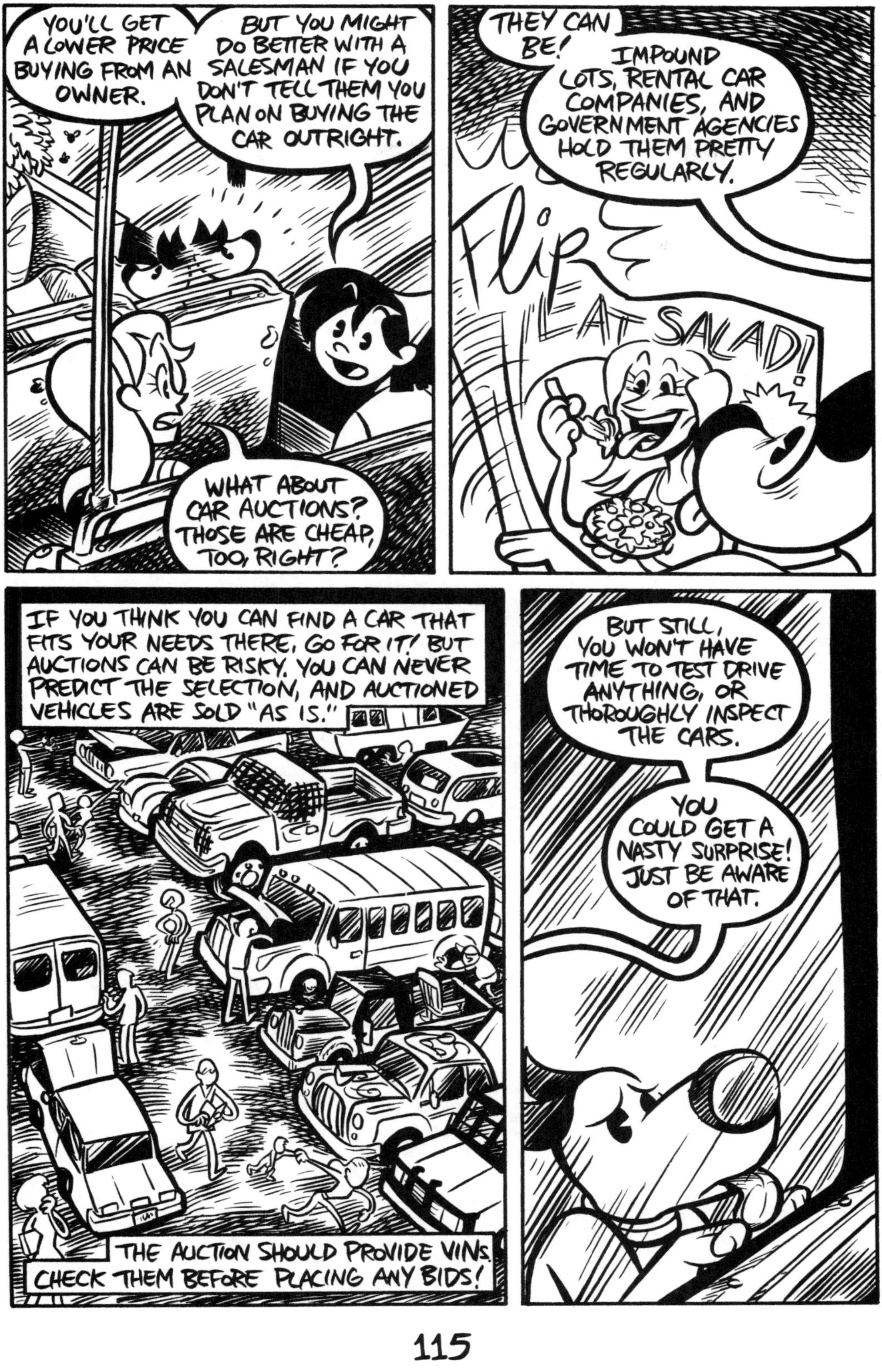

YOU'LL GET A LOWER PRICE BUYING FROM AN OWNER.
BUT YOU MIGHT DO BETTER WITH A SALESMAN IF YOU DON'T TELL THEM YOU PLAN ON BUYING THE CAR OUTRIGHT.
WHAT ABOUT CAR AUCTIONS? THOSE ARE CHEAP, TOO, RIGHT?
THEY CAN BE!
IMPOUND LOTS, RENTAL CAR COMPANIES, AND GOVERNMENT AGENCIES HOLD THEM PRETTY REGULARLY.
Flip
EAT SALAD!
IF YOU THINK YOU CAN FIND A CAR THAT FITS YOUR NEEDS THERE, GO FOR IT! BUT AUCTIONS CAN BE RISKY. YOU CAN NEVER PREDICT THE SELECTION, AND AUCTIONED VEHICLES ARE SOLD "AS IS."
THE AUCTION SHOULD PROVIDE VINs. CHECK THEM BEFORE PLACING ANY BIDS!
BUT STILL, YOU WON'T HAVE TIME TO TEST DRIVE ANYTHING, OR THOROUGHLY INSPECT THE CARS.
YOU COULD GET A NASTY SURPRISE! JUST BE AWARE OF THAT.

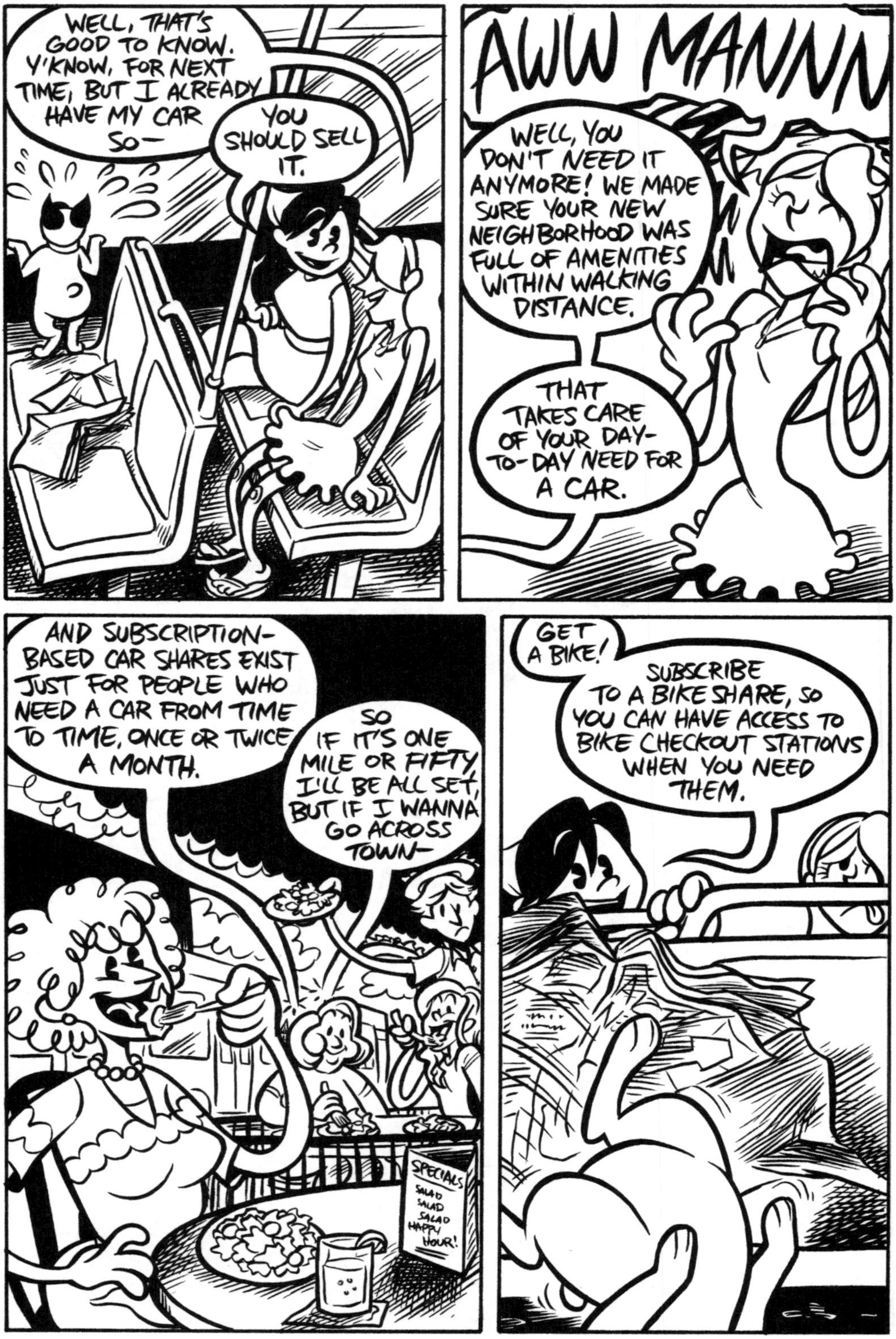
WELL, THAT'S GOOD TO KNOW. Y'KNOW, FOR NEXT TIME, BUT I ALREADY HAVE MY CAR SO—
YOU SHOULD SELL IT.
AWW MANNN
WELL, YOU DON'T NEED IT ANYMORE! WE MADE SURE YOUR NEW NEIGHBORHOOD WAS FULL OF AMENITIES WITHIN WALKING DISTANCE.
THAT TAKES CARE OF YOUR DAY-TO-DAY NEED FOR A CAR.
AND SUBSCRIPTION-BASED CAR SHARES EXIST JUST FOR PEOPLE WHO NEED A CAR FROM TIME TO TIME, ONCE OR TWICE A MONTH.
SO IF IT'S ONE MILE OR FIFTY, I'LL BE ALL SET, BUT IF I WANNA GO ACROSS TOWN—
SPECIALS
SALAD
SALAD
SALAD
HAPPY HOUR!
GET A BIKE!
SUBSCRIBE TO A BIKE SHARE, SO YOU CAN HAVE ACCESS TO BIKE CHECKOUT STATIONS WHEN YOU NEED THEM.

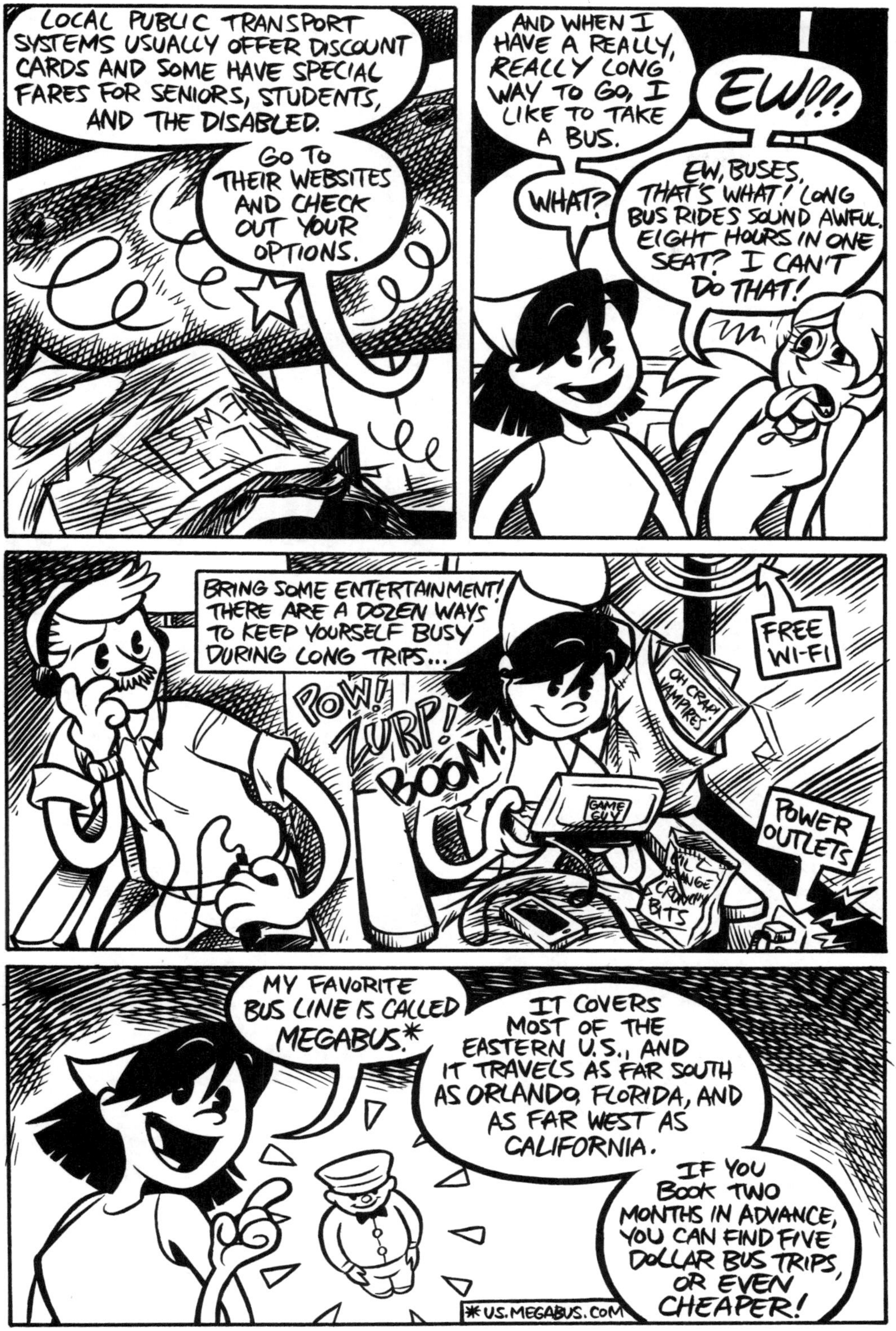
LOCAL PUBLIC TRANSPORT SYSTEMS USUALLY OFFER DISCOUNT CARDS AND SOME HAVE SPECIAL FARES FOR SENIORS, STUDENTS, AND THE DISABLED.
GO TO THEIR WEBSITES AND CHECK OUT YOUR OPTIONS.
AND WHEN I HAVE A REALLY, REALLY LONG WAY TO GO, I LIKE TO TAKE A BUS.
EW!!!
WHAT?
EW, BUSES, THAT'S WHAT! LONG BUS RIDES SOUND AWFUL. EIGHT HOURS IN ONE SEAT? I CAN'T DO THAT!
BRING SOME ENTERTAINMENT! THERE ARE A DOZEN WAYS TO KEEP YOURSELF BUSY DURING LONG TRIPS...
FREE WI-FI
OH CRAP! VAMPIRES
POW!
ZURP!
BOOM!
GAME GUY
POWER OUTLETS
ORANGE CRUNCHY BITS
MY FAVORITE BUS LINE IS CALLED MEGABUS.*
IT COVERS MOST OF THE EASTERN U.S., AND IT TRAVELS AS FAR SOUTH AS ORLANDO, FLORIDA, AND AS FAR WEST AS CALIFORNIA.
IF YOU BOOK TWO MONTHS IN ADVANCE, YOU CAN FIND FIVE DOLLAR BUS TRIPS, OR EVEN CHEAPER!
*US.MEGABUS.COM

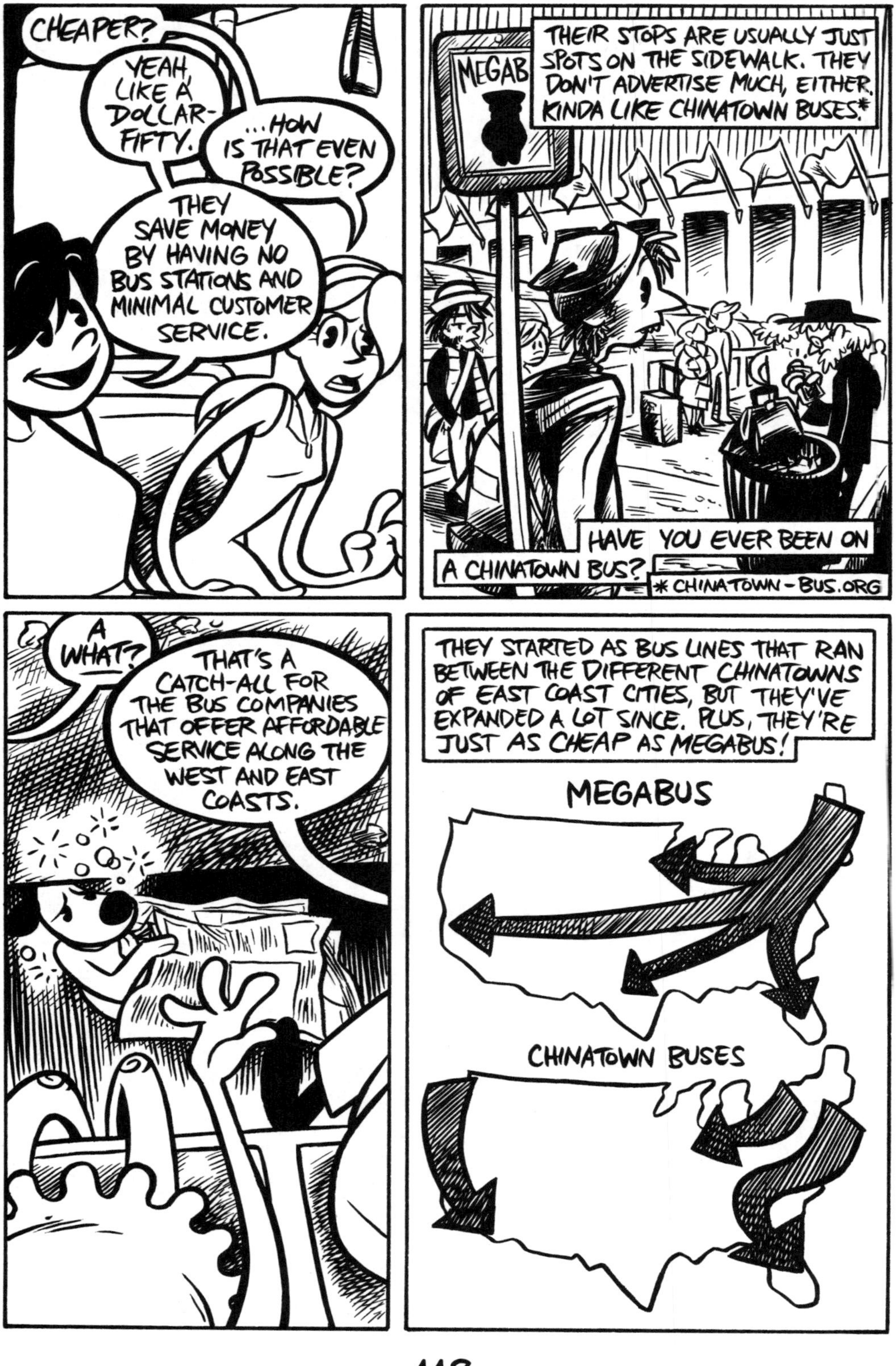
CHEAPER?
YEAH, LIKE A DOLLAR-FIFTY.
...HOW IS THAT EVEN POSSIBLE?
THEY SAVE MONEY BY HAVING NO BUS STATIONS AND MINIMAL CUSTOMER SERVICE.
MEGAB
THEIR STOPS ARE USUALLY JUST SPOTS ON THE SIDEWALK. THEY DON'T ADVERTISE MUCH, EITHER. KINDA LIKE CHINATOWN BUSES*
HAVE YOU EVER BEEN ON A CHINATOWN BUS?
* CHINATOWN-BUS.ORG
A WHAT?
THAT'S A CATCH-ALL FOR THE BUS COMPANIES THAT OFFER AFFORDABLE SERVICE ALONG THE WEST AND EAST COASTS.
THEY STARTED AS BUS LINES THAT RAN BETWEEN THE DIFFERENT CHINATOWNS OF EAST COAST CITIES, BUT THEY'VE EXPANDED A LOT SINCE. PLUS, THEY'RE JUST AS CHEAP AS MEGABUS!
MEGABUS
CHINATOWN BUSES

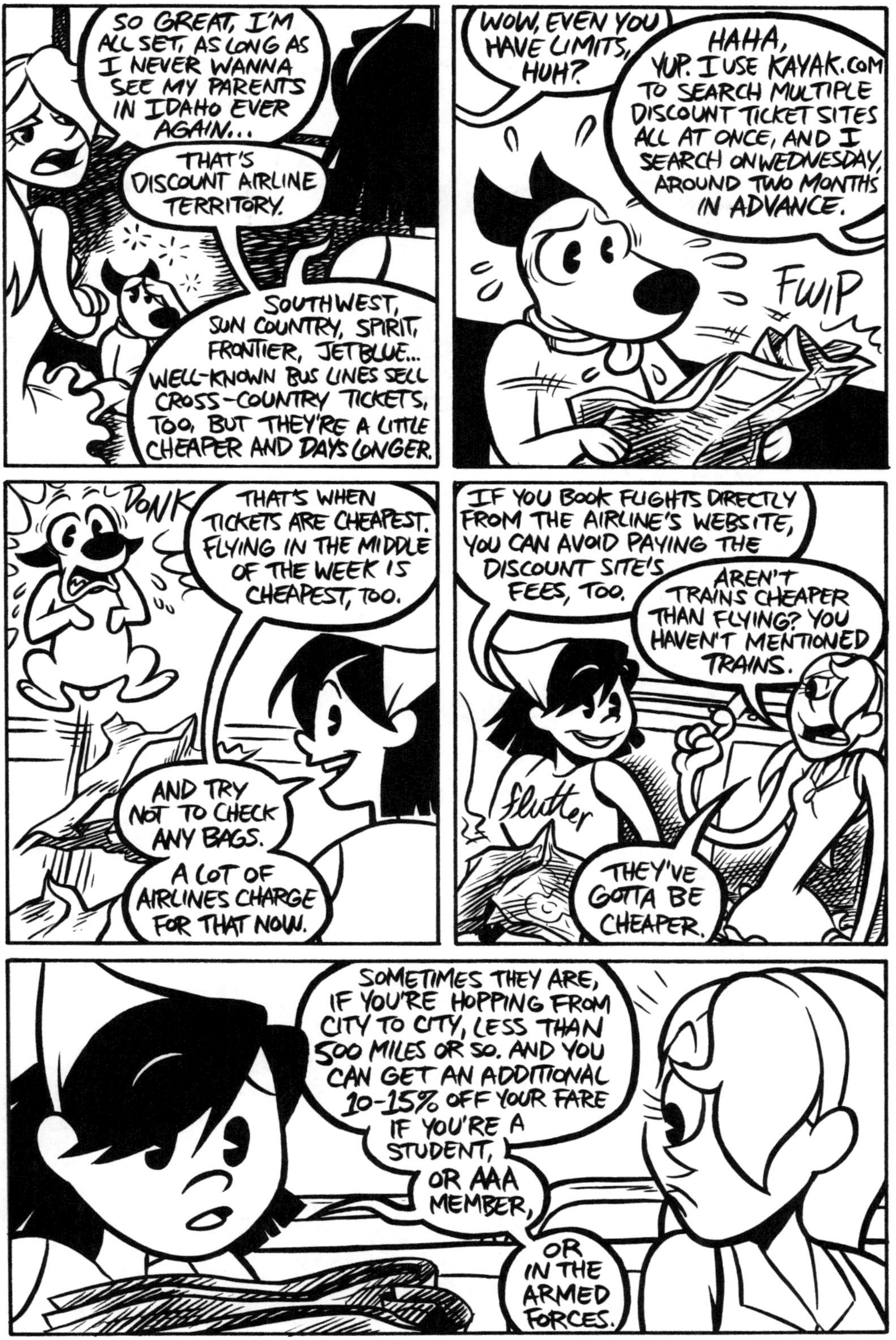

SO GREAT, I'M ALL SET, AS LONG AS I NEVER WANNA SEE MY PARENTS IN IDAHO EVER AGAIN...
THAT'S DISCOUNT AIRLINE TERRITORY.
SOUTHWEST, SUN COUNTRY, SPIRIT, FRONTIER, JETBLUE... WELL-KNOWN BUS LINES SELL CROSS-COUNTRY TICKETS, TOO, BUT THEY'RE A LITTLE CHEAPER AND DAYS LONGER.
WOW, EVEN YOU HAVE LIMITS, HUH?
HAHA, YUP. I USE KAYAK.COM TO SEARCH MULTIPLE DISCOUNT TICKET SITES ALL AT ONCE, AND I SEARCH ON WEDNESDAY, AROUND TWO MONTHS IN ADVANCE.
FWIP
DONK
THAT'S WHEN TICKETS ARE CHEAPEST. FLYING IN THE MIDDLE OF THE WEEK IS CHEAPEST, TOO.
AND TRY NOT TO CHECK ANY BAGS.
A LOT OF AIRLINES CHARGE FOR THAT NOW.
IF YOU BOOK FLIGHTS DIRECTLY FROM THE AIRLINE'S WEBSITE, YOU CAN AVOID PAYING THE DISCOUNT SITE'S FEES, TOO.
AREN'T TRAINS CHEAPER THAN FLYING? YOU HAVEN'T MENTIONED TRAINS.
flutter
THEY'VE GOTTA BE CHEAPER.
SOMETIMES THEY ARE, IF YOU'RE HOPPING FROM CITY TO CITY, LESS THAN 500 MILES OR SO. AND YOU CAN GET AN ADDITIONAL 10-15% OFF YOUR FARE IF YOU'RE A STUDENT,
OR AAA MEMBER,
OR IN THE ARMED FORCES.

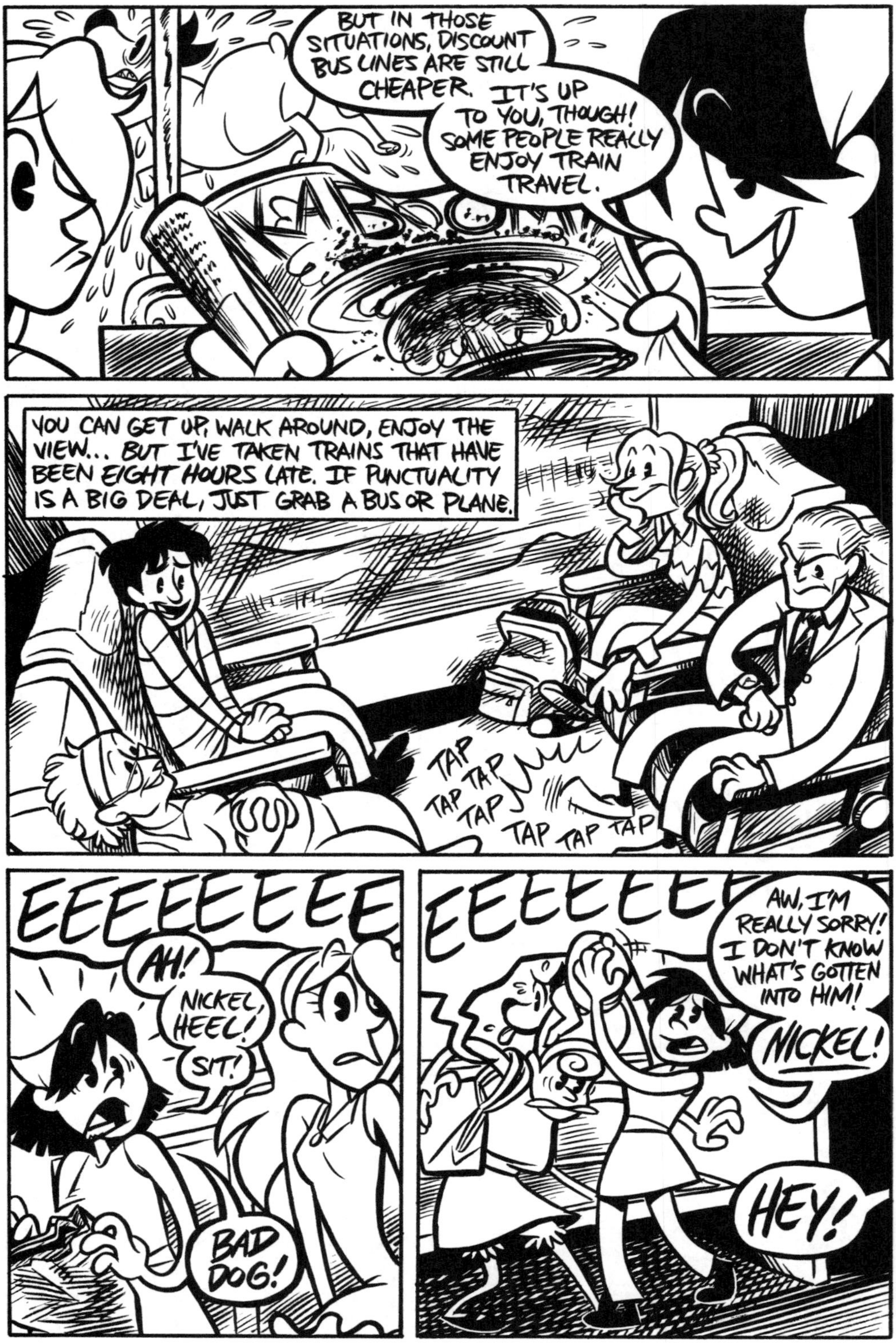
BUT IN THOSE SITUATIONS, DISCOUNT BUS LINES ARE STILL CHEAPER.
IT'S UP TO YOU, THOUGH! SOME PEOPLE REALLY ENJOY TRAIN TRAVEL.
KABOOM
YOU CAN GET UP, WALK AROUND, ENJOY THE VIEW... BUT I'VE TAKEN TRAINS THAT HAVE BEEN EIGHT HOURS LATE. IF PUNCTUALITY IS A BIG DEAL, JUST GRAB A BUS OR PLANE.
TAP TAP TAP TAP TAP TAP TAP
EEEEEEEEE
AH!
NICKEL, HEEL!
SIT!
BAD DOG!
EEEEEEE
AW, I'M REALLY SORRY! I DON'T KNOW WHAT'S GOTTEN INTO HIM!
NICKEL!
HEY!

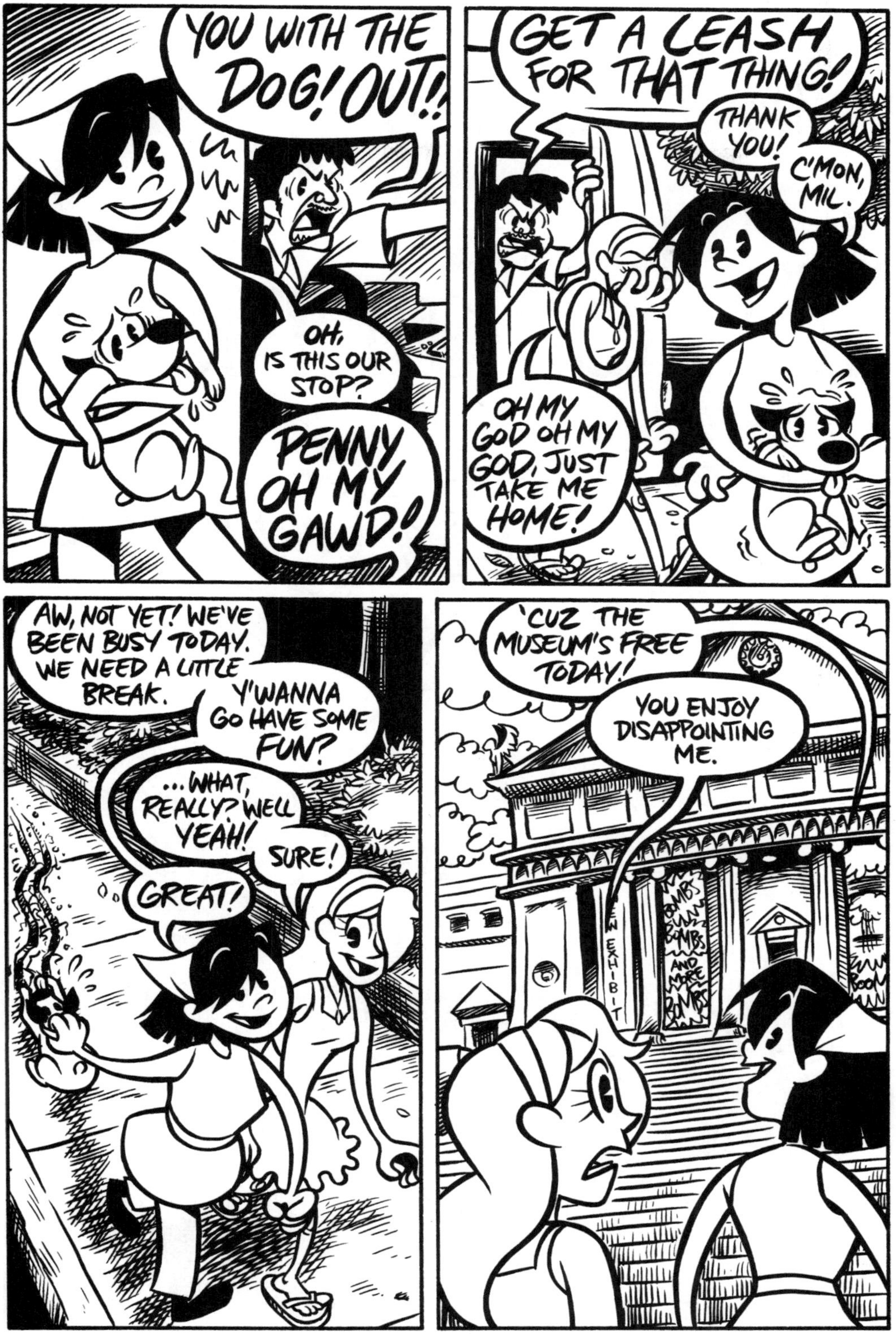
YOU WITH THE DOG! OUT!!
OH, IS THIS OUR STOP?
PENNY OH MY GAWD!
GET A LEASH FOR THAT THING!
THANK YOU!
C'MON, MIL.
OH MY GOD OH MY GOD, JUST TAKE ME HOME!
AW, NOT YET! WE'VE BEEN BUSY TODAY. WE NEED A LITTLE BREAK.
Y'WANNA GO HAVE SOME FUN?
...WHAT, REALLY? WELL YEAH!
SURE!
GREAT!
'CUZ THE MUSEUM'S FREE TODAY!
YOU ENJOY DISAPPOINTING ME.
NEW EXHIBIT
BOMBS BOMBS BOMBS AND MORE BOMBS

Chapter Seven

Entertainment

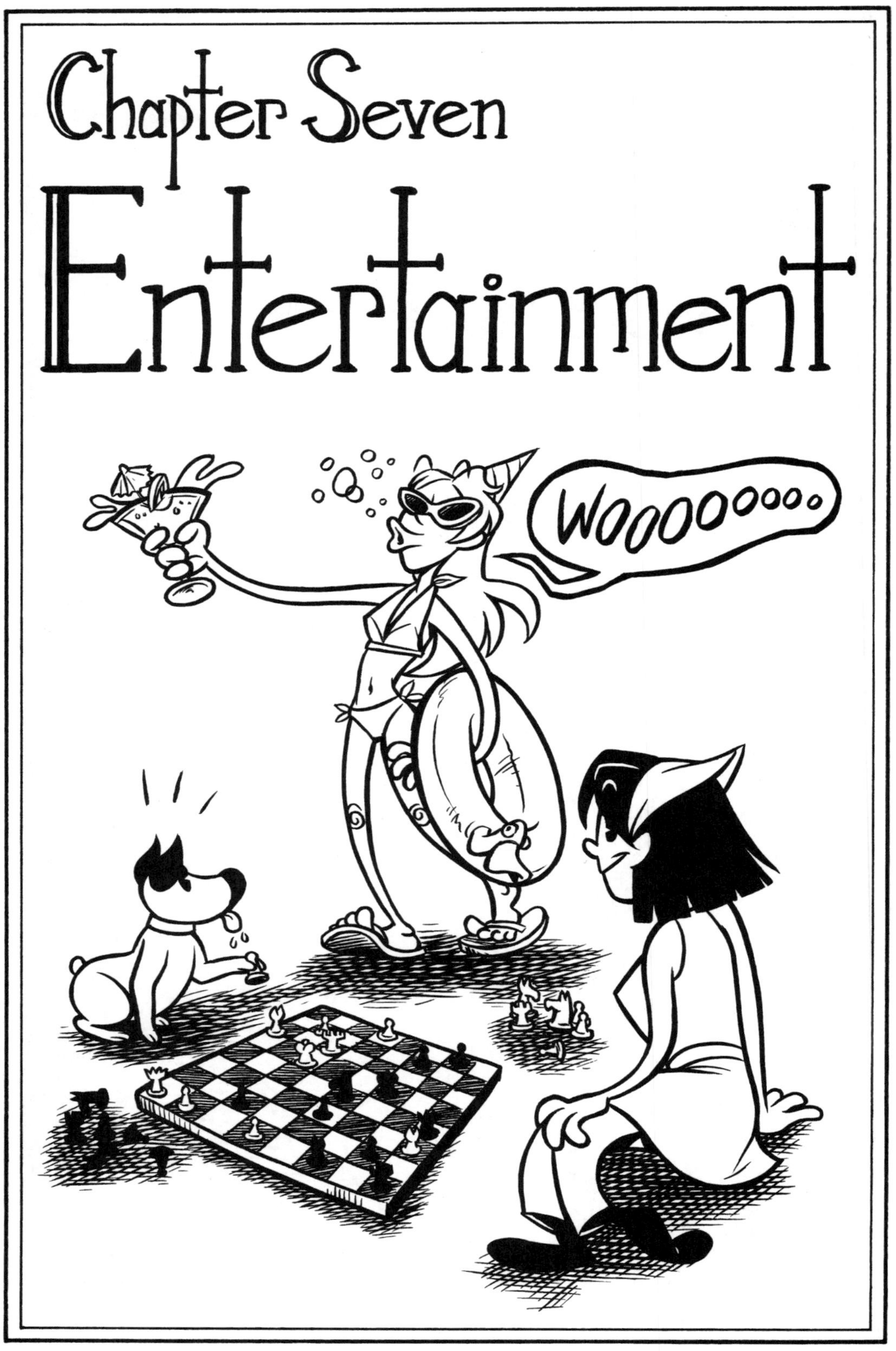
Woooooooo

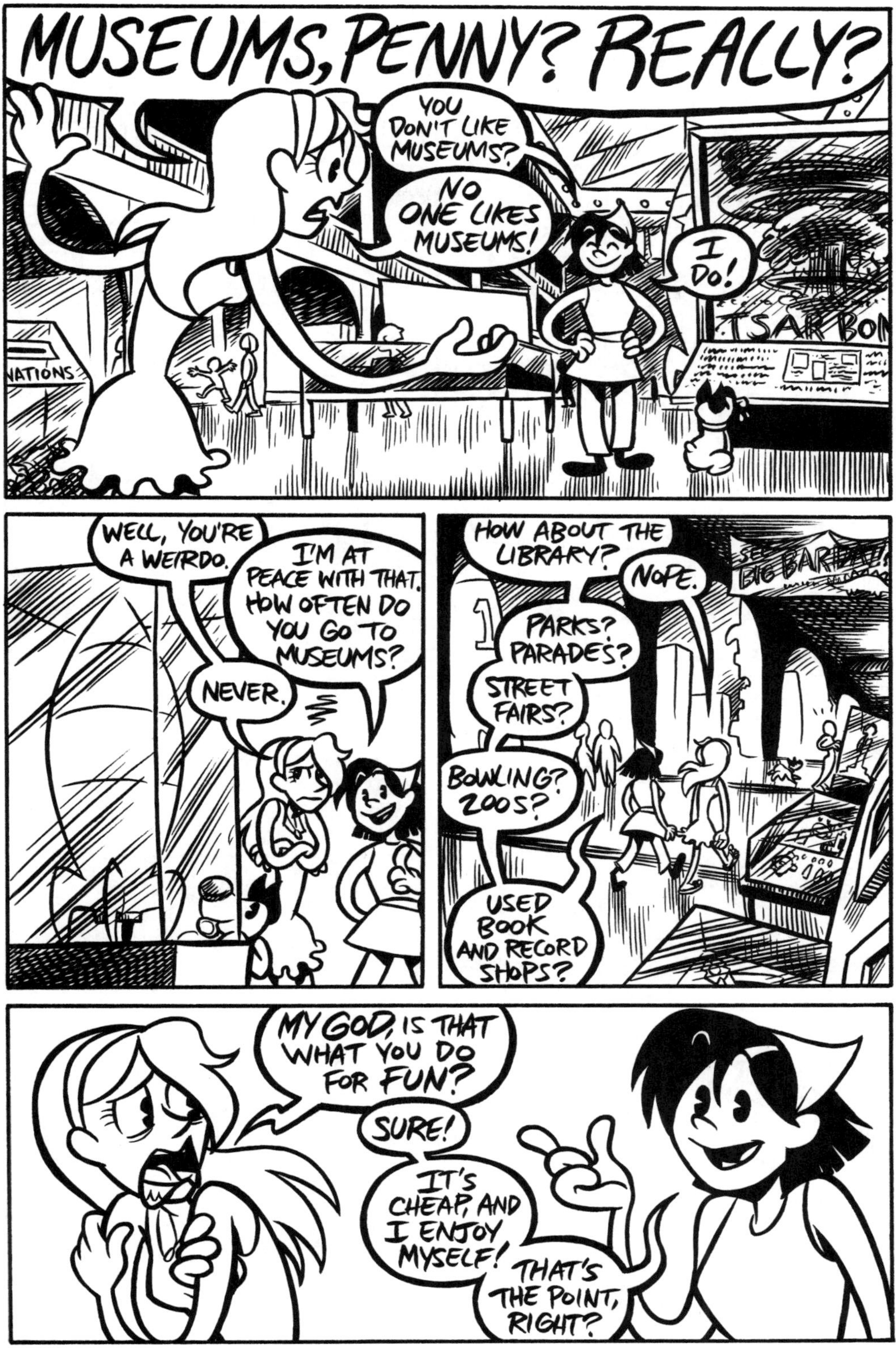
MUSEUMS, PENNY? REALLY?
YOU DON'T LIKE MUSEUMS?
NO ONE LIKES MUSEUMS!
I DO!
TSAR BOM
NATIONS
WELL, YOU'RE A WEIRDO.
I'M AT PEACE WITH THAT. HOW OFTEN DO YOU GO TO MUSEUMS?
NEVER.
HOW ABOUT THE LIBRARY?
NOPE.
PARKS? PARADES?
STREET FAIRS?
BOWLING? ZOOS?
USED BOOK AND RECORD SHOPS?
MY GOD, IS THAT WHAT YOU DO FOR FUN?
SURE!
IT'S CHEAP, AND I ENJOY MYSELF!
THAT'S THE POINT, RIGHT?

LOTS OF MUSEUMS ARE ALWAYS FREE, LIKE THE NINETEEN RUN BY THE SMITHSONIAN, BUT EVEN MORE HAVE SPECIAL FREE OR REDUCED ADMISSION DAYS. CHECK THEIR SITES FOR DETAILS, OR JUST CALL AND ASK.

MUSEUM of POINTY OBJECTS

FREE ON WEDNESDA

CHECK FOR SPECIAL ADMISSION PROGRAMS, TOO. SOME COMPANIES HAVE PARTNER-SHIPS WITH MUSEUMS, MEANING THEIR EMPLOYEES CAN GET IN FREE.

FICTION

MUSEUM of POINTY OBJECTS

FREE ADMISSION TO ALL SHARPCO EMPLOYEES!

AND MY LOCAL LIBRARY HAS MUSEUM PASSES YOU CAN CHECK OUT LIKE A BOOK! NEXT TO MUSEUMS, LIBRARIES ARE MY FAVORITE SOURCES OF ENTERTAINMENT, Y'KNOW.

TAXONOMY OF TIME TRAVELING

WHY AM I NOT SURPRISED?

I LOVE THE LIBRARY! THAT'S HOW I SEE MOST OF MY MOVIES, NOW. A LOT OF 'EM HAVE AUDIOBOOKS, TOO. ONES YOU CAN DOWNLOAD WITHOUT EVEN VISITING! AND WRITING WORK-SHOPS, AND BOOK CLUBS...

STAFF PICKS

POPULAR MUSIC

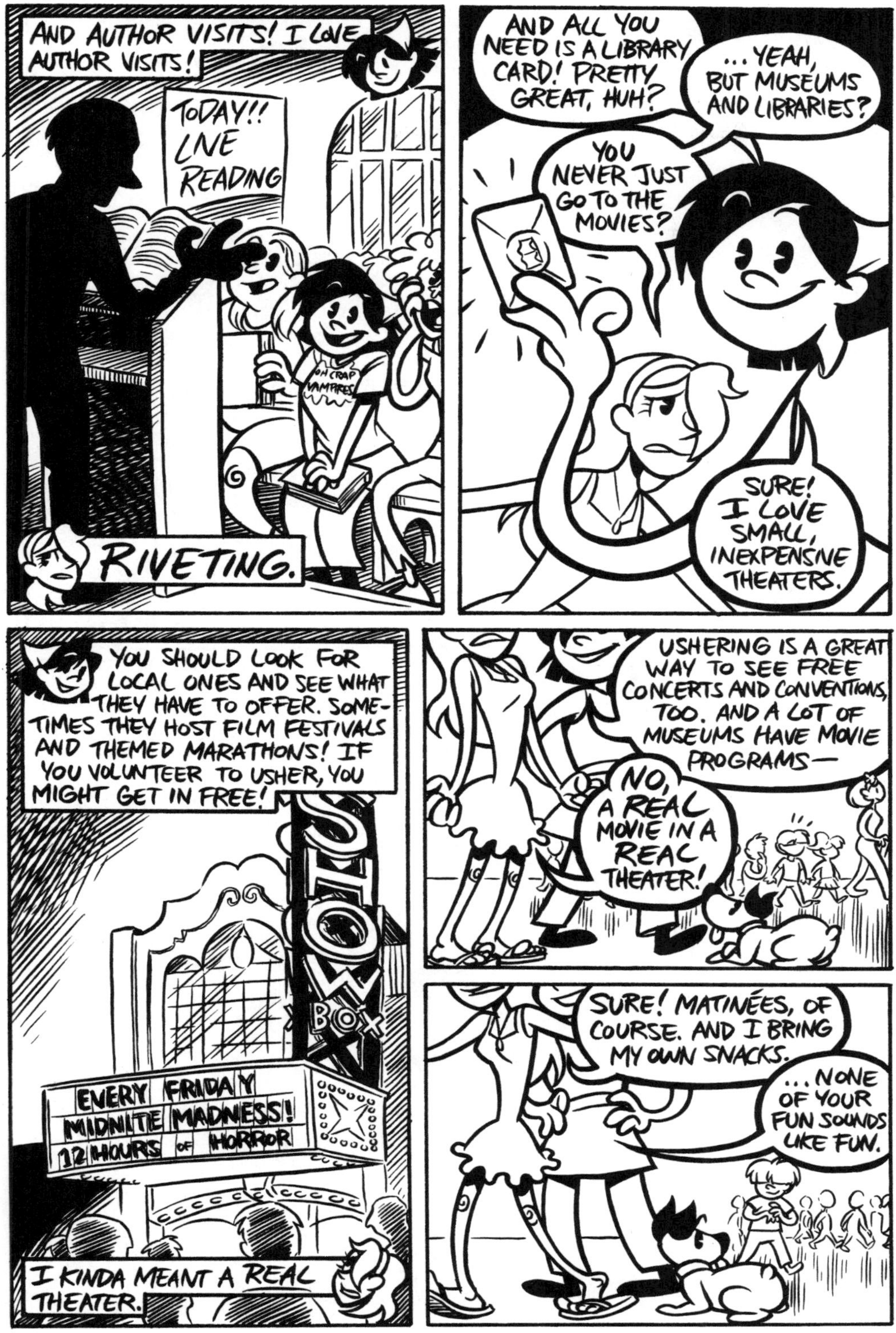
AND AUTHOR VISITS! I LOVE AUTHOR VISITS!
TODAY!! LIVE READING
OH CRAP VAMPIRES
RIVETING.
AND ALL YOU NEED IS A LIBRARY CARD! PRETTY GREAT, HUH?
...YEAH, BUT MUSEUMS AND LIBRARIES?
YOU NEVER JUST GO TO THE MOVIES?
SURE! I LOVE SMALL, INEXPENSIVE THEATERS.
YOU SHOULD LOOK FOR LOCAL ONES AND SEE WHAT THEY HAVE TO OFFER. SOMETIMES THEY HOST FILM FESTIVALS AND THEMED MARATHONS! IF YOU VOLUNTEER TO USHER, YOU MIGHT GET IN FREE!
EVERY FRIDAY
MIDNITE MADNESS!
12 HOURS OF HORROR
BOX
I KINDA MEANT A REAL THEATER.
USHERING IS A GREAT WAY TO SEE FREE CONCERTS AND CONVENTIONS, TOO. AND A LOT OF MUSEUMS HAVE MOVIE PROGRAMS—
NO, A REAL MOVIE IN A REAL THEATER!
SURE! MATINÉES, OF COURSE. AND I BRING MY OWN SNACKS.
...NONE OF YOUR FUN SOUNDS LIKE FUN.

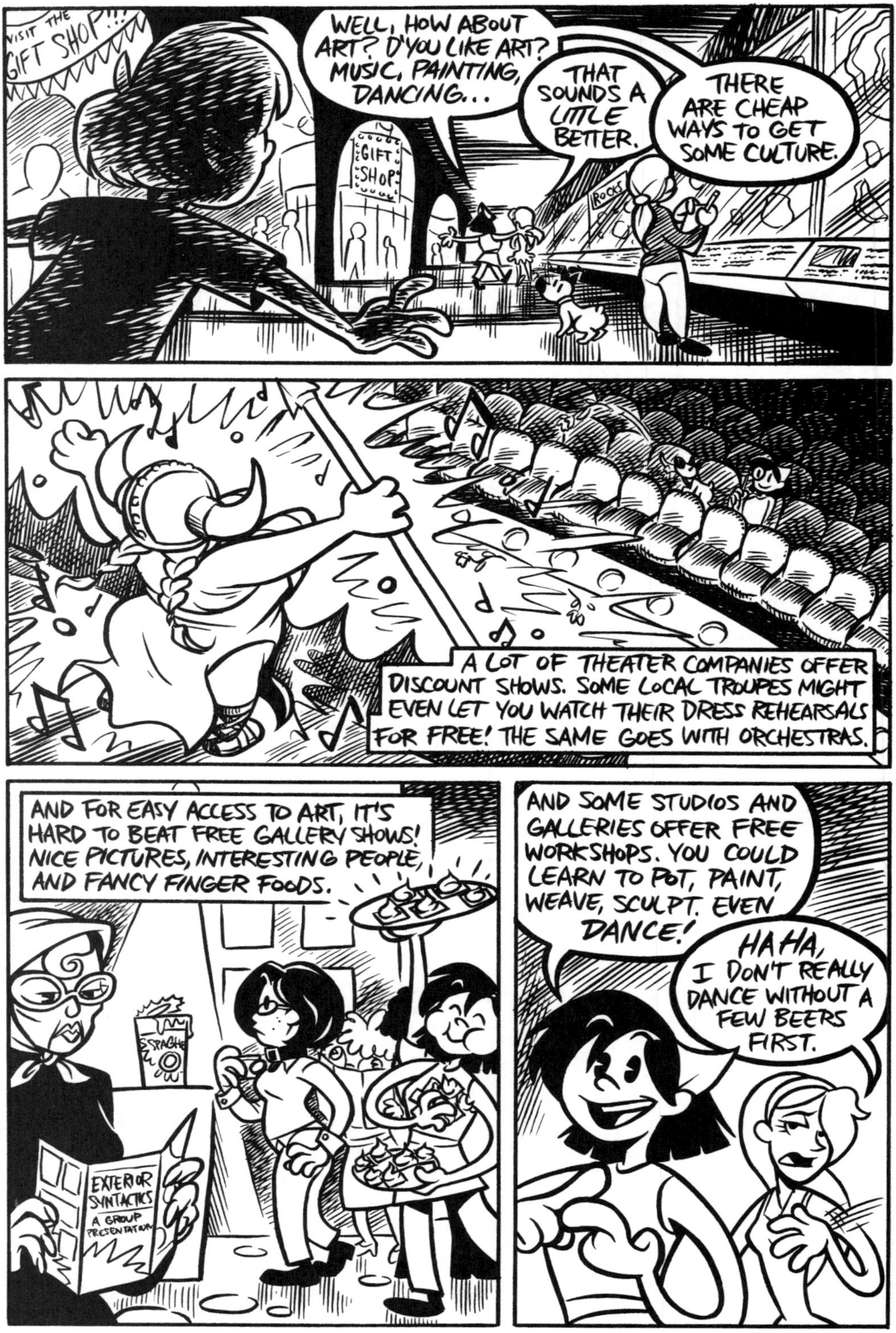
VISIT THE GIFT SHOP!!!
WELL, HOW ABOUT ART? D'YOU LIKE ART? MUSIC, PAINTING, DANCING...
THAT SOUNDS A LITTLE BETTER.
THERE ARE CHEAP WAYS TO GET SOME CULTURE.
GIFT SHOP
ROCKS
A LOT OF THEATER COMPANIES OFFER DISCOUNT SHOWS. SOME LOCAL TROUPES MIGHT EVEN LET YOU WATCH THEIR DRESS REHEARSALS FOR FREE! THE SAME GOES WITH ORCHESTRAS.
AND FOR EASY ACCESS TO ART, IT'S HARD TO BEAT FREE GALLERY SHOWS! NICE PICTURES, INTERESTING PEOPLE, AND FANCY FINGER FOODS.
EXTERIOR SYNTACTICS
A GROUP PRESENTATION
AND SOME STUDIOS AND GALLERIES OFFER FREE WORKSHOPS. YOU COULD LEARN TO POT, PAINT, WEAVE, SCULPT. EVEN DANCE!
HAHA, I DON'T REALLY DANCE WITHOUT A FEW BEERS FIRST.

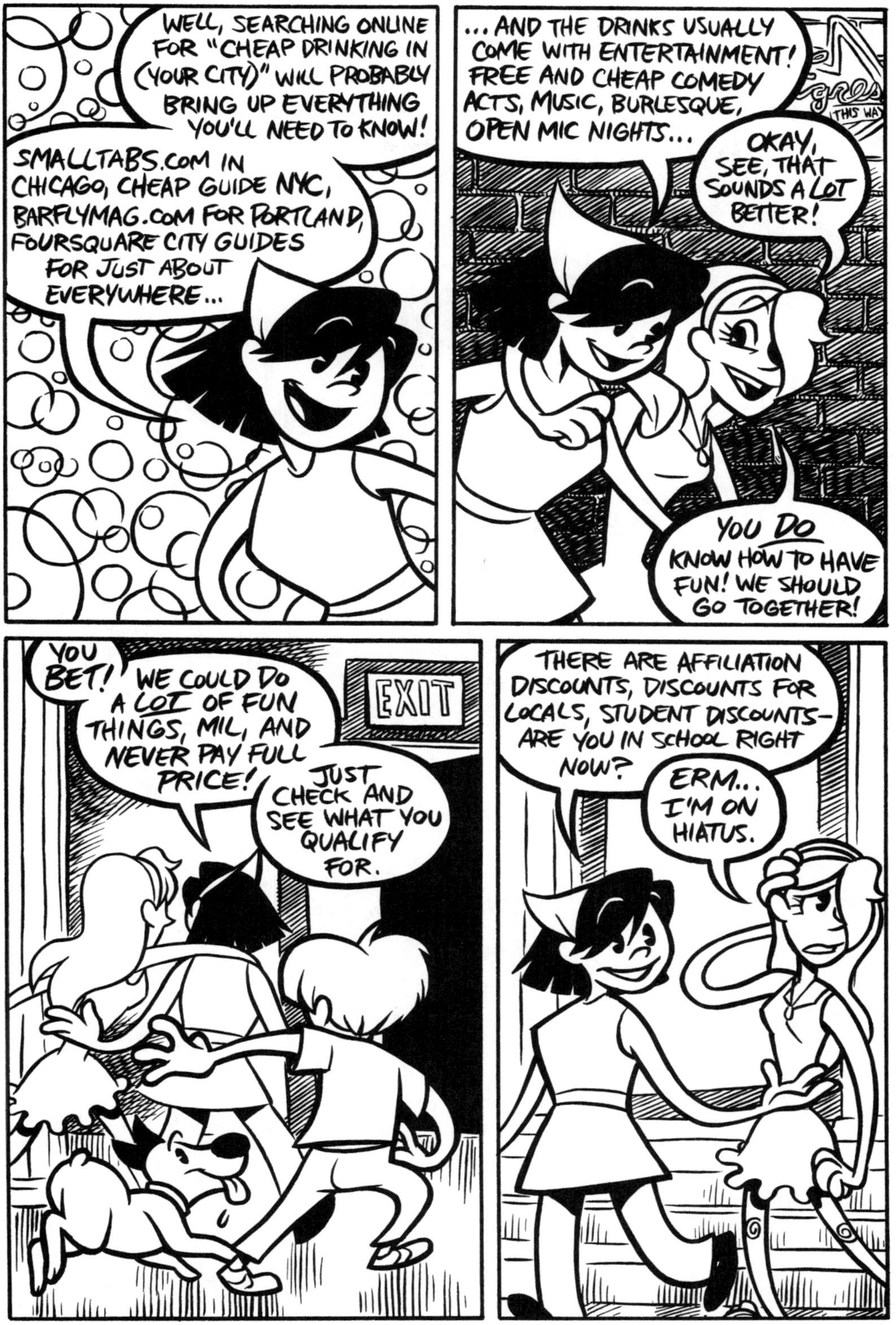
WELL, SEARCHING ONLINE FOR "CHEAP DRINKING IN (YOUR CITY)" WILL PROBABLY BRING UP EVERYTHING YOU'LL NEED TO KNOW!
SMALLTABS.COM IN CHICAGO, CHEAP GUIDE NYC, BARFLYMAG.COM FOR PORTLAND, FOURSQUARE CITY GUIDES FOR JUST ABOUT EVERYWHERE...
...AND THE DRINKS USUALLY COME WITH ENTERTAINMENT! FREE AND CHEAP COMEDY ACTS, MUSIC, BURLESQUE, OPEN MIC NIGHTS...
THIS WAY
OKAY, SEE, THAT SOUNDS A LOT BETTER!
YOU DO KNOW HOW TO HAVE FUN! WE SHOULD GO TOGETHER!
YOU BET!
WE COULD DO A LOT OF FUN THINGS, MIL, AND NEVER PAY FULL PRICE!
EXIT
JUST CHECK AND SEE WHAT YOU QUALIFY FOR.
THERE ARE AFFILIATION DISCOUNTS, DISCOUNTS FOR LOCALS, STUDENT DISCOUNTS- ARE YOU IN SCHOOL RIGHT NOW?
ERM... I'M ON HIATUS.

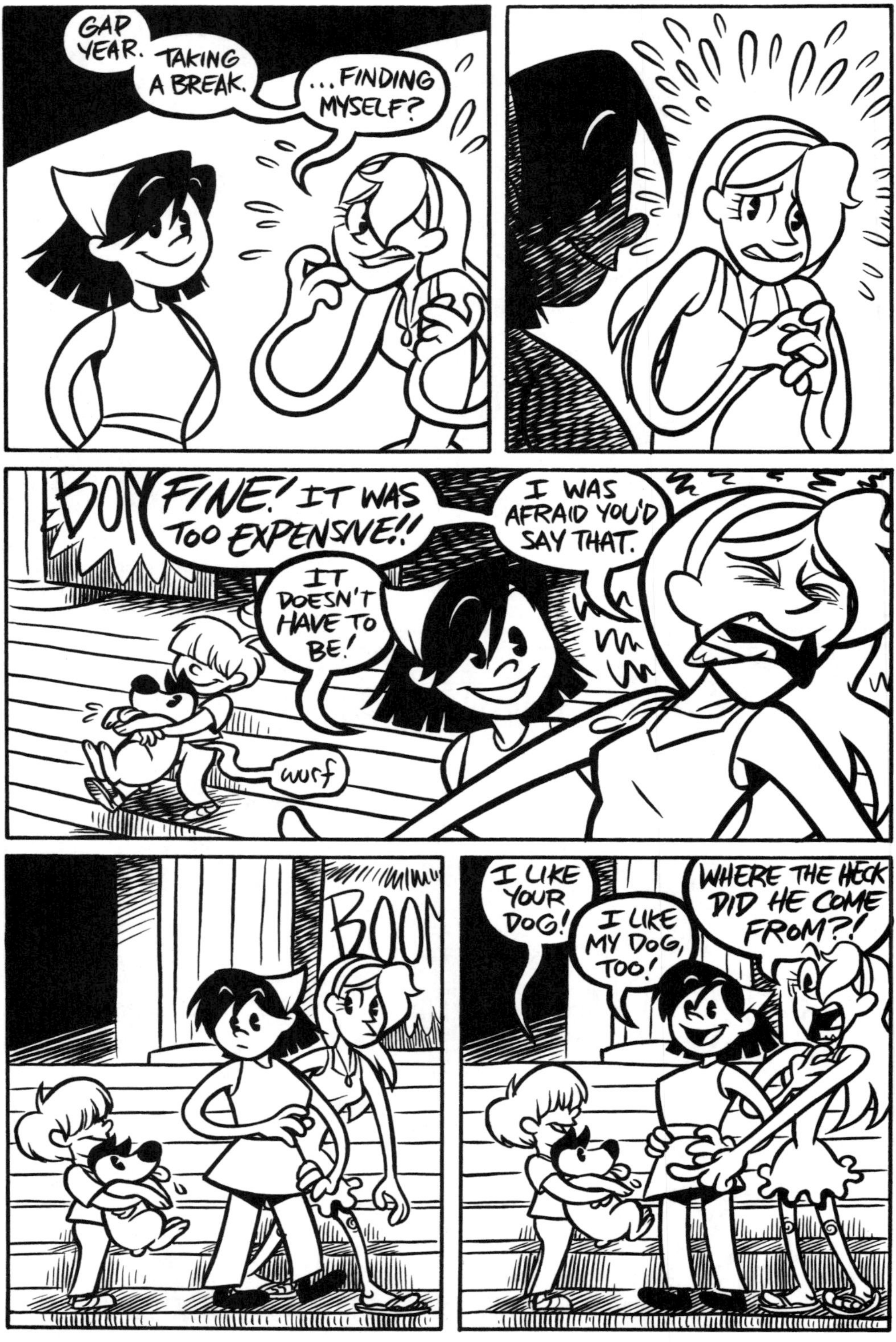
GAP YEAR.
TAKING A BREAK.
...FINDING MYSELF?
BOOM
FINE! IT WAS TOO EXPENSIVE!!
I WAS AFRAID YOU'D SAY THAT.
IT DOESN'T HAVE TO BE!
wurf
BOOM
I LIKE YOUR DOG!
I LIKE MY DOG, TOO!
WHERE THE HECK DID HE COME FROM?!

Chapter Eight

Education

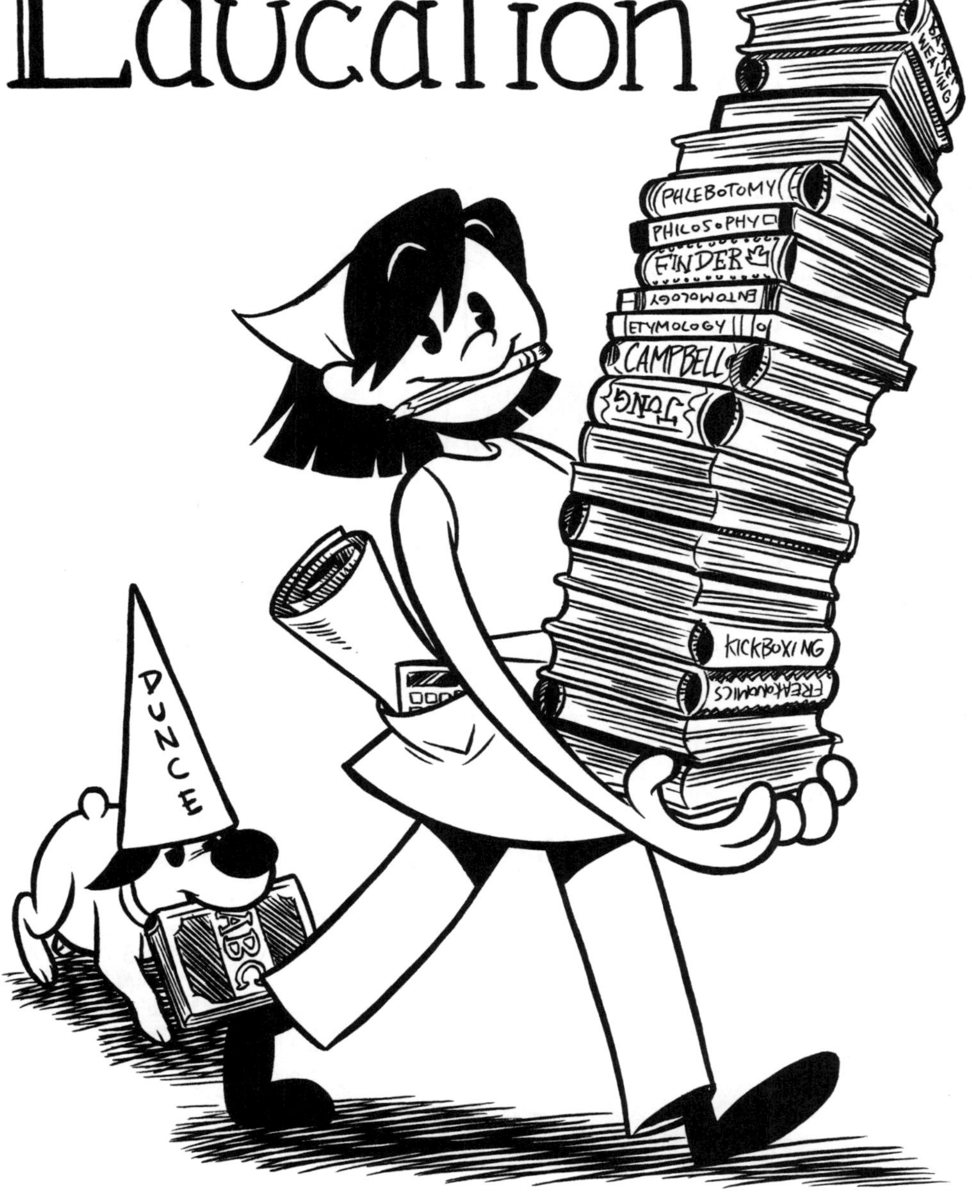
BASKET WEAVING
PHLEBOTOMY
PHILOSOPHY
FINDER
ENTOMOLOGY
ETYMOLOGY
CAMPBELL
JUNG
KICKBOXING
FREAKONOMICS
DUNCE
ABC

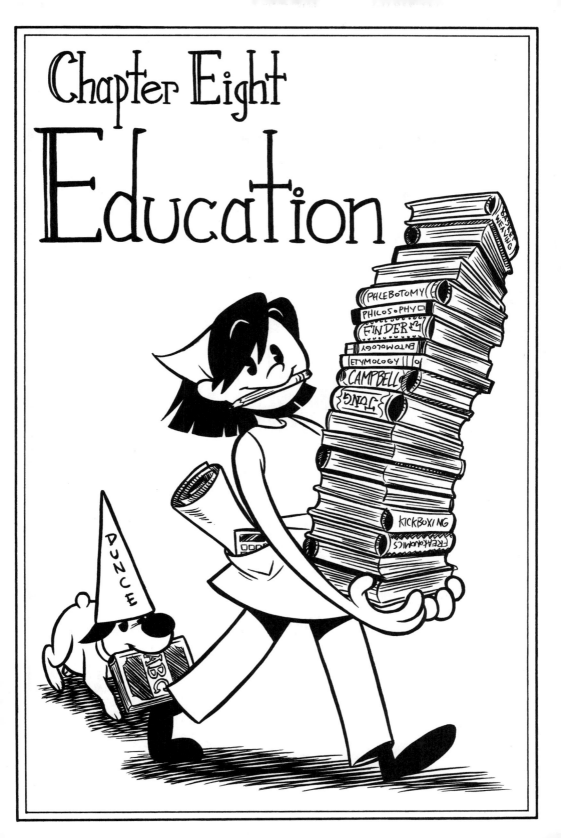

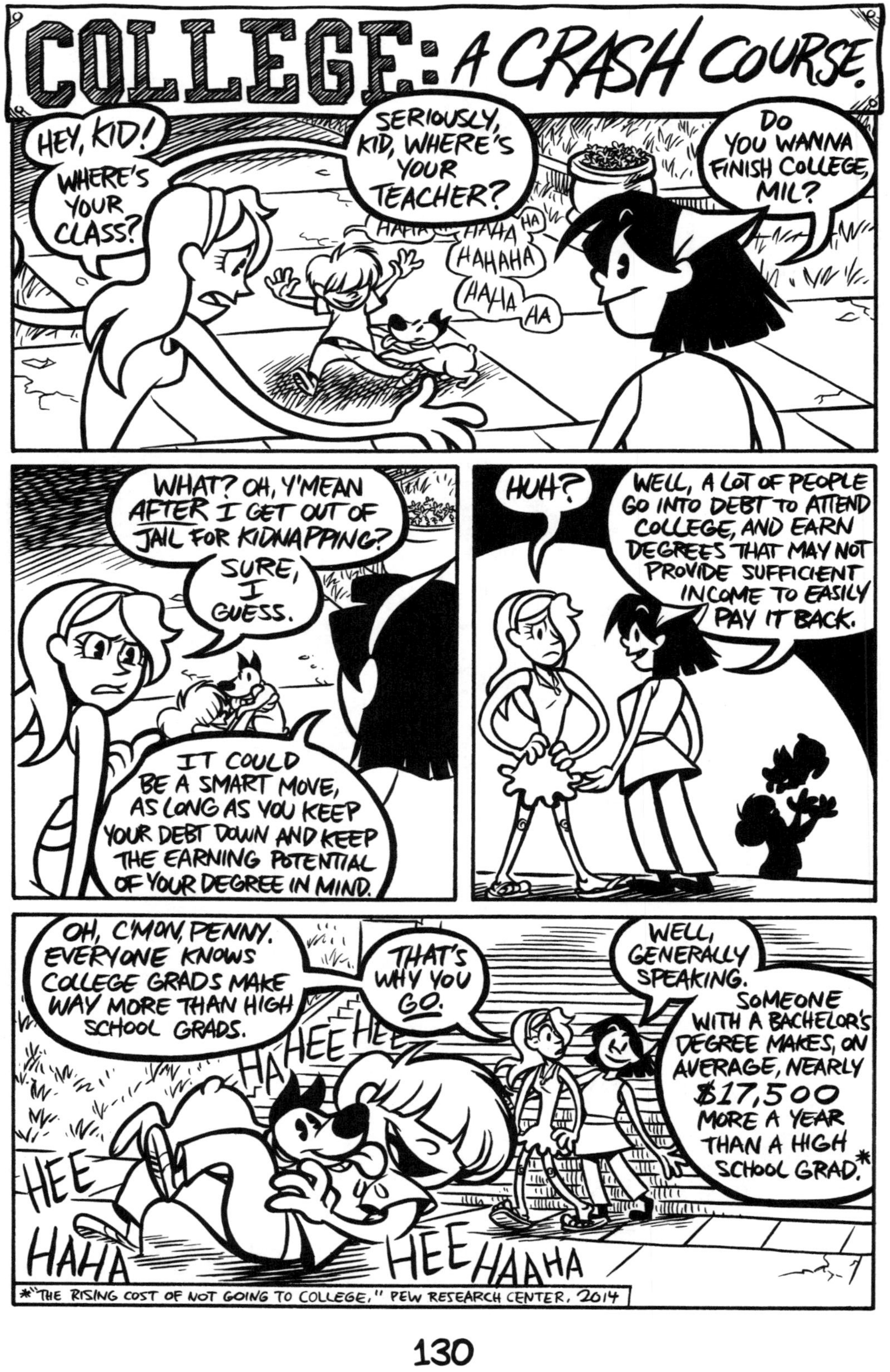
COLLEGE: A CRASH COURSE
HEY, KID! WHERE'S YOUR CLASS?
SERIOUSLY, KID, WHERE'S YOUR TEACHER?
HAHA HAHA HA HAHAHA HAHA HA
DO YOU WANNA FINISH COLLEGE, MIL?
WHAT? OH, Y'MEAN AFTER I GET OUT OF JAIL FOR KIDNAPPING?
SURE, I GUESS.
IT COULD BE A SMART MOVE, AS LONG AS YOU KEEP YOUR DEBT DOWN AND KEEP THE EARNING POTENTIAL OF YOUR DEGREE IN MIND.
HUH?
WELL, A LOT OF PEOPLE GO INTO DEBT TO ATTEND COLLEGE, AND EARN DEGREES THAT MAY NOT PROVIDE SUFFICIENT INCOME TO EASILY PAY IT BACK.
OH, C'MON, PENNY. EVERYONE KNOWS COLLEGE GRADS MAKE WAY MORE THAN HIGH SCHOOL GRADS.
THAT'S WHY YOU GO.
HAHEEHEE
WELL, GENERALLY SPEAKING.
SOMEONE WITH A BACHELOR'S DEGREE MAKES, ON AVERAGE, NEARLY $17,500 MORE A YEAR THAN A HIGH SCHOOL GRAD.*
HEE HAHA
HEEHAAHA
*"THE RISING COST OF NOT GOING TO COLLEGE," PEW RESEARCH CENTER, 2014

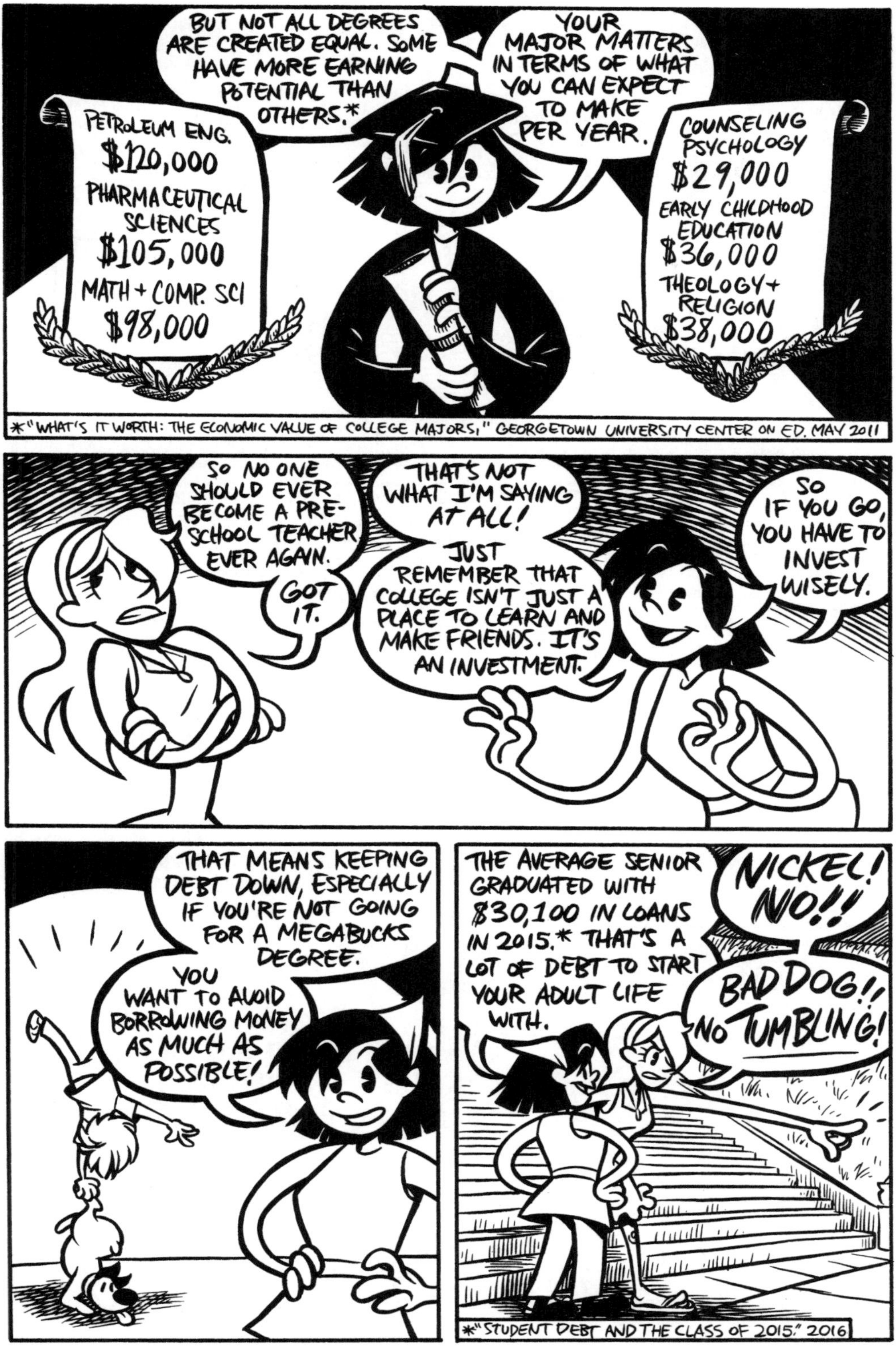
BUT NOT ALL DEGREES ARE CREATED EQUAL. SOME HAVE MORE EARNING POTENTIAL THAN OTHERS.*
YOUR MAJOR MATTERS IN TERMS OF WHAT YOU CAN EXPECT TO MAKE PER YEAR.
PETROLEUM ENG. $120,000
PHARMACEUTICAL SCIENCES $105,000
MATH + COMP. SCI $98,000
COUNSELING PSYCHOLOGY $29,000
EARLY CHILDHOOD EDUCATION $36,000
THEOLOGY + RELIGION $38,000
*"WHAT'S IT WORTH: THE ECONOMIC VALUE OF COLLEGE MAJORS," GEORGETOWN UNIVERSITY CENTER ON ED. MAY 2011
SO NO ONE SHOULD EVER BECOME A PRE-SCHOOL TEACHER EVER AGAIN.
GOT IT.
THAT'S NOT WHAT I'M SAYING AT ALL!
JUST REMEMBER THAT COLLEGE ISN'T JUST A PLACE TO LEARN AND MAKE FRIENDS. IT'S AN INVESTMENT.
SO IF YOU GO, YOU HAVE TO INVEST WISELY.
THAT MEANS KEEPING DEBT DOWN, ESPECIALLY IF YOU'RE NOT GOING FOR A MEGABUCKS DEGREE.
YOU WANT TO AVOID BORROWING MONEY AS MUCH AS POSSIBLE!
THE AVERAGE SENIOR GRADUATED WITH $30,100 IN LOANS IN 2015.* THAT'S A LOT OF DEBT TO START YOUR ADULT LIFE WITH.
NICKEL! NO!!
BAD DOG!! NO TUMBLING!
*"STUDENT DEBT AND THE CLASS OF 2015," 2016

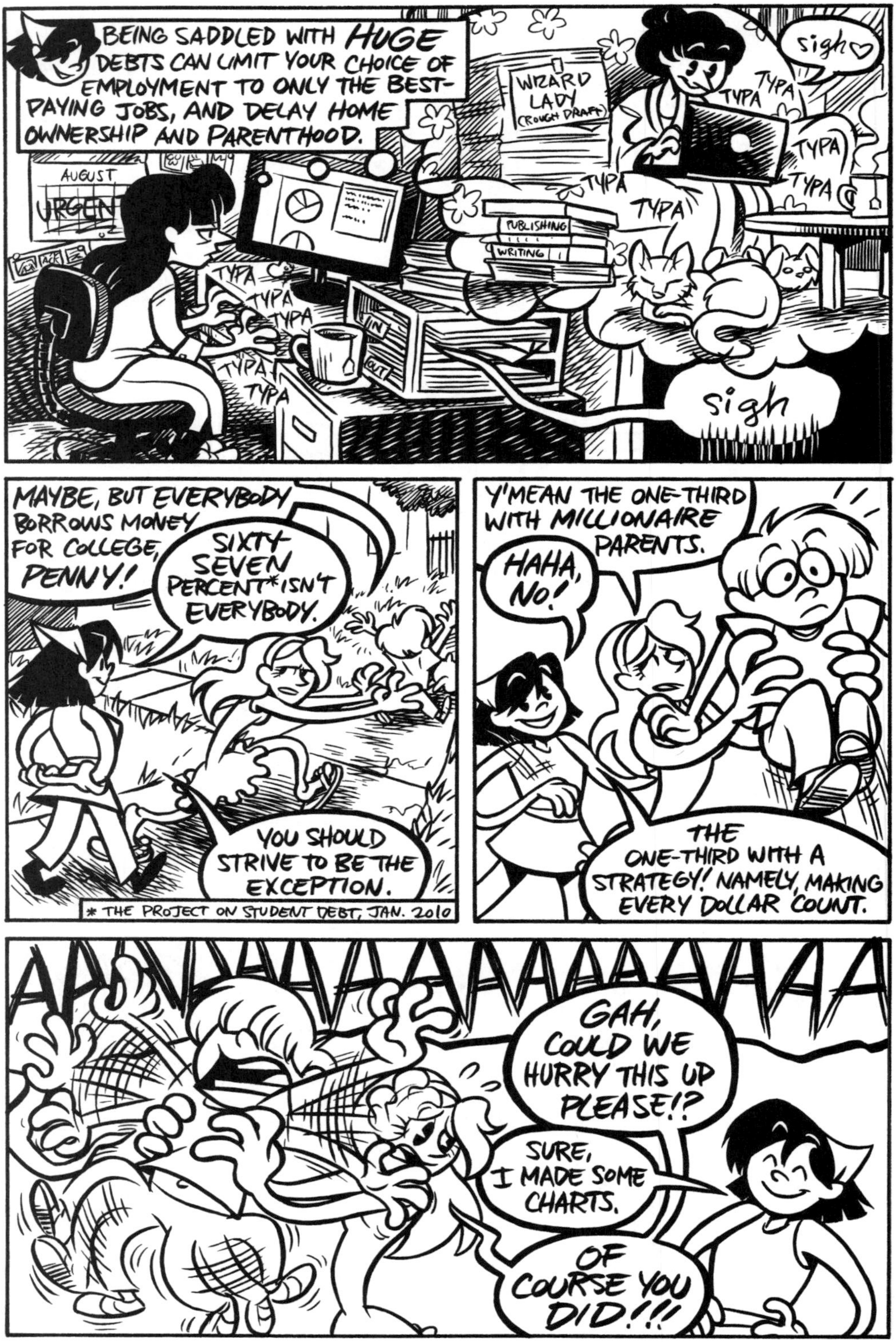

BEING SADDLED WITH HUGE DEBTS CAN LIMIT YOUR CHOICE OF EMPLOYMENT TO ONLY THE BEST-PAYING JOBS, AND DELAY HOME OWNERSHIP AND PARENTHOOD.
AUGUST
URGENT
WIZARD LADY (ROUGH DRAFT)
PUBLISHING
WRITING
IN
OUT
TYPA TYPA TYPA TYPA TYPA
TYPA TYPA TYPA TYPA TYPA TYPA TYPA
sigh♡
sigh
MAYBE, BUT EVERYBODY BORROWS MONEY FOR COLLEGE, PENNY!
SIXTY-SEVEN PERCENT* ISN'T EVERYBODY.
YOU SHOULD STRIVE TO BE THE EXCEPTION.
* THE PROJECT ON STUDENT DEBT, JAN. 2010
Y'MEAN THE ONE-THIRD WITH MILLIONAIRE PARENTS.
HAHA, NO!
THE ONE-THIRD WITH A STRATEGY! NAMELY, MAKING EVERY DOLLAR COUNT.
AAAAAAAAAAAAAAAA
GAH, COULD WE HURRY THIS UP PLEASE!?
SURE, I MADE SOME CHARTS.
OF COURSE YOU DID!!!

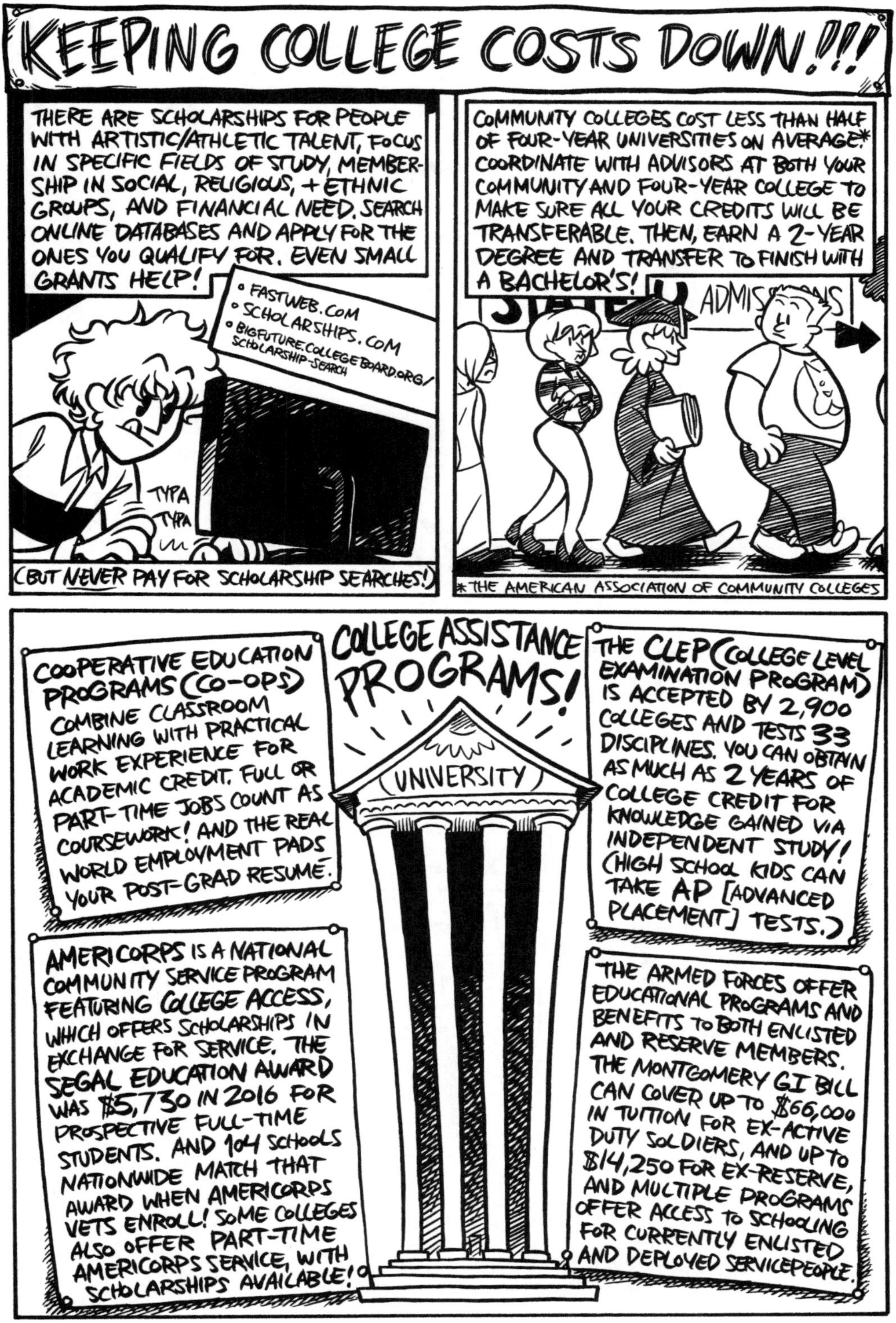
KEEPING COLLEGE COSTS DOWN!!!
THERE ARE SCHOLARSHIPS FOR PEOPLE WITH ARTISTIC/ATHLETIC TALENT, FOCUS IN SPECIFIC FIELDS OF STUDY, MEMBERSHIP IN SOCIAL, RELIGIOUS, + ETHNIC GROUPS, AND FINANCIAL NEED. SEARCH ONLINE DATABASES AND APPLY FOR THE ONES YOU QUALIFY FOR. EVEN SMALL GRANTS HELP!
• FASTWEB.COM
• SCHOLARSHIPS.COM
• BIGFUTURE.COLLEGEBOARD.ORG/SCHOLARSHIP-SEARCH
TYPA
TYPA
(BUT NEVER PAY FOR SCHOLARSHIP SEARCHES!)
COMMUNITY COLLEGES COST LESS THAN HALF OF FOUR-YEAR UNIVERSITIES ON AVERAGE.* COORDINATE WITH ADVISORS AT BOTH YOUR COMMUNITY AND FOUR-YEAR COLLEGE TO MAKE SURE ALL YOUR CREDITS WILL BE TRANSFERABLE. THEN, EARN A 2-YEAR DEGREE AND TRANSFER TO FINISH WITH A BACHELOR'S!
*THE AMERICAN ASSOCIATION OF COMMUNITY COLLEGES
COLLEGE ASSISTANCE PROGRAMS!
UNIVERSITY
COOPERATIVE EDUCATION PROGRAMS (CO-OPS) COMBINE CLASSROOM LEARNING WITH PRACTICAL WORK EXPERIENCE FOR ACADEMIC CREDIT. FULL OR PART-TIME JOBS COUNT AS COURSEWORK! AND THE REAL WORLD EMPLOYMENT PADS YOUR POST-GRAD RESUME.
THE CLEP (COLLEGE LEVEL EXAMINATION PROGRAM) IS ACCEPTED BY 2,900 COLLEGES AND TESTS 33 DISCIPLINES. YOU CAN OBTAIN AS MUCH AS 2 YEARS OF COLLEGE CREDIT FOR KNOWLEDGE GAINED VIA INDEPENDENT STUDY! (HIGH SCHOOL KIDS CAN TAKE AP [ADVANCED PLACEMENT] TESTS.)
AMERICORPS IS A NATIONAL COMMUNITY SERVICE PROGRAM FEATURING COLLEGE ACCESS, WHICH OFFERS SCHOLARSHIPS IN EXCHANGE FOR SERVICE. THE SEGAL EDUCATION AWARD WAS $5,730 IN 2016 FOR PROSPECTIVE FULL-TIME STUDENTS. AND 104 SCHOOLS NATIONWIDE MATCH THAT AWARD WHEN AMERICORPS VETS ENROLL! SOME COLLEGES ALSO OFFER PART-TIME AMERICORPS SERVICE, WITH SCHOLARSHIPS AVAILABLE!
THE ARMED FORCES OFFER EDUCATIONAL PROGRAMS AND BENEFITS TO BOTH ENLISTED AND RESERVE MEMBERS. THE MONTGOMERY GI BILL CAN COVER UP TO $66,000 IN TUITION FOR EX-ACTIVE DUTY SOLDIERS, AND UP TO $14,250 FOR EX-RESERVE, AND MULTIPLE PROGRAMS OFFER ACCESS TO SCHOOLING FOR CURRENTLY ENLISTED AND DEPLOYED SERVICEPEOPLE.

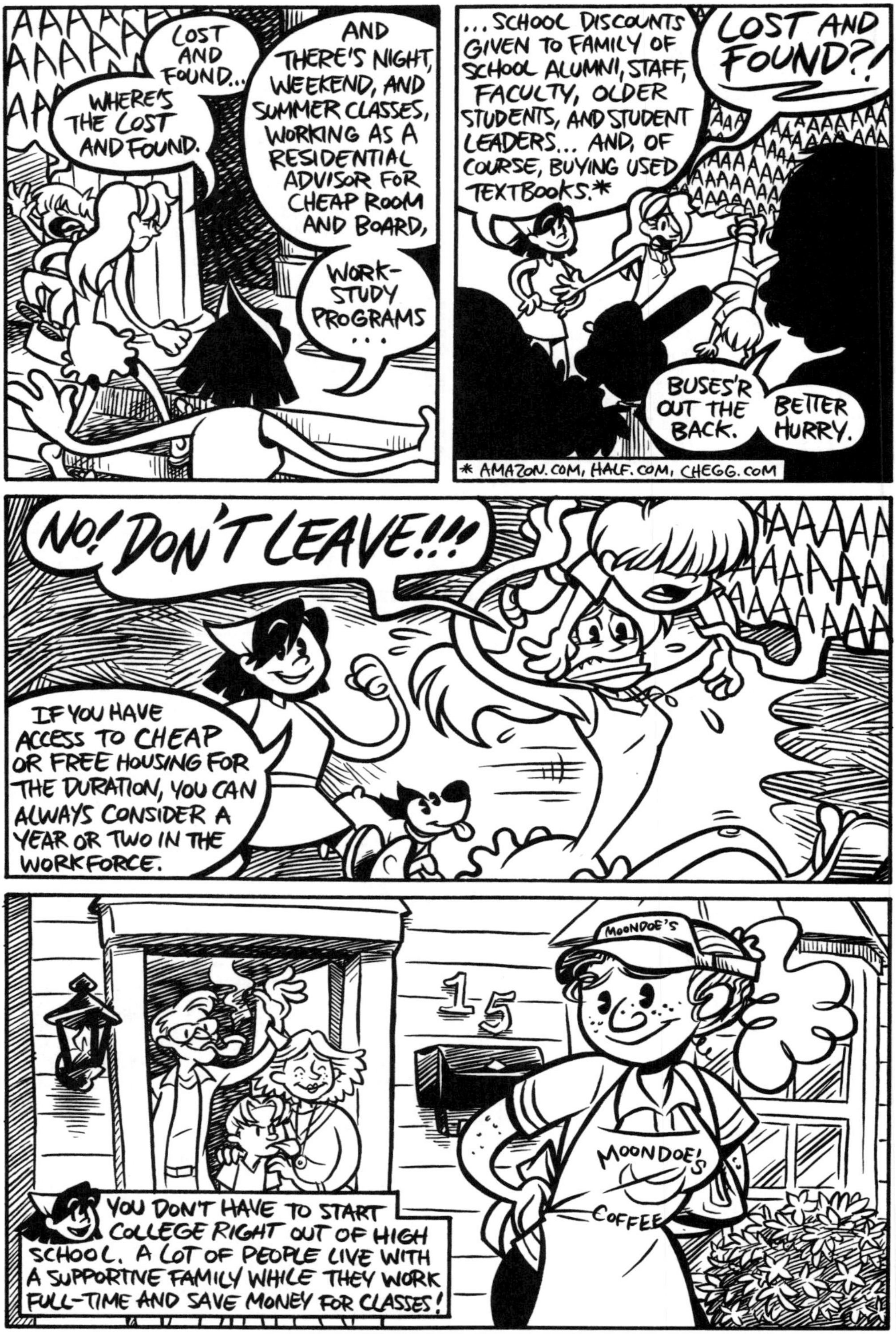
LOST AND FOUND...
WHERE'S THE LOST AND FOUND.
AND THERE'S NIGHT, WEEKEND, AND SUMMER CLASSES, WORKING AS A RESIDENTIAL ADVISOR FOR CHEAP ROOM AND BOARD,
WORK-STUDY PROGRAMS ...
...SCHOOL DISCOUNTS GIVEN TO FAMILY OF SCHOOL ALUMNI, STAFF, FACULTY, OLDER STUDENTS, AND STUDENT LEADERS... AND, OF COURSE, BUYING USED TEXTBOOKS.*
LOST AND FOUND?!
BUSES'R OUT THE BACK.
BETTER HURRY.
* AMAZON.COM, HALF.COM, CHEGG.COM
NO! DON'T LEAVE!!!
IF YOU HAVE ACCESS TO CHEAP OR FREE HOUSING FOR THE DURATION, YOU CAN ALWAYS CONSIDER A YEAR OR TWO IN THE WORKFORCE.
MOONDOE'S
15
MOONDOE'S COFFEE
YOU DON'T HAVE TO START COLLEGE RIGHT OUT OF HIGH SCHOOL. A LOT OF PEOPLE LIVE WITH A SUPPORTIVE FAMILY WHILE THEY WORK FULL-TIME AND SAVE MONEY FOR CLASSES!

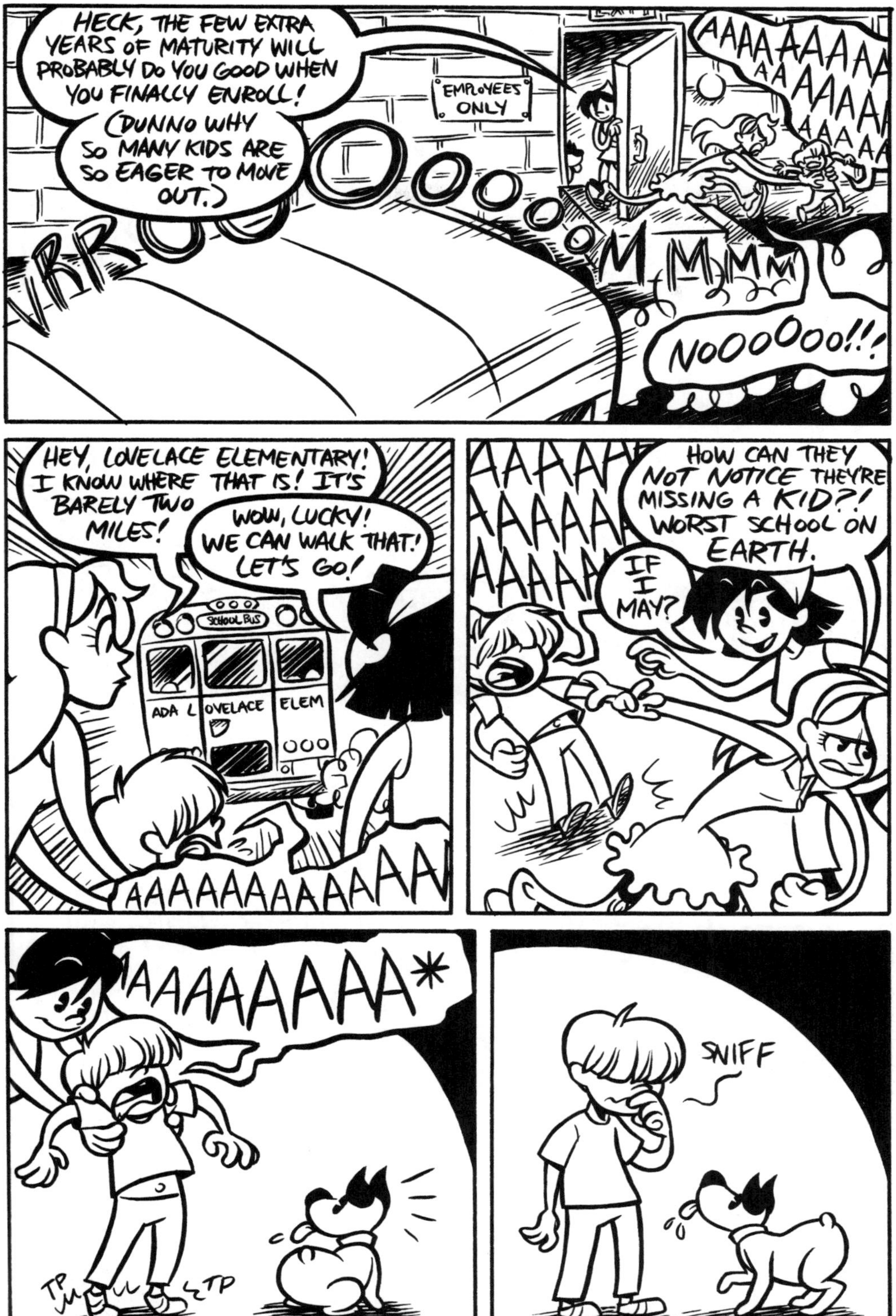
HECK, THE FEW EXTRA YEARS OF MATURITY WILL PROBABLY DO YOU GOOD WHEN YOU FINALLY ENROLL!
(DUNNO WHY SO MANY KIDS ARE SO EAGER TO MOVE OUT.)
EMPLOYEES ONLY
AAAAAAAAA AAAAAAA AAAAA
VRROOOOOOOOOOM MMM
NOOOOOO!!!
HEY, LOVELACE ELEMENTARY! I KNOW WHERE THAT IS! IT'S BARELY TWO MILES!
WOW, LUCKY! WE CAN WALK THAT! LET'S GO!
SCHOOL BUS
ADA LOVELACE ELEM
AAAAAAAAAAAA
AAAAA AAAAA AAAAA
HOW CAN THEY NOT NOTICE THEY'RE MISSING A KID?! WORST SCHOOL ON EARTH.
IF I MAY?
AAAAAAAA*
TP TP
SNIFF

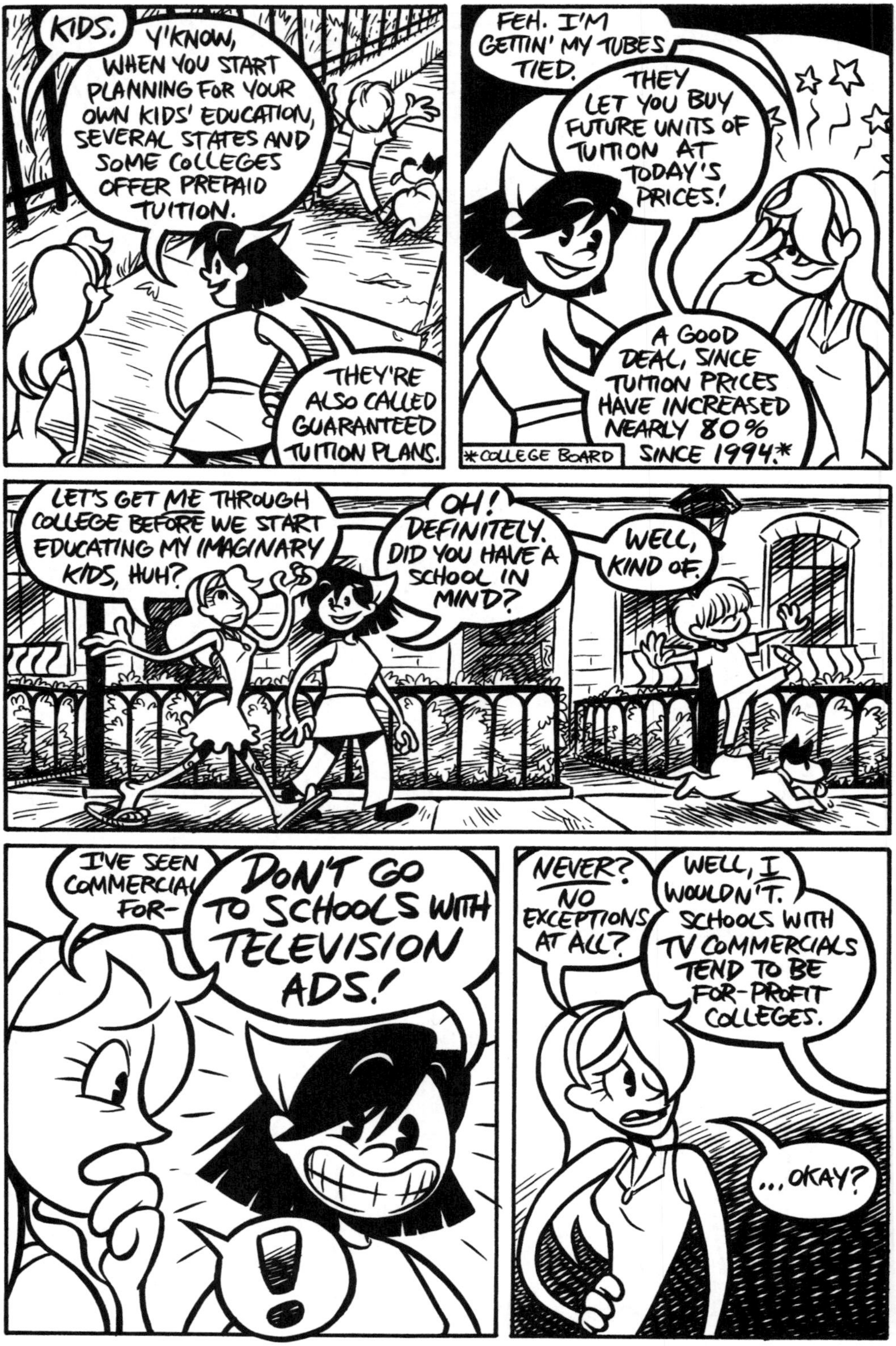
KIDS.
Y'KNOW, WHEN YOU START PLANNING FOR YOUR OWN KIDS' EDUCATION, SEVERAL STATES AND SOME COLLEGES OFFER PREPAID TUITION.
THEY'RE ALSO CALLED GUARANTEED TUITION PLANS.
FEH. I'M GETTIN' MY TUBES TIED.
THEY LET YOU BUY FUTURE UNITS OF TUITION AT TODAY'S PRICES!
A GOOD DEAL, SINCE TUITION PRICES HAVE INCREASED NEARLY 80% SINCE 1994.*
*COLLEGE BOARD
LET'S GET ME THROUGH COLLEGE BEFORE WE START EDUCATING MY IMAGINARY KIDS, HUH?
OH! DEFINITELY. DID YOU HAVE A SCHOOL IN MIND?
WELL, KIND OF.
I'VE SEEN COMMERCIALS FOR-
DON'T GO TO SCHOOLS WITH TELEVISION ADS!
!
NEVER? NO EXCEPTIONS AT ALL?
WELL, I WOULDN'T. SCHOOLS WITH TV COMMERCIALS TEND TO BE FOR-PROFIT COLLEGES.
...OKAY?

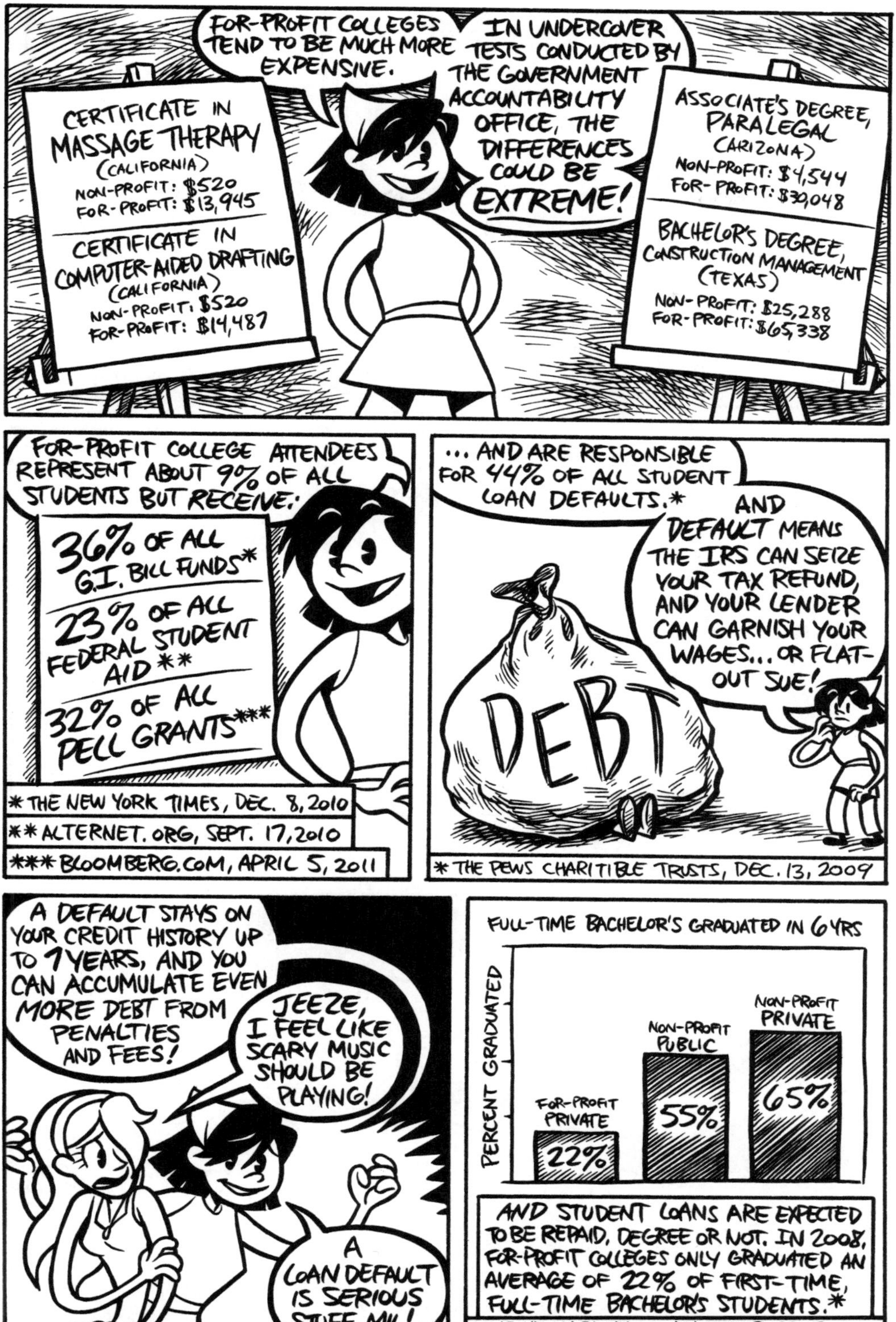

FOR-PROFIT COLLEGES TEND TO BE MUCH MORE EXPENSIVE.
IN UNDERCOVER TESTS CONDUCTED BY THE GOVERNMENT ACCOUNTABILITY OFFICE, THE DIFFERENCES COULD BE EXTREME!
CERTIFICATE IN MASSAGE THERAPY (CALIFORNIA) NON-PROFIT: $520 FOR-PROFIT: $13,945
CERTIFICATE IN COMPUTER-AIDED DRAFTING (CALIFORNIA) NON-PROFIT: $520 FOR-PROFIT: $14,487
ASSOCIATE'S DEGREE, PARALEGAL (ARIZONA) NON-PROFIT: $4,544 FOR-PROFIT: $30,048
BACHELOR'S DEGREE, CONSTRUCTION MANAGEMENT (TEXAS) NON-PROFIT: $25,288 FOR-PROFIT: $65,338
FOR-PROFIT COLLEGE ATTENDEES REPRESENT ABOUT 9% OF ALL STUDENTS BUT RECEIVE:
36% OF ALL G.I. BILL FUNDS*
23% OF ALL FEDERAL STUDENT AID**
32% OF ALL PELL GRANTS***
* THE NEW YORK TIMES, DEC. 8, 2010
** ALTERNET.ORG, SEPT. 17, 2010
*** BLOOMBERG.COM, APRIL 5, 2011
... AND ARE RESPONSIBLE FOR 44% OF ALL STUDENT LOAN DEFAULTS.*
AND DEFAULT MEANS THE IRS CAN SEIZE YOUR TAX REFUND, AND YOUR LENDER CAN GARNISH YOUR WAGES... OR FLAT-OUT SUE!
DEBT
* THE PEWS CHARITIBLE TRUSTS, DEC. 13, 2009
A DEFAULT STAYS ON YOUR CREDIT HISTORY UP TO 7 YEARS, AND YOU CAN ACCUMULATE EVEN MORE DEBT FROM PENALTIES AND FEES!
JEEZE, I FEEL LIKE SCARY MUSIC SHOULD BE PLAYING!
A LOAN DEFAULT IS SERIOUS STUFF, MIL!
FULL-TIME BACHELOR'S GRADUATED IN 6 YRS
PERCENT GRADUATED
FOR-PROFIT PRIVATE 22%
NON-PROFIT PUBLIC 55%
NON-PROFIT PRIVATE 65%
AND STUDENT LOANS ARE EXPECTED TO BE REPAID, DEGREE OR NOT. IN 2008, FOR-PROFIT COLLEGES ONLY GRADUATED AN AVERAGE OF 22% OF FIRST-TIME, FULL-TIME BACHELOR'S STUDENTS.*
* THE NEW YORK TIMES, NOVEMBER 23, 2010

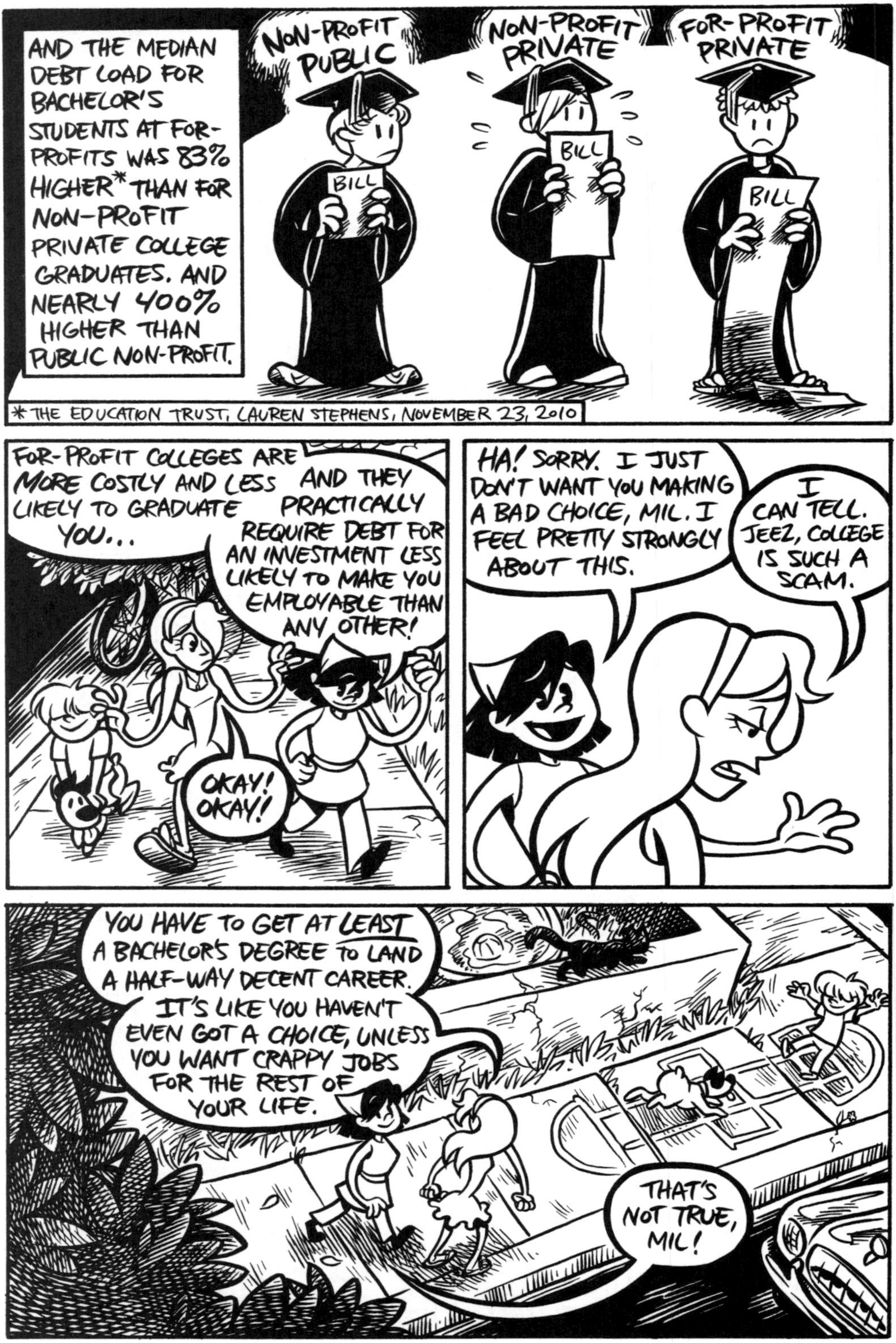
AND THE MEDIAN DEBT LOAD FOR BACHELOR'S STUDENTS AT FOR-PROFITS WAS 83% HIGHER* THAN FOR NON-PROFIT PRIVATE COLLEGE GRADUATES. AND NEARLY 400% HIGHER THAN PUBLIC NON-PROFIT.
NON-PROFIT PUBLIC
NON-PROFIT PRIVATE
FOR-PROFIT PRIVATE
BILL
BILL
BILL
* THE EDUCATION TRUST, LAUREN STEPHENS, NOVEMBER 23, 2010
FOR-PROFIT COLLEGES ARE MORE COSTLY AND LESS LIKELY TO GRADUATE YOU...
AND THEY PRACTICALLY REQUIRE DEBT FOR AN INVESTMENT LESS LIKELY TO MAKE YOU EMPLOYABLE THAN ANY OTHER!
OKAY! OKAY!
HA! SORRY. I JUST DON'T WANT YOU MAKING A BAD CHOICE, MIL. I FEEL PRETTY STRONGLY ABOUT THIS.
I CAN TELL. JEEZ, COLLEGE IS SUCH A SCAM.
YOU HAVE TO GET AT LEAST A BACHELOR'S DEGREE TO LAND A HALF-WAY DECENT CAREER.
IT'S LIKE YOU HAVEN'T EVEN GOT A CHOICE, UNLESS YOU WANT CRAPPY JOBS FOR THE REST OF YOUR LIFE.
THAT'S NOT TRUE, MIL!

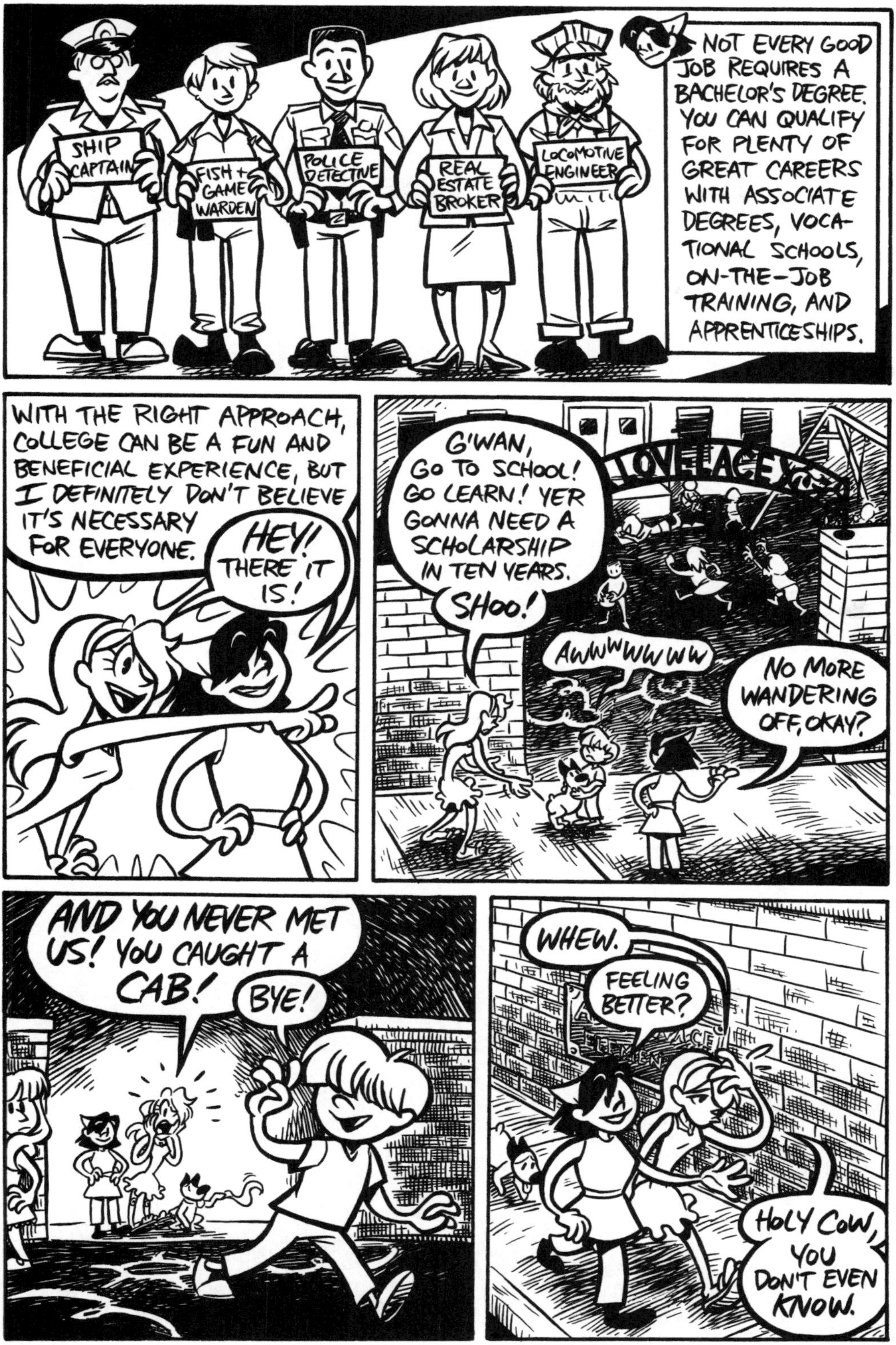
SHIP CAPTAIN
FISH + GAME WARDEN
POLICE DETECTIVE
REAL ESTATE BROKER
LOCOMOTIVE ENGINEER
NOT EVERY GOOD JOB REQUIRES A BACHELOR'S DEGREE. YOU CAN QUALIFY FOR PLENTY OF GREAT CAREERS WITH ASSOCIATE DEGREES, VOCATIONAL SCHOOLS, ON-THE-JOB TRAINING, AND APPRENTICESHIPS.
WITH THE RIGHT APPROACH, COLLEGE CAN BE A FUN AND BENEFICIAL EXPERIENCE, BUT I DEFINITELY DON'T BELIEVE IT'S NECESSARY FOR EVERYONE.
HEY! THERE IT IS!
LOVELACE
G'WAN, GO TO SCHOOL! GO LEARN! YER GONNA NEED A SCHOLARSHIP IN TEN YEARS.
SHOO!
AWWWWWWW
NO MORE WANDERING OFF, OKAY?
AND YOU NEVER MET US! YOU CAUGHT A CAB!
BYE!
WHEW.
FEELING BETTER?
HOLY COW, YOU DON'T EVEN KNOW.

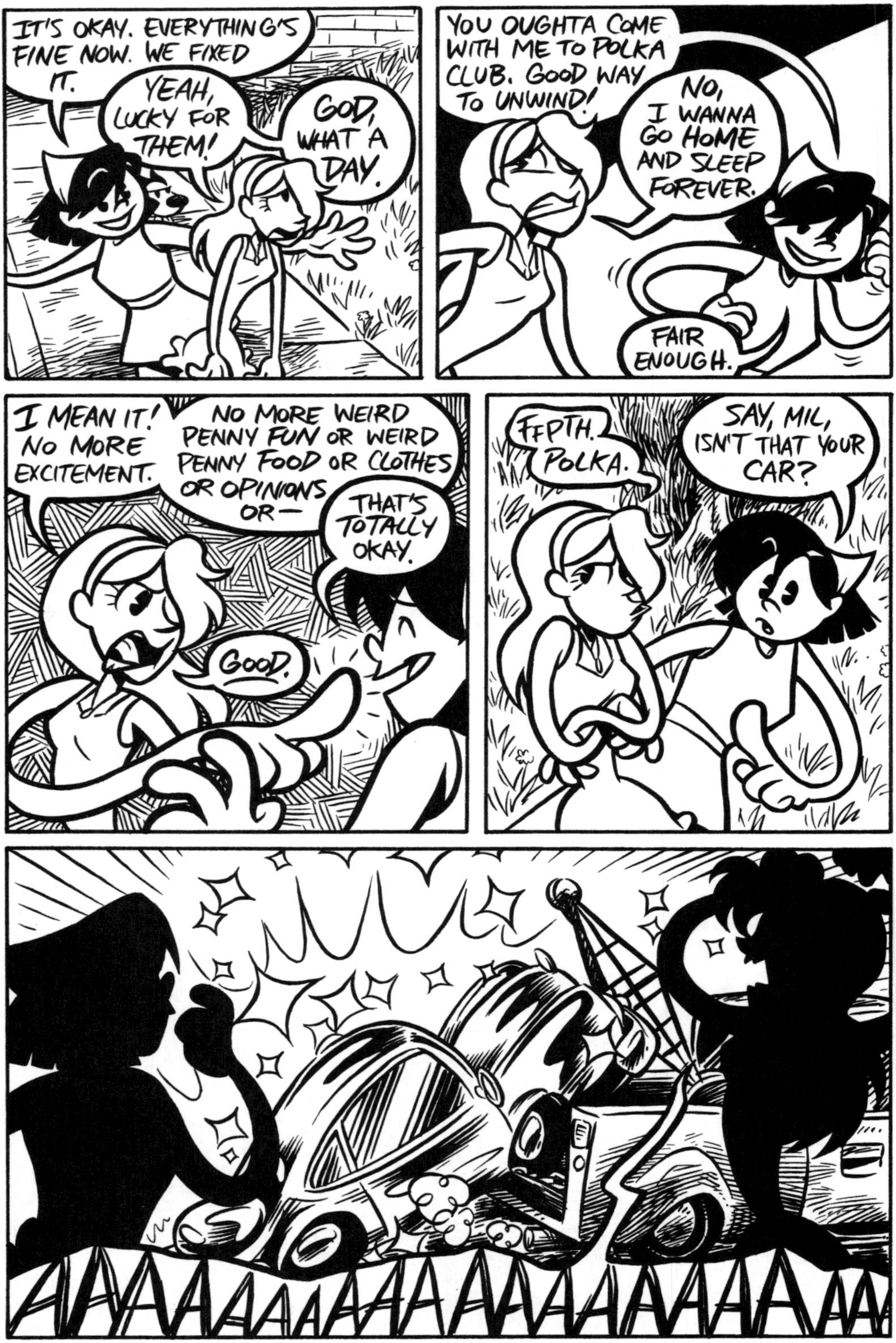
IT'S OKAY. EVERYTHING'S FINE NOW. WE FIXED IT.
YEAH, LUCKY FOR THEM!
GOD, WHAT A DAY.
YOU OUGHTA COME WITH ME TO POLKA CLUB. GOOD WAY TO UNWIND!
NO, I WANNA GO HOME AND SLEEP FOREVER.
FAIR ENOUGH.
I MEAN IT! NO MORE EXCITEMENT.
NO MORE WEIRD PENNY FUN OR WEIRD PENNY FOOD OR CLOTHES OR OPINIONS OR—
THAT'S TOTALLY OKAY.
GOOD.
FFPTH. POLKA.
SAY, MIL, ISN'T THAT YOUR CAR?
AAAAAAAAAAAAAAAAAAAAAAAAAAAAAAAAA

Chapter Nine
Emergencies

MISTAKES WERE MADE.

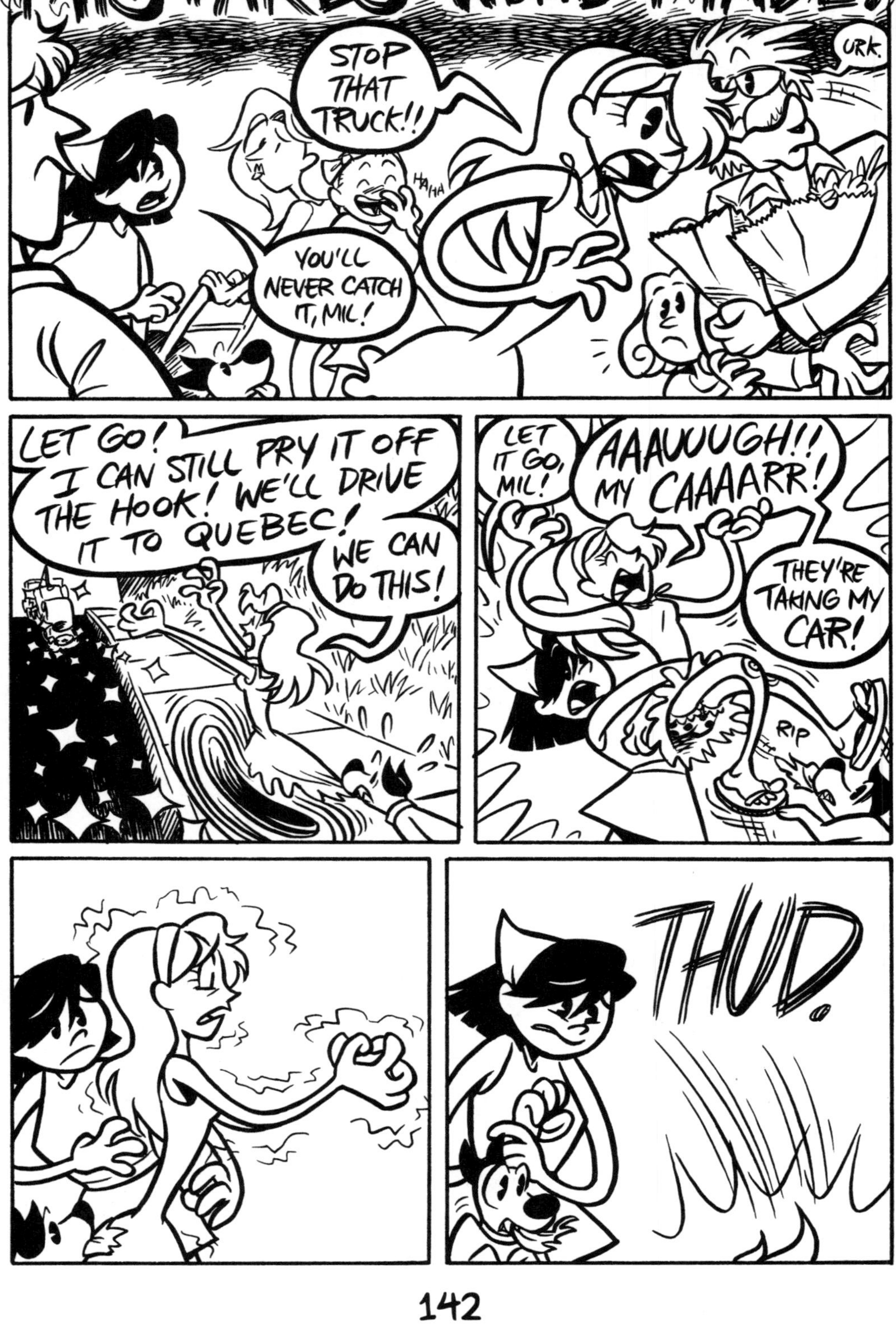

STOP THAT TRUCK!!
URK.
HAHA
YOU'LL NEVER CATCH IT, MIL!
LET GO! I CAN STILL PRY IT OFF THE HOOK! WE'LL DRIVE IT TO QUEBEC!
WE CAN DO THIS!
LET IT GO, MIL!
AAAUUUGH!! MY CAAAARR!
THEY'RE TAKING MY CAR!
RIP
THUD.

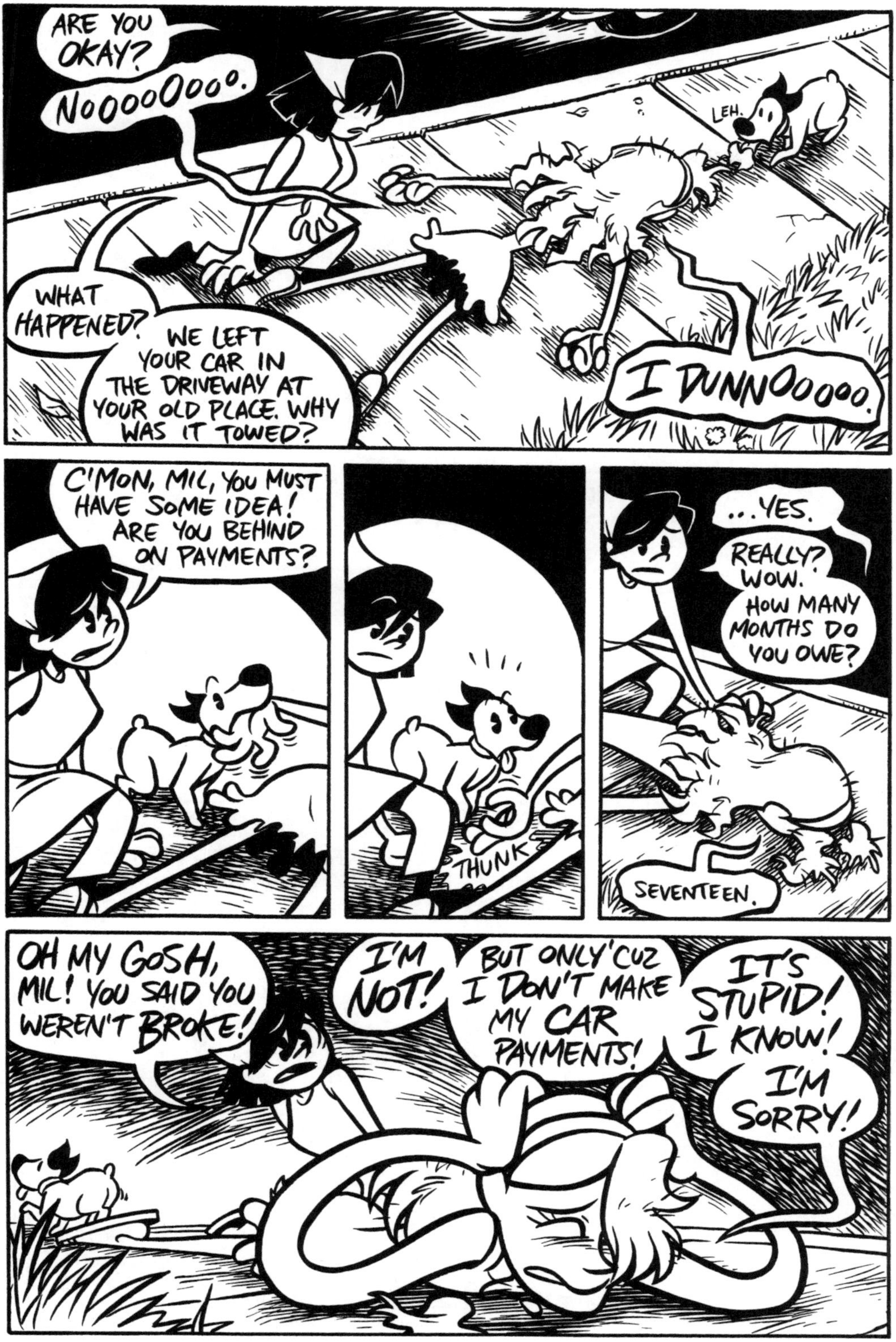
ARE YOU OKAY?
NOOOOOOOO.
LEH.
WHAT HAPPENED?
WE LEFT YOUR CAR IN THE DRIVEWAY AT YOUR OLD PLACE. WHY WAS IT TOWED?
I DUNNOOOOO.
C'MON, MIL, YOU MUST HAVE SOME IDEA! ARE YOU BEHIND ON PAYMENTS?
THUNK
...YES.
REALLY? WOW. HOW MANY MONTHS DO YOU OWE?
SEVENTEEN.
OH MY GOSH, MIL! YOU SAID YOU WEREN'T BROKE!
I'M NOT!
BUT ONLY 'CUZ I DON'T MAKE MY CAR PAYMENTS!
IT'S STUPID! I KNOW!
I'M SORRY!

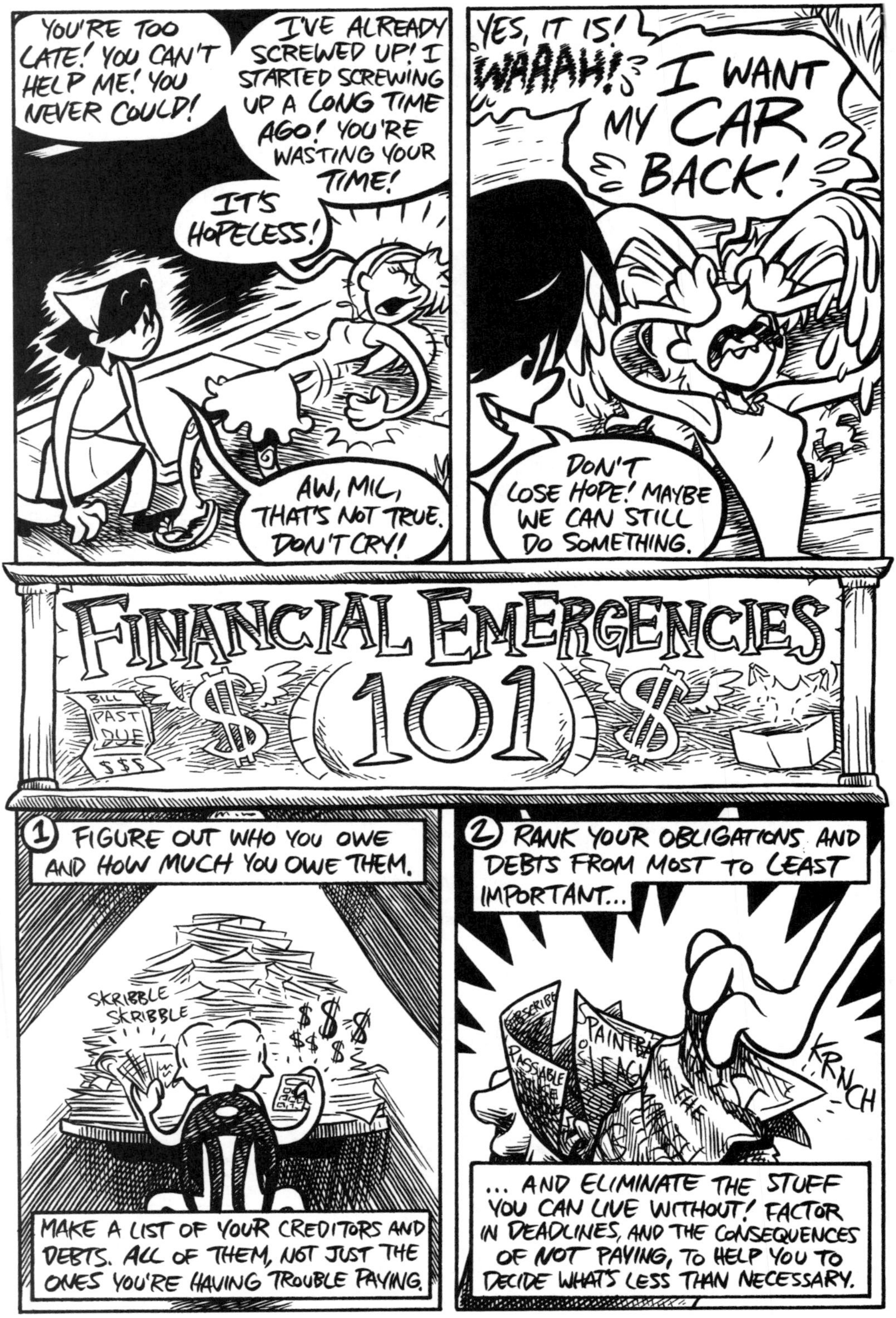
YOU'RE TOO LATE! YOU CAN'T HELP ME! YOU NEVER COULD!
I'VE ALREADY SCREWED UP! I STARTED SCREWING UP A LONG TIME AGO! YOU'RE WASTING YOUR TIME!
IT'S HOPELESS!
AW, MIL, THAT'S NOT TRUE. DON'T CRY!
YES, IT IS!
WAAAH!
I WANT MY CAR BACK!
DON'T LOSE HOPE! MAYBE WE CAN STILL DO SOMETHING.
FINANCIAL EMERGENCIES
$ (101) $
BILL
PAST DUE
$$$
1 FIGURE OUT WHO YOU OWE AND HOW MUCH YOU OWE THEM.
SKRIBBLE SKRIBBLE
MAKE A LIST OF YOUR CREDITORS AND DEBTS. ALL OF THEM, NOT JUST THE ONES YOU'RE HAVING TROUBLE PAYING.
2 RANK YOUR OBLIGATIONS AND DEBTS FROM MOST TO LEAST IMPORTANT...
KRNCH
... AND ELIMINATE THE STUFF YOU CAN LIVE WITHOUT! FACTOR IN DEADLINES, AND THE CONSEQUENCES OF NOT PAYING, TO HELP YOU TO DECIDE WHAT'S LESS THAN NECESSARY.

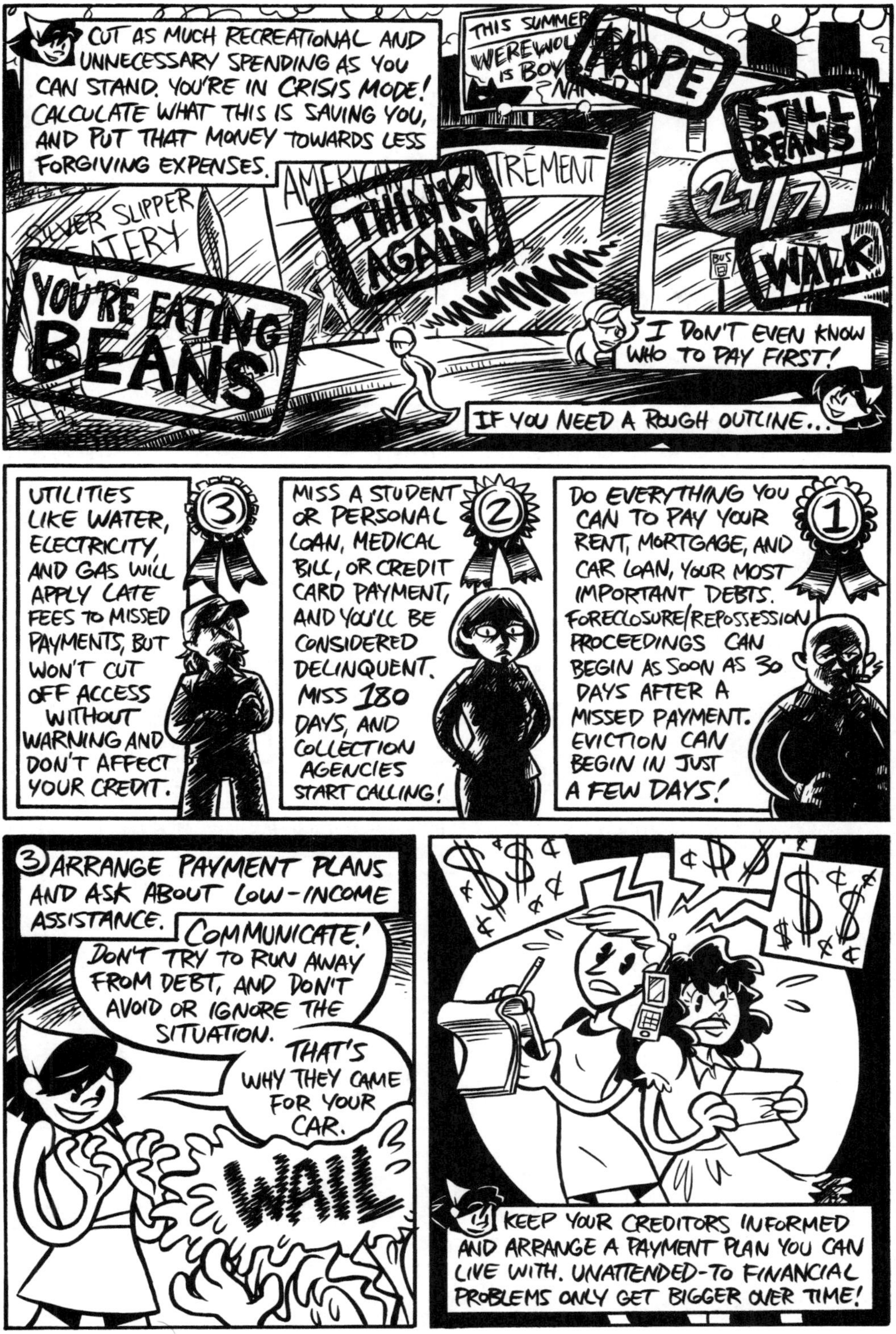

CUT AS MUCH RECREATIONAL AND UNNECESSARY SPENDING AS YOU CAN STAND. YOU'RE IN CRISIS MODE! CALCULATE WHAT THIS IS SAVING YOU, AND PUT THAT MONEY TOWARDS LESS FORGIVING EXPENSES.
SILVER SLIPPER EATERY
YOU'RE EATING BEANS
THINK AGAIN
NOPE
STILL BEANS
WALK
BUS
I DON'T EVEN KNOW WHO TO PAY FIRST!
IF YOU NEED A ROUGH OUTLINE...
3
UTILITIES LIKE WATER, ELECTRICITY, AND GAS WILL APPLY LATE FEES TO MISSED PAYMENTS, BUT WON'T CUT OFF ACCESS WITHOUT WARNING AND DON'T AFFECT YOUR CREDIT.
2
MISS A STUDENT OR PERSONAL LOAN, MEDICAL BILL, OR CREDIT CARD PAYMENT, AND YOU'LL BE CONSIDERED DELINQUENT. MISS 180 DAYS, AND COLLECTION AGENCIES START CALLING!
1
DO EVERYTHING YOU CAN TO PAY YOUR RENT, MORTGAGE, AND CAR LOAN, YOUR MOST IMPORTANT DEBTS. FORECLOSURE/REPOSSESSION PROCEEDINGS CAN BEGIN AS SOON AS 30 DAYS AFTER A MISSED PAYMENT. EVICTION CAN BEGIN IN JUST A FEW DAYS!
3 ARRANGE PAYMENT PLANS AND ASK ABOUT LOW-INCOME ASSISTANCE.
COMMUNICATE! DON'T TRY TO RUN AWAY FROM DEBT, AND DON'T AVOID OR IGNORE THE SITUATION.
THAT'S WHY THEY CAME FOR YOUR CAR.
WAIL
KEEP YOUR CREDITORS INFORMED AND ARRANGE A PAYMENT PLAN YOU CAN LIVE WITH. UNATTENDED-TO FINANCIAL PROBLEMS ONLY GET BIGGER OVER TIME!

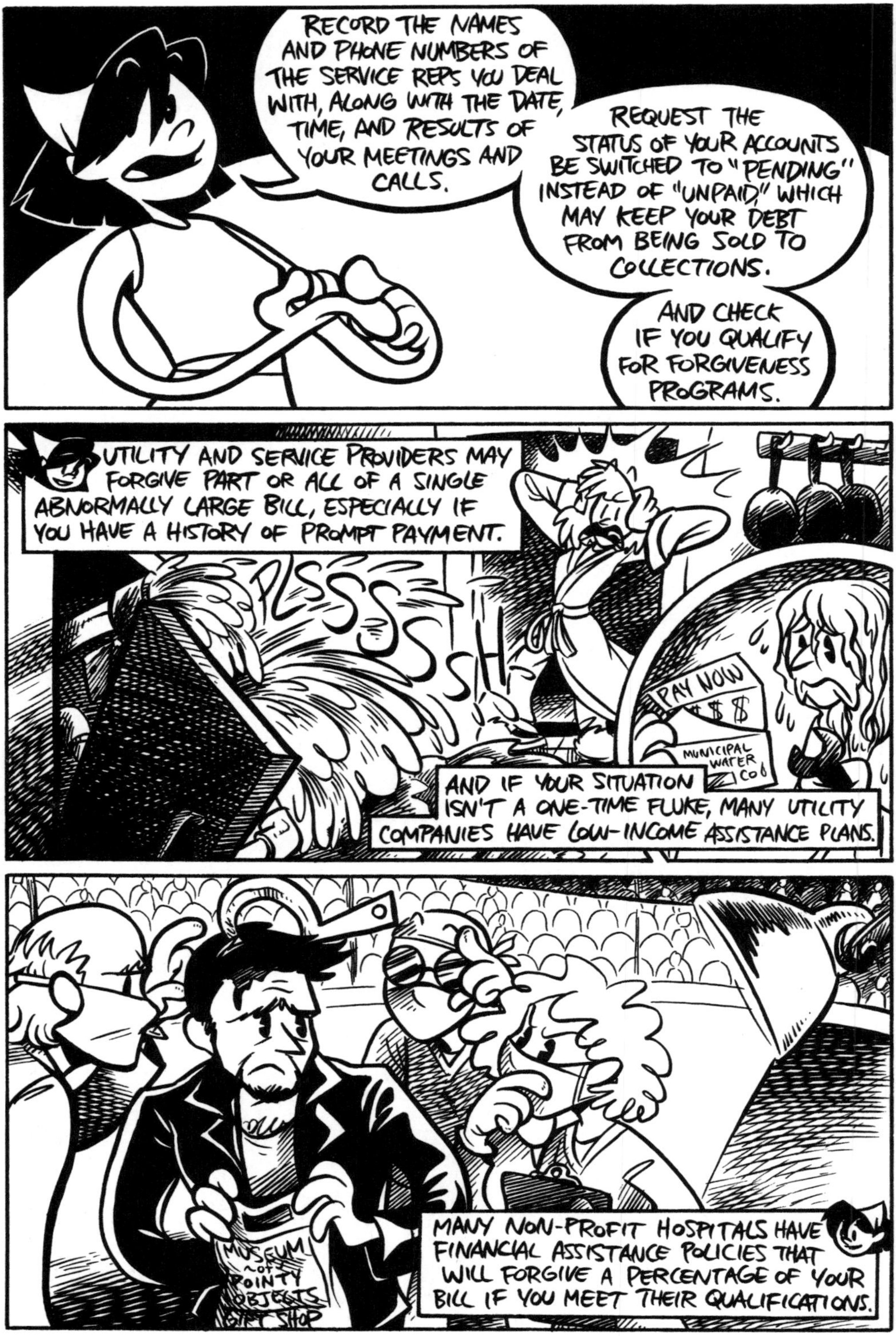
RECORD THE NAMES AND PHONE NUMBERS OF THE SERVICE REPS YOU DEAL WITH, ALONG WITH THE DATE, TIME, AND RESULTS OF YOUR MEETINGS AND CALLS.
REQUEST THE STATUS OF YOUR ACCOUNTS BE SWITCHED TO "PENDING" INSTEAD OF "UNPAID," WHICH MAY KEEP YOUR DEBT FROM BEING SOLD TO COLLECTIONS.
AND CHECK IF YOU QUALIFY FOR FORGIVENESS PROGRAMS.
UTILITY AND SERVICE PROVIDERS MAY FORGIVE PART OR ALL OF A SINGLE ABNORMALLY LARGE BILL, ESPECIALLY IF YOU HAVE A HISTORY OF PROMPT PAYMENT.
PLSSSSSSH!
PAY NOW $$$
MUNICIPAL WATER CO
AND IF YOUR SITUATION ISN'T A ONE-TIME FLUKE, MANY UTILITY COMPANIES HAVE LOW-INCOME ASSISTANCE PLANS.
MUSEUM OF POINTY OBJECTS GIFT SHOP
MANY NON-PROFIT HOSPITALS HAVE FINANCIAL ASSISTANCE POLICIES THAT WILL FORGIVE A PERCENTAGE OF YOUR BILL IF YOU MEET THEIR QUALIFICATIONS.

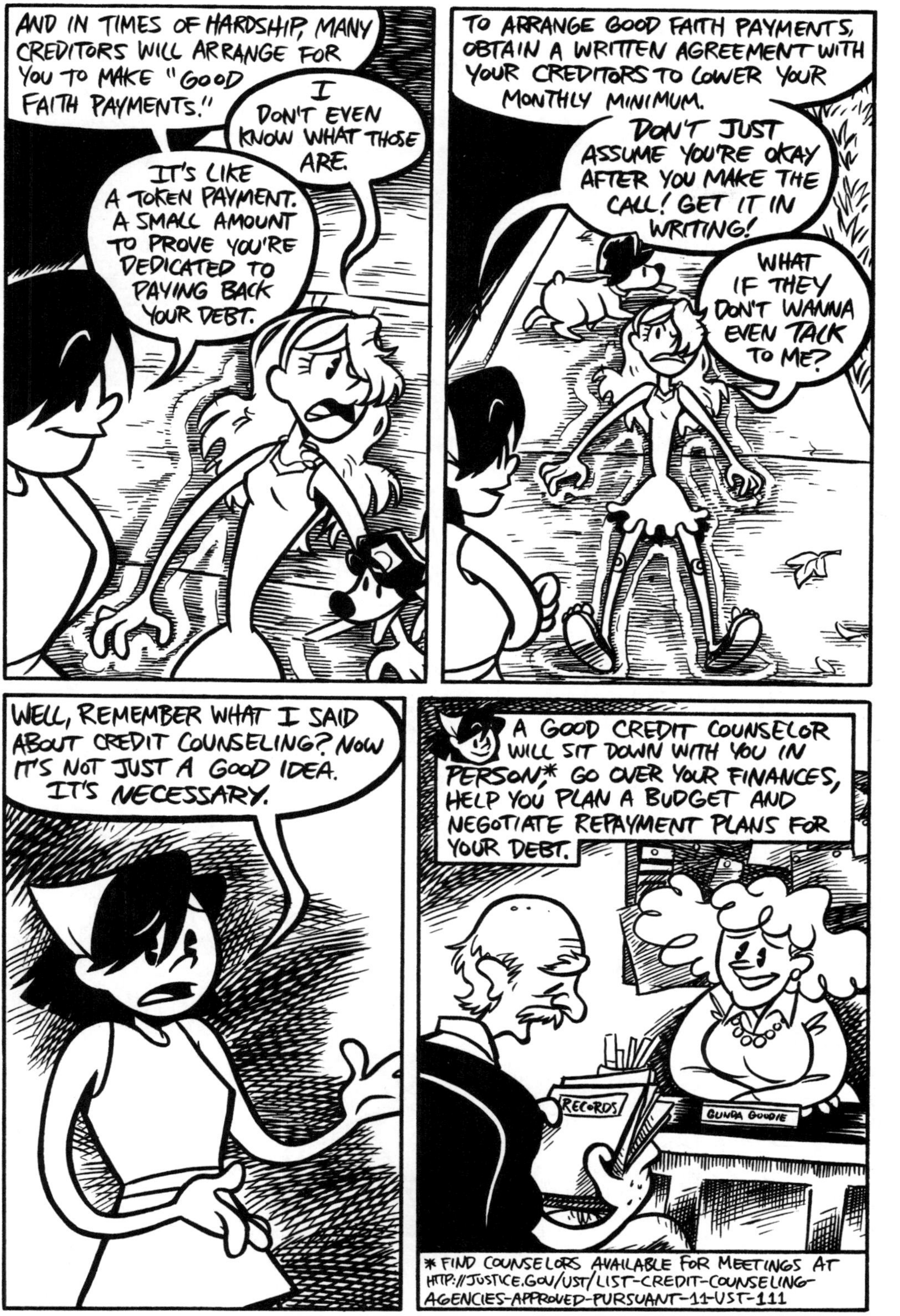

AND IN TIMES OF HARDSHIP, MANY CREDITORS WILL ARRANGE FOR YOU TO MAKE "GOOD FAITH PAYMENTS."
I DON'T EVEN KNOW WHAT THOSE ARE.
IT'S LIKE A TOKEN PAYMENT. A SMALL AMOUNT TO PROVE YOU'RE DEDICATED TO PAYING BACK YOUR DEBT.
TO ARRANGE GOOD FAITH PAYMENTS, OBTAIN A WRITTEN AGREEMENT WITH YOUR CREDITORS TO LOWER YOUR MONTHLY MINIMUM.
DON'T JUST ASSUME YOU'RE OKAY AFTER YOU MAKE THE CALL! GET IT IN WRITING!
WHAT IF THEY DON'T WANNA EVEN TALK TO ME?
WELL, REMEMBER WHAT I SAID ABOUT CREDIT COUNSELING? NOW IT'S NOT JUST A GOOD IDEA. IT'S NECESSARY.
A GOOD CREDIT COUNSELOR WILL SIT DOWN WITH YOU IN PERSON,* GO OVER YOUR FINANCES, HELP YOU PLAN A BUDGET AND NEGOTIATE REPAYMENT PLANS FOR YOUR DEBT.
RECORDS
GUNDA GOODIE
* FIND COUNSELORS AVAILABLE FOR MEETINGS AT HTTP://JUSTICE.GOV/UST/LIST-CREDIT-COUNSELING-AGENCIES-APPROVED-PURSUANT-11-UST-111

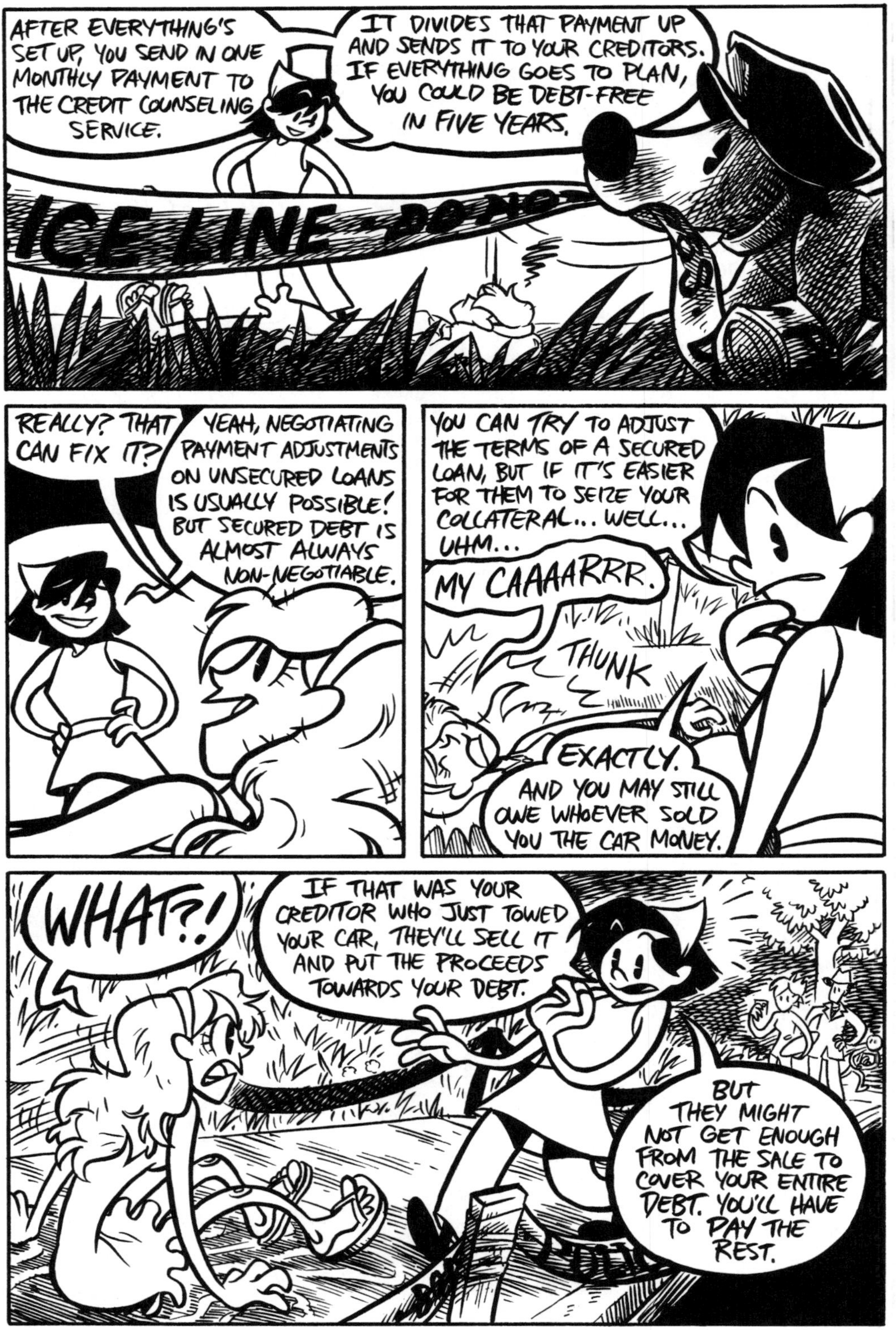
AFTER EVERYTHING'S SET UP, YOU SEND IN ONE MONTHLY PAYMENT TO THE CREDIT COUNSELING SERVICE.
IT DIVIDES THAT PAYMENT UP AND SENDS IT TO YOUR CREDITORS. IF EVERYTHING GOES TO PLAN, YOU COULD BE DEBT-FREE IN FIVE YEARS.
ICE LINE
REALLY? THAT CAN FIX IT?
YEAH, NEGOTIATING PAYMENT ADJUSTMENTS ON UNSECURED LOANS IS USUALLY POSSIBLE! BUT SECURED DEBT IS ALMOST ALWAYS NON-NEGOTIABLE.
YOU CAN TRY TO ADJUST THE TERMS OF A SECURED LOAN, BUT IF IT'S EASIER FOR THEM TO SEIZE YOUR COLLATERAL... WELL... UHM...
MY CAAAARRR.
THUNK
EXACTLY. AND YOU MAY STILL OWE WHOEVER SOLD YOU THE CAR MONEY.
WHAT?!
IF THAT WAS YOUR CREDITOR WHO JUST TOWED YOUR CAR, THEY'LL SELL IT AND PUT THE PROCEEDS TOWARDS YOUR DEBT.
BUT THEY MIGHT NOT GET ENOUGH FROM THE SALE TO COVER YOUR ENTIRE DEBT. YOU'LL HAVE TO PAY THE REST.

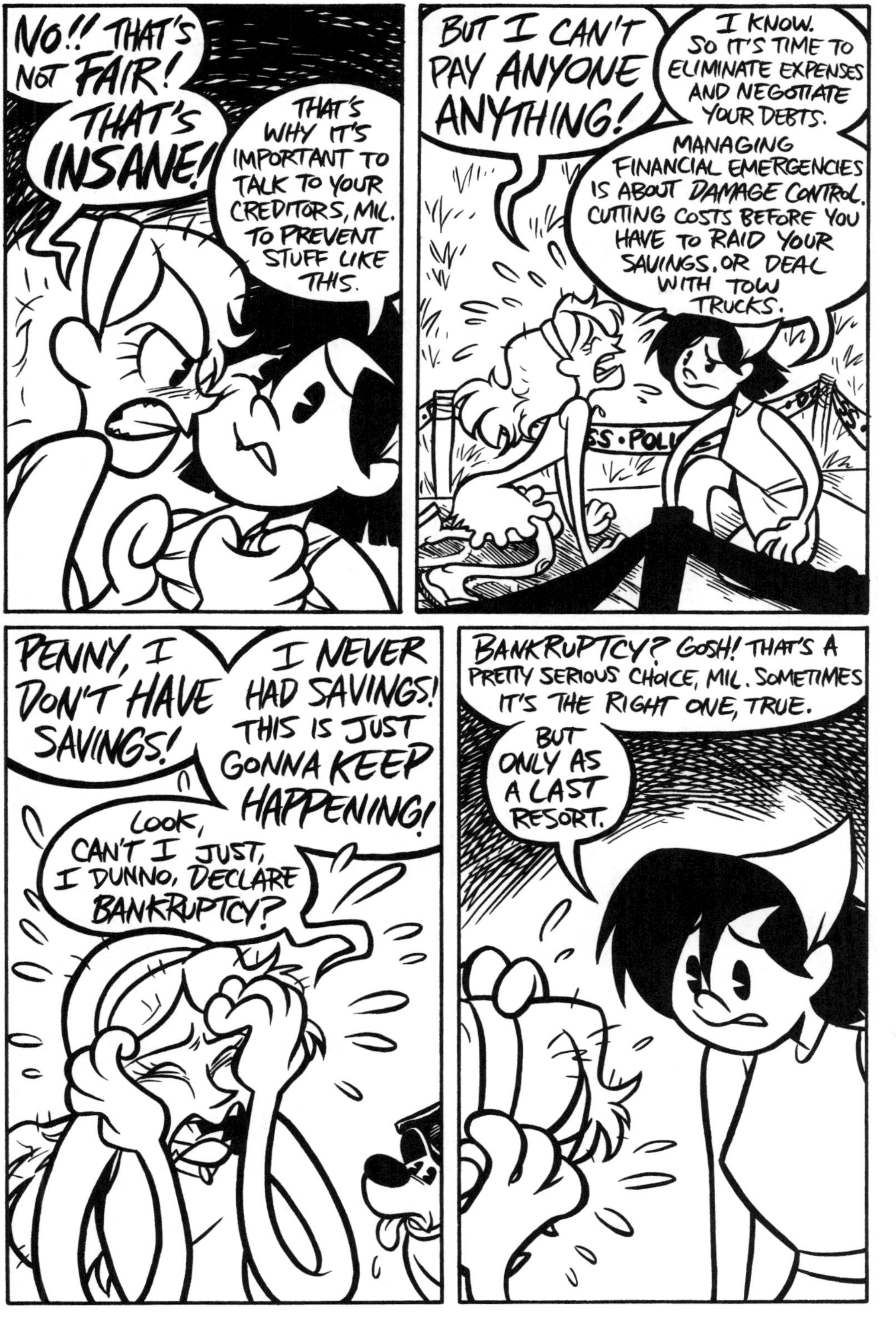
NO!! THAT'S NOT FAIR! THAT'S INSANE!
THAT'S WHY IT'S IMPORTANT TO TALK TO YOUR CREDITORS, MIL. TO PREVENT STUFF LIKE THIS.
BUT I CAN'T PAY ANYONE ANYTHING!
I KNOW. SO IT'S TIME TO ELIMINATE EXPENSES AND NEGOTIATE YOUR DEBTS.
MANAGING FINANCIAL EMERGENCIES IS ABOUT DAMAGE CONTROL. CUTTING COSTS BEFORE YOU HAVE TO RAID YOUR SAVINGS, OR DEAL WITH TOW TRUCKS.
PENNY, I DON'T HAVE SAVINGS!
I NEVER HAD SAVINGS! THIS IS JUST GONNA KEEP HAPPENING!
LOOK, CAN'T I JUST, I DUNNO, DECLARE BANKRUPTCY?
BANKRUPTCY? GOSH! THAT'S A PRETTY SERIOUS CHOICE, MIL. SOMETIMES IT'S THE RIGHT ONE, TRUE.
BUT ONLY AS A LAST RESORT.

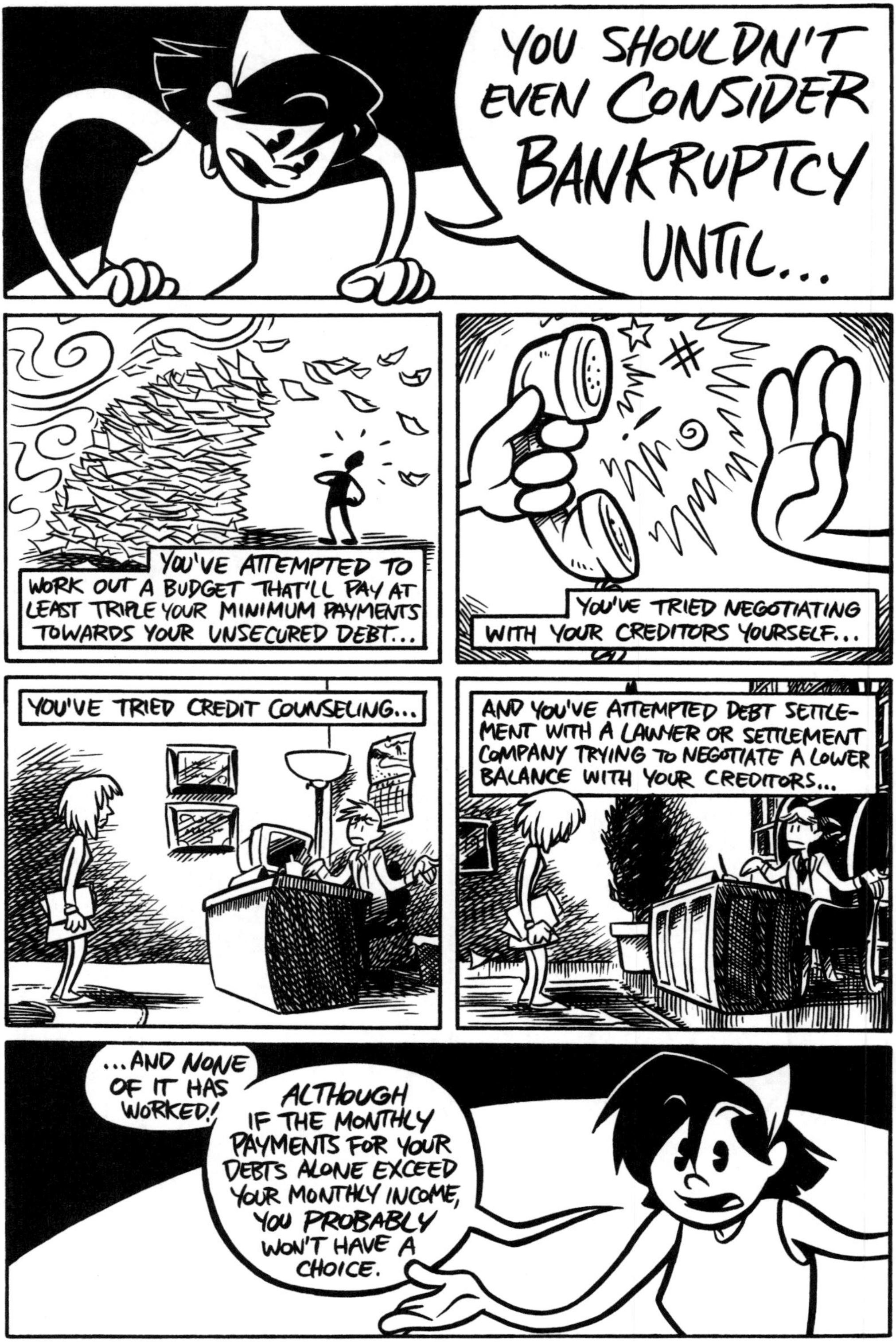
YOU SHOULDN'T EVEN CONSIDER BANKRUPTCY UNTIL...
YOU'VE ATTEMPTED TO WORK OUT A BUDGET THAT'LL PAY AT LEAST TRIPLE YOUR MINIMUM PAYMENTS TOWARDS YOUR UNSECURED DEBT...
YOU'VE TRIED NEGOTIATING WITH YOUR CREDITORS YOURSELF...
YOU'VE TRIED CREDIT COUNSELING...
AND YOU'VE ATTEMPTED DEBT SETTLE-MENT WITH A LAWYER OR SETTLEMENT COMPANY TRYING TO NEGOTIATE A LOWER BALANCE WITH YOUR CREDITORS...
...AND NONE OF IT HAS WORKED!
ALTHOUGH IF THE MONTHLY PAYMENTS FOR YOUR DEBTS ALONE EXCEED YOUR MONTHLY INCOME, YOU PROBABLY WON'T HAVE A CHOICE.

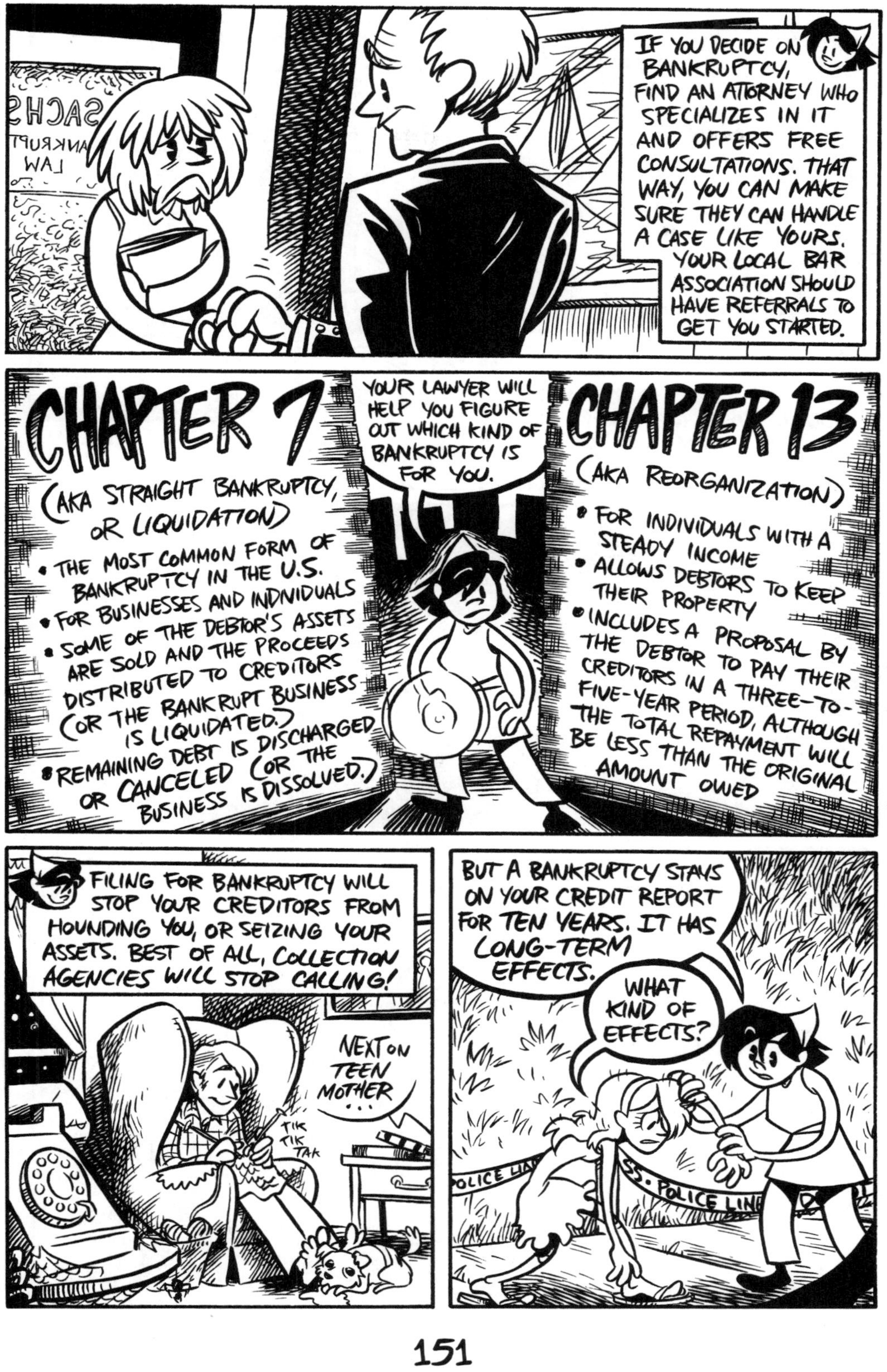
IF YOU DECIDE ON BANKRUPTCY, FIND AN ATTORNEY WHO SPECIALIZES IN IT AND OFFERS FREE CONSULTATIONS. THAT WAY, YOU CAN MAKE SURE THEY CAN HANDLE A CASE LIKE YOURS. YOUR LOCAL BAR ASSOCIATION SHOULD HAVE REFERRALS TO GET YOU STARTED.
CHAPTER 7
(AKA STRAIGHT BANKRUPTCY, OR LIQUIDATION)
• THE MOST COMMON FORM OF BANKRUPTCY IN THE U.S.
• FOR BUSINESSES AND INDIVIDUALS
• SOME OF THE DEBTOR'S ASSETS ARE SOLD AND THE PROCEEDS DISTRIBUTED TO CREDITORS (OR THE BANKRUPT BUSINESS IS LIQUIDATED.)
• REMAINING DEBT IS DISCHARGED OR CANCELED (OR THE BUSINESS IS DISSOLVED.)
YOUR LAWYER WILL HELP YOU FIGURE OUT WHICH KIND OF BANKRUPTCY IS FOR YOU.
CHAPTER 13
(AKA REORGANIZATION)
• FOR INDIVIDUALS WITH A STEADY INCOME
• ALLOWS DEBTORS TO KEEP THEIR PROPERTY
• INCLUDES A PROPOSAL BY THE DEBTOR TO PAY THEIR CREDITORS IN A THREE-TO-FIVE-YEAR PERIOD, ALTHOUGH THE TOTAL REPAYMENT WILL BE LESS THAN THE ORIGINAL AMOUNT OWED
FILING FOR BANKRUPTCY WILL STOP YOUR CREDITORS FROM HOUNDING YOU, OR SEIZING YOUR ASSETS. BEST OF ALL, COLLECTION AGENCIES WILL STOP CALLING!
NEXT ON TEEN MOTHER...
TIK TIK TAK
BUT A BANKRUPTCY STAYS ON YOUR CREDIT REPORT FOR TEN YEARS. IT HAS LONG-TERM EFFECTS.
WHAT KIND OF EFFECTS?
POLICE LINE

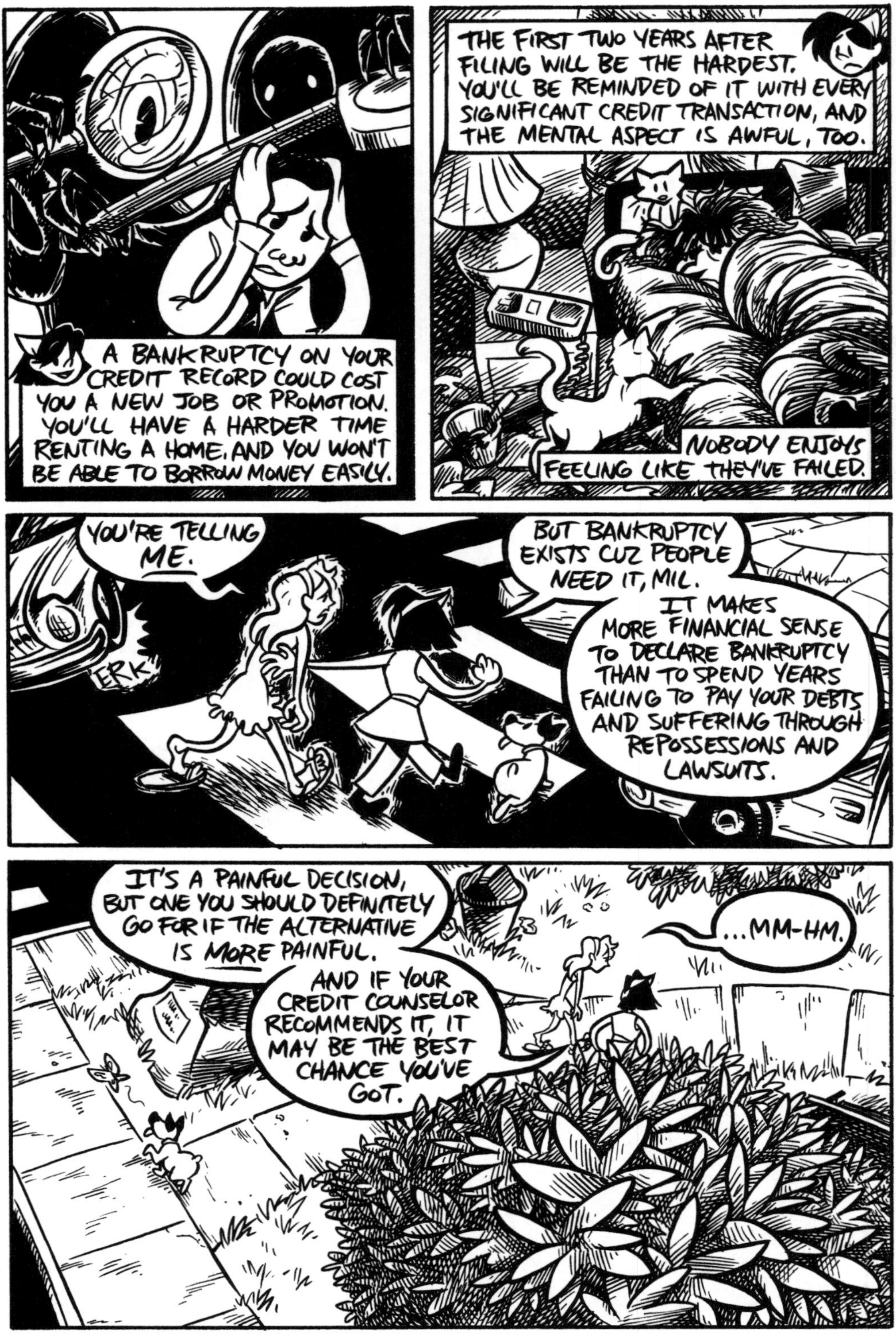
A BANKRUPTCY ON YOUR CREDIT RECORD COULD COST YOU A NEW JOB OR PROMOTION. YOU'LL HAVE A HARDER TIME RENTING A HOME, AND YOU WON'T BE ABLE TO BORROW MONEY EASILY.
THE FIRST TWO YEARS AFTER FILING WILL BE THE HARDEST. YOU'LL BE REMINDED OF IT WITH EVERY SIGNIFICANT CREDIT TRANSACTION, AND THE MENTAL ASPECT IS AWFUL, TOO.
NOBODY ENJOYS FEELING LIKE THEY'VE FAILED.
YOU'RE TELLING ME.
ERK
BUT BANKRUPTCY EXISTS CUZ PEOPLE NEED IT, MIL.
IT MAKES MORE FINANCIAL SENSE TO DECLARE BANKRUPTCY THAN TO SPEND YEARS FAILING TO PAY YOUR DEBTS AND SUFFERING THROUGH REPOSSESSIONS AND LAWSUITS.
IT'S A PAINFUL DECISION, BUT ONE YOU SHOULD DEFINITELY GO FOR IF THE ALTERNATIVE IS MORE PAINFUL.
AND IF YOUR CREDIT COUNSELOR RECOMMENDS IT, IT MAY BE THE BEST CHANCE YOU'VE GOT.
...MM-HM.

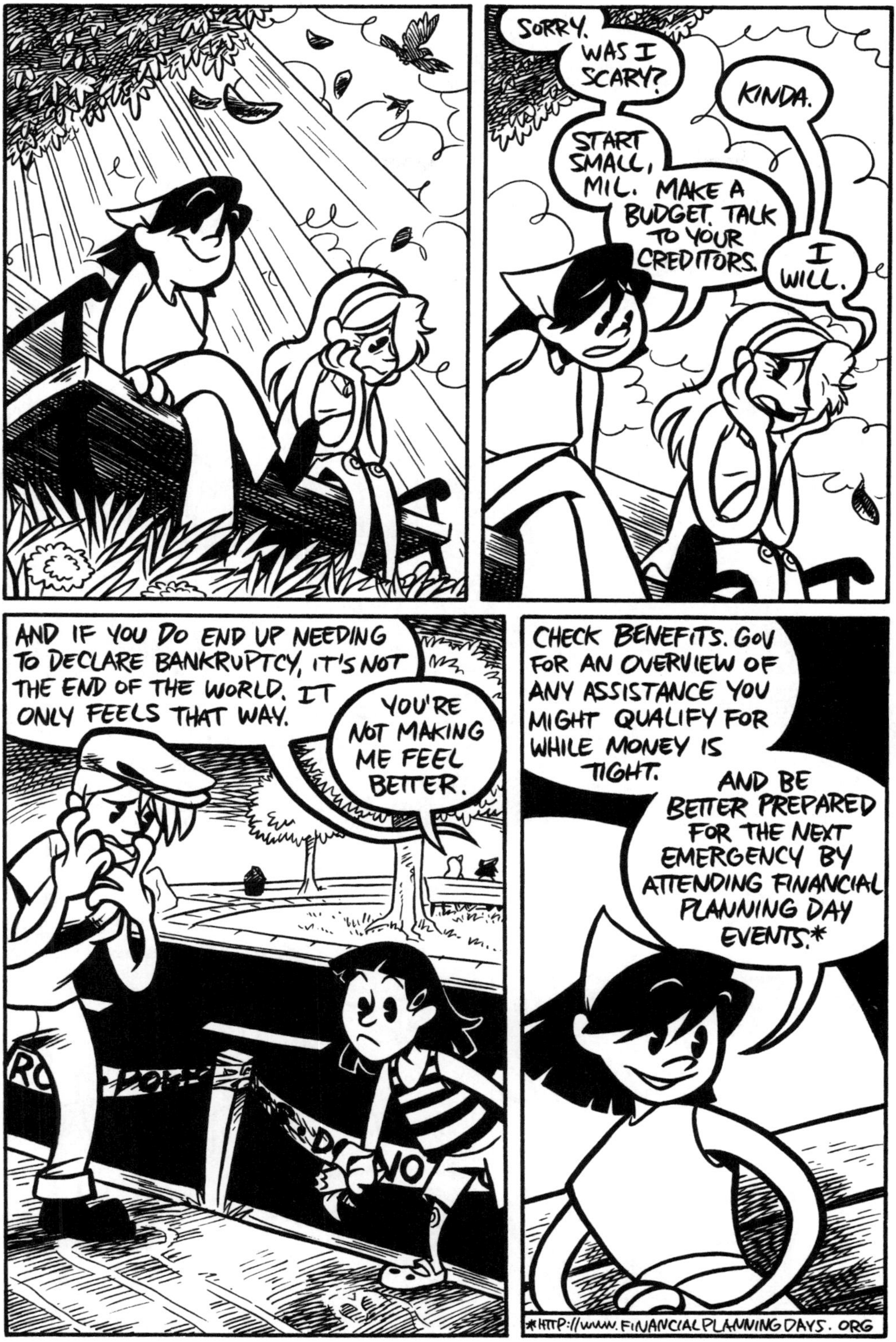
SORRY.
WAS I SCARY?
KINDA.
START SMALL, MIL.
MAKE A BUDGET. TALK TO YOUR CREDITORS.
I WILL.
AND IF YOU DO END UP NEEDING TO DECLARE BANKRUPTCY, IT'S NOT THE END OF THE WORLD. IT ONLY FEELS THAT WAY.
YOU'RE NOT MAKING ME FEEL BETTER.
CHECK BENEFITS.GOV FOR AN OVERVIEW OF ANY ASSISTANCE YOU MIGHT QUALIFY FOR WHILE MONEY IS TIGHT.
AND BE BETTER PREPARED FOR THE NEXT EMERGENCY BY ATTENDING FINANCIAL PLANNING DAY EVENTS.*
*HTTP://WWW.FINANCIALPLANNINGDAYS.ORG

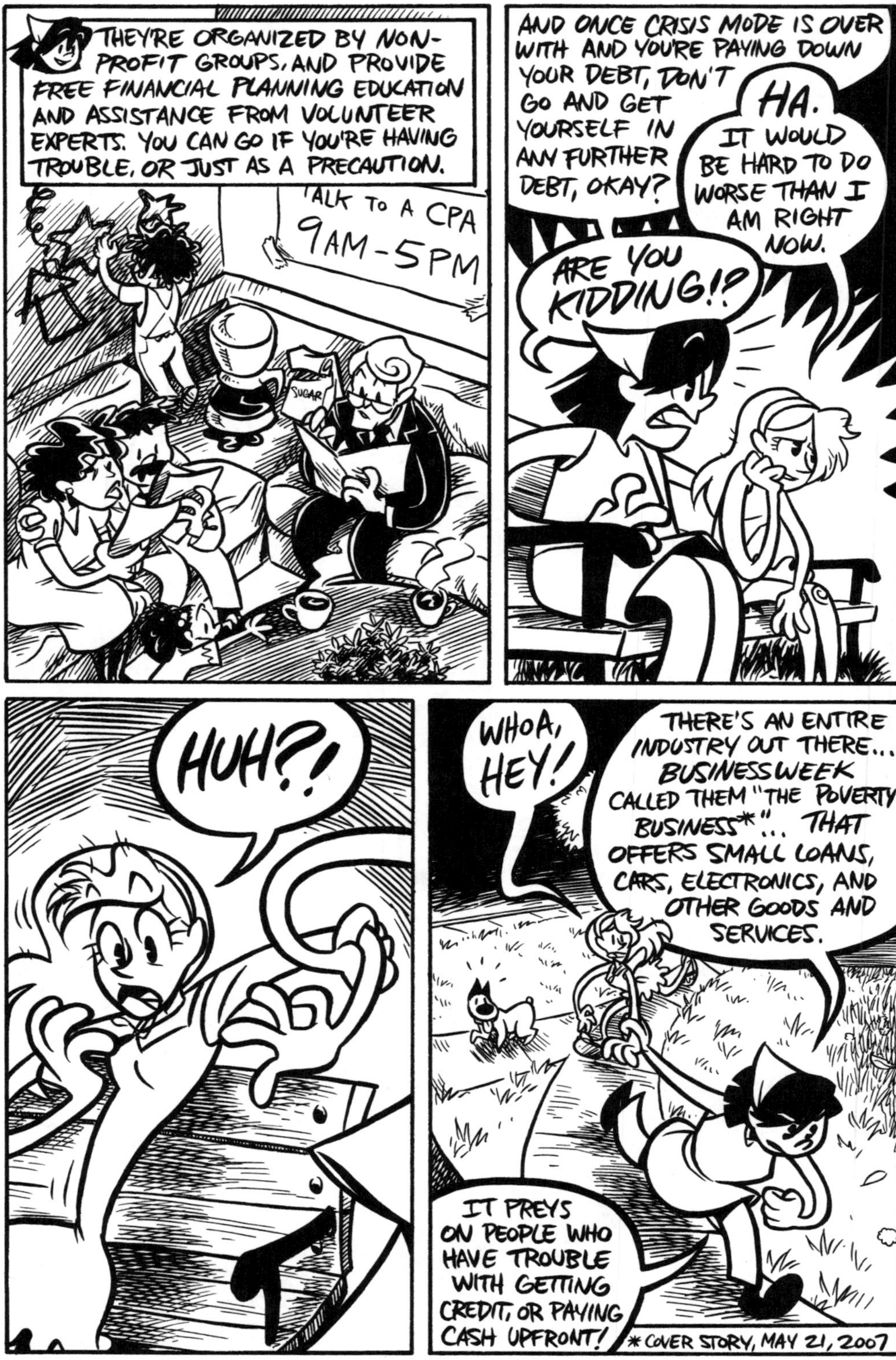
THEY'RE ORGANIZED BY NON-PROFIT GROUPS, AND PROVIDE FREE FINANCIAL PLANNING EDUCATION AND ASSISTANCE FROM VOLUNTEER EXPERTS. YOU CAN GO IF YOU'RE HAVING TROUBLE, OR JUST AS A PRECAUTION.
TALK TO A CPA 9AM-5PM
SUGAR
AND ONCE CRISIS MODE IS OVER WITH AND YOU'RE PAYING DOWN YOUR DEBT, DON'T GO AND GET YOURSELF IN ANY FURTHER DEBT, OKAY?
HA. IT WOULD BE HARD TO DO WORSE THAN I AM RIGHT NOW.
ARE YOU KIDDING!?
HUH?!
WHOA, HEY!
THERE'S AN ENTIRE INDUSTRY OUT THERE... BUSINESSWEEK CALLED THEM "THE POVERTY BUSINESS*"... THAT OFFERS SMALL LOANS, CARS, ELECTRONICS, AND OTHER GOODS AND SERVICES.
IT PREYS ON PEOPLE WHO HAVE TROUBLE WITH GETTING CREDIT, OR PAYING CASH UPFRONT!
* COVER STORY, MAY 21, 2007

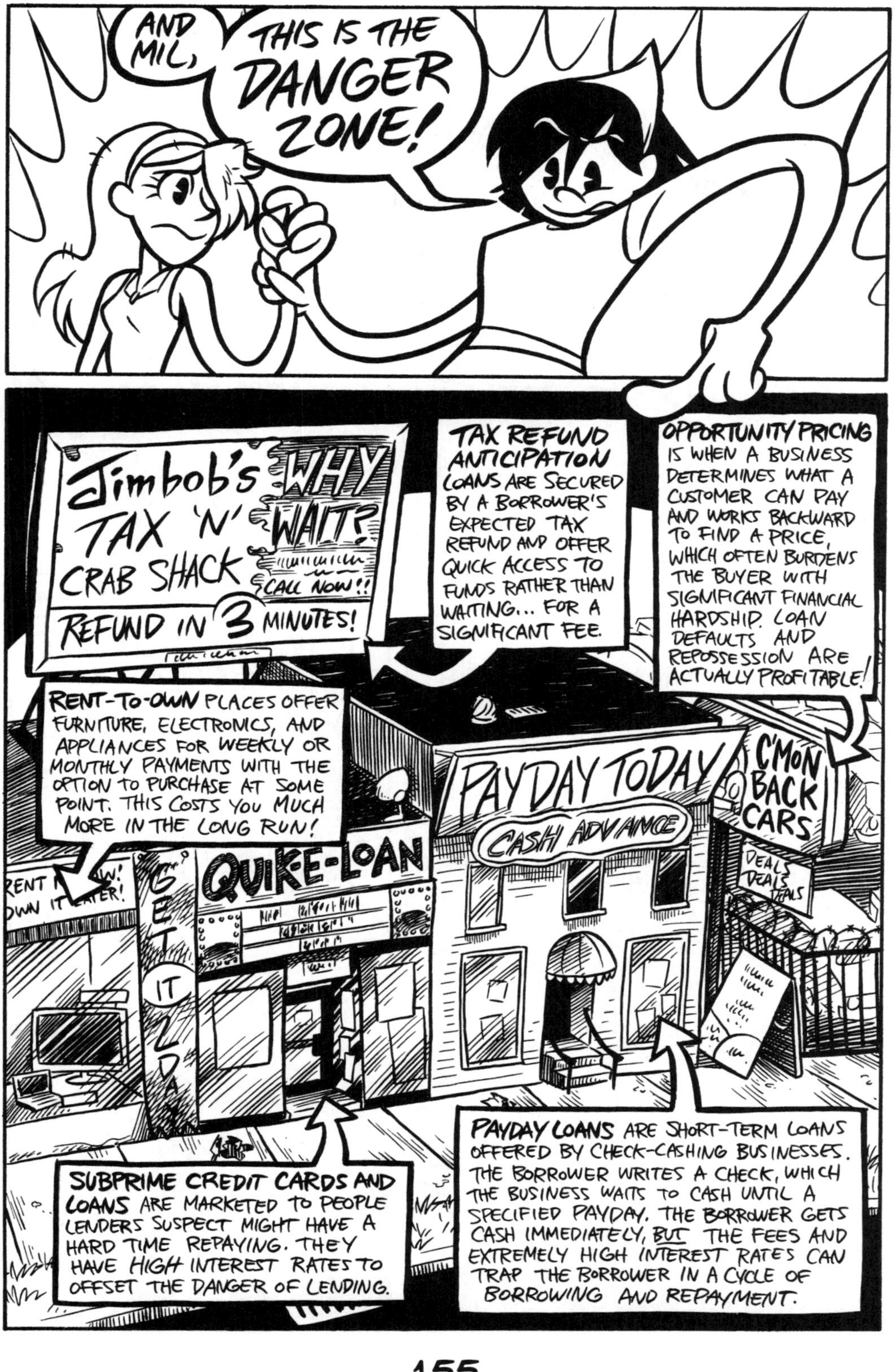
AND MIL,
THIS IS THE DANGER ZONE!
Jimbob's TAX 'N' CRAB SHACK
WHY WAIT?
CALL NOW!!
REFUND IN 3 MINUTES!
TAX REFUND ANTICIPATION LOANS ARE SECURED BY A BORROWER'S EXPECTED TAX REFUND AND OFFER QUICK ACCESS TO FUNDS RATHER THAN WAITING... FOR A SIGNIFICANT FEE.
OPPORTUNITY PRICING IS WHEN A BUSINESS DETERMINES WHAT A CUSTOMER CAN PAY AND WORKS BACKWARD TO FIND A PRICE, WHICH OFTEN BURDENS THE BUYER WITH SIGNIFICANT FINANCIAL HARDSHIP. LOAN DEFAULTS AND REPOSSESSION ARE ACTUALLY PROFITABLE!
RENT-TO-OWN PLACES OFFER FURNITURE, ELECTRONICS, AND APPLIANCES FOR WEEKLY OR MONTHLY PAYMENTS WITH THE OPTION TO PURCHASE AT SOME POINT. THIS COSTS YOU MUCH MORE IN THE LONG RUN!
PAYDAY TODAY
CASH ADVANCE
C'MON BACK CARS
DEALS DEALS
QUIK-E-LOAN
SUBPRIME CREDIT CARDS AND LOANS ARE MARKETED TO PEOPLE LENDERS SUSPECT MIGHT HAVE A HARD TIME REPAYING. THEY HAVE HIGH INTEREST RATES TO OFFSET THE DANGER OF LENDING.
PAYDAY LOANS ARE SHORT-TERM LOANS OFFERED BY CHECK-CASHING BUSINESSES. THE BORROWER WRITES A CHECK, WHICH THE BUSINESS WAITS TO CASH UNTIL A SPECIFIED PAYDAY. THE BORROWER GETS CASH IMMEDIATELY, BUT THE FEES AND EXTREMELY HIGH INTEREST RATES CAN TRAP THE BORROWER IN A CYCLE OF BORROWING AND REPAYMENT.

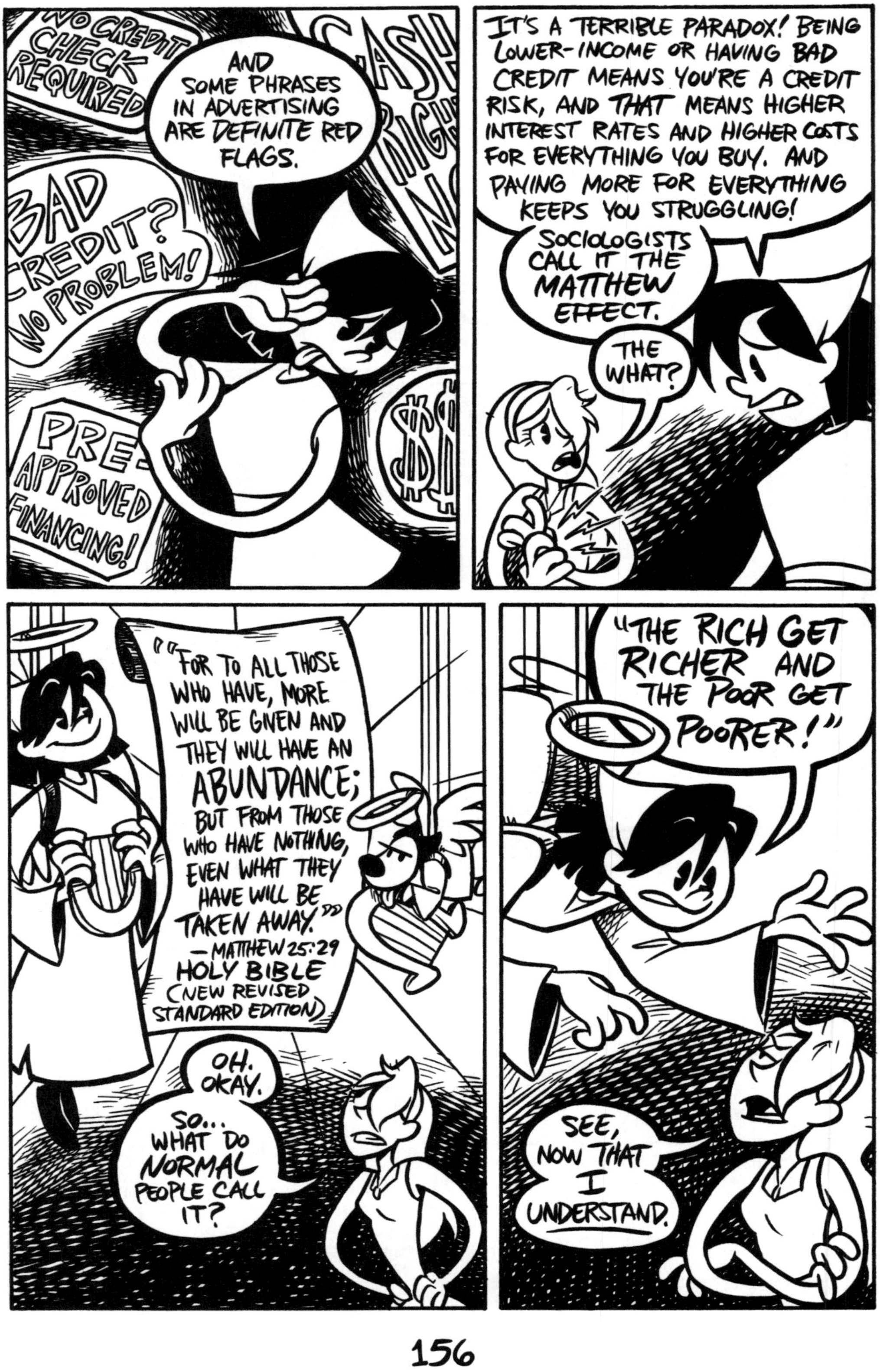

NO CREDIT CHECK REQUIRED
AND SOME PHRASES IN ADVERTISING ARE DEFINITE RED FLAGS.
BAD CREDIT? NO PROBLEM!
PRE-APPROVED FINANCING!
IT'S A TERRIBLE PARADOX! BEING LOWER-INCOME OR HAVING BAD CREDIT MEANS YOU'RE A CREDIT RISK, AND THAT MEANS HIGHER INTEREST RATES AND HIGHER COSTS FOR EVERYTHING YOU BUY. AND PAYING MORE FOR EVERYTHING KEEPS YOU STRUGGLING!
SOCIOLOGISTS CALL IT THE MATTHEW EFFECT.
THE WHAT?
"FOR TO ALL THOSE WHO HAVE, MORE WILL BE GIVEN AND THEY WILL HAVE AN ABUNDANCE; BUT FROM THOSE WHO HAVE NOTHING, EVEN WHAT THEY HAVE WILL BE TAKEN AWAY."
—MATTHEW 25:29 HOLY BIBLE (NEW REVISED STANDARD EDITION)
OH. OKAY.
SO... WHAT DO NORMAL PEOPLE CALL IT?
"THE RICH GET RICHER AND THE POOR GET POORER!"
SEE, NOW THAT I UNDERSTAND.

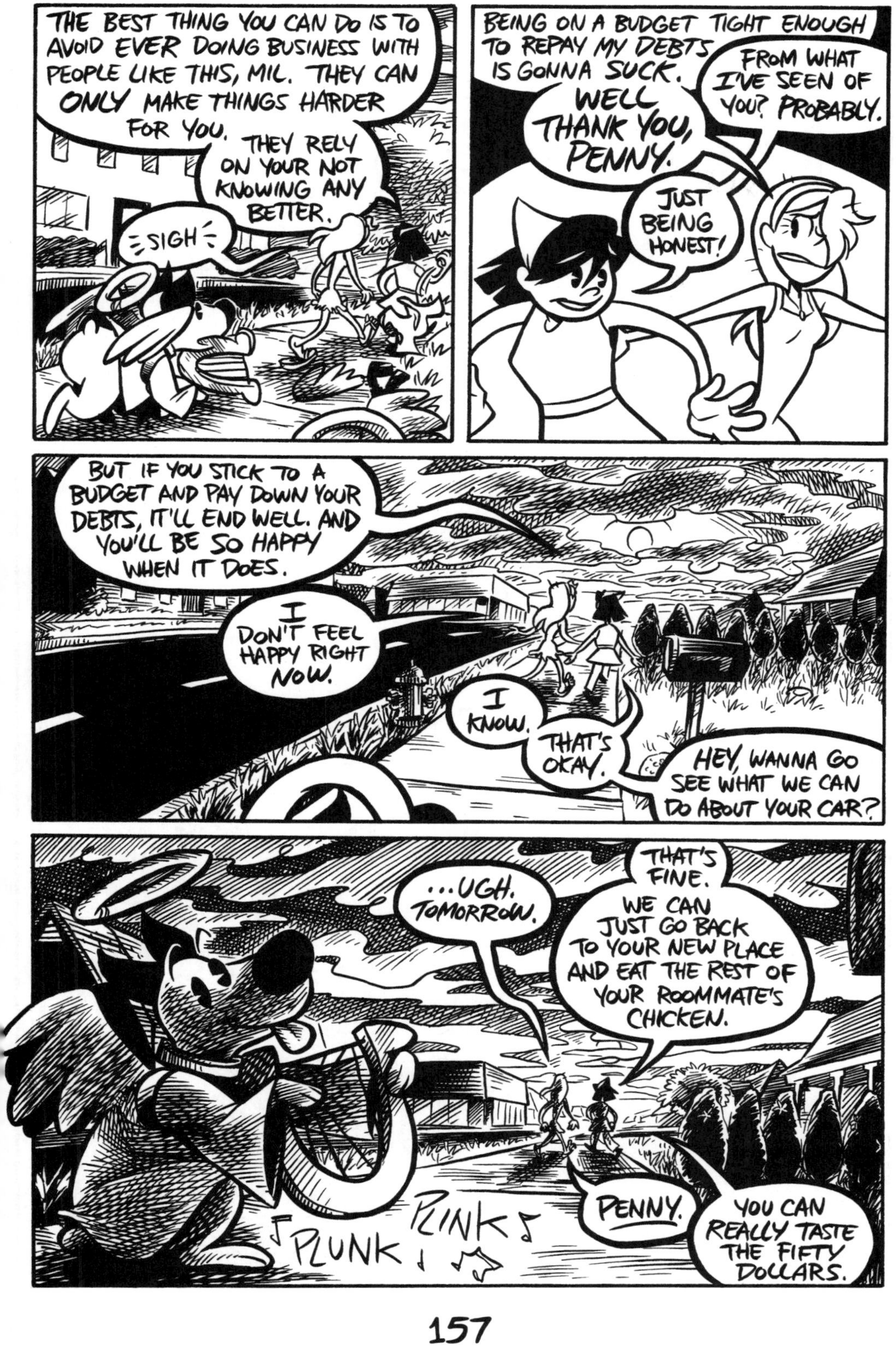
THE BEST THING YOU CAN DO IS TO AVOID EVER DOING BUSINESS WITH PEOPLE LIKE THIS, MIL. THEY CAN ONLY MAKE THINGS HARDER FOR YOU.
THEY RELY ON YOUR NOT KNOWING ANY BETTER.
SIGH
BEING ON A BUDGET TIGHT ENOUGH TO REPAY MY DEBTS IS GONNA SUCK.
FROM WHAT I'VE SEEN OF YOU? PROBABLY.
WELL THANK YOU, PENNY.
JUST BEING HONEST!
BUT IF YOU STICK TO A BUDGET AND PAY DOWN YOUR DEBTS, IT'LL END WELL. AND YOU'LL BE SO HAPPY WHEN IT DOES.
I DON'T FEEL HAPPY RIGHT NOW.
I KNOW.
THAT'S OKAY.
HEY, WANNA GO SEE WHAT WE CAN DO ABOUT YOUR CAR?
...UGH. TOMORROW.
THAT'S FINE.
WE CAN JUST GO BACK TO YOUR NEW PLACE AND EAT THE REST OF YOUR ROOMMATE'S CHICKEN.
PLINK
PLUNK
PENNY.
YOU CAN REALLY TASTE THE FIFTY DOLLARS.

In Conclusion...

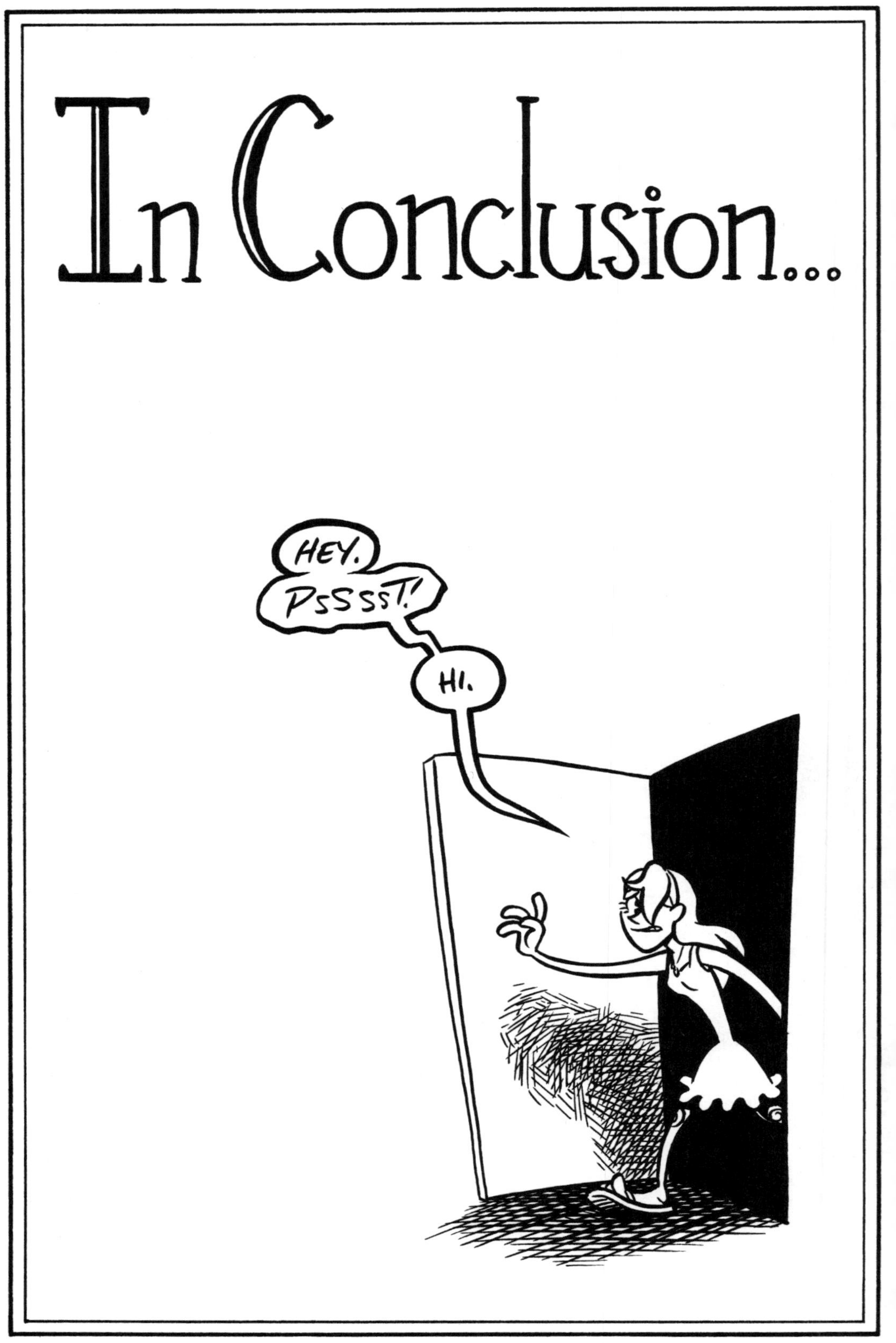
HEY.
PSSSST!
HI.

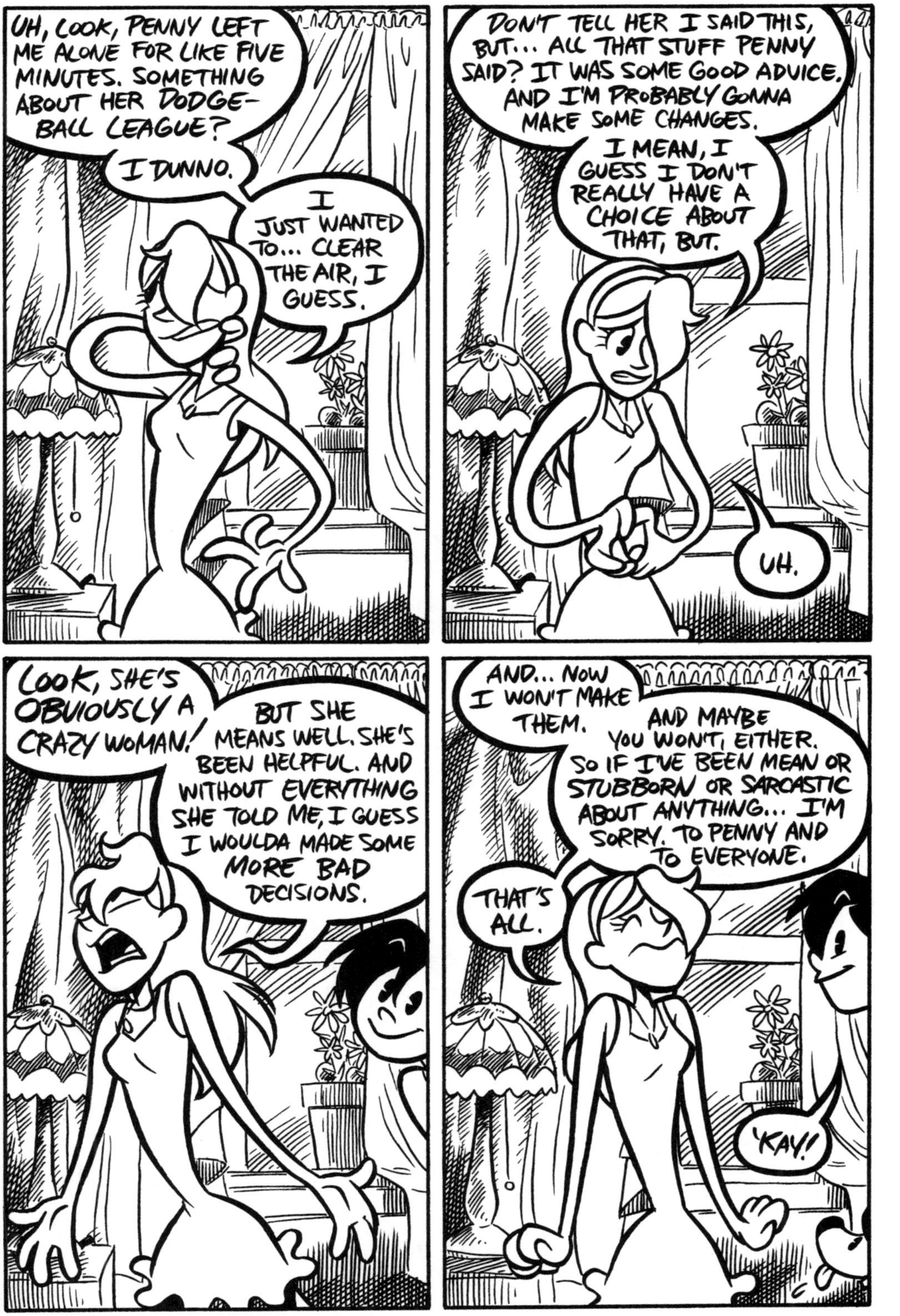
UH, LOOK, PENNY LEFT ME ALONE FOR LIKE FIVE MINUTES. SOMETHING ABOUT HER DODGE-BALL LEAGUE?
I DUNNO.
I JUST WANTED TO... CLEAR THE AIR, I GUESS.
DON'T TELL HER I SAID THIS, BUT... ALL THAT STUFF PENNY SAID? IT WAS SOME GOOD ADVICE. AND I'M PROBABLY GONNA MAKE SOME CHANGES.
I MEAN, I GUESS I DON'T REALLY HAVE A CHOICE ABOUT THAT, BUT.
UH.
LOOK, SHE'S OBVIOUSLY A CRAZY WOMAN!
BUT SHE MEANS WELL. SHE'S BEEN HELPFUL. AND WITHOUT EVERYTHING SHE TOLD ME, I GUESS I WOULDA MADE SOME MORE BAD DECISIONS.
AND... NOW I WON'T MAKE THEM.
AND MAYBE YOU WON'T, EITHER. SO IF I'VE BEEN MEAN OR STUBBORN OR SARCASTIC ABOUT ANYTHING... I'M SORRY. TO PENNY AND TO EVERYONE.
THAT'S ALL.
'KAY!

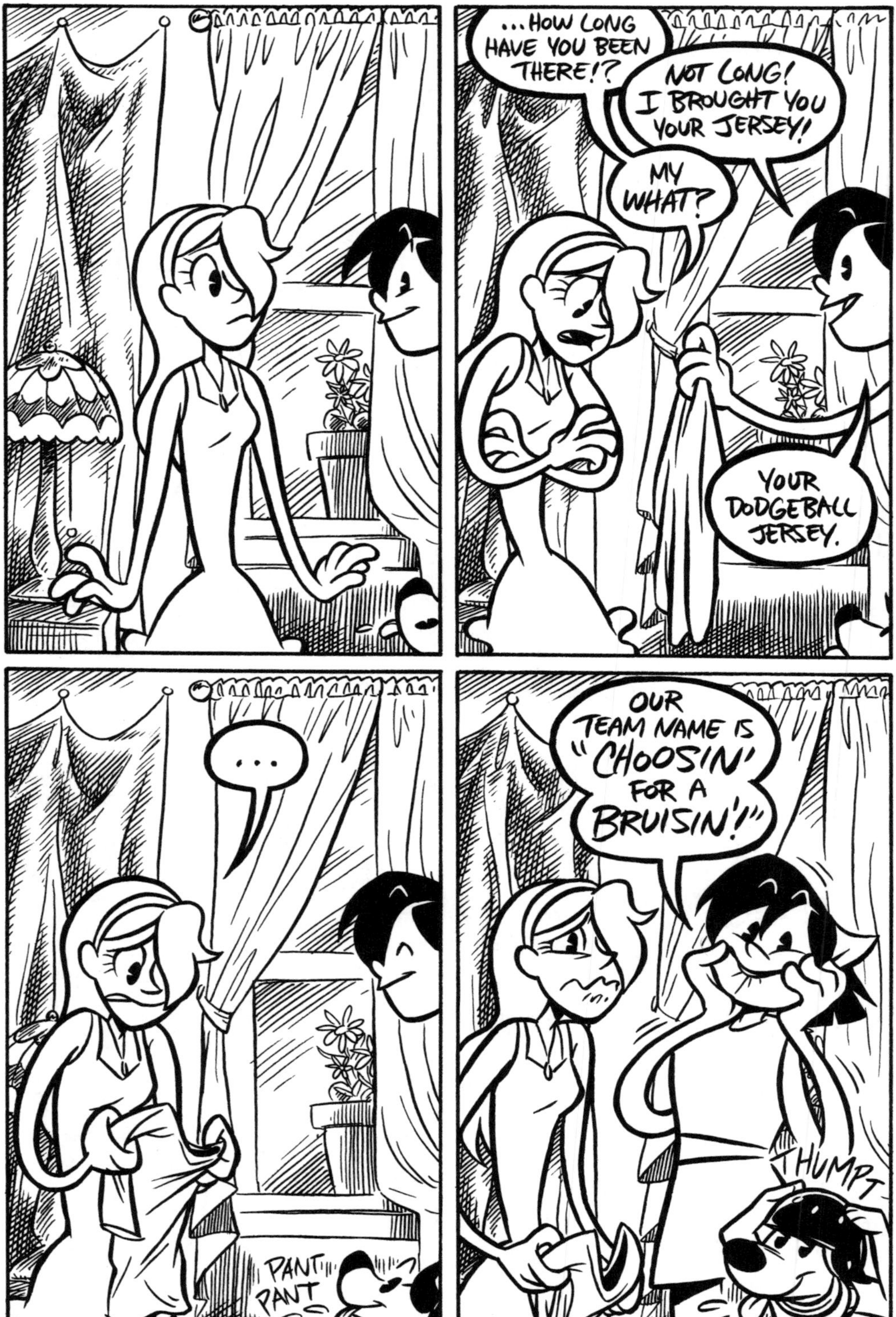
...HOW LONG HAVE YOU BEEN THERE!?
NOT LONG! I BROUGHT YOU YOUR JERSEY!
MY WHAT?
YOUR DODGEBALL JERSEY.
...
PANT PANT
OUR TEAM NAME IS "CHOOSIN' FOR A BRUISIN'!"
THUMP

Appendix:
Links and
Resources

Prologue

I'll admit it: I still eat ramen. I throw away the seasoning packet, boil up the noodle brick, mix in some homemade teriyaki sauce, and top it with tamagoyaki. It's delicious. But it's not healthy, and it's not something I do every day.

If you really, truly have no choice other than to stock up on instant noodles, offset the nutritional shortfalls of ramen by mixing in lean proteins and vegetables. And if you need ideas, there are a dozen online archives of creative ramen recipes. My favorite:

The Official Ramen Homepage
http://www.mattfischer.com/ramen/

Not really official, but probably the best. I've been consulting it for years. Over 500 recipes, neatly organized. (The "Prison" category is the most interesting, in a strictly anthropological sense.)

Chapter 1

Page 10

More examples of non-discretionary expenses: yearly doctor and dentist check-ups, tuition, your monthly subway pass, car insurance, utility bills . . . you get the idea. The unavoidable costs of your existence. They can vary in size—you can decide to spend less on groceries, or use less electricity—but you'll always have to pay them.

Page 11

The National Foundation for Credit Counseling Budget Worksheet
http://nfcc.org/tools-and-education/budget-worksheet

This is the easiest budget worksheet I've ever found. I recommend starting here.

The NFCC site also has a tool to help you calculate how long it would take you to save a million dollars. Because hey, why not.

Chapter 2

Page 21

Walk Score is the best thing to happen to apartment hunters, ever. Do not discount its power. Do not sign any sort of rental agreement until you've plugged your new potential address into Walkscore. I cannot say that enough.

Page 23

In case the third panel of "Sharing Space" was too subtle . . . find out if your potential roomies use drugs recreationally. Especially illegal ones. Enthusiastic social drinkers and smokers might just make your new place tougher to live in, but making sure you're not even in the same home as certain pills and powders is a matter of self-preservation. This is about making sure you don't come home to the cops tossing your room, one day.

Be polite and neutral-toned when you ask. But definitely ask.

Page 27

Really, really be careful about curbside furniture, particularly upholstered stuff. Bedbugs are back with a vengeance, especially in big cities. To be absolutely safe, never scavenge mattresses, bed frames or headboards, and don't bring home anything you can't give a good wipedown with soapy water or a boric acid solution.

Page 32

Prepare food for your helpers the day before the move, then warm up dinner after moving is over and done with. Trust me, you'll be in no mood to cook for a crowd after a day of hauling boxes.

Page 37

The only homebrew cleaning product webpage you'll ever need.

> **Eartheasy Non-Toxic Home Cleaning**
> http://eartheasy.com/live_nontoxic_solutions.htm

If you decide to start making your own cleaning supplies, you're gonna go through a lot of vinegar and baking soda. They're basically magic. You'll be shelling out for gallon jugs of vinegar and 64-ounce boxes of baking soda, but that will still be cheaper than buying multiple spray bottles of specialist cleansers for each individual task.

And if you can get bored, you can make a science fair volcano.

Especially handy? The tip on this site about cleaning windows. Nothing works better than wet newspaper. I skip the vinegar and just use water.

Page 47

If I ever recommend that you get help or instruction first, get help or instruction first. I want everyone who reads this book to become capable home repair and maintenance types. But I don't want anyone losing thumbs.

I particularly recommend hiring professionals to do any electrical work or complex plumbing. And if you don't have a landlord to appeal to, check yelp.com and the Better Business Bureau site (bbb.org) for good candidates. The building you live in might also have preferred service providers; ask the management company or the building superintendent.

If you're handy enough to build your own furniture (or just hope to be one day), ana-white.com is going to become your new favorite website. Free, step-by-step, comprehensive plans for everything from DIY storage beds to picnic tables.

Chapter 3

Page 58

I have cartoonist Joe Matt to thank for the four frugal staples. A notorious miser, one of his books included a page about how to be as cheap as he is. Beans, pasta, rice and potatoes figured prominently.

I don't recommend sticking to starchy carbohydrates exclusively, though. I don't think anyone would.

Page 64

I had friends literally gasp in horror when I told them I would be suggesting mushrooming and foraging as a legitimate food source.

Where I grew up, there were tons of wild blackberry bushes in the woods. One summer, my family spent an afternoon filling entire grocery bags with blackberries. Good memories! And not dangerous. I'm not even sure why anyone would think it is.

In addition, a lot of people have a hugely disproportionate idea of how life-threatening eating wild mushrooms can be. There are certainly poisonous mushrooms, even deadly ones, but with a little instruction, they're easy to avoid. It's not difficult to distinguish a tasty morel from a killer amanita. You just need to learn how. So buy a guidebook, download a foraging app, and join a mushrooming club! And remember the mantra of mushroomers everywhere: can't identify it? Don't eat it.

When in doubt, chuck it out.

Page 66

Big thanks to Rustin H. Wright of Streetcar Press for this container garden set-up. I've used it to grow sage, rosemary, and oregano!

Chapter 4

Page 88

When the armpits of your favorite shirts bet stiff, yellow, and crusty with caked sweat and deodorant, soak the garments in a sink full of cool water for half an hour, or get some baking soda, add enough hydrogen peroxide to make a paste, scrub it into the stains with a toothbrush, and leave it to work for half an hour as well. Then, launder as usual. And start wearing undershirts!

Chapter 5

Page 101

Medical bill sharing is how the Amish cover their hospital tabs. They have a religious conviction against insurance of any sort, and pay for medical services out of a community pool.

Similar plans exist outside Pennsylvania Dutch country. They also tend to be religious, so much so that the practice is occasionally referred to as "Christian healthcare."

Page 102

This book went to press in February of 2017, with Donald Trump newly elected president and vociferously dedicated to gutting the most necessary provisions of the ACA. There's no telling how much any of the current laws will change, or how fast. As always, it's a good idea to do your own research, and double-check anything recommended here. (Also, vote.)

Chapter 6

Page 118
I know cartoonists who swear by the east coast Chinatown buses during convention season, when they're traveling frequently and costs need to be kept down. If I didn't live in Chicago, I'd do the same.

Page 120
I do not like trains. I have never been on a train that arrived on time. America's current train system does not impress me, and it will not impress you. If you decide to chance it, don't make any tight schedules about when you're going to be where.

I could overlook that if they were significantly cheaper than any other mode of long-range transportation, but the ten dollars I may save by choosing a train over a plane? Not worth it.

Chapter 7

Page 126
Gallery shows are practically how I fed myself during my ill-fated, short-lived stint in art school. I judged galleries by their catering. I don't remember much about the art I saw, but you can bet I remember which galleries served steamed shrimp dumplings and butter-soaked stuffed mushrooms.

Mmm. I love art.

Chapter 8

Page 137
For-profit college company Education Management Group (owner of The Art Institutes and Brown Mackie College, among other chains) settled a 95.5 million dollar fraud case against them in 2015, triggered by whistleblower ex-employees. And in January of 2017, the U.S. Department of Education released statistics detailing the debt-to-earning ratios of multiple secondary education programs. For-profit schools represented 98% of the 800 programs that failed to meet Gainful Employment regulations, requiring schools that receive federal funding to achieve:

- A student loan repayment rate of at least 35%,
- A ratio of no more than 30% between debt that must be repaid each year and annual discretionary income,
- And a ratio of no more than 12% between debt and overall income.

In all seriousness: the data is there. Do not attend a for profit school. You'll pay more. You're less likely to graduate. And you're less likely to find work in your degree's field if you do.

Chapter 9

Page 146
In 2011, I spent a weekend in Toronto. The entire time I was there, my smartphone was acting very strangely. The battery was draining abnormally

fast, and nothing I did could fix it. When I came back home, I eventually ended up taking the phone to an Apple Store to have it reset completely.

Shortly afterwards, I was informed by my service provider that I'd racked up around $5,000 in roaming fees.

To this day, I'm not sure what happened. I suspect an app spent that entire weekend stuck in some bizarre updating loop, constantly downloading. In any case, it took three mildly hysterical explanatory phone calls to have the bill bumped down by about 90%. My phone company was inclined to believe my story, because I'd been a customer for years and had never racked up that kind of bill before. And it probably helped that I was relatively calm during the calls.

Do I have to mention that? Don't be nasty, don't yell at people, and don't demand things? Especially when you're hoping for a little sympathy?

Well, don't.

Page 148

I had to include this page to counter the advice people in financial straits are sometimes given to simply "walk away" from their debts. Let them take the car, let them take the house, et cetera. With "them," of course, being the bank or dealership.

Not a good plan. Your lenders don't want your car or home. They want money. And if your collateral won't give them enough, they'll still want money from you to make up the difference.

In addition, your lender is under no obligation to sell seized property for its absolute maximum worth. If you want to be rid of your home or car and the debt it carries, you're much better off selling it yourself and putting the proceeds towards the loan.

Page 150

Some credit counselors are dead-set against their clients declaring bankruptcy, regardless of circumstances. They tend to be the ones who work at for-profit organizations, organizations who won't receive their cut if you give up on ever hammering out a repayment plan. Avoid this potential conflict of interests by finding a non-profit counseling service.

Page 151

There are actually six different kinds of bankruptcy in the United States, not two. But these two are the ones most likely to apply to anyone buying this book. For the curious, the other chapters concern farmers, fishermen, governing bodies, business reorganizations, and international bankruptcies. Probably not the kind of thing you have to worry about.

And that's that.

Thank you for reading, and I hope this book does you as much good as writing it did me.

Spike

April, 2017

SPECIAL THANKS

HALEY MILLMAN · KAOLIN FIRE
WEIRDLING · DIANA · JAMES DONLAN
LOUISA SMITH · BRIAN SEBBY
JR M · JAMES VOOGHT · OMEGA HOWELL
ILLUMINATI PICTURES · MICHAEL GIVENS
FORREST NORVELL · MIKE MEYER
ABENI GARRET · PHILIP LUDINGTON
MATT PARKER · MARC KEVIN HALL
NICH MARAGOS · DAVID W. WOODWARD
TIFF HUDSON · MINZOKU · MICHAEL LERNER
THE WATCHER · AMANDA · WENDY CLERY
JENNIFER MURPHY · GEORGE OLIVE
KEL McDONALD · SARAH CHAVIS
UPHOLSTERY · PHILIPP PALMER
EMILY HUFF · DAN KOZLOW

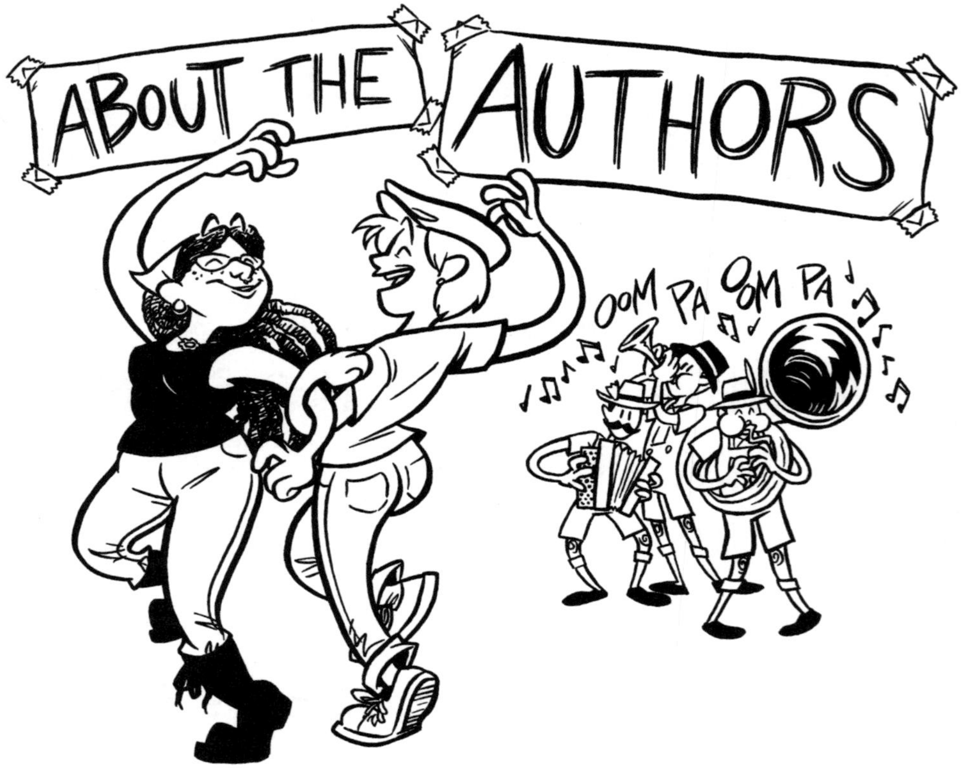
ABOUT THE AUTHORS
OOM PA OOM PA

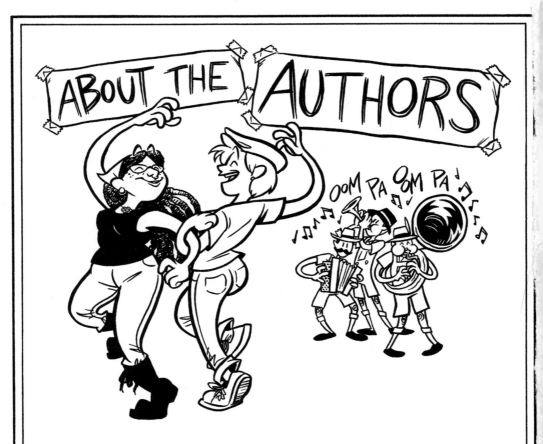

Spike is not an alias.

Spike was born in Washington D.C., grew up in suburban Maryland, and learned to draw because there was nothing else to do. She now lives in Chicago, Illinois, where there is penty to do, with a friendly dog and a very accommodating man. She is the founder of Iron Circus Comics, the city's largest comics publisher. It will be ten years old this year. You can find it at ironcircus.com.

Spike wrote *Poorcraft*, and she hopes you liked it.

Diana Nock is a freelance cartoonist, illustrator, and designer, with a BFA in Comic Art from the Minneapolis College of Art & Design. She spends most of her time hunched over a drawing board *in a dark basement* drawing funny pictures. Her other comics projects include *Wonderlust* (wonderlustcomic.com) *and The Intrepid Girlbot* (intrepidgirlbot.com).